THE
RIFLE BRIGADE
1939—1945

In Two Volumes

The Naval & Military Press Ltd

Published by

The Naval & Military Press Ltd
Unit 5 Riverside, Brambleside
Bellbrook Industrial Estate
Uckfield, East Sussex
TN22 1QQ England

Tel: +44 (0)1825 749494

www.naval-military-press.com
www.nmarchive.com

*Cover illustration:
A Universal Carrier crew of the 8th Battalion, Rifle Brigade hands out chocolate to Dutch civilians during the advance of 11th Armoured Division in the Netherlands, 22 September 1944.*

In reprinting in facsimile from the original, any imperfections are inevitably reproduced and the quality may fall short of modern type and cartographic standards.

THE
RIFLE BRIGADE
1939—1945

Volume 1

Contents

	PAGE
MESSAGE TO THE REGIMENT FROM H.R.H. THE DUKE OF GLOUCESTER, K.G., ETC., COLONEL-IN-CHIEF	v
THE 1ST BATTALION AT CALAIS, 1940. By MAJOR A. W. ALLAN, D.S.O.	1
TWO YEARS IN THE DESERT WITH THE 1ST BATTALION. By CAPTAIN R. FELLOWES	19
THE 1ST BATTALION WITH THE B.L.A., 1944	36
A SONG BEFORE SUNRISE, THE 2ND BATTALION. By MAJOR-GENERAL J. M. L. RENTON, D.S.O., O.B.E.	45
THE 2ND BATTALION AT EL ALAMEIN AND THE ACTION OF THE SNIPE POSITION	60
WITH THE 7TH BATTALION, 1942. By MAJOR A. DUDGEON, M.C.	71
THE 7TH BATTALION IN THE MIDDLE EAST. By LIEUT.-COLONEL D. L. DARLING, D.S.O., M.C.	84
THE 8TH BATTALION IN NORTH-WEST EUROPE, 1944 ...	95
THE FIRST WITHDRAWAL IN CYRENAICA, 1941 (9TH BATTALION). By LIEUT.-COLONEL E. A. SHIPTON, O.B.E., M.C.	100
TWO YEARS IN BRIEF (9TH BATTALION). By CAPTAIN F. J. M. SCHUSTER AND CAPTAIN E. N. SARGEANT	105
TUNISIAN TURNTABLE (10TH BATTALION). By LIEUT.-COLONEL R. A. FYFFE, D.S.O., M.C.	110
10TH BATTALION, 12TH MARCH, 1944 TO 19TH MARCH, 1945, By MAJOR N. C. SELWAY AND MAJOR J. F. LONSDALE, D.S.O.	126

Illustrations

	FACING PAGE
LIEUT.-COLONEL V. B. TURNER, V.C.	1
DINNER, CHRISTMAS DAY	20
MY CREWS, CHRISTMAS DAY	21
AFTER THE ACTION, SNIPE POSITION	62
SNIPE POSITION. THE GENERAL'S CONGRATULATIONS	63
GENERAL SIR H. M. WILSON'S INSPECTION	64
SNIPE POSITION	65
INSPECTION BY GENERAL SIR H. M. WILSON	85
ARMY COMMANDER' INSPECTION	85

Foreword

On the conclusion of the War, the following message was received from

H.R.H. THE DUKE OF GLOUCESTER, COLONEL-IN-CHIEF, THE RIFLE BRIGADE

"*N*OW *that the war in Europe is over, I wish, as your Colonel-in-Chief to send my warmest congratulations to all ranks. From the dark days of Calais, through the Western Desert and then on to Tunisia where Battalions from North Africa met those who had advanced from Egypt through bad times and good, one thing has never varied. This is the spirit of the Regiment and its reputation for close co-operation with other arms for the purpose of defeating the enemy. Since those days you have fought in Italy and in North West Europe from the start of that campaign till, at the end you led the pursuit over the Rhine and into the heart of Germany. From my present appointment in Australia, I have watched these closing scenes with admiration and pride. Whatever the future holds in store, you can be certain that never in all the splendid history of the Regiment have your achievements been surpassed. I am proud to be your Colonel-in-Chief.*"

(*Signed*) HENRY,
Colonel-in-Chief.

June, 1945.

[*Speaight.*

LIEUT.-COLONEL V. B. TURNER, V.C.

CALAIS
(The 1st Battalion, 1940).

By Major A. W. Allan, D.S.O.

Readers of the " Chronicle " who followed in its pages the fortunes of the 1st Battalion in the busy pre-war years of its pioneering activities as the first Motor Battalion of the Army will have gleaned some idea of the magnitude of the task involved, as well as the success achieved. Much of the credit so justly given to the motor battalions of the 8th and other British Armies during the war years can fairly be attributed to the hard groundwork of 1937/1940. But, however much their role was changed, the men of the old 1st Battalion took it in their stride, remaining essentially the same riflemen as ever. The following pages are designed to give a short sketch of how this unit came temporarily to pass from ken in the days of the Defence of Calais, where such success as was achieved against Germany's best trained and equipped troops was attributable still in the main to the rifle and the spirit of the man behind it.

On Tuesday, 21st May, 1940 the Battalion dispersed in Suffolk villages, had done a hard day's work constructing road-blocks in the anticipation of the German invasion of England, then regarded as imminent. Orders received at 1900 hours for an immediate move to Southampton resulted in the whole unit being under way in fully packed vehicles at 2315 hours. An exhausting drive in pouring rain ended at Southampton at midday on the 22nd, where a scratch meal was served to the men on the Avenue. Vehicles were taken straight to the docks and loaded as they were, with all ammunition, weapons, etc. (except for 40 rounds S.A.A. per man and 8 Bren guns) on to the vehicle ship. Some two hours later the Battalion marched in hot sunny weather to embark on a personnel ship, *s.s Archangel*, passing *en route* a cricket match, a typical scene of peaceful England. The German armoured thrust was then at, or approaching, Abbeville. The men spent the night packed like sardines, only those not on duty being able to get a few hours' fitful sleep, as the convoy of two personnel and two vehicle ships, with 2nd/60th Rifles and 1st R.B., steamed up-channel to Dover. Here, Brigadier Nicholson received his orders to move, on disembarkation at Calais, to operate somewhere beyond St. Omer on the right flank of the B.E.F. It was known that 3rd R.T.R. had gone to Calais the previous night with similar orders. The third unit of 30th Infantry Brigade (1st Q.V.R., previously billeted in Kent) had crossed from Dover on the 21st and were awaiting the arrival of the rest of the Brigade at Calais. The convoy sailed from Dover under escort of one destroyer and during the crossing the Brigadier issued orders for the battalions to move to dispersal areas clear of the harbour on disembarkation, and to await the unloading of vehicles, etc. As vehicles arrived, units were to concentrate right and left of the Calais—Boulogne road, the first unit to disembark to take the right. This order had, in the event, the effect of determining the tasks of 60th and R.B. For, as the personnel ships steamed into Calais harbour at 1300 hours on Thursday, 23rd May (after an ineffectual attempt by German aircraft to bomb them and amid depth charges dropped by the escort), the 60th's ship berthed first.

From the moment of arrival it was plain that the battle for Calais was on. A movement control staff officer, a D.S.T.O. and a few khaki-clad figures were only there to handle the warps and one or two short gang planks. Broken glass from the station and hotel buildings littered the quays and platforms, in which many bomb craters were visible besides overturned and bombed trucks on the lines. As he stepped ashore, the Brigadier was informed by movement control staff officer that all telephone communications at the quay with England and France were cut by Fifth Columnists and Germans; that the town was full of snipers; that the location of B.E.F. H.Q., last heard of near Hazebrouck, had not been known for some time and could not be conjectured; and that German armoured columns were already operating between Boulogne and Calais. 3rd R.T.R. were still unloading the last of their " B " Echelon, but the regiment had already moved south of Calais, and were rumoured to have met opposition. The Brigadier departed for the town to find the Base commandant, and battalions filed off the ships to their dispersal area, the men gazing curiously at the piles of abandoned kit lying on the quays jettisoned by crowds of soldiers and airmen who were being shepherded on to the ship, recently vacated by 3rd R.T.R., homeward bound. These troops were in the main, non-combatant personnel, R.A.F. ground staff, H.Q. clerks, etc., who had suffered a severe battering by the Luftwaffe on their travels to the coast. They bore every sign of this, and made a far from cheerful welcome to the theatre of war.

The dispersal area for 1st R.B. was in the sand dunes to the east of the harbour mouth. The C.O. was quickly called away and Major J. A. Taylor, who had temporarily taken over Second-in-Command in the absence of that Officer on special duty, set companies, after a hasty meal, to digging trenches. It was well that he did so, for such protection as was then prepared was used throughout the battle and it was in this area that the last rounds were fired. The afternoon wore on with the vehicle ships still churning up the mud in the falling harbour tide in the absence of tugs to haul them into the quays, and it was not until 1700 hours that the 60th vehicle ship berthed and unloading began. She got the benefit of three cranes while the Rifle Brigade ship, last in, had only one. Soon after unloading began the first enemy shells fell on the far side of the harbour. This shelling, combined with an excited mob of civilians, yelling " Les Allemands," was in full view of the Battalion, which could also see that some form of scrap was taking place down the coast towards Boulogne. Now came the news that 3rd R.T.R. had fought an action only a few kilometres south of their position, and were withdrawing into Calais itself and officers began to feel more than impatient for the arrival of their weapons and equipment.

Unloading proceeded very slowly. The British stevedores had worked for thirty-six hours at unloading a supply ship of rations for the B.E.F. on to lorries, and were almost too tired to stand. There was no French dock labour, with the exception of the operators of the crane. Parties from each company standing by to take away vehicles did what they could to help, but it was found that unskilled labour was more inclined to delay unloading than otherwise. So darkness fell, with little that was required ashore, and already there were new orders for the Rifle Brigade requiring the use of all transport urgently.

It would be convenient here to anticipate a little and to explain that there were really four phases of the action at Calais, corresponding with fresh orders received by Brigadier Nicholson. These orders varied in accordance with information as it was collated by higher authority. The first, as has been said, was the preparation for concentration south-west of the town, with a view to advancing inland and operating against enemy light troops on the flank of the main battle. At this time it was believed that enemy armoured cars only were operating in the areas Abbeville—Calais. Next, the urgency of the supply situation for the B.E.F., now withdrawing on Dunkirk, pressed for the delivery of the 350,000 rations unloaded on 22nd May, at Calais, and the Rifle Brigade was ordered to escort them half-way to Dunkirk, while 60th and Q.V.R. held the enemy from Calais. The enemy was now realized to be stronger than formerly supposed (for Boulogne was to be evacuated), but only light armoured forces were still estimated. Thirdly, early on 24th May orders were received for the defence of Calais, but the Brigadier was informed that evacuation of defending troops would probably be undertaken that night. Later, this evacuation was postponed until the 25th. Lastly, some time on the 25th, Brigadier Nicholson received the order to hold out to the last, and that every moment the enemy could be held off was of the utmost importance to the safety of the B.E.F. This last order reached 1st R.B. some time shortly before midnight on the 25th and was repeated continually throughout the 26th by various means.

Now, as the evening of the 23rd drew on, Lieut.-Colonel Hoskyns gave out the orders to " A " and " I " Companies for concentration areas north of the Calais—Dunkirk road preparatory to picketing the route for some twelve miles, after which protection would be taken over by troops from Dunkirk. " B " Company was detailed as escort to the supply column, with a detachment of 3rd R.T.R. under command. The column was to start at midnight. These orders were not destined to be carried out for various reasons, the first being the desperately slow rate of unloading of vehicles. " A " Company's scout platoon (2/Lieut. A. P. R. Rolt) was made up to strength, and drove to its rendezvous some seven miles to the east. On arrival there, local information indicated that enemy tanks were already in the area and surrounding the platoon. A dispatch rider arrived from Captain P. Peel, who had taken over " A " Company, with withdrawal orders, but, as the D.R. only gave these orders verbally, Rolt asked for confirmation and laagered for the night with all-round defence. During the night, a number of fires were lit in his neighbourhood on all sides. These proved to be the enemy forward tanks, lighting signals to show their aircraft the limit of their advance. It was only by the exercise of considerable skill that this platoon extricated itself without loss the following morning, after receiving confirmatory orders to withdraw. Meantime, as vehicles slowly became available, Major G. L. Hamilton-Russell, O.C. " B " Company with Captain C. M. Smiley as his Second-in-Command, received four composite platoons made up from all companies, and was ready at the appointed hour for his escort duties. The Tank Commander, however, insisted on delaying the start until first light, and it was not until nearly 0500 hours on the 24th that the column got under way (3rd R.T.R. had, as stated, fought an action on the outskirts of Calais on the 23rd, in which they had lost about a squadron strength of their tanks).

Rifle Brigade Companies still awaited their vehicles, but " I " Company's scout platoon (2/Lieut. D. R. Sladen) mounted in trucks, and 2/Lieut. C. R. C. Weld-Forester's platoon (dismounted), were placed to the east of Calais, the 60th having by now taken up positions to the west and south-west on the outer defences of Calais with their left about the St. Omer road. 1st Q.V.R. still held the thin line of advanced positions west and south of Calais to which they had been directed on arrival. During the night a complete hiatus had taken place on the quay; all the staff having gone away to sleep in utter exhaustion, and the essential men who worked the cranes had disappeared after several shell splinters had landed in the holds of the ships. It was mainly by the super-human efforts of Captain T. R. Gordon-Duff that the cranes were got working again, and unloading resumed slowly. Sundry ships of the Royal Navy came in during the night, one destroyer bringing Major-General McNaughton, commanding 1st Canadian Division, to reconnoitre. Despite desultory shelling and bombing during the hours of darkness, the Battalion suffered no loss so far as is known, and the first casualties occurred in " Boy " Hamilton-Russell's column. This met opposition within some two miles of Calais amongst the surbuban " ribbon development " and allotments. A strong enemy road-block defeated the advance-guard tanks, which found flanking movement impossible. A gallant effort by 2/Lieut. J. F. H. Surtees, with carriers, was also unsuccessful, but while he pinned the enemy so far located, 2/Lieut. E. A. Bird's

Platoon of " B " Company was sent round the right flank, while P.S.M. Stevens covered the left flank with " I " Company troops. Touch was lost with Bird (who in fact had become involved with enemy infantry posts south of the road) and several casualties were incurred from well-directed enemy mortar fire on the reserve platoons, a motley-mounting truck receiving a direct hit. Hamilton-Russell's orders were interrupted by accurate fire wherever his command post was moved.

The Commanding Officer and Brigadier were present during a considerable part of the five hours effort to break the passage, and, after reports from David Sladen, and other posts, which strongly confirmed that the " Boy's " command was rapidly being surrounded by superior forces, he received orders to withdraw. Bird's platoon rejoined just as the withdrawal began, well pleased with having inflicted ten or more casualties on the enemy. They had lost, however, Cpl. Cross killed and three or four riflemen were carried back wounded. The column was back in Calais by 1100 hours on 24th and " B " Company (less No. 6 Platoon) now took up positions in reserve near the Cellulose Factory, while the remainder joined their Companies.

Much had occurred during their absence. 60th vehicle ship, which carried Brigade H.Q. vehicles, completed unloading at about 0430 hours and was then filled with wounded from the first of two hospital trains which had been standing in the station before its arrival. Unloading of Rifle Brigade ship continued, but at about 0730 hours orders were given by the quay staff, who stated that they had Brigadier Nicholson's permission, to close down the holds and load with the wounded of the second hospital train. Both trainloads of patients were transferred by Rifle Brigade personnel, but more than twenty men who had died in the train were left on the quay, which had now for some hours been under shell-fire. The stevedores and their officers and some of the quay staff embarked, and the ship sailed at about 0830 hrs. followed some time later by the 60th vehicle ship, which carried the remainder of the quay staff (except D.S.T.O.), as well as the Brigadier lately commanding Boulogne base, and other persons who had escaped from that place. The ships were shelled from a south-east direction as they left the harbour, but not hit.

1st R.B's. deficiency in equipment was now severe. All scout cars and the six Bren guns they carried had been handed to 1st Armoured Division just before embarkation, and the premature departure of the vehicle ship left them some 50 per cent. short of weapons and equipment ; the Signal Officer (Lieut. J. P. Duncanson) had only one (No. 9) truck, only " B " Company had its W./T. truck ; carriers were barely enough to make up two scout platoons ; the M.O. had no medical stores or transport, and " B " Echelon no tools. Fortunately, the reserve ammunition had come ashore. A lot was done to remedy this state of affairs. By 2/Lieut. R. G. L. Tryon's (T.O.) and others' efforts, vehicles were, in many cases, replaced from the mass of abandoned material in Calais, several Bren guns even being "scrounged" and at least one scout car. "Wally" Straight was most successful in finding rations in various places under sniping and other fire, and in distributing them. The men, in fact, were never short of food, but rather of time in which to eat any. A limited amount of 3-inch mortar ammunition (not issued to the Battalion up to the time of embarkation) was brought in by the Royal Navy as well as quantities of petrol and gelignite for demolition. The Royal Navy demolition party reported however, that the primers brought were the wrong size, and at about 1300 hours they, as well as the D.S.T.O. and the Admiralty wireless ship, left Calais; the quay now being entirely deserted of officials. For some time the increasing enemy fire had added considerably to the difficulties in movement and "sorting out." Fires were blazing everywhere; oil tanks smoking. Gordon-Duff, who had been put in charge of the protection of the quays with two scratch platoons of spare drivers, was hard put to it to keep them clear of refugee civilians. He and his men also succeeded in saving some light tanks out of several set on fire, but 3rd R.T.R. were already sadly reduced in tank strength by the afternoon of the 24th. One squadron had been sent to reconnoitre the coast road through Gravelines. The Germans had already reached the coast, and this squadron, after a sharp action in which it is believed the Germans lost heavily, was absorbed into the Dunkirk defences. During the morning, 60th had been fighting in the outer defences of Calais in extended positions interspersed with two companies of Q.V.R. The remaining half of that regiment was put under Lieut.-Colonel Hoskyn's command, and was reinforced by platoons of 1st R.B. 2/Lieut. F. Reed, with No. 10 Platoon of "C" Company, had put himself under command of Capt. Bower of the 60th at the point of junction with that regiment. Here at 0500 hours two German prisoners were taken, and at 0600 hours two light tanks driven off.

Nothing is known of the adventures of Lieut. W. M. Welch's platoon ("B" Company) posted on the Dunkirk exit, from the time the column returned until 1600 hours. David Sladen (No. 13 Platoon) reported at about 1100 hours large enemy forces moving from south to north across his front, and the C.O. ordered this and No. 14 Platoon posts to be withdrawn to the line of battlements. This was effected by No. 13 Platoon withdrawing through No. 14 Platoon (who also towed in an anti-tank gun taken under command) and covering its retirement in turn. The enemy took no action. At 1145 hours, after Q.V.R. had reported the outer perimeter no longer tenable, the C.O. ordered "I" and "A" Companies to occupy the inner perimeter: "I" Company on the right from the end of the bridge under the Mairie clock tower (in touch here with 60th Rifles), then southwards 400 yds. to the canal junction, thence 800 yds. eastwards to the junction of battlements with the canal (here "I" Company was in touch with "A" Company). "A" Company held from this corner (inclusive of the bridge) facing east along the battlements to the Bassin des Chasses, with their scout platoon (2/Lieut. Rolt) from there to the sea, but this platoon was kept as a reserve under the C.O's. hand. Both companies had an uncomfortably long frontage, and 2/Lieut. F. T. F. C. G. Fletcher's platoon of " B " Company (about half strength only) and later Willy Welch's platoon also were sent to Peter Peel. H.Q. and the remaining two platoons of " B " Company were held in reserve near a large heavily bombed building south of the quays, known as the Cellulose Factory. " C " Company (Major V. C. Knollys) were still digging in on the dunes, held in reserve, while Major H. Coghill, with H.Q. Company was never required to leave his original position to the east of the harbour entrance throughout the battle.

Before midday on the 24th, the 30th Brigade was clearly involved in phrase three referred to above ; that is, in a desperate attempt to defend the town and harbour of Calais. To do this, Brigadier Nicholson had few troops and all too little material. There was no artillery. Some execution had been done the previous evening and earlier this day by French shore artillery turned inland, but the personnel manning these weapons had put them out of action and departed to sea in a fleet of tugs before midday. A detachment of an anti-tank unit under a R.A. Officer had arrived with eight 2-pdr. anti-tank guns. These were all out of action by the afternoon of the 25th. 1st R.B. had two or three 3-inch mortars, and 60th presumably one per Company. A few anti-tank mines were landed by the Royal Navy and distributed by 2/Lieut. A. G. H. Bampfylde equally between the two regiments' fronts on a lorry drive which he must have found somewhat hectic. For the rest, apart from the machine guns in the few tanks left, and two Vickers brought by the Royal Marines, reliance had to be placed on Bren guns, " Boy's " anti-tank rifles and the rifle.

Large numbers of troops continued to make their way into Calais on the 24th from L. of C. bombed out A/A and Searchlight positions, R.A.S.C. units, etc., but the large majority of these were unarmed except for revolvers. Useful work was, however, done by many in the heavy fighting to come. It was clear that demolition material was of the first importance, for Calais was intersected by canals which in those days made excellent anti-tank obstacles if the bridges could be destroyed or well blocked. It had been arranged that demolition would be the responsibility of the French, with the exception of the docks area, for which the Royal Navy were to make arrangements. The French had no material and no demolitions were in the event carried out. Most of the many bridges were, of course, of heavy masonry and considerable size, and the plan advanced by the French commander at the Citadel for attempting their destruction by placing under them some prodigious shells, which he said existed in his store, and having them fired in some mysterious way by officers prepared to sacrifice themselves *pour la patrie* was adjudged to be at that stage of the battle, impracticable. H.M.S. *Wolfhound* tied up to the outer jetty during the early afternoon with a view to spotting for some destroyers which were engaging German batteries on the coast between Boulogne and Calais. At least one such battery was put out of action. The C.O. went aboard with the Adjutant (Lieut. T. H. Acton) to ask for demolition material, and was offered the ship's complement of gun-cotton, with any other assistance the Captain could give. Unfortunately, so many urgent calls on the C.O's. attention intervened then and for the rest of the day that the matter was not pursued. H.M.S. *Wolfhound* remained until the evening, several times coming into action against attacking enemy aircraft.

At about 1800 hours a M.T.B. brought the P.S.T.O. Channel Ports, a Commodore, who once more took over Naval control of the docks and, having brought the necessary primers, wirelessed for the naval demolition party to return. Now a swing bridge over the docks was prepared for demolition, and the party returned home, the Commodore himself remaining until the 26th. During the afternoon the enemy attacks on the 60th front had intensified to such a degree that Lieut.-Colonel Hoskyns deemed it necessary on several occasions to send assistance from his reserves. Gordon-Duff took a platoon of spare drivers with which he held a section of the 60th front being about the last to be withdrawn from the outer perimeter at dark. At 1600 hours Hamilton-Russell with No. 8 Platoon (P.S.M. Eason) and half his scout platoon, was sent in trucks through " I " Company's position into the town to support 60th and Q.V.R. There was sniping by Fifth Columnists in " I " Company's area at this time, and a part of Brigade H.Q. withdrew past the Mairie to its new location at the Gare Maritime. At about 1600 hours also Tony Rolt received an order through the Intelligence Officer to take his mortar section and No. 11 Platoon, " C " Company (P.S.M. Criss) to the 60th area. There he was to get into touch with C.O. 60th (whose H.Q. were not known to 1st R.B.) and put down mortar fire on an area of the Rue Gambetta which 2/Lieut. Price showed him on the map. On passing through No. 15 Platoon, Rolt was told that enemy tanks were already in the 60th area, and that he was likely to meet them at any moment. All parties of 60th and Q.V.R. met confirmed that the enemy had got a footing in the town. After reconnaissance the area indicated was plastered with thirty bombs at long range from the gardens near the Mairie Square. This somewhat doubtful shoot actually had helped a party of Q.V.R's. according to information given later by an officer present to Tony Rolt. However, he rightly decided to use no more ammunition and withdrew to report to the C.O., Hamilton-Russell returned through " I " Company at about 1730 hours to the roadblock near the Cellulose Factory. His Company (" B ") still had two platoons detached (No. 6 and No. 7) and was destined to remain so for the remainder of the battle. At 1900 hours these platoons were both in position with " A " Company and at about the same time, No. 12 Platoon " C " Company (2/Lieut. Fellows) and No. 11 Platoon " C " Company (P.S.M. Criss) were sent to reinforce " I " Company. Both these platoons were placed by Major E. J. A. H Brush in reserve about 200 yards in rear of No. 16 Platoon on the transverse road (and yet they were in a front-line position as the Battalion was forward of the 60th line here from now onwards). 60th were fighting in the Rue Gambetta about 300 yards south-west of " I " Company while withdrawals from the battlements south-west and south of the town were taking place. Q.V.R. less two companies were withdrawing to the neighbourhood of H.Q. Rifle Brigade and the 60th (the majority of whose retirements did not take place until dusk) were brought back to the shorter line in the old town ordered by the Brigadier. By 2100 hours the new positions were taken up, leaving, as arranged, " I " Company R.B. in a forward salient with the nearest 60th post in view of No. 15 Platoon bridge overlooking the Hotel de Ville. At midnight enemy activity in the town ceased apart from isolated bombing and shelling, Rifle Brigade H.Q. having some close " overs " of heavy stuff which fell in the Bassin nearby at about 0100 hours on the 25th.

Friday, the 24th had been a day of great tension. At about 1900 hours, the C.O. sent a message to companies that positions then occupied were to be held to the last man and the last round. Apart from enemy action, the general confusion as to the situation, the fantastic stories put about by enemy agents (in a letter to the Colonel-in-Chief from hospital in England, Lieut.-Colonel Hoskyns drew particular attention to the effect of the so-called " Fifth Column " activities on this and the next day), and the fact that no commander ever had a moment from the time of landing to look around him and think and plan for more than the immediate future, all tended to intensify fatigue. Nobody had slept except for a few hours on the ships, or ceased to work hard since the morning of Tuesday the 21st.

1st R.B. stood to at 0330 hours on Saturday, 25th May. After the successful repulse of the enemy on Friday, and the lull of the hours of darkness, Brigadier Nicholson asked 60th and Rifle Brigade whether there were signs of enemy withdrawal. Brush reported that he had himself patrolled the Rue Gambetta from 0530 hrs. in a car and discovered no sign of the enemy.

Peel reported little activity on the eastern face, and 60th reported similarly. Sundry forward moves were ordered by the Brigadier, but these soon met German anti-tank guns and infantry. Advanced Brigade H.Q. had left the Gare Maritime for the Citadel with a view to close liaison with the French Commander there at 0600 hours. At 0700 hours Germans were reported by " I " Company in the Rue Gambetta. Sniping began from the western side of the canal, and a bombardment of " A " Company's position also took place at about this time, as well as a certain amount of small-arms fire from the woods to its front, coupled with Fifth Column sniping from the houses behind them. Rolt's 3-inch mortar (Cpl. Blackman) engaged Germans in the Rue Gambetta at 0745 hours from No. 11 Platoon position. At 0800 hours Peter Brush was shot through the throat by a sniper, but refused to leave his H.Q. At 0830 hours a German tactical reçonnaissance plane flew along " I " Company's positions and indicated them to their artillery by a line of smoke. At 0930 hours the enemy strafe came down with accuracy. At 1000 hours John Taylor arrived with orders to send Brush to the R.A.P. and to take over his command. All positions were now under intense fire, except the north-east portion of the defences from which the company of Q.V.R. extending " A " Company's left nevertheless reported observations of considerable enemy movement. Throughout the remainder of the morning, enemy pressure was very strong at the southern face and 2/Lieut. C. J. J. Clay (Liaison Officer, 30th Brigade) took a situation report to the Citadel at about 1130 hours with a map marked by the C.O. Apparently a German W/T message was intercepted by the French indicating that if the attacks now being launched failed they proposed to attack heavily on their left, *i.e.*, 60th right. The Brigadier decided to attempt a diversion in rear of the enemy from Rifle Brigade's left, and at 1300 hours 2/Lieut. Clay returned with Col. Holland (formerly Base Commandant) with duplicate orders to Lieut.-Colonel Hoskyns to take a mobile column of all A.F.Vs. (tanks and carriers) and at least two motor platoons through the perimeter east of the Bassin des Chasses, and to sweep round to attack the enemy's right rear in order to relieve pressure on the 60th. All reserves had become involved from the previous day with the exception of H.Q. and two platoons of " C " Company. " I " Company relied particularly on their three carriers and Cpl. Blackman's mortar section of Rolt's carrier platoon to cover bridges on their extended front, and both these and " A " Company's bridges were now in momentary danger of being forced. The C.O. made a formal and energetic protest which was rejected by Colonel Holland, and preparation for collecting the necessary troops was put in hand. Lieut.-Colonel Hoskyns stated that he would try to start at 1430 hours. The Adjutant, having written the necessary messages, made a personal reconnaissance of the route along the south edge of the Bassin des Chasses, and finding it impracticable, returned to report and to get the vehicles, now collected, turned round and in order (for the only other way out was by the sand dunes and beach), a very difficult task on the narrow road past the railway yards, which was all this time under heavy fire. At this time, Tony Rolt while engaged in collecting 2/Lieut. Sanderson and his carriers from " I " Company's line, became involved in the streets behind the main position with enemy infantry, who had infiltrated. Meeting three light tanks of 3rd R.T.R., he led them with his carriers in a successful counter-drive to clear the streets, inflicting several casualties, and finding particularly good targets down the streets across the canal to the west of David Fellow's[1] houses and south of the 60th left. Jerry Duncanson shot down a German reconnaissance plane with a Bren gun in " A " Company's area.

Meanwhile the C. O. had already sent Knollys with " C " Company (less two platoons) on foot along the dunes to the eastern end of the Bassin, but now, realising the practical impossibility of taking wheeled vehicles through the heavy sand, he at last succeeded in getting through to Brigade by wireless and receiving Brigadier Nicholson's permission to cancel the column. The leading tanks and carriers had already started, and were in trouble in the sand. Where possible the return of troops to their previous locations began, but the damage was already done when the defence was weakened by the collection of the column and the C.O's. attention distracted from fighting his command, and Battalion H.Q. never really assembled and functioned as such again. Indeed, before the C.O. left finally to start the movement (taking practically all Battalion H.Q. with him) he had already received reports that breaches had been made in the front line and left the Second-in-Command to organize another position through " B " Company's main road block. This was accomplished, the troops used being H.Q. " B " Company, with one Bren gun section ; H.Q. and one company, Q.V.R. ; the remains of an A/A battery half armed with rifles ; about thirty men of a searchlight battery ; and rear brigade H.Q. The enemy had by 1500 hours succeeded in breaking through the forward positions in two places and, working through the streets in getting round the back of Company H.Q. and platoons holding the front line. Desperate close fighting took place, during which John Taylor was severely wounded and David Sladen killed while attacking the enemy in one of the many small counter-actions which took place. The Second-in-Command of " I " Company, 2/Lieut. A. J. B. Van der Weyer, was eventually killed defending the point of junction with the 60th where P.S.M. Williams had already lost his life, and 2/Lieut. Thomas was killed in circumstances not known. Small detachments continued to defend houses in this area after being surrounded, and P.S.M. Stevens (No. 16 Platoon) with some sixteen men of " I " and " C " Companies, having fought until all their ammunition was exhausted, hid in the houses round their positions for fourteen days before starvation forced them to surrender. Few of " I " Company and the two platoons of " C " Company attacked, were extricated from this imbroglio in spite of a determined effort on the part of Brush, who had left the R.A.P., and had received the C.O's. permission to attempt to retrieve the situation on his company's front with the assistance of Lieut. Bird's platoon of " B " Company (now returned from the cancelled column) and the remaining tanks. None of the latter were, however, made available, and the small party were brought

---

[1] 2/Lieut. Honbl. J. D. C. Fellowes.

to a stop a short distance beyond "B" Company's block by intensive L.A. fire. While trying to deal with this a French camion appeared full of wounded men belonging to "I" Company in charge of Cpl. Lane, and driven by a Fifth Columnist at the point of the revolver. In spite of being waved on, the driver stopped under fire, and while the wounded who could were getting out to try to crawl across the road, Edward Bird ran forward, climbed into the driver's seat, and endeavoured to restart the lorry. In this gallant effort he was shot in the head, dying soon after. After this, Peter Brush having only a handful of No. 5 Platoon unwounded men left, was forced to abandon the attempt to reach the original company area. "A" Company although suffering many casualties was still fairly intact and was fighting the enemy on three sides of it ; P.S.M. Johnstone being killed at the road-block formed to protect the rear of Peter Peel's H.Q. But the two attached platoons of "B" Company were overwhelmed by enemy tanks on this evening while attempting a flanking movement to retake the bridge which had been lost at the junction of "I" and "A" Companies front. Willy Welch was killed in circumstances not yet known during this counter-attack.

At about 1530 hours a shell had landed in one of H.Q. Company's trenches where the C.O. was with Coghill and Taylor, who had been brought there. Taylor was again wounded, as was C.Q.M.S.Clifton, by the same shell, and "Chan" Hoskyns received such severe wounds that he subsequently died in England. A young D.R. reported to the Second-in-Command, near the Cellulose Factory, that the C.O. was killed, and Brush and Acton "blown to bits." The Second-in-Command duly reported to Brigade that he had taken over, and in time he, Hamilton-Russell, and Brush became aware of each others' presence ; each having received false reports that the others were casualties and believing himself to be the senior officer left. This was a critical moment in the battle. Between 1530 and 1630 hours Rolt's carrier platoon (dismounted after the cancellation of the column) was now remounted and sent by the acting C.O. on a foray into the old town across the Place de l'Europe as a result of reports that enemy tanks had broken in and the danger of a breakthrough between the two regiments. At about 1630 hours the bombardment intensified upon the whole Brigade's position, and soon the Citadel was a vast sheet of flame. From this time advanced Brigade H.Q. were out of touch on W/T. While Tony Rolt was away, Hamilton-Russell reported with a well-worked-out scheme for ordering and covering the withdrawal of "A" Company, the company of Q.V.R. extending "A" Company's left, and as many elements of "I" and "C" Company's platoons as possible to a shorter line behind the Cellulose Factory.

He already had arrangements in hand at his H.Q., and the acting C.O. now approved the plan and ordered Hamilton-Russell to take charge of this operation, while he himself dealt with the point of pressure at the junction with the 60th and O.C. " B " Company's right flank. Subsequently withdrawal proceeded with little interference from the enemy, Captain Smiley directing platoons to their new positions as they came back. The Q.V.R. reported that they would not be able to get all their men in before dark, and in fact some elements did cross the canal in the wrong direction and, becoming involved with the Germans on the dunes to the east, were not recovered. 2/Lieut. Hon. T. C. F. Prittie came back via the beach with a few men of " A " Company and, reporting to Duncanson with H.Q. Company, was ordered to join Surtees in " C " Company's old trenches. Surtees, after his carriers had become stuck in the sand, had been informed of the cancellation of the column during the evening by Acton, who was not, however, able to retrieve the rest of Knollys' command from the dunes east of the Bassin, where the C.O. had sent them early in the afternoon. Knollys, joined by some Q.V.R. from the eastern perimeter referred to above, had moved to positions farther east for the night. On the following morning he engaged the enemy, who had A.F.V's. in this area, for some hours before being surrounded and overwhelmed. During this action 2/Lieut. G. J. Kane carried out a most successful fighting patrol amongst the sandhills, in which he, with Rifleman Eagle as his Second-in-Command destroyed three enemy L.A. Sections. Kane, when disarming a fourth with an empty revolver, was severely wounded by a German N.C.O. who appeared from behind a knoll at the wrong moment.

At about 1700 hours the acting C.O., who had failed to speak to the Brigadier, did succeed in speaking to Lieut.-Colonel Miller (O.C. 60th) and ascertained that he was being very hard-pressed everywhere, and was still very nervous about his right flank. Not long after this enemy aircraft dropped showers of leaflets on and around the Gare Maritime giving an hour's grace for surrender from 1800 to 1900 hours. In the hot weather of these days and the dust and grime of battle drinking water was of importance, and trouble was caused from Saturday onwards by damage to the mains in the town and Gare Maritime area, but this difficulty was overcome by recourse to wells which were found and by constantly repairing main supplies. Water had to be carried for some distance to sand dune positions. As on previous nights, enemy activity died down at dark and the Battalion now settled in its new positions for the night, breathed again. Enemy attacks had all but succeeded this evening, and great credit is due to the 60th for their magnificent defence of the Old Town. Hoskyns and Taylor were found in the R.A.P. at the station, both in a bad way, but the former expressed his delight at the way in which the enemy had been held off. It is difficult to write more of this fine officer who had now seen the last of the Battalion he had loved and commanded so well. Taylor, who had been a tower of strength throughout, was a grave loss to the Battalion at this time. Though damaged beyond complete repair, he fortunately recovered enough to do much more for the Regiment during the war.

At about 2330 hours W/T communication with the 60th was again got with difficulty, for many batteries were now low. Lieut.-Colonel Miller had gone to the Citadel to find the Brigadier whose fate had not been known for some time. The Brigadier, however, at this moment arrived at the station yard and expressed himself in most complimentary terms on the Battalion's efforts.

He then received the C.O's. rather meagre reports (for patrols sent out to locate troops beyond the Bassin and on the beach were not yet back) and approved his proposed dispositions for the following day. The Brigadier now gave the latest order from home that Calais was to be held to the last, and this was duly repeated during the night to responsible commanders. He then asked if the C.O. considered it possible, in the event of 1st R.B. and other troops in the vicinity being heavily attacked, to withdraw them all into the town and make, with the 60th, an all-round defensive ring to include the Citadel. The C.O. replied that he did not think so, and the Brigadier agreed that it would be most difficult especially in view of the failure so far to locate the remnants of 3rd R.T.R. " C " Company Rifle Brigade (less two platoons) and some of the Q.V.R. Permission was given to wireless for a hospital ship, and this was done by Commodore, R.N., later in the night. The Brigadier wished the Battalion luck and said good-night, returning to the Citadel. No further order was received from Brigade, except for a repetition of the Government and War Office message to hold to the last, brought by Colonel Holland the next morning. At dawn a small yacht took off Hoskyns, Taylor and other wounded from the R.A.P. on the quay, where Surgeon-Lieut. Waind, R.N., had done wonderful work, and was to do more on the 26th when he was the only Medical Officer present. The R.A.P in the tunnel was shared by Captain Cameron, R.A.M.C. the Rifle Brigade Medical Officer, and Lieut. Gartside, M.O., of Q.V.R. helped by the two padres, Wingfield-Digby and Heard. Here they had been intensely busy for two days. All their efforts deserve the highest praise. Unfortunately, this R.A.P. had been moved, together with its patients, by order of an officer of 3rd R.T.R. urgently expressed, along the beach during the afternoon without the knowledge of the respective C.Os. of the Rifle Brigade and Q.V.R. During Saturday 1st R.B. had used all its ammunition, including reserves, and had issued 20,000 rounds more brought by the Royal Navy, most of which had been used up. There was, besides, a grave shortage of weapons available for the next day's battle, a shortage more serious than man power, which in itself, so far as the Battalion was concerned, was now serious. Expectations of an enemy dawn attack on the 26th were fortunately not realized. Apparently the two defeats suffered by the enemy on the Friday and Saturday imposed on the enemy Corps Commander such caution that he decided to relieve his forward troops (probably for the second time) and stage a new full-dress attack with more extensive artillery preparation, continuous dive-bombing attacks and heavy mortar and machine-gun support—certainly a compliment to the tired defenders. Subsequent accounts of German origin made much of the resources called upon. Artillery of a complete corps was stated to have been in action since early on the 24th, and a lot was made of the fine supply effort which replaced their ammunition expenditure. In consequence of this extended preparation, some measure of reorganization was possible on the Rifle Brigade fronts. New forward positions on either side of the Bassin des Chasses were manned by the least tired of the troops available, with as much advantage taken of cross-fire positions as possible. Bren guns were very short, and though thoroughly cleaned during the hours of darkness became, like the rifles, badly clogged with sand in the positions held on this side of Calais, and many excellent targets must have been inadequately dealt with on this account during Sunday's fighting while weapons were recleaned again and again. Ammunition, however, was now so short that few rounds can have been wasted ; and the capable efforts of R.S.M. Goodey, Sergt. Phillips and Sergt. Welch, of the new skeleton H.Q. formed, eked out what was left for replenishment to the best effect. The last 3-inch mortar rounds were fired during the morning with accurate results by " Sandy " Sanderson, who had, with Cpl. Morton, already done good execution with a salvaged machine gun. There were no other weapons to use. It can be stated with some pride that the heavy German strafing preparation referred to above had the minimum effect on the riflemen, who fired from their exposed positions at the attacking Stukas as coolly as participants in a pheasant shoot. That some positions became, as the day drew on, untenable goes without saying, but on no occasion was a withdrawal made of more than a few yards, and more than once the original position was retaken. The space between the portions of the defence on the Battalion's front entailed great difficulty of control and communication, and distances between sub-units were greatly increased by battle obstacles. In this kind of fighting a man often knows nothing of what is occurring within ten yards of him. Smoke, fires, dust and falling masonry ; line after line of track holding scores of goods wagons and other rolling stock ; thin but high cement walls ; heavy sand on the dunes and bunds—made movement as fatiguing as observation was difficult. In spite of all this, the defence, by no means badly damaged or deterred by the preparatory bombardments, continued throughout the morning to hold the enemy's attack which was now being pressed very strongly at all points ; but from about 1300 hours onwards, the situation deteriorated. Accurate German heavy mortar fire was mainly responsible for helping on their infantry.

It had been hoped that these and other enemy support weapons might be dealt with by naval bombardment and this had been asked for at 1045 hours, on 26th, in the last message sent over the air from the Gare Maritime. Targets considered easily recognizable were indicated as well as a clear line beyond which it was safe to shoot. In the evening, an effective bombardment was in fact carried out by the Royal Navy on this line, but it was by then too late. Lieut. Millet, R.C.S., who, with his section of Brigade H.Q. Signals, had been of inestimable value throughout, was ordered to be prepared to destroy all W/T installations and files early in the afternoon. Later this was done for him, before the final order was given, by enemy mortar fire, all vehicles of value in the station yards being burned out. By 1630 hours or thereabouts the last rounds were fired, and all organized resistance ceased. The enemy infantry had indeed treated the exhausted defenders with respect and taken their time in coming to grips. This they eventually did at all points simultaneously, from the 60th right, into the Citadel itself, and all along the circle of attack to the beaches in the rear of the Rifle Brigade positions. Men of the Rifle Brigade were shot from across the harbour mouth at the end.

Much more could be written of the fighting on this last day; of the tough resistance put up on the right by Rolt's scout platoon, P.S.M. Easen's Platoon of " B " Company (he later died of wounds) and others; of Arthur Hamilton-Russell, mortally wounded in an attempt to gain observation from the most exposed point near him, after as hard a four days' fighting and work as ever a soldier did; of Tony Rolt's final gallant effort, almost alone, to seize a possible point of vantage; of the accurate fire still being directed from the French shore battery emplacement by men of " A " Company, Royal Marines and others, including Major Coxwell Rogers, the Staff Captain, who was killed here while firing a Bren gun at Germans on the beach behind this position; of the hours of steady and accurate shooting put in by Peter Brush's command based on Surtee's trenches on the sand dunes, where Rifleman Gurr (one of the Battalion's best Bisley shots) got badly wounded in the leg he was to lose; Sergt. Welsh, shot through the jaw, Rifleman Murphy, who had found and got into working order a Lewis gun; David Fellows of " C " Company, with a large hole in his head from the fighting in " I " Company's area the day before; Peter Peel and John Surtees, both wounded, and Brush wounded again, with Forrester, Price and a few other riflemen sniped and hit (for that was all that was now possible) to the end—until Jerry Duncanson, who had never for a moment ceased to chivvy the enemy at every possible opportunity, and who had enjoyed every moment of it, stood up to kill the last German to be shot in this area, and inevitably received his mortal wound. But it is surely invidious to dwell upon individual efforts when all did their utmost. Of those who died, although the deeds of some are not yet known in full, it would be impossible to write too much. They will be

THE 1ST BATTALION AT CALAIS, 1940

remembered. Of those who survived a great number were wounded, most of whom had to recover as best they could in German hands. If all ranks of the 1st Battalion who had reached by keenness and hard work such a high standard of training for mobile warfare with armoured divisions, were disappointed of their fun in a war of movement, they at least still enjoyed the excitements of the early days of this action, and in the grim realities of the last days took pride in their discipline and fighting qualities as Riflemen under any conditions of war. It would not be easy to find any who regret the days of Calais.

* * *

The recently awarded decorations to the Regiment for the Defence were : D.S.O., 2 ; M.C., 4 ; D.C.M., 2 ; M.M., 7 ; Mention in Despatches, 32.

* * *

On 4th June, 1940, the Prime Minister made the following statement to Parliament:—

" However, the German eruption swept like a sharp scythe around the right and rear of the armies of the North. Eight, or nine, armoured divisions, each of about four hundred armoured vehicles of different kinds, but carefully assorted to be complementary and divisible into small self-contained units, cut off all communications between us and the main French armies. It severed our own communications for food and ammunition, which ran first to Amiens and afterwards through Abbeville, and it shored its way up the coast to Boulogne and Calais, almost to Dunkirk.

" Behind this armoured and mechanized onslaught came a number of German divisions in lorries, and behind them again there plodded comparatively slowly the dull brute mass of the ordinary German army and German people, always so ready to be led to the trampling down in other lands of liberties and comforts which they have never known in their own. I have said this armoured scythe-stroke almost reached Dunkirk—almost, but not quite. Boulogne and Calais were the scenes of desperate fighting. The Guards defended Boulogne for a while, and were then withdrawn by orders from this country.

" The Rifle Brigade, the 60th Rifles and the Queen Victoria's Rifles, with a battalion of British tanks and one thousand Frenchmen—in all about four thousand strong—defended Calais to the last.

" The British brigadier was given an hour to surrender. He spurned the offer, and four days of intense street fighting passed before silence reigned over Calais, which marked the end of a memorable resistance.

"Only thirty unwounded survivors were brought off by the Royal Navy, and we do not know the fate of their comrades. Their sacrifice was not, however, in vain. At least two armoured divisions, which otherwise would have been turned against the British Expeditionary Force, had to be sent to overcome them.

"They have added another page to the glories of the Light Division and the time gained enabled the Gravelines Walnlieu to be flooded and to be held by the French troops; and thus it was that the Port of Dunkirk was kept open."

* * *

The following message to all riflemen of the Rifle Brigade was received from Field-Marshal H.R.H. the Duke of Connaught K.G., K.T., etc., the Colonel-in-Chief :—

Bagshot Park,
2nd June, 1940.

"I am prouder than I can say of the manner in which the Battalion I once commanded acquitted themselves in the defence of Calais. In the glorious record of the Regiment there is little, if anything, that has been finer than the part they took in this action.

"The defence contributed enormously to the successful evacuation of the British Expeditionary Force from Dunkirk.

"The superb conduct of àll ranks in an operation attended by the greatest difficulty was worthy of the highest traditions of the Regiment.

"England is proud of this magnificent action, and as an old Commander of the Battalion, I am equally proud. I am sure that this glorious passage in the history of the Regiment will live in the history of the Army.

"My sympathy goes out to all the relations and friends of those who fell."—ARTHUR, Colonel-in-Chief.

TWO YEARS WITH A BATTALION IN THE DESERT
(1st Battalion)

By Captain Robert Fellowes

ABOUT six weeks after we had first heard that we were for overseas, we were moving out of our last billets, and heading for our port of embarkation.

The voyage started off with everyone very tee-ed up, and anxious to get cracking. A few days passed whilst the convoy gradually formed up, and boat drill was practised with quite a show of attention to detail—very different from those peace-time boat-drill practices.

Although, to most people, our destination was practically a certainty, there was a lot of betting on it—and bets were laid on such widely separated spots as Norway, Italy, India, Singapore, and naturally Egypt.

Redfern quoted against Egypt in an unguarded moment, and was eagerly snapped up by three betting men, whom he finally had to pay out, on reaching Suez.

We expected some forms of excitement during the first week of the voyage ; all we had were a few " action stations," and once a plane came and had a look at us, but nothing followed him up.

About the third day out, rough seas started and many of the troops began to go down, to say nothing of the officers, on whom a sweepstake was run for the first to go down from sea-sickness. It was a selling sweep, and evinced huge interest—a deadline was decided on at 6,30 one evening. Those who had drawn, or bought, probable good things tried every known device to make their selection win this race. The padre and the medical officer were both strongly supported, but the Jepson-Turner brothers made a race of it, Dick winning by four minutes from his elder brother.

From then on sweeps were run on every conceivable and inconceivable thing.

Training of various sorts took place every morning till eleven, and we had quite a number of interesting and amusing talks by our own officers and those from other units. Vic. Turner gave a very good series on regimental history. Sorbo Soboleff told us tales of his quite extraordinary times in Russia, China and elsewhere. Lentaigne stirred and terrified us with his talks and demonstrations with knives.

Various sports meetings and boxing matches were arranged, and altogether time did not drag too much.

We had two poker schools in our saloon, and much time, and not a little money, was spent there. Culme-Seymour and Raphael started a backgammon session as well, and Price, the 9th Lancers, and Kerr were chief exponents of a dice school.

Several days were spent refuelling at a port, where the bumboat men were in great form, and the riflemen in better form, very often getting the better of a bargain with them in their deals for bananas, while the blacks, diving for pennies, certainly amused the troops with their repartee in the " vernacular."

At Capetown our ship was first into port early one evening, and to everyone's delight we were allowed shore leave. Passes were made out at a terrific pace and issued, but as everyone (a matter of a few thousand) wanted to get off at once, there was certain chaos. Everyone eventually got off, and we all started the most monumental five days you could ever imagine.

The hospitality was truly terrific, dances, shows, visits to homes, drives around the magnificent countryside, and entertainment of every sort was laid on for everyone. Capetown took to the troops, and they in turn had the time of their lives.

Kenilworth Races with the Great Metropolitan, the South African Derby, was the climax, and the paddock might have been in England, with so many of the English " regulars " in attendance.

Most people got around to the " Bohemia " during their stay.

A large parade was held one morning at which the G.O.C., South Africa, took the salute. The Battalion found some difficulty with the fast step, of bringing up the rear, and shortly before the saluting base we halted (as we had done once or twice previously) so we could go by at our own pace, and not crowd up on those ahead. All went well until, when within about thirty yards of the base, a band started up in slow time, which finished us.

Many good friendships were formed during those five days, and it was with genuine sorrow that we sailed away from the view of Table Mountain.

Time did not drag, and as we sailed north we heard of the start of the new offensive, and feared we might have missed the bus.

Aden was our next port of call, and we had some shore leave in that grim, desolate spot, and saw all the so-called sights, and found the Club, on the front, the only reasonable spot, and everyone wanted to push on.

We were delayed several days in Aden, and our hopes fell and a suspicion arose that we might be sent to the Far East, the scanty news we were getting suggesting that Rommel's men might have been finished off for good. Then we sailed and our destination was still uncertain ; but we turned up the Red Sea, and our minds were at rest, as we felt we were reaching our scene of action.

We disembarked at Suez in rain ! There was no small confusion unloading the essential kit and getting the various units more or less together, but finally the ship was cleared, leaving the baggage parties in solitary state. Dorrien-Smith and I were with the baggage party,

Rfn. Baker, Allen, Siddle. Lieuts. F. P. Tindall and R. Brand
DINNER, CHRISTMAS DAY

1st BATTALION

RFN. ABBOTT

(*Standing*) Rfn. Channell, Rfn. Eldon, Rfn. Beasley, Rfn. Collier
(*Seated*) Cpl. Lee, Rfn. Abbott, Cpl. Allen, Rfn. Humphreys, Rfn. Ames

MY CREWS, CHRISTMAS DAY

which entailed a lot of hard work and many good laughs, the best being when we found the Gyppey dockhands eating and thoroughly enjoying a tin of axle grease, which they found broken open. Our journey, lasting two days and nights in an open goods truck, proved stimulating, and by the last night we made ourselves reasonably comfortable.

Amriya camp was, to say the least of it, a bad introduction to the desert, but we were hectically busy, and the short while we were there passed very quickly. Collecting our vehicles, getting desert modifications fitted—Baron, our O.M.E., did incredible and absolutely non-stop work—going out on short trips in the local desert to learn compass marching and learning all about desert life from Poole and Cubitt, who came to us for a few days to give us invaluable tips, and of course getting used to sand, which seemed worse and blew more at Amriya than anywhere.

Then eventually time came for the move up, and on the 13th December the brigade started off up the coast road to Mersa Matruh, where we harboured by night, and to this day I cannot forget the muddle of that move in the dark. The whole scene was just a mass of twinkling red rearlights and lots of people shouting directions and vehicles getting stuck ; so losing touch with their columns. Perhaps it was good experience, certainly such chaos never occurred again, and although farther up lights were never used we never had such a muddle as that first night at Mersa Matruh.

After a few days we began to form up in our armoured regimental groups near Khanayis, and then started our approach march. They were long marches, tiring, and no real fun, and then in a real bad sandstorm we reached the wire, which was naturally quite a big event to us. Soon afterwards our plans were altered and we stayed several days, firstly around Bir Gibni, and thence at Bir Harmat, including Christmas, which for most was the plainest and dullest one on record—just another day and just some more bully and biscuits, although it must be said that personally, my crew and I did have a most wizard meal, including tinned Christmas pudding.

Tobruk was near, and everyone was anxious to get in, have a look and see, and above all get well stocked up at the " Naafi."

Although it was very interesting for us newcomers to see the town just after it had been relieved, my chief impression was of depression —it was so derelict, so desolate, and the endless dumps of destroyed vehicles, aircraft, stores and general disorder. The " Naafi " was being besieged by people on the way up, people resting, people on the way back, many old friends met and chatted, but could we get what we wanted ? I should say not. I had gone hopefully with a three-tonner, but all the stores I got could easily have been taken away in a dingo !

I met Culme-Seymour there, and we went back together, and *en route* we had to go and help a truck which had been blown up on a thermos mine some distance from our track.

The approach march was continued up to near Antelat, where we broke up and re-formed into four " Jock " Columns, which were to relieve those that were already out ahead of us. " A " and " C " Companies went into these columns. " C " Company in a column under the Colonel.

Some night training was carried out, and quite a bit of shooting of gazelles and more trips to " Naafi " or other haunts in Benghazi, where a quantity of excellent tinned Italian food and vegetables was picked up.

By this time we were reasonably accustomed to desert life, and beginning to learn some of the tricks of the trade.

Edwardes and Kerr went ahead of their companies to join up with Jock Campbell's H.Q. and see his columns in action, and we formed up and waited whilst it poured with rain and was generally unpleasant.

We moved on South and passed one of our other battalions coming back ; our General came to see us, and wished us good luck.

Then came the Stukas for the first time, and everyone bit the dust at their first outing ; and vehicles got a bit more dispersed than previously ; but, as so often, the German bombing was not oversuccessful, providing one was well dispersed, but certain folk who bunched up came in for a packet of trouble.

Our company commanders rejoined us, and had good tales to tell of their experiences, especially the Stuka-ing, which was most methodical, being carried out to a regular daily time-table.

Our column was in reserve at first, and Sorbo, having everything well organized, with an abundant supply of water, organized baths for us, a most welcome event, to say nothing of a special brew-up with the bath.

Then we moved up ; the day was sunny and peaceful to a degree, when Rommel started his counter-attack. Everyone had a pretty hectic time.

Two incidents I remember vividly—a direct hit on a bolting camel, and a most welcome swig of whisky given me by some of the South Africans whose 25-pounder we had just dragged from some soft sand with a carrier.

We leaguered what remained of our column that night ; then later we saw, for the first time, that sight which was to become so familiar—German Verey lights—and as they began to close in on us we moved off and travelled until the moon set. Trucks began to get stuck, and we pushed and pulled, and progress, to say the least, was slow. Then the whipping-in vehicle became stuck, and was left behind ; the crew dug with their shovels and their hands, and at last managed to get clear, but lost the column till next morning, finding instead two other " missing " vehicles. This leaguer of three vehicles, before dawn next morning, had to make a quick move when tanks were heard starting up, also the sound of voices ; a driver whispered,

" they don't sound very English ! " Later the column was discovered, and a long detour was made before the main body was joined.

Our column commander, who was out when the attack started, had quite a trip rejoining the column ; his truck got stuck with engine trouble and had to be abandoned, and after some lengthy hitch-hiking, some vehicles were seen, identical to our own, even to the markings ; on closer examination they proved to be British all right, but fully laden with Boches !

We went back, passed that well-known landmark, the Well with Windpump—took part in what became known as the " Races "—the " Sauna and Suburban," the Msus Stakes and the Charruba Handicap. We ended up at Mechili, where a depot was found from which we obtained blankets and coats, food, water and a little petrol. This was all remarkably lucky, as the nights were still terribly cold, and those without any form of cover at night had a very unpleasant time, and with the vehicle casualties we had had, a lot of this kind of equipment had been lost.

We heard about " B " Company for the first time here at Mechili and how they had leagured, and in the morning after Rommel's break-through found enemy leaguers around them. Most of the company did manage to break out, splitting into two groups and pushing it.

Vehicles were beginning to bear traces of their buffeting despite, in mileage, no great distance having been covered. We moved then west again to Charruba—a most terrible night drive, ending with heavy rain, but only stayed a few hours before going back towards Mechili, and farther east towards Bir Harmat area, where the Gazala line began to be formed.

Kerr, at this time, was sent off with " A " Company and some gunners and worked around Bir Zeidan for several days. The first move of this small force was on compass bearings, and on arriving at its destination everyone was pleased to see there was a large well with good water in the midst. On examination a concrete plaque was found, announcing the well as Bir Zeidan and the names of some Italian units and the dates they had been stationed there.

We looked at our maps and found this Bir should have been miles away and were rather worried. But, trusting ourselves, and not the preliminary map issued, we marked all our bearings and trips from where we estimated we and the Bir were situated and found it correct, and the next map was issued with the Bir correctly marked.

As the Gazala line was being formed " A " and " C " Companies remained in the line, while " B " went back to re-form as the anti-tank company, and " I " re-formed in Tobruk, where the transit camp became overflowing with men of every unit who were re-organizing after the withdrawal.

Vic. Turner arrived back many days overdue, together with Geoffrey Fletcher and several riflemen, all of whom had escaped ; they had walked back by night while lying up by day. After a few days and nights, including times of torrential rain, it was realized that they could not continue indefinitely without water and food, so Turner laid an ambush across a track along which several German vehicles had been seen moving east. However, as luck would have it the party waited for two days, and not a single vehicle appeared. Then a German staff car was seen on the third day, and the Germans, stopping to investigate, were caught. Everyone boarded the car, which, mercifully, was full of petrol, and had a reserve as well, and made off. The last view they had of their victims was that they were still standing with their hands up, completely bewildered.

When it became obvious we were likely to be staying around the Gazala line for quite a time, everyone began to try and make life more agreeable.

Battalion headquarters was with brigade, where a good mess was quickly functioning, but became so overcrowded that a junior mess was found to be necessary. Wills, the 9th Lancers, was made mess president, and our own Mess Corporal, Fletcher, put in charge, and things were magnificently done, even down to candle lighting, a very nice touch.

Invitations to the junior mess were thereafter eagerly sought by members of the senior mess !

Sorbo Soboleff procured so many tents of every conceivable type that his platoon area became known as "Sorbo City," a landmark for miles around, and so conspicuous that an order to camouflage it was received. This, like everything managed by Sorbo, was so well done that the landmark became completely invisible, and people traversing the desert in those parts became lost, failing to see the " City."

" A " Company H.Q. at Sidi Muftah blossomed forth with a marquee, and the company commander and second-in-command each had a tent apiece in addition.

Any little wadi, or slope, became full of ingeniously devised " homes."

" C " Company, on the escarpment, overlooking the Trigh Capuzzo and " Sorbo City," were lucky in finding a number of suitable spots provided by nature for their homes. Culme-Seymour, in particular, discovered a huge extinct water-hole, where his three-ton truck could be driven in under cover, as well as good accommodation for his platoon H.Q.

After their refit, " I " Company moved up to " B " Echelon area, and finally took over from " C," who retired to the hardly peaceful " B " Echelon position. " A " Company stayed up, and had two carrier sections permanently out on patrol at the minefields.

The strains of " The Bays " dance band used periodically to break the stillness of the desert nights, while one or other of the squadron messes had a " gala," and then " A " Company gave a party in return.

Our brigade at this time sent out a column, working in conjunction with a Guards column, towards Mechili. " A " Company were in the column—" Barcol "—and had a very good time, and carried out several successful night patrols, being away just about three weeks. Lentaigne, who had just joined the company, thoroughly enjoyed himself, never resting for a moment, doing patrols by night and keeping on the go all day, either having a " look and see " at something miles away, or gazelle shooting, which usually was one and the same thing. It was on one of Lentaigne's patrols that German watchdogs, guarding a leaguer, were encountered. They proved most effective and the patrol found it impossible to approach anywhere near enough to observe without attracting the dogs' attention.

About this time we were reasonably near to Martuba and Tmimi aerodromes, and we used to watch with delight the bombing of these places by the R.A.F. First, one parachute flare would go down, and if it were right over the target many more would follow, and then the bombing, with the " ack-ack " tracer tearing into the sky like their Veréy lights. German tracer fire at night was easily distinguishable from British. And here around Mechili we could compare the " ack-ack " over Martuba and Tmimi with that over Tobruk in the far distance. But what a packet used to go up from Tobruk—a really colossal barrage.

Sorbo, with Sergt. Bowsher and one rifleman, did one astounding night patrol, when they visited and actually entered three Italian leaguers, and kept observation for a long time on a German one.

The Italians had a motor-cycle patrol encircling all three leaguers —not a very good scheme as the sound of the engines drowned any small noises made by men on patrol.

The first leaguer Sorbo and his party encountered were in good heart, many singing Italian opera ; the while Sorbo observed all he needed ; at the second they were spotted but not caught, and after laying up for nearly an hour moved on again, checking up on that and a subsequent leaguer easily, and finally observed a German tank leaguer.

For their return all the leaguers had to be passed again, so Sorbo might get back to his truck on the back-bearing he knew. As a final gesture, the party pinned up an English newspaper by an Italian leaguer, which no doubt shook them a little the next morning.

Following this patrol, a plot was hatched to revisit the scene in a couple of nights, lay some mines on the edges of the leaguer area, and have a shoot with all our Bren guns, but the gunners wanted to bring their 25-pounders into action as well, which would undoubtedly have been more effective. But their observers failed to find us in the dark, the guns also did not arrive on time at the right meeting point, a place known as the " Dancing Doodle," and the whole plan went astray. Soon after this our time was up and we came back, being relieved by another column in which " I " Company took part.

These columns passed through each other near Rotunda Segnali, and as we were actually marching through each other both columns were subjected to machine-gunning from ME. 109's.

Leake, who had just come to the Battalion, went on this column to get accustomed to the desert, and " have a little excitement," as he put it.

He had terrible bad luck, and certainly more than his share of excitement ; he went out to contact another column and, coming over a ridge, ran straight into some Boches, who machine-gunned him well and truly. They got away, but one wireless operator was killed and another badly wounded. Not undaunted, Leake came back for a day, collected more signallers and rejoined the column, still with the same very old truck.

Within forty-eight hours of his previous experience, he met trouble once again ; a Stuka came out of the skies and let him have it. This time Leake was badly wounded and two signallers were killed.

On " Barcol " reaching its own area again, we were told we were going out on another column in two days, so before the crew had unpacked our truck we set off for Tobruk and the " Naafi " to restock the company with anything we could get. I proceeded direct to Tobruk to collect money and pay from the field cashier, while Lentaigne went direct to the new " Naafi " we had to deal with down the El Adem Axis track.

He was to get first in the queue in the morning, order the goods, and then I would arrive with the money. However, with unbounded enthusiasm, he bought nearly everything he could see, so when I turned up we were short of cash, and another trip had to be made to the field cashier. On the way back to our area by Sidi Muftah, going along the Trigh Capuzzo just west of the Knightsbridge cross tracks in the early afternoon, my truck was attacked by three ME. 109s'. It was the only vehicle in sight and the three planes, which were presumably out on another job, came down to well under two hundred feet, taking us utterly by surprise, yet not one bullet-hole could be found on the truck. Fortunate for us, but very poor shooting !

Having been out on column for three weeks it was very humiliating to be strafed well back in one's own country, and came as quite a shock.

Our repeat column was postponed more or less day by day, and finally dropped all together.

Time passed, and many ways of passing the time were indulged in.

All ranks began to find tortoises, which became pets and also gave a chance for a gamble ; races being organized with all the tortoises in the centre of a large circle scratched in the earth, the winner being first out of the circle. The reptiles were so well camouflaged for the desert that they were frequently lost, and then names were painted on their backs in vivid reds or yellows. " Stuka Joe," " Bardia Bill," and the like.

Football pitches were cleared, and in very hot weather games were organized; troopers, gunners and riflemen all taking part.

Kerr used to have daily water parties go out, which proved a boon, and we were never short of water in quantity for washing and, having early on realized how vastly superior the German water and petrol containers were to anything we possessed, all "Jerricans," as they were later called officially, were collected, and the entire company was equipped with these weeks before an order was issued that they were to be collected and used in certain proportions, the remainder to be sent back to base.

A few lucky people began to get some bathing about this time on trips to Tobruk, or elsewhere, and what an experience it was after about four months to get one's body well, and truly, in the sea. I shall never forget my first bathe at El Auda, near Tobruk, in a little bay nicknamed Palm Beach, where one walked through a gap in a minefield on the edge of the beach into the warm blue sea of the little bay. That, just after the sticky heat and foul sand of a Khamsin, was a never-to-be-forgotten experience.

Edwardes, just before leaving us, gave a farewell party in his mess, to which we were all invited, and all had a very enjoyable time.

Around this time a divisional scheme was put on, and our brigade taken out of the Gazala line for a rest and refit. We moved to a spot midway between El Gubi and Gambut and leave, which had just previously been started, got well under way, and courses, too, loomed large on the horizon. Messes were set up in the best possible manner, and here again Sorbo proved his worth and arranged a stupendous affair. In addition to a marquee a special attached tent was added and became "Beasley's Bar," with quite a variety of drinks obtainable and suitable pictures adorning the walls.

The one and only batman, Beasley, found himself in his real element, and presided over the entire mess in his own inimitable way.

H.R.H. the Duke of Gloucester paid the Battalion a visit—the first occasion he had met any of the Regiment since becoming colonel-in-chief—and the Battalion was inspected in two parts: "B" and "H.Q." Companies in one parade and "A," "C" and "I" Companies in another. The riflemen, after five unbroken months in the desert, turned out looking very smart, and the drill, on both parades, was sufficiently satisfactory to receive special praise in a letter from our brigadier, who said "what a pleasure it was to see really good drill once again."

One sidelight on the parades was the matter of cap badges—during our time in the "blue" naturally enough many badges had been lost, but the quartermaster had the matter in hand, and had six hundred small badges on order, due to arrive well in time for the Colonel-in-Chief's inspection; but, alas, they were lost on the journey from the delta and no more could be obtained in time, despite most frantic efforts being made. So, for the parades, front rank men wore badges, centre rank and rear rank men none at all. Obviously the rear rankers were quite a little disappointed, and thought they would not be inspected, but the Duke went right down all ranks during his visit, which pleased the men immensely.

The night of the inspection the Colonel and Baring came to dinner with " A " Company, which we felt officially opened our mess, and a memorable evening was spent.

Bathing parties, combined with training, were now the order of the day, and platoons went off in turn to Marsa Lukkh, where actually some lucky folk were encamped, but we were about thirty miles distant—thirty miles of the most atrocious going you could ever imagine for trucks.

Courses, instruction and leave being the order of the day, nearly everyone got away on one or other of these—and away to the delta ; Lentaigne, alone, attended a physical training course at Capuzzo.

Soon I, in my turn, went off to the delta, and for my sins had to spend a night at that wretched transit camp, Fort Capuzzo. Luckily, I was able to continue down to Mersa Matruh by road, and did not have to face the uncomfortable train journey. At Mersa Matruh the organization was quite good and provided a real meeting place. Beavis had a job there during the summer months, and was always helpful to all riflemen.

Everyone seemed in good form at Mersa Matruh, those going to the delta, feeling leave and civilization about to start and those returning to the desert still having happy memories of their leave.

Shepheard's Hotel, Cairo, resembled a regimental mess, as many as twenty of our officers, from the various battalions, were counted at one time.

Seeing Crowder, whom I had not met since Tidworth days, and who since had been badly wounded at Sidi Rezegh, was one of the best pleasures of all during my three week-end visits from Khataba, where I was instructing. His sister Anne's flat was always a meeting place for Greenjackets in Cairo. Then one Saturday night I saw the Colonel at Shepheard's, and he said " Collect John Witt (who was at Mena doing a similar job as myself,) and get back to the Battalion—the party is about to start."

So that was that. I found Witt and arranged transport in the shape of a brand new lorry, which was loaned to us, and which did not allow of high speed. Tuesday found us breakfasting amongst some newly made pill boxes, and a proper position, which was being built by our troops and Egyptian labour. We facetiously made some remarks, and checked our position before moving off, and found we were at a spot called El Alamein. In exactly a month later we were back there, and now the whole world has heard of that place, which to us, that morning, meant absolutely nothing.

The Battalion moved from around El Gubi, and companies returned to their armoured regimental groups in the area, just north of Knightsbridge Box, and on the first day of the battle moved south towards the oncoming German Panzer divisions, and were in action by the afternoon. " A " Company, following up and occupying the battlefield, took over three hundred prisoners that afternoon. Witt and I hit the El Adem Axis track around noon on the first day, and asked the Red Cap there if he knew the latest whereabouts of our brigade—he did not, but thought it might be near Acroma and said nothing was happening at all. We stopped, and noticed that the stream of vehicles heading east was heavy, and travelling fast. By the end of our meal the flow was heavier, and going much faster—a very bad sign we thought and something must be up. We continued, and going up the El Duda escarpment came on two Grant tanks obviously coming out of battle, and sure enough on top of the escarpment we found a battery of guns just going into action against six German tanks, and some motorized infantry. So the battle was on. We spent some hours there trying to get news, filled up with petrol, water and food from a nearby depot, and collected two lorry loads of troops from our brigade returning from leave, who were also trying to rejoin their units. Our travels were long and wearisome and it was not until after eleven next morning we rejoined our companies just around Bir Bellefa, having done various jobs for various units *en route*, and once being taken definitely for the enemy and a troop of Cruisers sent off to deal with us.

That day all went well with the Battalion, and in the evening we were chasing the retreating Germans towards the west, and near Bir Aslagh our carriers were out late supporting sappers who were blowing up German tanks found damaged, or abandoned, on the battlefield which we held. Redfern returned joyfully with a grand German " Mercedes " staff car in going order, but with an obstinate starter, as well as a Morris truck, which had been captured, and now, resplendent with an Afrika Corps emblem, was being used as an officers' mess truck, and when captured was full of the most wonderful array of food.

All the evening Lentaigne begged to be allowed to go out on patrol, and upset the Germans' sleep.

If that policy had been adopted, of harassing the enemy all that night, perhaps things might have turned out differently, as it was the third day brought us the big tank battle, which raged till late in the afternoon despite the most appalling sandstorm. Casualties began to mount, as was inevitable. One of our trucks was actually run over by a tank during the morning—and alas Redfern's staff car, driven by Beasley, developed further starter trouble, and had to be abandoned. Companies were well split up, and we saw nothing of each other, everybody having their own excitements during the time the battle swayed around the Knightsbridge Box. After about a week, while " B " Company was down near El Harmat, they bagged their first victim with their anti-tank guns—an eight wheel armoured car.

At a later stage " I " Company became very bunched up when rejoining a 25-pounder battery, and had very severe casualties from a Stuka raid that caught them near Bir Bellefa.

And all through, the carriers by day and the motor platoons by night, continued their incessant patrolling. Redfern, Culme-Seymour and Dorrien-Smith earned unstinted praise from all quarters for the magnificent work carried out by their carriers.

One of our carriers whilst returning from a patrol south of Bir Harmat, stopped to fill up with water and whilst there the corporal spotted an enemy column approaching from the south-west, and passed on this vital information, which nobody else had reported, over the wireless, and then while rejoining his section verbally handed on the news to a brigade headquarters which knew nothing of it, and without this chance knowledge would undoubtedly have been captured.

Our supplies came up regularly by night, in spite of the most appalling difficulties.

With the fall of Bir Hacheim, it became obvious that the Gazala line could not be held and that soon the Knightsbridge Box would have to be evacuated. And so we began to fall back to the Righel Ridge, where nearly the whole Battalion had already at various times during the last two weeks, been in action.

It was near here that Jepson-Turner, the younger, won his D.S.O. in a magnificent stand with his 2-pounders against a large force of German tanks. He was firing the gun himself at the finish, until he was hit and lost his arm. It was a truly magnificent show against vastly superior odds. Then on one night patrol Lentaigne found a tank very badly ditched, but apparently in going order, and the wireless working. He switched on the set, and using the correct code, he called up the Bays, calling his set " Derelict." To hear over the air a voice saying " Hullo Bolo—Derelict calling " was one of the funnier incidents of this period. Lentaigne was very anxious to go out immediately with a truck, and unditch the tank ; it was not possible then, but two nights later he took out a Scammel breakdown lorry with a patrol and brought it back to our lines.

The Knightsbridge Box was duly evacuated, and then we fell back to the Acroma escarpment around Eluet El Tamar, and the South Africans began their withdrawal from Gazala down the coastal road ; things did not look too good.

A box in front of " A " Company gave way under heavy shelling, and the first we knew of it was swarms of infantry coming across open country at us. Our tanks nearly opened fire on them, but waited, and Soboleff decided he would investigate, and went out alone in his truck, found they were British, loaded his truck with the wounded, and brought them in ; then, asking permission, he took all his platoon trucks well forward of our tanks, and collected our casualties from right under the noses of the Germans. It was a grand show, saving about two hundred of our troops, and a most inspiring sight to those who witnessed it.

Things were getting sticky ; we received orders to withdraw, and

"A" and "I" Companies started off; "I" Company was unlucky, and having sent their vehicles well back, could not get them up in time, a great number of the company being taken prisoners. Corporal Guise, however, saw the trouble one of the platoons was in, went back with his carrier, and brought up a score of riflemen, a performance which deservedly won him the D.C.M.

The only gap in the minefields, near Acroma, was apparently closed, and so it meant going over the escarpment somehow, somewhere. Our colonel took command of what remained of our various groups—two batteries R.H.A., some anti-tank guns, some Bofors, and "A" and "I" Companies. A reconnaissance showed a possible route down part of the slope, and a plan was made. Suddenly Milner appeared, together with "A" Company ration lorry complete with three days' food and water. What a wonderful sight it was; water was woefully short, and doubly pleasant.

How amazed four Italian prisoners were, whom we picked up a few days previously, and had not been able to send back, to see those rations arrive. They had realized things were not going any too well with us, but that ration lorry, and the huge quantity of water, of which they apparently were always short, shook them more than somewhat. We started to move off for the escarpment at eleven o'clock, and for seven hours we bumped, crashed, stopped, restarted, stuck on boulders and helped unditch guns, or our own vehicles. Everyone was dead-beat, and fell asleep on the slightest chance. Vehicles with no brakes, crashed down the track and only stopped on hitting the vehicle ahead. The drivers that night did really magnificent work, and of the whole outfit only one Bofors gun got irretrievably ditched, or broke down. About half-way down the route became completely impassable, and Baring was sent on a hurried reconnaissance to find an alternative way down. Time was vital, as if we were caught stuck on the escarpment at dawn, it would be very awkward indeed. Another route was found which meant going along the ridge we were on, then to the flat ground and the coast road; it was all very tricky. As first light broke the rear of the column was still only half-way down the escarpment, when Lentaigne whose platoon was acting as rearguard, rushed up shouting "There are twenty Boche tanks on the top of the ridge." We got down that last bit pretty quickly and being well spaced out made a bolt for the road; just as all seemed clear we found a minefield along the edge of the road, so everyone had to close up to go through a gap, but luck was with us, and where we bunched was just out of range of the tanks' guns. One carrier was lost by a direct hit, but the whole crew escaped. It had taken just over seven hours to do a distance of three miles. What a trip! We all collected outside the Tobruk perimeter and received orders to proceed to a brigade area near Gambut aerodrome. The South Africans were still pouring down the road in every kind of conveyance, and the outlook seemed far from healthy. The road was packed with cars, as far as could be seen—a perfect

Stuka, or strafing target ; but the R.A.F. had such complete control of the whole situation that during the entire day one never saw, or heard, a Boche aeroplane. We dumped our four Italian prisoners, who had been with us several days, at the prisoners of war cage before going into Tobruk to get some money, and see if the " Naafi " was still functioning. As we drove into the town we met Lentaigne who was on a similar errand, and we arranged to meet at the " Naafi," and pool our resources.

While at the " Naafi," stacking up with all the food and drink we could buy, the shelling of Tobruk area began, and we pushed on with the " Naafi " goods. Near Gambut, the Battalion was getting together, and stray sections, or supply trucks, were coming in late. Everyone was in good heart, and it was nice to meet old friends one had not seen, or heard of, for nearly a month, and have a real old laugh about the " incidents."

The next day the Brigade moved on again with the intention of going through the wire, for a refit somewhere around Sofafi, and then return to engage Rommel again. We crossed the aerodrome at Gambut, and the R.A.F. became rather worried, thinking everybody was in full retreat, which fear we did our best to put at rest. We ourselves had one further minor scare. just beyond the aerodrome when enemy tanks and transport were reported south-east of us, which meant they had overtaken us, and were astride our direct route. A little investigation proved this to be our own stuff, and all was well. Just short of Libyan Omar, one of our carriers broke down, and I stayed behind to bring it along to the Shefergen Gap, where I was to pick up a message if the Battalion was going on for a night march. By now many of our vehicles were in very poor condition and mechanical breakdowns were fairly frequent, and in the short distance from where our carrier broke down to the Shefergen Gap, there were no less than seventeen belonging to the Battalion, which had either had mechanical trouble, or lost touch with their company. Several were on tow, and the speed made was not impressive, but the military police at Shefergen were most impressed by our arrival—we were nicknamed " Dodgy-Col." The next day much the same performance took place, but our area had been altered, luckily for us, and we were to tee-up by the blue sea at Buq-Buq ; what a wonderful relief it was, after that three hectic weeks, followed by that very dreary march back, to get down on the beach and have a glorious bathe. But it was by no means all rest—order, counter-order followed quickly one after the other. One Company was to go into the box at Sollum—"A" and " C " Companies, the most complete—tossed for it, and " C " won, and we worked late bringing " C " up to strength from " A." Then the next order was two companies to go out on column, so " C " returned men and vehicles to " A " and both got ready to move out. Then that was cancelled, and we heard about Tobruk—which came as a shattering blow to us all—it seemed unbelievable. We had just collected some new vehicles from a park near Sollum, which improved matters as regards further operations.

But even with all these worries and troubles, those only too few days along the seashore at Buq-Buq gave us the rest we needed, and really were wonderful days. Fishing, or trying to catch fish, by throwing Italian grenades into the sea, bathing, scrounging, mad rushes to Sidi Barrani to see the field cashier and the " Naafi."

After these various alarms, and excursions, we finally moved down towards Thalata where the Battalion took over the guarding of an aerodrome, which almost as soon as we arrived to do this duty, decided it was time to evacuate and so very little was done.

En route there, a final visit was paid to Sidi Barrani, where we managed to get as much tinned beer as there was money to pay for ; no rationing was bothered about, thank heavens, at that period. Near Thalata a large supply dump was to be abandoned and all stores burnt so the quartermaster and others visited the spot and made up their stocks. It was a terrible sight to see so much stuff about to be burnt—even if the stores were not of great importance—owing entirely to lack of available transport. We continued our march eastwards, moving now as a division, and travelling by night. A huge column it was, and very easy in such a mass of vehicles to go astray from one's own unit.

Around Khayanis once again we split up into some columns, and fought various delaying actions in the area, while Mersa Matruh prepared for a hasty evacuation.

One column was formed very hurriedly with tanks, guns and " A " Company late one evening ; none of the units had worked together before, which caused certain delay whilst forming up, and eventually we all went into close leaguer in rather a mixed state. We knew we were very close to two German leaguers, and our listening posts were well teed-up. So were the R.A.F. who unfortunately spotted a leaguer approximately in the position of which they had been notified, and dropping flares found tanks, which were their target, and let go all their stuff. Lit up by these flares, we, on the ground, felt absolutely naked, and very frightened. Quite a lot of bombs were dropped, and the leaguer actually moved out into open formation, but all to no avail, as we were still caught in the light of the flares. Then, at last, a recognition signal was let off, and all was well. It was only a slight bombing, and a mistake, but it did give us all a good idea of what the R.A.F. could put over and we were very pleased then that the Luftwaffe was not so good.

This column was dissolved next day, and we moved east once more, and came very near to El Alamein. About 5 o'clock one evening " A " Company were called out to rejoin some of the Bays in another column.

We were by now well accustomed to these sudden changes of formation, but this one came quite as a surprise ; yet it was a pleasure to be rejoining the Bays again. All " doubtful " vehicles were sent back with our echelon and the company hastily re-formed with the remaining vehicles and men turned west to their rendezvous, while the remainder of the Battalion continued towards the El Alamein line. We met the gunners, but no sign could be found of the Bays. We used the wireless without avail, but there was a station on practically the same frequency as us, and using a very similar code name to that which we had been given for the Bays, but there was no response to our repeated calls. It was decided to leaguer as we were for the night, and go on trying to get them on the wireless. The other station kept on the air, and they, too, were obviously trying to locate someone, and suddenly the very familiar voice of Alex. Barclay was heard. I gave our code name, and said " Is that Alex." The reply was very guarded, and a long conversation ensued trying out several recognition signals and various names, and finally a voice replied, " Is that Bob," and so final contact was made. We found out their position and joined them at first light, and had quite a good time harassing the Boches, and " B " Company's 6-pounders under the elder Jepson-Turner and Sergt. Mulford had a really good day's shoot, and we bagged a few prisoners, but at sunset had to make a quick move, and go farther westwards to avoid trouble. The question of supplies now loomed very large as we were well out, and isolated Boche units were between us and the echelon, and it seemed foolhardy to risk them trying to contact us, and it was decided to move east again next day, and so go back to them ourselves. That night, whilst in leaguer, one of our listening posts warned us suddenly of a large movement of vehicles, and sure enough a huge column began rumbling past about one thousand yards from the leaguer, and within a quarter of a mile of our listening post. Everyone prepared to move, expecting we had been spotted, and were about to be encircled ; but no, the column kept moving, and going due east, nothing deviating in our direction. This seemed too good to be true, but it continued in all for four solid hours, everything heading due east. This was all right, but it meant we had to overtake the whole outfit before we could reach our own lines again. The next morning, however, was a picnic, as the desert seemed littered with broken-down, or temporarily lost, vehicles, whose crews had bedded down for the night, and all we had to do was to go up next morning, wake the said crews, and inform them they were " in the bag " ; of course that did not go on indefinitely, and opposition soon began. But it was a wonderful feeling, and the surprise of the Germans or Italians was a sight well worth seeing ; they thought we were on the run, in and around Alexandria. They just could not understand it.

Once again the " B " Company guns did magnificent work, and we were all quite cheery that night.

Then the plan was told us of how we were going to drive through the night, and get back to our lines by first light. We were driving on compass bearing, which in over thirty miles would bring us in just north of Ruweisat Ridge ; we would try to evade the enemy who had passed near our leaguer the previous night. If lucky, we would pass them exactly as they had passed us, otherwise we were to keep going as fast as possible with the crews of outside vehicles of the column firing on anyone who tried to deal with us.

Before moving off, however, any spare petrol was pooled, from all vehicles, and split up amongst the tanks—the wrong petrol but better than nothing. Even then it was thought several would not do the distance. All was set, and we moved, but almost at once came upon a very bad escarpment, which was unmarked on the few maps of this area. Who, after all, even two weeks previously, had thought we'd ever need maps of Fuka-el Daba, and beyond? It was nearly three hours before we had done as many miles. Then all went well, and good progress was made. I dozed off, then Abbott, my driver, shook me and said, " Sir, who are these chaps ? " I wearily said, " Oh, some of our outposts "—and having said it noticed we had begun to travel quite quickly, and the pace was getting faster, in fact very fast. People were shouting at us, and vehicles were crashing in and out of slit trenches ; this was undoubtedly opposition, and peering at the stationary vehicles, as we sped past, I spotted them as Italian. We continued on at our fast pace, and passed, literally, hundreds of vehicles in open leaguers before we reached clear country again ; yet not a shot had been fired, and not a vehicle lost.

One sergeant, thinking, as I had at first, that he was in our own lines again stopped and changed a wheel on his truck quite unmolested, and an officer stopping to ask a man in the dark what unit he belonged to found himself face to face with an Italian, gripped him, dragged him into the truck, and brought him in.

We seemed to be through it all, and we looked forward to dawn, but when that came we saw that we were the centre column of three, almost each the same size, and all heading east. That seemed strange, and it turned out it was—the other two were German.

One German cooks' lorry, and another car, uncertain of their whereabouts, decided to join the centre column, and approached very close before finding out their mistake, but soon disappeared, being well peppered by our machine-guns, but they escaped.

The alarm then being given, an 88 mm. came into action against us, but we were too quick for them, and although the rear of the column came under pretty heavy fire, no hits were scored.

And so we came across, at last, our own outposts, and into the El Alamein position " in nice time for breakfast" as someone so nicely said.

THE 1st BATTALION WITH THE B.L.A., 1944.

Our last letter ended with the Battalion shivering in their dismal and ill-constructed Nissen huts in a dank pine wood near Brandon, Norfolk. By the beginning of May our re-equipping was largely complete and the English climate became more tolerable. Waterproofing was, next to leave, our chief pre-occupation, and much training and instruction in this were carried out : we were told we must expect to drive through at least three and a half feet of water.

Around the middle of May we moved to our assembly area near Brentwood and began the actual waterproofing of the whole of the Battalion vehicles. The camp was overcrowded and our time there was a nightmare, relieved from time to time with a few hours' respite in London. But after we had been briefed as to our destination, even this was officially denied us and we were, at least theoretically, wired in.

At the very end of May we moved down to the docks. The vehicles had already been loaded and we were driven to Tilbury in R.A.S.C. transport and embarked on our M.T. ships during the first days of June.

We had been warned that we should be crowded, but I don't think anyone expected that the packing would be quite so tight. But once out in the Thames Estuary we had a grandstand view of the invasion fleet which stretched to the horizon. The voyage was uneventful and early in the morning of D plus 2 we anchored off the coast of Normandy, opposite Arramanches.

Arramanches looked unexpectedly peaceful from the boat and only distant gunfire from farther inland could be heard. There seemed, though, to be a great dearth of landing-craft apart from a large number high and dry on the beaches. During the time we spent at anchor in the M.T. ship there was an almost eerie calm ashore and a serious lack of any unloading of the many hundreds of ships awaiting unloading.

However, at length after delays of as much as eighteen hours in some cases, the Battalion began to come ashore. Enormous time and attention had been spent in waterproofing, but most people's hearts were in their mouths as they took to the water to drive ashore, for the prospect of losing one's vehicle and all one's belongings was by no means attractive. Those landing on the high tide were the luckiest, for their landing was almost dry-shod. But those at half or low tide had a longer and deeper drive and occasionally disappeared completely from view through driving into holes up to 18 feet deep, made where ships had beached on previous tides. The driver and crew had to bale out quickly and make a sad and ignominious way to the beach. On the whole, there were remarkably few cases of drowned vehicles in the Battalion, and such as there were were for the most part quickly rescued by the R.E.M.E. beach detachments which did splendid work with their specially waterproofed bulldozers.

We concentrated inland a few miles short of Bayeux still without sign of any but distant sound of enemy activity. We were not, however, ready to go forward as a complete battalion when the Armoured Brigade moved, as "C" Company (Bill Jepson-Turner) and the Support Company, "B" Company (John Witt) were far from complete. Nevertheless, when the advance did start on D plus 4, "A" Company (James Wright) and "I" Company (Bill Apsey), each with an anti-tank platoon under command, were ready to join 4th C.L.Y. and 5th R. Tanks, the two Armoured Regiments with which they usually work.

We soon learned the nature of the "Bocage" country with its banks and thick hedges every hundred yards or so. You could not imagine closer country, and it was difficult, if not impossible, to spot enemy anti-tank guns, Spandau positions or even tanks themselves if they chose to lie up and keep still. It was hopeless country for an Armoured Division and our hopes of a rapid "swan-through" faded rapidly. "I" Company found themselves clearing one small set of houses no less than three times in the day since small parties of Germans kept filtering back. Whilst doing so they were unlucky enough to lose Sergt. Hines (M.M.), who had a distinguished record both in the old 9th Battalion and in this Battalion. "A" Company were plugging along with the leading Armoured Regiment and finding it necessary to watch every approach along which enemy infantry might try to stalk the tanks, and all night had to guard the tank leaguer.

All this seemed far removed from the rapid dash some twenty miles inland for which we had been briefed, with its first objective Villers-Bocage and its final objective Mt. Pincon and the high ground near it dominating all the surrounding country. However, after a few days of imperceptible progress towards Tilly la Campagne it was decided on the 12th June to switch the Armoured Brigade by small side roads to pass through the Americans on our right and to approach Villers-Bocage from the west and to capture some high ground to the south and east of the town. Speed was to be the essence of the party and rapid progress was made by the 4th Sharpshooters (County of London Yeomanry) and "A" Company, with Roger Butler's anti-tank platoon under command which formed the leading Armoured Regimental Group.

The group passed through Villers-Bocage early on the morning of the 13th and reached their objective some two miles to the east of the town by 9 o'clock that morning, and halted on the road in close column ready to take up dispositions for holding the ground gained. At that moment the front half of the column was attacked by German tanks, the tanks of the Regimental H.Q. were knocked out, and a number of the motor company's half-tracks brewed up by enemy tank fire at point-blank range. Dense clouds of smoke from burning tanks and vehicles added to the general confusion, which was increased by the fact that the platoon commanders of the company were forward at the time getting orders from James Wright and so were not with their platoons. Many of the company managed to get away from the burning vehicles, but a number were not so fortunate. By about 1 o'clock the leading squadron of tanks had been overwhelmed and the enemy had appeared at the rear of the column in Villers-Bocage itself. Of the whole company only one officer and thirty other ranks finally returned during the next few days and we lost Alfred de Pass and Roger Butler killed, James Wright, Charles Parker, Bruce Campbell were taken prisoner, and Peter Coop is missing still.

Meanwhile the rest of the Brigade took up an all-round position some two miles west of the town and dug in. "C" Company arrived the same day and dug in to the north, other machine-guns and anti-tank guns of the support company plugged various holes in the position. "I" Company were on the southern flank and the next day had a very busy time, and the whole area was fairly heavily shelled and mortared. At about eight in the evening the enemy put in an attack on "I" Company's area and got quite near to "I" Company's position before being seen off magnificently by the company, admirably assisted by 5th R.H.A. firing air bursts over open sights and a special concentration (the code word for which was "pandemonium") laid on by some self-propelled 155's of the American Artillery who had an O.P. officer with us.

Although this attack was repulsed with heavy enemy losses, higher authority decided that the Division must be pulled back that night to a less isolated position. It was pitch black that night, but the move was a triumph of good driving and road discipline, and was completed with the minimum of enemy interference. Only a few shells came over, but one unluckily landed on John Foreshew's carrier and killed him and his crew instantly. "I" Company had already had a most unfortunate time in officer casualties with Geoffrey May killed and Gerald Pritty and Dennis Matthews badly wounded, as well as losing C.S.M. Jefford also killed.

We were only given a few days' respite (with the exception of the remnants of "A" Company which was sent back to refit) and the Battalion was concentrated and sent up to fill a gap in the line near Le Pont Mulot some four miles south of Caumont. The frontage was about 2,500 yards and with only two motor companies and the support company there was no depth to the position whatever. We remained in position for eleven days and found the long hours of daylight desperately trying. Stand to in the morning was at 4.15 and in the evening at 10.30, each for an hour, so that there was no opportunity for a good night's rest. Still there were certain compensations in the form of delicious Camembert and Port de Salut cheeses from Bayeux, eggs and fresh butter from the farm houses, and plenty of Calvados, a highly potent and lethal form of apple jack which tasted like fire water.

It was during the time at Pont Mulot that " B " Echelon, away back near Balleroy, was heavily shelled at night. " A " Company was there re-forming and re-equipping and Francis Dorrien-Smith had just taken over command. Unhappily Francis and James Caesar were killed by one of the first shells and shortly afterwards Gilbert Talbot commanding H.Q. Company was also killed. It was a desperately tragic affair and the Battalion suffered a loss of exceptionally able and experienced officers whom it will be indeed difficult to replace.

We were relieved at Pont Mulot by the Glosters and went back to Ellon, some five miles south of Bayeux, for two weeks. We spent the time pleasantly enough and the motor companies tried various schemes in conjunction with the tanks to decide on the best method of advancing with the tanks in close country. Eric Sargeant joined us from home to take over " A " Company and shortly afterwards " A " Company was brought up to strength with a large batch of reinforcements.

Early on the 17th July we came under command of 8 Corps to take part with 11th Armoured Division and the Guards Armoured Division in the big attack which was to be made to break out south of Caen. For this purpose we crossed the Orne, north of Caen, and moved southwards. We had a good view of the terrifically heavy bombing of Caen and the enemy-held villages to the south, when some 7,000 tons of bombs were dropped. We moved in regimental groups, but there was much congestion and long delays when no forward movement was possible. There was a lot of Nebelwerfering, the noise of which often causes much alarm and despondency, though fortunately the splinter effect is surprisingly small. But progress was slow in spite of the air bombardment and artillery barrage, for well-concealed enemy tanks and anti-tank guns were hard to dislodge and the armour never succeeded in gaining freedom for manœuvre. The weather broke too and it became plain that the operation would not succeed. There was a lot of enemy shelling and all that we could do was to disperse our vehicles, dig deep and hope for the best. The G.A.F. were also active at night with an unpleasant kind of anti-personnel bomb. Bill Apsey was, unfortunately, wounded by a mortar bomb and he will be a sad loss to " I " Company. Norman Griffiths (" B " Company) and Tony Crassweller (" I " Company) were both slightly wounded by shell splinters. Peter Luke, who had been Second-in-Command " B " Company, took over " I " Company.

Meanwhile a new plan had been evolved which placed the Division under command of the Canadians, through whom we were to pass on their reaching their second objective in the hopes of a break-through in the direction of Falaise. Unfortunately, the Canadians were held up and the Brigade found itself in the early morning on an extremely exposed slope within some 3,000 yards of the enemy. The inevitable reaction on the enemy's part was not long delayed and the Battalion suffered some casualties before less vulnerable positions could be found. Nevertheless, the number of untenanted reverse slopes was all too small and considerable overcrowding again resulted. Once again some days of inaction followed with shelling by day during which we lost Robin Birch, and air bombing by night until we were relieved by a Canadian Motor Battalion. We were delighted to leave the Caen area with its open cornfields and destroyed villages which had a most depressing effect on everyone. The bridge at Caen had been repaired, so we drove through the town and could see the full extent of the devastation caused by the air bombing. On the 30th July we found ourselves back again in Ellon and delighted to be back among the green and fertile pastures of the Bocage country.

But it was not for long, for on 1st August we returned to 30 Corps and were on the move again in the direction of Villers-Bocage and Aunay-sur-Odon. 5th Royal Inniskilling Dragoons had replaced the Sharpshooters in the Brigade and we were shortly to lose our universally admired, respected and beloved Brigadier Hinde, a blow from which the Brigade took long to recover. While in addition to this, it was decided to change the Divisional Commander, Bobby Erskine, and his loss was felt deeply throughout the Battalion, whose good friend he had been for so long. For the next two days the motor companies were fully occupied with their armoured regiments pushing forward in difficult country against determined enemy rearguards. Aunay itself had been bombed completely and utterly flat with the sole exception of the church tower, which still stood an erect and gloomy sentinel over the devastation.

We were then moved from the Aunay area to a position west of the main road from Caen to Falaise, and the Division became part of the First British Corps of the First Canadian Army. We moved eastwards and took over a small bridgehead near Livarot. There was another river obstacle a few miles ahead and the Battalion was ordered to seize the one bridge that was supposed to be intact at Fervaques. In the failing light " I " Company were hastily mounted on tanks and succeeded in rushing and capturing the bridge. The rest of the night they had a good harvest ambushing enemy vehicles, some of them horse drawn, who were unaware that the use of the bridge had been denied to them. The most satisfactory prize was the capture of a German cook's lorry with a hot breakfast destined for the German garrison. However, the enemy were not prepared to give up Fervaques without a struggle, and in the evening a vigorous infantry counter-attack was put in. " A " " B " and " I " Company Commanders had taken up their headquarters in the local chateau, a splendidly constructed building with walls at least five feet thick. There was a prodigious expenditure of small arms ammunition on both sides, but a well-timed and well-directed D.F. by the Gunners and a generous use of ·5 Brownings by " I " Company's Scout

Platoon and plenty of M.M.G. fire from "B" Company proved decisive and the attack was repulsed.

The advance continued with the object of forcing the enemy into the big loop of the Seine, south-west of Rouen, and involved much clearing of woods and orchards in which all the scout platoons especially had satisfactory bags of prisoners, and booty.

We crossed the Seine on 31st August, and by last light were well on the way to the Somme. We kept going all night, although at one moment the whole of our column had to turn round in its tracks on a narrow road owing to an alteration of plan and route. We, like most of the Army, had run off our maps and the best that was available was scale 1/100,000 to the tune of about one per company. A Canadian Armoured Division then decided to use our narrow centre line and delayed our progress considerably. However, we crossed the Somme soon after first light on the 2nd September and pushed on eastwards. By this time we could only raise maps of scale 1/250,000, and the difficulties of navigation sensibly increased. The enthusiasm of the local inhabitants was prodigious in this part of France and Company Commanders (and perhaps even the C.O.) from their Olympian seats in their half-tracks could not help but envy the D.Rs., so vulnerable on their lowly machines to the embraces of the local ladies. Prisoners were becoming a considerable problem and often outnumbered many times those who had taken them. But the Maquis were very active and helpful and always ready to take them off our hands and it was a real pleasure.

The Maquis were particularly useful in Lillers, which was cleared and held by 1st R. Tanks and "C" Company. Unfortunately John Young, who was commanding their Scout Platoon, was wounded on the way there and Norman Deveson killed in the street fighting, but a good number of prisoners were taken. Germans continued to try to filter back into Lillers, and it was unfortunate that we should have been ordered to push on and so leave the inhabitants to the risk of German reprisals. The only consolation was that the Maquis were by this time both numerous and well armed, and it is to be known thay they were able to give a good account of themselves.

That evening we pushed on to the La Bassee Canal near Bethune, but our intended centre line was never finally cleared, of enemy and so we moved the next day through Bethune, which by then was reported clear, to Mazingarbe near Lens, where the Battalion rested for a few days and tried to catch up on some much needed maintenance. "A" Company was not so lucky and joined the remainder of the Brigade who by then had moved up to the area of Ghent.

By the 8th September we were on the move again, passed to the east of Lille, crossed the frontier into Belgium, through Tournai to south of Termonde. We found the Belgians even more delighted to see us than the French, and were met everywhere with a happy admixture of eggs and enthusiasm. Belgian beer was there for the asking, and made up in quantity what it lacked in quality.

We pushed on towards Antwerp and stopped to hold St. Micolas, a delightful old town some five miles west of Antwerp. Here we were joined by "A" Company and 5th D.G. who had taken part in the operations around Ghent. The population were beside themselves with joy at the disappearance of the "Moffe," the Flemish word of affection for the German, and could not do enough for us. The local White Brigade were busy rounding up collaborators of both sexes, shaving the heads of the women and making the men get on their hands and knees and scrub out Nazi emblems from the pavements before clapping them into prison. In fact an enjoyable time was had by all, and we were sorry when we were ordered to move on to a village five miles north of Malines. Here we celebrated the Regimental Birthday with the aid of casks of beer from Malines, and most people managed to get into Malines for a few hours.

The Battalion was then ordered to join the Lorried Infantry Brigade in holding a stretch of some twenty miles of the Albert Canal. We were well spaced out but had the canal between us and the enemy, and things on the whole were reasonable quiet. After this we returned to our own Brigade which was split up, 5th D.G. with "A" Company going off to join the 53rd (W) Division and 5th R. Tanks and "I" Company joining the 15th (S) Division. The rest of us moved up to the Meuse-Escaut Canal north of Moll where we took over the defence of the canal. Here the anti-tank platoons of the support company parked their anti-tank guns and took over as ordinary riflemen, aided by the machine-gunners, the defence of a large factory area bordering the canal. When the Germans finally pulled out, Michael King, with some of his platoon accompanied by a Belgian officer, went off on a special patrol. This involved commandeering bicycles from some most reluctant onlookers who could hardly be prevailed upon to part with such valuable articles. The party was then ferried across the canal and cycled to Rethy some four miles north of the canal and there organized civilian bicycle patrols in all directions, and when these had reported, the patrol cycled back with some really valuable information.

On 24th September we crossed into Holland and moved up to Eindhoven and then on to St. Oudenrode. Just to our north there was acute centre line trouble : a German column had cut the road and brewed up a number of 3-tonners. But the situation was later restored and we moved on to Dinther and Heeswijk where we were joined by "A" and "I" Companies. The enemy were rather accurate with their mortars and we were not sorry when we were relieved and moved north to Heesch, some eight miles east of s'Hertogenbosch.

We stayed in the area of Heesch for three weeks, our task being to prevent any eastwards thrust by the enemy which might have cut the centre line of the troops in the area north of Graves and Nijmegen. We were spread over a wide front and there was much night patrolling to be done. " A " Company had a highly successful battle when a night attack of battalion strength was put in against their positions in the small nearby village of Geffen : they drove the enemy off with gusto and heavy losses to him, and George Burder won a richly deserved M.C.

We left Heesch on 20th October, the Battalion coming under command of the Lorried Infantry Brigade (131st) whose task it was to protect the left flank of the 53rd (W) Division which was attacking s'Hertogenbosch. The Battalion was not heavily engaged, though John Poole and Ian Bancroft had a good indirect shoot with their Vickers on to some enemy positions on a canal bank. We then returned to the Armoured Brigade and moved westwards to cut the northern roads out of Tilburg. The motor companies went with their armoured regiments and did some good work patrolling and clearing woods. The Brigade was, however, held up beyond Udenhout by a strongly defended position in front of some woods at a cross-tracks near De Heidebloom. The plan was for " I " Company to put in an attack with the riflemen riding on the backs of the tanks of the 5th D.G. The attack was to be preceded by a heavy concentration of artillery and supported by covering fire from John Poole's Vickers machine-guns. Unfortunately, when still some 300 yards from their objective, several of the troop-carrying tanks got bogged : one went up on a mine and another was knocked out by an anti-tank gun. The attacking infantry came under heavy spandau fire and had no alternative but to gain the temporary shelter of a small wood. Later, " I " Company went in again in a different place followed by " A " Company, and there was a very satisfactory bag of some 120 prisoners.

We had forty-eight hours much needed rest before taking over the town of Ramsdoncksveer, which lies some 1,000 yards south of the River Maas, from the 51st (H) Division which had just captured it. The take-over had in fact to be partly postponed until darkness owing to enemy interference, but was satisfactorily completed during the night. The enemy were just across the canal in the adjoining town of Getruidenberg and there was much mutual shelling, mortaring, sniping and patrolling, which ended up considerably to our advantage. Finally, the Poles came up from the south and captured Getruidenberg, and we were relieved partly by them and partly by the Canadians, and moved back to Belgium again to the area some way south of Venlo.

While we were at Ramsdoncksveer, Bill Jepson-Turner went home to the Training Battalion for a rest, and Cyril Suter, who had been second-in-command of " B " Company, took over " C " Company. Gilbert Williams came out from the Training Battalion and became second-in-command to " B " Company.

We arrived at Neeroteren, a small village a few miles from the Maas just opposite the narrowest point of the Maastricht appendix, on the 13th November. We were all in comfortable billets and with no operational commitments, settled down to a rest and a good time. After some days the matter of training began to rear its ugly head and Company Commanders were invited to make out a training programme for a fortnight. This was clearly tempting providence too far and just when we were thinking we might spend Christmas in peace and comfort we were ordered to move across the Maas to take over from the Guards Armoured Division who were holding the villages of Nieuwstadt and Holtum, two miles north of Sittard and on the German-Dutch frontier.

We arrived there on the 1st of December and took over with one motor company and part of the support company in each village and one motor company and the rest of the support company in reserve. The enemy was disagreeably close to our F.D.L.s—only 200 yards at one point—and was quite aggressive in his patrolling and accurate with his shell and mortar fire. We suffered occasional casualties from shelling, especially at Nieuwstadt, but gave back a good deal better than we got. Shortly before Christmas the Germans sent over a lot of leaflet shells containing propaganda leaflets and Christmas cards. They were mainly fired from 105 mms. and as ill luck would have it, one of the empty metal containers had a direct hit on Eric Sargeant's H.Q. in Nieuwstadt and killed Gilbert Williams, Eric's second-in-command, and wounded the Gunner O.P. officer and two signallers. It was the most tragic luck and cast a gloom over the Christmas festivities.

Everyone spent Christmas as best they could and there was some enjoyable if impromptu parties, Shortly before Christmas David Clive, who had returned to the Battalion from Brigade H.Q. and became second-in-command of the support company, went off to Rheims and came back with excellent stocks of champagne. The P.R.I. produced some good Christmas fare and the N.A.A.F.I. some beer and brandy, so there was no lack of alcoholic encouragement.

As we bring this letter to an end with the close of the year we hope that we shall read this letter when it appears in the CHRONICLE, with our feet on the marblepiece of our respective homes back in the one and only street many of us ever want to live in—Civvy Street.

A SONG BEFORE SUNRISE

2nd BATTALION

The Cyrenaica, Libya Operations, 1940-41, and the Operations of the 7th Motor Brigade, during the Summer, 1942.

BY MAJOR-GENERAL J. M. L. RENTON, D.S.O., O.B.E.

IN January, 1940, the 2nd Rifle Brigade arrived in Egypt, from Palestine, and was posted as part of the Support Group of the 7th Armoured Division. The Support Group performed a very definite role in the Armoured Division and was supposed to be the pivot of manœuvre from which the force would eventually fight. It consisted of two motor battalions, the 1st/60th and 2nd Rifle Brigade, 3rd R.H.A. (Anti-Tank Bofors guns) and 4th R.H.A. (25-pounders). Owing to the shortage of equipment the Rifle Brigade during the first year of the war never had more than eight carriers per platoon and they were invariably short of transport and trucks for the motor platoons. The necessity of including reserve rations of water and petrol made it necessary to reduce the sections below the full eight men of the establishment.

The Battalion carried out training for six weeks in the Ribiqi Desert under the general supervision of Brigadier (later Lieut.-General) W. H. E. Gott, who had just finished command of the 1st/60th and assumed command of the Support Group. This officer had evolved the system of motor tactics in the desert ; these tactics have been invariably successful and his training of all units under him justified.

The Battalion came back from training in the middle of April and were preparing on the 1st May to celebrate the 90th Birthday of the Duke of Connaught, together with the 60th anniversary of H.R.H. assuming the Colonelcy-in-Chief of the Regiment. This was to be celebrated by a photograph of all officers, N.C.Os. and men, of the Battalion under the Colonel Commandant, General Sir Maitland Wilson, at that time G.O.C.-in-C., Egypt. The photograph was due to be taken at eleven. Just before that hour the Commanding Officer was rung up and told that the General could not come till one o'clock. On his arrival, when asked whether he would like lunch or photograph first, he said we should have the photograph first as we should be leaving after the lunch for the desert. Information had reached G.H.Q. that an Italian attack was imminent and the Support Group was to be sent up to Matruh forthwith to cover the detrainment and deployment of the Armoured Division. Luckily a practice mobilization had been held during the previous week and all arrangements worked smoothly and in two hours under the specified time (eight hours) the Battalion was ready to move. We moved out to Matruh at first light next morning, orders having been in the meantime received that black-out that night was to be strictly observed. The British barracks were conspicuous as the whole of the rest of Cairo was brilliantly illuminated.

On arrival at Matruh, the Battalion was ordered to take up a covering position on an eight-mile front along the Wadi Halazin, about 40 kilometres west of Matruh. Positions were dug and for a fortnight an attack was expected almost every day. But after that fortnight the Battalion was withdrawn to camp at Matruh and the tension appeared to have relaxed. While in camp at Matruh the Battalion was sent up to Bir Fuad, about sixty miles south of Matruh on the Siwa road, to dig dumps of petrol and supplies, which were later to become very useful for the retreat in September, 1940.

On 4th June the 1st/60th were having an Old Etonian party in their mess when news arrived of the Fall of Calais and the Prime Minister's speech of the part played by the Rifle Brigade and the 60th Rifles in its defence was heard over the wireless. Four days later news arrived of the declaration of war with Italy and the Battalion was moved up one hundred and twenty miles to a position twenty miles west of Sidi Barrani where it had its first taste of war, when the Italian air force came over and bombed and machined-gunned it every day. About three days after this the first " Hurricane " was seen in the desert scattering a force of eight Savoyas by itself and was greeted with cheers by the whole battalion.

The plan of campaign adopted by General Wavell and General Wilson was as follows. It had originally been decided to hold Matruh as a fortress and for the Armoured Division to operate south of it, but this was cancelled, much to the surprise of the Italians who were fully aware of the previous plan, and the two armoured brigades were sent straight up to the frontier to operate between Maddalena and Sollum and mop up various frontier posts there, while the Support Group was to hold Sollum and the escarpment above it as a pivot, one battalion in the Sollum area and one back at Buq-Buq. the Rifle Brigade were chosen to hold the forward position, being relieved by the 1st/60th every three weeks. The main job at Sollum was night patrolling against the Bardia defences. General Gott was anxious that all the information possible about Bardia should be discovered, and officer patrols went out every night. Officers usually had two nights out, out of three, owing to the shortage of numbers, while the men went out every fourth night. The average patrol can be described as follows.

They drive eight to ten miles in the dark across the desert on a compass bearing and speedometer reading. A two to three-mile march on a compass bearing checked by pacing. Contact to be gained with the enemy, if possible mines to be laid, information as to dispositions obtained. Then back again on the bearings to the trucks and a drive back in the dark to our own lines ; all this had to be accomplished before daylight.

By means of these constant and incessant patrols we remained masters of " No Man's Land," although there was never more than one battalion opposed to three Italian divisions in Bardia.

In addition to these, small reconnaissance patrols would go out to the escarpment for two days at a time to watch enemy movement. This life continued until 19th August when a change had to be made in the dispositions owing to the fact that the armour was wearing out. Armoured formations cannot operate indefinitely at a long distance from their workshop, and it was decided to go back, with modification, to the original plan. The Armoured Brigade was withdrawn to positions south of Matruh where it was intended to fight. The Support Group battalions were to cover the frontier and to fight a delaying action in the event of an enemy advance until a real resistance should be made one hundred and thirty miles back from their position. This meant that the front to be covered by the Battalion, from Maddalena to Sollum, was approximately fifty miles and, as can be seen, we were very thin on the ground.

On 13th September the enemy advance started. Large columns of tanks and motor infantry advanced against our position. At that time the Rifle Brigade was holding the forward position, with the 60th in depth behind them on the Buq-Buq—Sòfafi line and the Coldstream at Sollum on the right. After fighting a delaying action for three days, we leap-frogged behind the 60th and they in turn leap-frogged behind us two days later on the line of Sidi Barrani—Bir Murman. During this withdrawal the conditions under which the day patrols operated must be described.

During the first period this had been carried out by armoured cars, but after the change of plan the 11th Hussars had been withdrawn, except for one squadron. The job had to be carried out by infantry and trucks ; most of these trucks were very worn out and it was by no means unusual for a patrol to go out with one truck on tow. These patrols often operated behind the enemy columns and two particular patrols, one commanded by Captain A. G. D. Palmer, and another by Captain R. A. A. Franklyn (since killed in action) operated behind the enemy columns for two whole days, shadowing them, reporting their dispositions, and keeping both the battalion and the divisional headquarters fully informed of the speed and direction of the advance. This action was most valuable.

On 17th September the enemy advance halted on the Sidi Barrani line and it was obvious that they were beginning to dig in. General Gott decided on a form of tactics which became the basis of those employed ever since by the 7th Armoured Division. It was clearly essential that the earliest possible information should be obtained of any hostile thrust, and a screen of armoured cars was pushed forward to gain contact with the enemy and gain possession of any high ground affording observation of his movements. The desert is not flat ; it is a series of undulations, hills and escarpments and all over it there are very definite points of observation which must be held if the enemy movements are to be forecast. It is important that the armoured car screen should not be driven in by small opposing forces gaining possession of high ground affording observation and thus denying us observation of the movement of their main forces. Only the main thrust must be capable of driving in the screen. This screen requires fire power to support it, and for this the " Jock " columns were invented, called after Brigadier Jock Campbell, V.C., who commanded the original one. These columns consist of a battery of 25-pounders, two to three troops of anti-tank guns, two companies of motor infantry, one troop of light anti-aircraft, and a regimental or battalion headquarters, to provide the necessary communications. They are put forward in close support of the armoured car screen, near important high ground, and their O.Ps. are either in or very close to the armoured car patrols. The job of these columns is to take on any threat to the armoured cars, to carry out night harassing, to be masters of " No Man's Land " and to discover the enemy fixed dispositions by means of night patrols, to harass by artillery fire enemy camps and posts, but not to get so committed that they cannot be extricated without assistance—that is, they must not allow themselves to get cut off by enemy tank columns getting round their flanks. It can be seen that for these a very wide field of vision is necessary and that the qualities of a column commander are such that he must be capable of making instant decisions whether to go forward, or back, at a minute's notice. These qualities were held in the highest degree by Brigadier Campbell, and the success of the columns throughout the last two years has been due to the original example that was set by him and to his unerring tactical genius and flair.

In September 1940, when the columns first started, they consisted of two who were found alternatively by the 1st/60th and the 2nd Rifle Brigade, the northern or coastal column, in the area east of Sidi Barrani, and the southern or escarpment column, on the top of the escarpment operating west of Bir Mumin. These columns continued till the 9th December and the life they led was the same as has been described on the escarpment, but varied with more daylight work in the way of artillery and harassing parties, usually consisting of a troop of 4th R.H.A., with a motor company, who went forward to harass before dawn.

On 22nd October the Battalion was given a new and extremely difficult role to carry out. It had been decided that the enemy camp at Maktila should be attacked and raided, and this was to be done by the Cameron Highlanders, who were to come up from behind Matruh to carry it out, a distance of well over one hundred and fifty miles and in country they had never previously seen. The task allotted to the Battalion was :—

(1) To guide the Cameron Highlanders' lorries up over sixty miles of country to a concentration area by day.
(2) To guide them another thirty miles to a detrucking area by night.
(3) To capture the starting line fifty yards from the enemy position.
(4) To tape the starting line.
(5) To guide the Cameron Highlanders up to the starting line.
(6) To cover their withdrawal after the raid.
(7) To guide them back, after the embussing, to their original positions.

As will be seen, the task of neither battalion was easy. The Camerons had to carry out an unreconnoitred attack by night, while the Battalion had a most complicated task for skilled troops, which was not made any easier by the fact that the drivers of the lorries to bring up the Camerons were all Indians who did not speak, or understand, one word of English.

The raid took place as ordered and the entire defensive fire of an Italian division was brought down to repel it. Every form of coloured light, shot and shell was fired off, and it looked more like a firework display than anything. The smallness of the casualties was more the result of Italian bad shooting than anything else. But although the raid was a success and prisoners captured, it was sufficient to determine the High Command that it was necessary to employ " I " tanks with a heavy concentration of artillery to take on the Italian fortress camps which they had established on the Nibeiwa—Sidi Barrani line.

At the end of November the Battalion was ordered to find out all that was possible about the approaches to, and the minefields covering, the Nibeiwa—Tumar camps. These were at a distance of some twenty miles from the column positions. A series of night patrols were sent out and more or less complete plans of the minefields obtained before the attack. Two particularly good patrols were carried out by Lieutenant C. H. Liddell with his platoon. This particular patrol first of all discovered an unsuspected minefield round Nibeiwa camp. Returning next night, they crawled in among the mines and eventually discovered enemy tanks ; rightly assuming that this was a passage through the minefield, they crawled in among them and discovered the width and exact position of the gap, and on 9th December successfully guided the " I " tanks through it.

The Tumar patrols were heavily handicapped by the very long distance—a seventy mile turn round—they had to do each night before they could actually carry out their job, but, under 2nd Lieutenant Carter, they discovered the minefields and gave a fairly accurate description of the defences, which was of great use when the attack was finally made.

All these preparations were carried out with great secrecy and no one in the battalion had any idea that anything more than a raid was being planned.

On 8th December the columns were withdrawn and concentrated south of the escarpment, and on the 9th December General Wavell's attack with the " I " tanks and the 4th Indian Division was made, while the Support Group was in reserve ready to operate behind the Armoured Division, which had been instructed to cut the main Sollum—Sidi Barrani road somewhere in the neighbourhood of Buq-Buq. This day, 9th December, was the first day the Support Group were not in actual contact with the enemy since war had started on 10th June, 1940.

Next day the Support Group resumed contact while the 60th Rifles were told to move forward to Sofafi and the Rifle Brigade were told to move round south and occupy a position just west of Sofafi and cut off any enemy that could be seen. A good many prisoners were captured on that day. On the following day the 2nd Rifle Brigade was told to move off down the Buq-Buq road as the armoured divisions had been withdrawn from there and had been sent round to deal with the Italian forts on the frontier wire.

The Battalion arrived on the road at about eight in the morning and pressed forward in two columns, one on the coast road and the other on the main Italian one. Contact was gained about nine o'clock and masses of prisoners captured, and by the evening the battalion line was established about fifteen miles from Sollum. Next day the advance was continued, Halfaya was captured and touch was gained with the 1st/60th on the top of the escarpment. Next day the Battalion occupied Sollum and pressed forward towards Bardia.

The operations of these three days were curious as there was no artillery whatever in support of the Battalion, while the enemy rearguards were particularly strong in that particular arm. It showed the great use of carriers, which were handled by the platoon commanders with great ability and were almost invulnerable to shell fire.

On arrival at the Bardia defences the enemy resistance stiffened. A particularly successful patrol by 2nd Lieutenants Salmon and Cooke shot down about twelve Italian O.Ps. from their ladders—it was rather like coconut shies at a fair—without suffering any casualties themselves.

The following day the Battalion was withdrawn with the rest of the Support Group to the wire and its place was taken by the Australian Division, who had been moved up on captured Italian transport. The next day the support group was ordered to proceed by night to cut the road between Bardia and Tobruk and prevent either (1) the enemy escaping from Bardia, or (2) being relieved from Tobruk. The 1st/60th were on the north, from the sea to the road exclusive, and the Battalion had the road inclusive to the escarpment. The 3rd and 4th R.H.A. were in support of both battalions. This role of facing both ways was not easy, and it was only due to the lack of Italian initiative that it was successfully carried out.

The usual night patrolling started again, accompanied by carrier patrols and artillery demonstrations by day to try and draw the enemy attention from the concentration of the 6th Australian Division to the east. Several prisoners were captured and some good raids made.

On 21st January, 1941, the Australian Division attacked and the role of the Battalion was to make a feint attack from the west to draw off the enemy shell fire ; this was done by carriers. The following day, after the fall of Bardia, the support group was moved south to El Adem and then moved north to cut the road between Tobruk and Derna and played the same role as at Bardia, only in this case its western flank was covered by the 7th Hussars. In this particular case the 60th Rifles were responsible for the road and the Rifle Brigade for the area south of the road and the main track from Acroma to Tobruk. When the attack on Tobruk came, the same role of making a feint attack was allotted to the Battalion, but on the second day we were ordered to press the carrier attack home.

The carriers on the south were held up by very heavy fire from Medawwar fort. The carriers in the north, however, under 2nd Lieutenant Bird, with a troop of 1st R.H.A. in support and an O.P. officer in the carriers with the platoon, were much more successful and the message that eventually came from the platoon commander was as follows :—" Have got round behind Medawwar and have taken nine big guns, 2,000 prisoners and about 40 small guns. I have found the Italian officers' mess. Whoopee. Off." Wireless discipline is strict in the Rifle Brigade, but this lapse from it was overlooked.

As soon as Tobruk was captured—in fact, before this had finally been done—the Support Group was again moved off to Segnali, south of Mechili, and two days later was brought up to Mechili only just in time to see the Italian garrison evacuate it. We were then told—this was the 3rd February—that no possible advance could be taken before the 15th and several senior officers, including the Brigadier, prepared to go on leave.

That afternoon, however, General Wilson arrived and told the Commanding Officer the enemy appeared to be evacuating the whole of Cyrenaica and we must cut them off. " The code word, boys, is Gallop." And that evening the Commanding Officer received orders that the Battalion was to form part of a mobile column under the 4th Armoured Brigade which was to try to get to the road along the Gulf of Sirte and cut off the enemy retreating from Benghazi.

The Battalion and the 4th R.H.A. were put last in the order of march in the 4th Armoured Brigade column, but at 11 o'clock next day the column was halted and the Commanding Officer received orders that the Battalion and one battery of the 4th R.H.A. and one battery 106th (Liverpool) Territorial anti-tank guns were to move ahead of the main body under Colonel Campbell and join up with the 11th Hussars, who were one hundred miles ahead in a place near Msus.

On arrival there, all the troops would come under the command of the Colonel commanding the 11th Hussars. The force started off, but at last light they came to large patches of thermos bombs, and Colonel Campbell decided to halt for the night while he himself went on to gain contact with the Colonel of the 11th. He drove alone from this minefield with full headlights on, not knowing the whereabouts of the enemy, throughout the night and contacted the Hussars at first light next morning. All then moved on and reached the neighbourhood of the road in the afternoon. Orders were then given.

The Rifle Brigade's main role was (1) protection of the guns, (2) to cut the road. The leading company, under Captain T. C. H. Pearson, was sent forward to cut the road, where it engaged about one thousand infantry and repelled an attempted attack by them. The remaining three companies were left with the guns about six miles from the road. The O.Ps. were put with the leading company. After personal reconnaissance that evening, the Commanding Officer brought up one more company to work on the left of the road, the whole of the road party being under the command of Captain Pearson, who decided, that night, to send out a patrol of anti-tank guns and two platoons under 2nd Lieutenant M. H. Mosley with orders to harass the length of the enemy column, which was now advancing down the road. This patrol had a very great effect as the enemy imagined there were guns all along the road instead of the same guns firing at different places. Three to four thousand Italians surrendered.

Next morning the Commanding Officer decided to move the whole Battalion (less half a company with the prisoners) up, as the 4th Armoured Brigade had arrived about ten miles to the north and the danger to the guns no longer existed.

The position was then—two companies on the road, another in depth about a mile behind, and one company from the coast to the road. The front was about five miles. Nine separate attacks were made during the ensuing thirty-six hours, all headed by tanks and with artillery and guns. The Battalion had only one battery of the 4th R.H.A. in support and a battery of the 106th (Liverpool) Territorial anti-tank guns. It was due to the magnificent shooting of both these batteries that the attacks were finally repelled. One Liverpool Territorial, with only five rounds left for his gun, accounted for one tank with each of them, holding his fire till they were within a range of about one hundred yards.

After the last attack on the morning of the 7th, General Bergonzoli surrendered. The total bag was 6 generals, 27 medium tanks, about 15,000 prisoners and well over 100 guns of all descriptions and innumerable cars and trucks.

The proceedings at the end were highly amusing. First the Italian generals, then the English generals arrived, and one almost expected an umpire's pow-wow to finish up with. Supplies of food and drink were obtained from the stores captured and the affair was reminiscent of a rather badly run point-to-point lunch.

One of the most satisfactory aspects of this campaign was that in the last hundred and fifty miles' rush across the desert on February 4th and 5th, over some of the worst and most rooky going in Cyrenaica, only one truck out of a hundred and forty broke down. The Battalion had had no new trucks since September, and no fresh spares since November. Maintenance had proved itself.

THE SEVENTH MOTOR BRIGADE
SUMMER, 1942

After the advance to Benghazi, in the autumn of 1941, it was decided to withdraw the 7th Armoured Division to the Delta to re-equip. A lesson of the autumn campaign had been that the German tank was infinitely superior to the English tank in armour, gun-power and mechanical reliability, and it was accordingly necessary for the fire-power of the Armoured Divisions to be considerably increased, if they were to take on the German Mark III and Mark IV tank.

The 7th Armoured Division was accordingly to be reorganized as follows :—

Into two Brigade Groups :
1. 4th Armoured Brigade Group, consisting of three regiments of tanks ; R.H.A. ; and the K.R.R.C. as the Motor Battalion.
2. 7th Motor Brigade Group, with the 4th R.H.A. and three Motor Infantry Battalions.

The fire-power of these battalions was very high, while their assaulting power with the bayonet was small.

The Division was completed in the Delta by the beginning of February and the intention was to give it ten weeks' training before proceeding to rejoin the 8th Army. The regiments in the 7th Motor Brigade were the K.R.R.C. and the Rifle Brigade.

In the 7th Motor Brigade Group, the Rifle Brigade and the 4th R.H.A. had been together since the beginning of hostilities. The other units had not previously served in the Support Group.

The tactical handling of the division was to be as follows :—

An armoured car screen would be extended twenty or thirty miles ahead, and then would come the Motor Brigade Group. The idea was that on approach to the enemy, the Motor Brigade Group was to de-truck and " bristle " ; that is, take up a position with all-round defences where its fire-power could be used to the greatest advantage.

The trucks were to be sent away on the signal " Lead horses " with a bearing and a distance, to a distance of five or six miles.

It was hoped that the enemy would then attack the Motor Brigade and himself be attacked by the Armoured Brigade whilst doing so.

This form of tactics was never actually tried out by the division for reasons that will be explained later, but it had been used, and used successfully, by the Rifle Brigade and the 4th Armoured Brigade at Sidi Saleh and Beda Fomm in February, 1941, and by the 60th Rifles and 7th Armoured Brigade at Sidi Rezegh in November.

For the employment of these tactics it is essential that ground vital to the enemy be seized, otherwise the Motor Brigade would be by-passed.

In both the cases mentioned, this vital ground was seized—in the first case the main road for the retreating Italian Army, and in the second the main line of supply of the troops investing Tobruk.

At the end of February it became obvious from the intensity of the air attack on Malta, that large supplies were reaching General Rommel, who had in the meantime forced the 8th Army back to the Gazala—Bir Hachiem position. By March, it had become so obvious that the 7th Armoured Division was sent up to join the 8th Army without any further training, and took its position with the fighting units in the middle of April.

The Division was employed under the following conditions :

The 8th Army held a defensive line from the sea to Bir Hacheim. Minefields and dummy minefields covered the whole line. These minefields, however, were only covered by fire for half the length of the line, owing to shortage of troops. The responsibility for the southern half, about twenty-five miles, was that of the 30 Corps, which consisted of the 1st and 7th Armoured Divisions. In front of 13 Corps, that is the northern half of the minefield, the enemy was at a distance of some eight miles from our forward lines ; on the 30 Corps front, the enemy swung back westwards to Segnali and Asida, sixty or seventy miles from Bir Hacheim. Bir Hacheim itself was garrisoned by a brigade of Free French who were well dug in and possessed considerable gun-power. This Free French garrison was under 30 Corps, who had placed it under command of the 7th Armoured Division.

In addition, on the 24th of May—twenty-four hours before the German attack started—an Indian Motor Brigade had been placed under command of the 7th Armoured Division and had been ordered to form a " box " about three miles south of Bir Hacheim.

There appeared to be three courses open to the enemy :—

    (i) An attack astride the coast road against our main defences directed on Tobruk on the front of 13 Corps.

    (ii) A penetration of the minefield on the main axis of the Trigh Capuzzo.

    (iii) An outflanking movement, south of Bir Hacheim, whilst detaching a force to mask that place, and the surrounding neighbourhood.

A SONG BEFORE SUNRISE, THE 2ND BATTALION 55

In any case his main objective was likely to be Tobruk. In the event of (i) 30 Corps would counter-attack northwards to attack such a penetration in the flank before it reached Acroma. For (ii) and (iii) there was ground vital to the enemy which he would have to take, and different hull down positions were carefully prepared and reconnoitred by the Armoured Brigades so as to deny this ground to the enemy forces. Because of the length of time it takes for armoured brigades to take up fighting positions it was vital that the earliest possible information as to the direction of the enemy's main thrust should reach the higher command.

In consequence, a screen of armoured cars was put out to keep contact with the enemy along the whole 30 Corps front from Mteiffel to Asida, and at a distance of seventy to one hundred miles from the armoured brigade positions.

Rather to the disappointment of the Motor Brigade, who had hoped to be employed concentrated, they were once more split up into columns to support the armoured car screen ; this dispersion was inevitable under the circumstances.

The distance of the screen from the ground of our own choosing, where the armour intended to fight, and the extended front rendered support to the armoured car regiments imperative. It must be added, however, that small independent commands gave great latitude of manœvre. It was essential that any armoured car screen must be backed up by a sufficient force to resist anything except the enemy's main thrust.

Three " Jock " columns from the Motor Brigade, one column from the Free French forces, and two armoured car regiments (the 4th South African Armoured Cars and the K.D.Gs.) were allocated to cover the 30 Corps front of about one hundred and thirty miles, all of which were placed under command of the 7th Motor Brigade. One battalion of the 7th Motor Brigade and one battery 4 R.H.A. were retained under direct command of 7th Armoured Division in the El Retima area.

Considerable harassing was undertaken both by day by artillery, and by night by motorized infantry, but the main responsibility of the columns was to ensure that observation was maintained on Segnali and the high ground of Asida and to ensure that no enemy thrust could be made without adequate warning being given to the armoured brigades.

Much has been said about these columns. They have been spoken of as the only way of fighting desert war, or alternatively as the one way of losing it. In fact, in defence, or withdrawal, they are used for the definite purpose of supporting the armoured car screen to enable sufficient warning to be given to the armoured brigades of any really strong enemy attack. In an advance they are used in the same way to locate the main, as distinct from the subsidiary, enemy positions. In fact, they merely represent on a wide front the fire-power of an advance, or rear guard. This has always formed part of the tactical organization of the British and other armies.

The support to the armoured car screen was not formed from Armoured Regiments for the following reasons :—

(i) The long distance from workshops and other repair facilities (it was obviously undesirable to site these forward of the main battle positions).

(ii) The wear and tear on our tanks and expenditure of tank mileage which would be entailed. These had a very limited mileage life compared with the German Mark III and Mark IV tanks.

(iii) The dissipation which would be caused to the very limited tank strength available.

(iv) The necessity for secrecy in regard to the General Grant tank and 6-pounder anti-tank gun.

Life on these columns is extremely strenuous. The column cannot leaguer until after dark. By first light the O.Ps. must be in position and in contact with the enemy, so they must leave at least an hour before first light. They are out all day and cannot withdraw to leaguer until after dark. Leaguers must be six to eight miles from the day position. Rations and ammunition, etc., have to be distributed after arrival in leaguer, and in the short summer nights there is little sleep to be obtained. Night patrolling is continuous ; most officers are out alternate nights. When it is remembered that the 7th Motor Brigade was in continuous contact with the enemy from 23rd April to the 17th September, it will be realized that they had some degree of strain.

Perhaps the main reason for the success of the 7th Motor Brigade was the fact that they all knew each other well. Motor infantry subalterns were quite capable of shooting the battery when the Gunner O.P. officer was wounded. R.H.A. subalterns were equally capable of commanding motor infantry platoons and companies, should conditions be reversed. Columns were commanded by motor infantry and gunner officers without reference to the arm of the service to which they belonged. Everyone knew everyone else, and if you are fighting the Germans that is the only way to succeed. Against the Italians it is not so important.

Night patrols during this period entailed a drive of anything up to fourteen miles each way on a compass bearing and consisted of locating enemy advances, capturing enemy prisoners, and raiding and harassing enemy leaguers. This patrolling was incessant and continued nightly throughout the operations until 17th September when the 7th Motor Brigade was withdrawn to refit.

On 25th May, at 1530 hours, the main enemy advance started. By 1900 hours, German tanks as distinct from Italian had been identified, and by 2130 hours large German armoured columns were reported to be advancing southwards. The columns, with the armoured car screen, withdrew in front of them. They kept in touch with them and reported throughout the night. Between 1530 and 2130 hours, twenty-three messages were sent by the 7th Motor Brigade reporting the German advance, and between 2130 hours and 7 o'clock next morning another thirty were dispatched by the 7th Motor Brigade.

In the meantime, it was impossible to get any further orders as Divisional Headquarters had been overrun, and touch was not established with 30 Corps until the late afternoon when the brigade was ordered to take over the defence of the F.M.C.S. in that area. Next afternoon, the 28th, orders were received from 30 Corps that the 7th Motor Brigade would be responsible for the defence of Bel Hamed, where the forward base was situated, the armoured car regiments reverting to command of 30 Corps. Shortly after this position had been taken up the brigade was ordered north to prevent the investment of Acroma and came again under command of 7th Armoured Division. Next day, however, the brigade was withdrawn and concentrated south of El Adem, with 4th S.A. Armoured Cars and K.D.Gs. once more under command.

There the situation was painted that the enemy had been more, or less, decisively defeated, that he was trapped opposite Mteiffel in a cauldron between our armour and the minefields and that he was trying to pick up the minefields with a view to escaping. The 7th Motor Brigade were ordered round the minefields to try to prevent him doing this. The brigade moved round that night and arrived in the Mteiffel area early next morning. It was one of the most successful days that the columns and 4th South African Armoured Cars have ever had. Much of the enemy lines of supply were at their mercy. Tanks and transporters and over one hundred trucks were knocked out, large numbers of guns captured, five hundred of our own prisoners released, three hundred prisoners taken.

It was obvious that we could work havoc on the enemy lines of supply ; equally obvious that the cauldron was not a cauldron but a bridgehead, that the enemy was not trying to get out of it but to get through it. Next day, it had been hoped to carry on with the same role, but orders were received directing the withdrawal of all columns to assist the French, who were being invested in Bir Hacheim. Permission to go on operating against the Axis lines-of-communication was refused until four days later, when one column only was allowed to go. The Rifle Brigade, under Lord Garmoyle, then had a success as great as that of the first day.

In the meantime, the Germans had surrounded Bir Hacheim with a screen of some seventy enemy guns and little could be done to assist the French with the smaller gun-fire of the 7th Motor Brigade. However, it was possible to send supplies into Bir Hacheim each night until the French refused to take any more. Liaison officers and small parties of the motor brigade were in Bir Hacheim the whole time. It was a considerable surprise when on the evening 12th June, orders were received that Bir Hacheim was being evacuated that night and that the 7th Motor Brigade would cover the evacuation. Nothing was known about plans or where the French troops were coming out. However, more by good luck than good management, nearly four thousand were evacuated. The commander of Bir Hacheim was the first to escape and arrived back at Bardia, seventy miles away, by 1000 hours on the following morning.

Before then the Rifle Brigade column had been withdrawn from the Mteiffel area, where it had had a most successful three days, and orders were received that as soon as the evacuation of Bir Hacheim had been completed the 7th Motor Brigade should concentrate near El Gubi and " make a supreme effort " to interfere with the investment of Tobruk. The news that Tobruk was in danger was a definite shock. As nothing had been received by the Motor Brigade, little was known of the battles farther north. The Motor Brigade advanced towards El Adem, which was still holding out, and three good days were had by the columns. Much enemy transport was destroyed, guns were captured and tanks knocked out.

It is emphasized that much of the success of the columns was due to the complete drill that had been established. On a code word everyone knew where to go and what to do. Everyone had code words to go forwards, or backwards, fifty miles, or anywhere else between. The consequence was that they stayed on longer and inflicted many more casualties than would have been possible had no such plans existed. Much punishment was inflicted on the enemy with the slightest of casualties to ourselves.

Two days later El Adem was evacuated at night by an Indian Brigade covered by the columns of the Motor Brigade, who assisted in the concentration of the Indians after evacuation and covered their withdrawal.

On 19th June, orders were received that 7th Armoured Division would come under 13 Corps, who were taking up a position along the escarpment outside Sollum, while the 7th Armoured Division, consisting of the 4th Armoured Brigade, much depleted in numbers, and the 7th Motor Brigade were to do all they could to prevent the investment of Tobruk and to cover the occupation of the Sollum position. Orders were given to carry on with the harassing when the following day it was heard that Tobruk had fallen. Orders were then received to cover first the occupation of the escarpment and about two hours later to cover the withdrawal of the Corps, and, in fact, the whole of the 8th Army from the escarpment. But the escarpment had to be held for three days until the Indian Division could be successfully withdrawn.

The plan was to operate the 4th Armoured Brigade close to the escarpment north of El Hamra, while the 7th Motor Brigade were to operate farther west against the southern flank and especially to deal with his advance through the frontier wire. This plan was successful and the Indian Division was withdrawn safely ; the 4th Armoured

Brigade was then taken back, under command of the 1st Armoured Division, to the Matruh area, the 7th Armoured Division covering the 8th Army withdrawal, with the Indian Motor Brigade, the 7th Motor Brigade and an infantry brigade coming under command at various periods. During the withdrawal the columns were in constant contact with the enemy who advanced in strong columns headed by tanks, always endeavouring to outflank our communications. The enemy being in much greater force than we were, this was not difficult.

On arrival at Matruh, the 7th Motor Brigade came under command of the 1st Armoured Division, and the 7th Armoured Division Headquarters were sent off to the 8th Army reserve to re-form. Matruh was not held, however, and at the beginning of July, the 7th Motor Brigade, the 4th Light Armoured Brigade and 3rd R.H.A., together with the 4th South African Armoured Cars, came under command of the 7th Armoured Division. The orders were to cover the southern flank of the El Alamein line and to act as rear-guard in the event of any further withdrawal and to protect the desert track between Himeinat and Cairo. Orders were issued for all these eventualities.

During the month of July several attacks were made on our positions and repelled and active harassing was carried out by the division, including one raid where a complete Italian post was captured by Major Bird, Rifle Brigade, without any casualties. An attack was attempted also with an infantry brigade, under command of 7th Armoured Division, towards the Taqa Plateau. It was intended to be subsidiary to a main attack in the north, and had this been successful the 4th Armoured Brigade would have been pushed north to cut off the enemy's retreat. The only lesson to be learned from this particular attack was that armoured divisions are not the best formations to handle infantry brigades. The communications are different, and the artillery and the O.Ps. were not trained to work with infantry.

This account cannot be closed without a further reference to one of the greatest of Greenjackets, Lieut.-General Gott. As our brigadier, divisional, and corps commander, he trained and inspired us from the time of our arrival in Egypt until his death. We were always all right under his skilful leadership.

EL ALAMEIN AND
THE ACTION OF THE SNIPE POSITION

2nd BATTALION

26th—27th October, 1942

The following account is compiled from letters received from the Battalion.

The action fought on 26th—27th October, 1942, at the Snipe position, when the Commanding Officer, Lieut.-Colonel V. B. Turner was awarded the Victoria Cross, will be an outstanding one in the annals of the Regiment.

The Victoria Cross awarded to the Colonel was not only for great gallantry and endurance, but for the example which he set to his officers and men, an example which they acted up to and enabled the Battalion to bring to a successful conclusion an action which might easily have been critical both to the Battalion and the Army.

The 2nd Battalion prior to the operation, had been taken out of its brigade and formed the infantry of the Minefield Task Force, its duty being to ensure the safe passage of the division through any enemy minefields that might be encountered on the divisional objective, 5,500 yards in from the enemy's F.D.Ls.

To cover the Minefield Task Force the divisions were to put in an infantry attack to this depth in front of this force. The attack of one of the divisions was successful, but in the case of the other a number of enemy strong points were missed, and had to be cleared by the Battalion, in addition to its other duties.

The Battalion was organized in three Parties :

" A " Company   Basset took the Right
" B "   ,,   Mosley ,,   ,, Centre
" C "   ,,   Liddell ,,   ,, Left

" B " and " C " Companies met with fairly strong opposition at the first enemy minefield, which had to be overcome before gapping operations could be commenced ; all this took place during the night 23rd—24th October.

Dawn on the 24th found the Battalion in the face of strong opposition from 88 mm. guns and medium artillery, trying to gap the second enemy minefield.

By this time there was great congestion in the area and dispersion was impossible on account of minefields on either flank, the second minefield was fully gapped by 0700 hours, but it was then found that a third and fourth existed, covering a depth of 2,000 yards, and to

THE 2ND BATTALION AT EL ALAMEIN

make matters worse the position was overlooked by a strongly held ridge to the west, on which were about 30 Mark III and Mark IV Specials.

Gaps were pushed forward under cover of an infantry attack, but casualties began to mount up, " B " Company lost C.S.M. Nobel, and three other sergeants, at this period of the action. By last light gaps had been made mainly due to the fine work of a field squadron, R.E., and the carrier platoons of " B " and " C " Companies, under Innes and Flower.

Innes had just completed his job when he was badly wounded, having both legs broken.

Flower and his party, managed to get through in the face of direct fire from 88 mm. guns and machine-guns, and were able to report the way clear for Armour.

All that night the Battalion had to provide traffic control at all the gaps, so no sleep was possible for anyone for the second night running.

The next two days were fairly quiet and the night 25th—26th the officers and men had their first sleep since the operation commenced.

During the night 26th—27th the Battalion was ordered to take up a position two miles west of our F.D.L's. which were not beyond the last minefield, and to hold it till the tanks came up at first light.

The position the Battalion was ordered to take up was at that time in the enemy's possession but was taken with small loss and the capture of forty German prisoners.

The Battalion's anti-tank guns and vehicles were now fetched up and an all round defensive position organized ; no sooner were the guns in position than the enemy counter-attacked with about fifteen tanks from the south and six others from the west ; three of the fifteen tanks were knocked out at point blank range and the remainder drew off.

When daylight came on the 27th it was found that the Armoured Brigade which was to have arrived to assist the Battalion, had not done so and were unable now to get through on account of enemy fire ; as a result the Battalion was isolated and left to bear the brunt throughout the day of continual attacks by a Panzer Division and part of another. To make matters worse no artillery support was given and the position was under direct observation from enemy strong points.

The day ended with an attack on the position by the full weight of the Panzer Divisions.

To quote in full from an Officer's letter :—

" Vic was magnificent, he was always where the action was hottest and continually took the place of wounded gun members. Tom Bird commanding ' S ' Company (A/Tank) was the same, and the example set by Jack Toms, Jimmy Irwin, Barry Holt Wilson and Geoffrey Merrick was an inspiration to their troops.

" Hugo Salmon was killed towing a gun across the position to replace one knocked out when an 88 mm. scored a direct hit on his Jeep. All the numbers one on the guns fought magnificently, and in particular Sergt. Calistan who, with Vic doing loader, knocked out nine enemy tanks, the last three with the last three remaining rounds, and turned the enemy's attack.

" The position was only penetrated once by two tanks which were both dealt with.

" We tried to run up more ammunition to the position in carriers but the enemy had two 88 mm. between our F.D.Ls. and the position which made this impossible. The position held till dark, and as the ammunition was nearly exhausted and the enemy were closing in, the Battalion withdrew on its left and got away all its arms including machine-guns and mortars, but it had to leave the 6-pounders behind, though these were put out of action before leaving.

" Vic was wounded in the head in the closing stages but remained in command till the position was evacuated.

" The official log was thirty-five tanks burnt out, but subsequent check has shown that at least fifty-seven were burnt out and many others were knocked out but did not burn.

" The Motor Platoons did great work picking off the tank crews when they baled out and stopped any infantry attack that formed up against the position. The wounded were all brought back when the Battalion withdrew."

It is hard to do justice to individuals in an action in which the whole Battalion distinguished itself.

The following awards were made in connection with the action.

It was for service during the period covering this action that a bar to his D.S.O. was awarded to Brigadier T. J. B. Bosvile. A paragraph of the citation for the award reads :

" His constant desire to be aggressive, his anxiety to maintain the offensive, his quick decisions and his calm and considered judgment were largely responsible for the destruction of over sixty tanks and a large number of enemy personnel."

Major T. A. Bird, the younger brother of Lieutenant E. A. Bird, who was killed in action with the 1st Battalion at Calais, 1940, while trying to save life, had already been awarded the Military Cross with bar, was given an immediate award of the D.S.O.

During the action he was in command of the anti-tank defence of the position ; in the words of the official citation " he paid no heed to his own safety but went from gun to gun under intense fire, giving encouragement and when necessary taking the place of wounded men in gun crews."

He himself was wounded in the head early during the afternoon 27th October, but in spite of concussion and a hot sun carried on until last light.

A bar to the Military Cross was awarded to Second-Lieutenant J. E. B. Toms ; he was commander of a troop of 6-pounder anti-tank guns. On the second day of the action it was the only surviving gun

2nd BATTALION

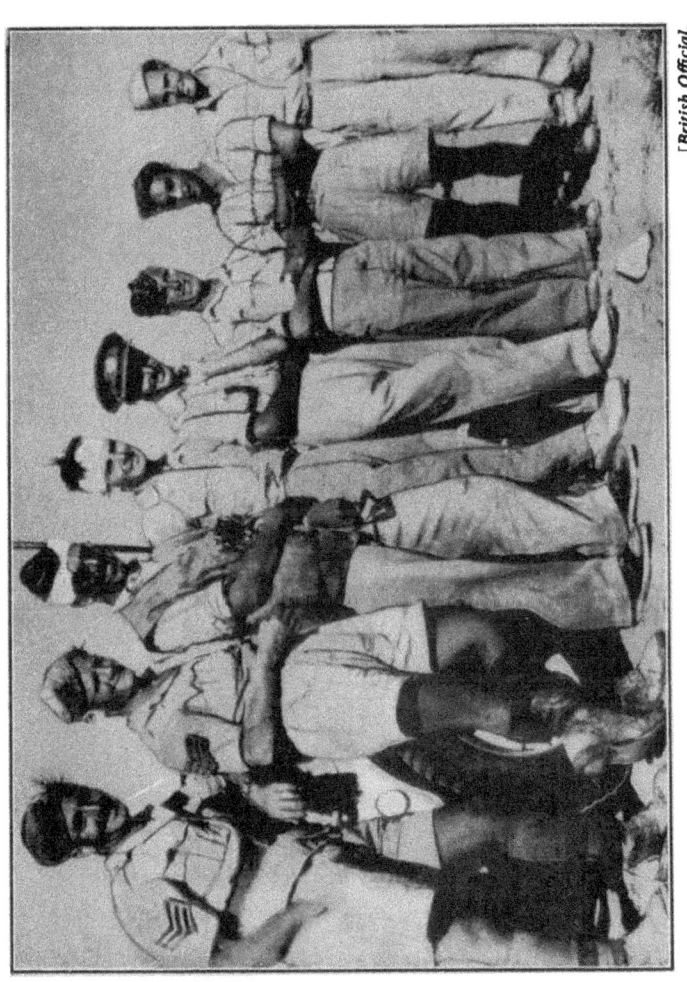

[*British Official.*]

Sergt. Avris, Sergt. Miles, M.M., Lieut. J. B. D. Irwin, M.C., Major T. A. Bird, D.S.O., M.C., Lieut. A. B. Holt Wilson, M.C., Sergt. Hine, M.M., Sergt. Calistan, D.C.M., M.M., Rfn. Chard, D.C.M.

AFTER THE ACTION OF THE SNIPE POSITION

2nd BATTALION

[*W.O. Official.*

THE SNIPE POSITION—THE GENERAL'S CONGRATULATIONS

of his troop which, manned by its No. 1 and the Colonel, remained in action. Toms acted as observer and kept the gun supplied with ammunition. Although wounded he remained at duty, his troop accounting for twenty-three enemy tanks burnt out as well as many other vehicles and guns hit. The Military Cross was awarded to Captain D. W. Basset, Lieutenants A. B. Holt-Wilson and J. B. D. Irwin.

Sergt. C. V. Calistan, M.M., was awarded the Distinguished Conduct Medal. His courage was outstanding amongst that of many courageous non-commissioned officers ; he was sergeant commander of a section of 6-pounder anti-tank guns on the west flank of the position. He was attacked both by day and night, all his guns except his own were knocked out, and was the only survivor of his own gun crew, the troop were almost out of ammunition, but Calistan held on, keeping his gun in action with deadly effect. He was assisted by the Colonel, who acted as loader until hit. Attacked by fifteen tanks he hit nine, then out of ammunition waited calmly for more to arrive ; when it came he hit three more tanks with as many shots.

After receiving orders to withdraw he proceeded to walk the 400 yards back to Company H.Q. carrying a wounded man. The wounded man was again hit and killed. Calistan returned to his old position and fetched away the last remaining wounded man whom he brought back through an intense and accurate fire.

The official citation concludes : " When the last point of human endurance and ability to continue to fight had been reached, Sergt. Calistan took on a new lease of courage : this he communicated to all around him and with their help he saved the day."

The D.C.M. was also awarded to Col.-Sergt. J. E. Swann and Rfn. D. A. Chard.

A bar to the Military Medal was awarded Sergt. J. A. Hine, and the Military Medal to Corpl. J. W. C. Barnett, Rfn. S. H. Burnhope, L/Sergt. E. W. Cope, L/Sergt. A. Francis, Corpl. S. W. Fulton, Sergt. H. H. Miles, Sergt. D. Newman.

The full official citations for these awards will appear in VOLUME II.

The following account of what was described by the General Commanding the 8th Army, 10 Corps, as " one of the finest actions of the war " is reprinted from the 8th November number of " The Crusader," the 8th Army weekly.

" We moved up to occupy the post at night. We're used to moving when the sun's gone down—we've been doing it for more than two years.

" There was a very yellow moon and as we advanced we came in for a spot of bother from some German 88 mm. guns. Our post was on a small ridge and diamond shaped. The Germans had not long left and it was in a filthy state. From the moment we got there until we left we were pestered by flies !

" After we had our twelve 6-pounders ready to do their stuff there was a chance to take a good look at the ground. It was just flat open desert, with the usual scrub.

" The enemy started machine-gunning us and sending over mortar bombs. In the brilliant moon I could see the tail of smoke trailing behind the bombs.

" We knew something big was starting—you get a funny sort of instinct after you've been through scraps. A thousand yards away I could see the lumpy shape of the leading German tank. It was a Mark IV Special. We held our fire. Those were the orders. They came rumbling on, spurting at us with their machine-guns and backed by shells and mortar bombs.

" They came on and on—they weren't more than five hundred yards away. There were fifty-odd tanks and a staff car leading them. Still we held our fire. I could almost hear my heart pounding and it seemed louder than the bursting bombs and rumbling tanks."

Sergt. Calistan's personal narrative of the action is now given.

" I let go at 150 yards. You couldn't miss. All our guns seemed to be firing at once. My target burst into flames but came on for another fifty yards before it halted. Suddenly the night was bright with burning tanks. Over on my left one blew up at two hundred yards.

" We were giving them hell, but we weren't by any means getting away with it. Our position was rather exposed and they let us have everything they had got. They even attacked us with lorried infantry.

" It was our twelve guns against fifty tanks, and when they turned about and retired we knew that for the moment our guns had won. Some of the enemy tanks tried to hide by mixing up with knocked-out tanks and derelict vehicles—but we are used to most of Jerry's tricks. The crew of one German tank tried to repair it on the spot. We picked them off with a rifle. I heard an 88 mm. banging away at us on a flank—then silence as one of our guns scored a direct hit.

" All this time the enemy never let up ; nor did we. Time seemed to be lost in the battle. My gun had smashed up five tanks in that first attack—and I am only counting those that ' brewed up '—that's our way of saying they burnt out.

" Some of our guns were out of action. Some had run out of ammo. I can't remember how many. The thing that sticks out is the Company Commander saying that we were cut off and that there wasn't anything that could get through to us. We would fight it out. Keep on firing as long as we had a shell or bullet. Yes. We understood.

" And when you had time to listen it was only then you realized that you had fewer and fewer guns firing. We were also short of water, but somehow you didn't think about that.

" Two of my gun crew crept out on their bellies—right into the open to get to some ammo. They were under enemy fire the whole time and their progress was terribly slow. Then our platoon

2nd BATTALION

GENERAL SIR H. M. WILSON'S INSPECTION

2nd BATTALION

Sergt. C. V. Calistan, D.C.M., M.M.

Major T. A. Bird, D.S.O., M.C.

Rfn. D. A. Chard, D.C.M.

W.O. Official

The Snipe Position

The 2nd Battalion at El Alamein

officer decided to reach his Jeep, which had four boxes of ammo on board.

" God knows how he got to it—they were machine-gunning the whole way. He started coming towards us and then they hit the Jeep and it caught fire, but he kept on coming. We got the ammo off and then I had an idea. We hadn't had a thing to drink and we naturally hadn't been able to light a fire but here was a perfectly good one. So I put a can of water on the Jeep and it brewed up well enough for three cups of tea !

" Our Colonel kept going from gun to gun. How he inspired us ! The enemy tried to shift us with an infantry attack but we soon sent them on their way with our Bren-carriers and our infantry, who were in position in front of us.

" When the next tank attack came in the Colonel was acting as loader on my gun. He got wounded in the head—a nasty wound and we wanted to bind it up but he wouldn't hear of it. Keep firing—that's what he wanted and we didn't pause. When the gun ran short of ammo he got it from one of the others.

" When the Colonel was too weak to refuse attention we bound up his head and put him behind some scrub. He called out that he wanted to know what was happening and my officer kept up a running commentary. We hit three tanks with three successive shots, and the Colonel yelled out : ' Good work—a hat trick ! ' Another gun got two tanks with one shell—they were one behind the other and it passed right through the nearest one into the other and knocked both of them out.

" The ground in front of us was littered with broken tanks. We had been fighting for nearly thirty-six hours. I've been talking most of the time about my own gun but what I've said goes for all of them. There was a rifleman and a sergeant who had fourteen tanks to their credit ; and a sergeant who had four and so on. The officers were all of them working on the guns with us.

" Suddenly I realized that my gun was the only one firing and that we had only two rounds of ammunition left ... We took a line on two tanks and got both of them.

" Then came the order to make our way back to our own lines as best we could. We had to go under fire the whole way for two and a half miles. We removed the breech blocks and the sights of our guns.

" We had men with tommy-guns leading and we carried the wounded in the centre. Before we moved off I did something you may think rather stupid—I went back and kissed my gun.

" I carried one of our wounded on my back. Freddie—that was his name. He had volunteered to come out here. Been out only a few weeks. He had a wife and four children. He had been wounded trying to help someone else. They got him on the way back—shot him through the head.

" It took us four hours to do that two and a half miles and then we reached our own lines. We had had about thirty-three casualties and we had had to destroy our guns—but there were at least thirty-seven enemy tanks smashed beyond hope of recovery and about twenty more knocked out.

" To-day I heard that some of our troops are back on our position. I hope they have our guns—we still have the breech blocks you know ! "

23RD OCTOBER—17TH NOVEMBER, 1942.

During the period that the action at the Snipe position was being fought by the 2nd Battalion, the 1st Battalion was engaged not far away.

The following is compiled from accounts received.

Before the battle started, 23rd October, 1942, the 8th Army Line ran from the sea, at El Alamein, to a point about thirty-eight miles south and six miles west of a large hill known as Himeimat, which dominated the whole of the southern sector. This hill was held by the enemy. The Battalion held a position about six miles north-west of Himeimat. The position consisted of two minefields known as " Nuts," the forward one ; and " May," the rear or eastern one. Two companies were on " Nuts " and two on " May." The distance between " Nuts " and " May " was about 8,000 yards. The Battalion formed part of an armoured brigade in an armoured division.

About 10,000 yards west of " Nuts," the enemy held two similar minefields, known as " January " and " February." For a month before the battle the Battalion had been employed patrolling and observing the enemy positions on " January," and much valuable information had been sent back to Division : information which operations subsequently proved to be correct in almost every detail. This reflects a very high standard of training on the part of the young officers who were employed to collect this information. It was nearly all done at night and often in the face of bitter opposition. As a result of these patrols it was possible for a complete map of both minefields to be issued, showing the extent of the minefields and the position of the enemy troops holding them. The troops opposite the Battalion consisted of the Folgore Division. These were Italian paratroops which were being used as ordinary infantry ; they were very well equipped with automatics, anti-tank guns, and artillery. They were about the best Italian troops encountered in the desert, although they did not come up to the standard of the best class German divisions. Nevertheless, they fought well, and proved themselves worthy opponents.

On the night of 24th—25th October, which was full moon, the Brigade was to advance through gaps which had been made. The advanced guard included Battalion H.Q. plus " A " and " B " Companies, and the Royal Scots Greys. The remainder followed with the main body. " I " and " C " Companies were put under command of the R.T.R. The Divisional Reconnaissance Regiment, assisted by the Royal Engineers, was to make four gaps in " January," corresponding precisely to those in " Nuts " and " May." As soon as these gaps were complete, " A " and " B " Companies were to push through and take up flanking positions—" A " Company to the north—" B " to the south, facing outwards and thus forming a corridor through which the Divisional Reconnaissance Regiment could repeat the operation on " February." The Greys were to support the action of the advanced guard throughout, and, as soon as the gaps in " February " were complete, the whole Brigade was to be passed through to take up a battle position on the far side of the minefield. The Battalion was then to hand over the whole of the minefield position to another brigade who would then become responsible for both minefields, and " A " and " B " Companies with Battalion H.Q. were to rejoin the Brigade in their battle position to the west.

Battalion H.Q. followed by " A " Company was to go through No. 1 Gap and " B " Company was to go through No. 4 Gap. The attack was preceded by an artillery barrage which crept forward about 200 yards in front of the Divisional Reconnaissance Regiment.

At 1900 hours, 22nd October, a squadron of cavalry, under Major Ferris St. George, took over a line of observation on " Nuts " minefield, and the Battalion was withdrawn to a concentration area behind " May." At 1830 hours, 23rd October, the Brigade was drawn up in four lines, ready to move up in accordance with the plan. At 1845 hours the advance guard moved forward, closely followed by the remainder of the Brigade, with " C " and " I " Companies. At 2100 hours the advance guard went through " Nuts " and entered " No Man's Land," where there was a delay for half an hour. The enemy realized that something was up and there was a certain amount of shelling. At 2200 hours our artillery preparation opened up on " January " and the head of the advance guard reached the eastern edge of " January." At 2300 hours " A " and " B " Companies, and Battalion H.Q., reached the eastern edge of " January." No. 2 Gap was now showing signs of being completed. No. 1 had not been started and it looked as though No. 2 was our best chance. There was a very heavy artillery fire from the enemy and " A " Company were suffering casualties, as there was very little room to manœuvre. At 2330 hours " B " Company reported that No. 3 Gap was impassible owing to soft sand, but that No. 4 Gap was progressing slowly. At 2350 hours No. 2 Gap looked as though it was complete, though the enemy fire from a gun, whose flashes could be seen, was making the gap a very unpleasant place. Orders were therefore given for the machine-gun platoon of " A " Company to come into action and engage this gun, which could be seen in the moonlight about 2,000 yards away. The platoon, under Sergt. Buxton, came into action very quickly and opened up smartly with four guns. The effect was quite instantaneous, and the gun stopped firing, and orders were given for " A " Company to go straight through the gap. As " A " Company went through, a wireless message from Brigade was received ordering the Battalion to turn south and clear the western end of No. 3 and No. 4 Gaps. On arrival at the western end of No. 2 the position was very unpleasant. However, " A " Company wheeled to their left and over-ran two posts and formed a temporary bridgehead. Progress to the south was slow, but at 0130 hours " B " Company reported No. 4 Gap slowly proceeding. At 0135 hours " B " Company appeared at the head of No. 4 Gap and tried to make progress to the south and west. At this moment the Royal Scots Greys were ordered to come up to support us, which they did, but the congestion of men and vehicles and tanks on the western end of the gap was very great. The enemy kept up a very heavy fire but it made dispersion and manœuvre a matter of great difficulty.

By 0230 hours " A " Company had reorganized, but very little progress had been made with " February " minefield owing to enemy strongpoints, well equipped with machine-guns sited between " January " and " February." Two points then became obvious. One, that it was unlikely that the Battalion would get through " February " that night ; two, that if they remained in their present position on the western end of " January," they would be destroyed as soon as it got light. Orders were therefore given for " A " Company and " B " Company to fan out at all costs and to extend the bridgehead 1500 yards to the south and west. The O.C., the Greys, was asked to support this action, but was unable to give support before it began to get light. However, at first light both companies went forward with no other support than their own machine-guns and, in the face of very heavy fire, over-ran three very strong Italian posts. By 0715 hours the bridgehead had been extended to " February " minefield on the west and south almost to the slopes of Himeimat. " A " Company had suffered badly, but " B " Company was largely intact. The bridgehead was consolidated by 0900 hours and " A " and " B " Companies were amalgamated into a composite company, under Palmer. The Battalion had taken about three hundred prisoners and had over-run the offending anti-tank gun of the previous night. The crew was found dead and the gun was turned round and its entire stock of ammunition was fired at an enemy strongpoint with considerable effect. A very unpleasant day was spent being shelled.

On the night 24th—25th an unsuccessful effort was made to get through " February." The gaps were made, but owing to heavy fire the armour could not be passed through. " I " Company took part in this venture, fortunately without serious casualties.

The 25th was spent in the same position, and very unpleasant it was too. On the night 25th—26th it was decided to relieve the Brigade. The armour was withdrawn at last light and the O.C. Battalion H.Q. was left in command of the rear party, which force took over the bridgehead just before the armour withdrew and, about 2200 hours, the relieving brigade started to come in. The enemy realized that something was up, and shelled the relief heavily all night. However, thanks to real energetic action by the Kent Brigade they strongly dug themselves in by 0400 hours, and the rear party was able to withdraw and rejoin the Brigade on " Nuts " minefield at first light. The 26th —27th—28th were spent in reorganizing.

On the 30th a still further withdrawal was made and the Battalion had another day's rest.

On the 31st the Battalion was moved to a brigade concentration area in the northern sector on the Coast Road, near Ilymayid station. That day ten officers and forty other ranks joined as reinforcements. The Battalion was organized into " A " and " B " Companies, now known as the " Composite Company," almost two hundred strong, with " C " and " I " Companies still with their armour.

On 3rd November the Battalion moved about twelve miles along the Coast Road, and it became obvious that we were going to be pushed through in this sector, as soon as the situation allowed.

On the night 3rd—4th November the 51st Division did a night attack, south of the main road and achieved their objective. The Armoured Brigade followed up this attack on a very trying night approach march, and by 0600 hours next morning, went through the Highlanders, through two minefields and into the open desert beyond. By 1200 hours the Brigade came up against a strong rearguard of the enemy and a tank battle developed. The Battalion took little part that day, and it was largely a tank *v.* tank battle, with the Battalion waiting for a chance to go in and shoot up the German antitank screen. It was a very unpleasant day, and the Battalion got most of the overs from the tank battle and their full ration of the enemy fire, without being able to do much about it. The tanks had a good day and cleaned up twenty-two enemy tanks ; the enemy withdrew at night. " C " Company followed up and took about six hundred prisoners in the darkness and reported that the ground was clear of enemy for four miles to the front.

The next morning, 5th November, the Battalion was astir at first light, with the whole Brigade. It was realized, for the first time, that the enemy was off, and as the Battalion had had no vehicle replacements since arrival in the desert in November, 1941, it was wondering how far they would get. Meanwhile the very welcome news was received that their friends in the Kent Brigade had broken through on " February " and were mopping up Folgore as fast as they could. The Brigade did sixty miles that day and took about four hundred prisoners. They moved off again on the 6th and connected with a large enemy column at about 1100 hours, but the tanks were short of petrol and could not take full advantage of the target. The Battalion got at them with 6-pounders and machine-guns and managed to round up sixteen lorries, all full of prisoners.

Total prisoners for that morning's action was just under one thousand. In the evening, the weather broke and it rained hard and the Brigade came up with what remained of the 21st Panzer Division, and a very confused battle developed in the rain and mist. As the sun went down the light cleared for a few minutes and five enemy guns, forming part of the enemy rear-guard, showed up clearly on the skyline in the evening light. Machine-gunners did not take long to take advantage of this and, in the last quarter of an hour before sunset they fired off ten thousand rounds and the carriers had no trouble in over-running these guns. All the crews were dead. The action had been successful and thirteen tanks, twelve guns and a large number of transport vehicles were found destroyed.

On the 7th the pursuit was pushed forward, but the country was water-logged and there was trouble with bogged vehicles.

On the 8th the pursuit continued a further thirty miles west and four hundred prisoners were picked up without much trouble.

On the 9th only thirty miles were done and the enemy were not contacted.

On the 10th the Battalion covered forty miles and crossed the wire into Libya. That evening we were warned that we were coming up with a strong hostile column. It was a most exciting chase, and we flogged our vehicles in the hopes that they would overtake them before dark. But no such luck and we camped about four miles short of them. The Battalion was now travelling almost due north.

On the morning of the 11th we bumped his rear-guard on the line of the railway, just west of Fort Capuzzo, where the tanks had a successful engagement. The Battalion did not take a great part in this, being detailed to watch the eastern flank, which was quiet throughout. By this time we were some miles in front of any other unit in the 8th Army and the state of the vehicles was beyond description. That was the last we saw of the enemy. On the afternoon of the 11th we were ordered to go into Bardia and clear the place up. There was no one there, but all the roads and streets and approaches to the town were mined and, to avoid loss of vehicles, the Battalion went in on foot. The men did an excellent day's work there as they had to clear the place of wreckage, much of which was booby trapped, and hand it over to the New Zealanders, without any R.E. assistance. On the evening of the 12th they rejoined the Brigade.

On the 14th the Battalion found itself outside Tobruk, without having any sign of the enemy. On the 15th the Composite Company came under command of the 11th Hussars and was ordered to go forward on a harassing column, west, to Msus.

" C " Company was also ordered forward on the 17th to a job in the Beda Fomm area, while " I " Company and Battalion H.Q. remained in the Tobruk area.

The Commanding Officer writes : " The Battalion is in great heart and the cheerfulness and good spirit shown by all ranks at the end of the year's almost continuous fighting is an object lesson to many units who have been in the desert half that time. The way the Quartermaster and the Battalion " B " Echelon kept the Companies supplied with petrol throughout the five-hundred mile pursuit is beyond all praise. The men behaved wonderfully throughout. Often they were driving and fighting all day and maintaining the vehicles all night.

" During the pursuit they had little more to eat than bully and half a gallon of water per man to drink, and most of that water went into the radiators."

The 7th Battalion of the Regiment was also engaged during this period and the following month, and as usual gave a good account of itself.

The Military Cross was awarded to Captains J. A. Dudgeon, S. R. Trappes-Lomax, and Lieut. K. J. Fish, and the D.C.M. to C.S.M. R. M. Jones.

The citations for these awards will appear in VOLUME II.

WITH THE 7th BATTALION OF THE REGIMENT, 1942.

BY MAJOR A. DUDGEON, M.C.

WE reached Aden one afternoon towards the end of June, 1942. News at the time was scanty. Tobruk had fallen and the army was moving east ; these facts were only too clear and they acted as stimuli to the normal crop of ship's rumours which had, according to the ship's staff, been well up to standard. Our ultimate destination was the one and only topic of conversation, and when we left Aden a few hours later—it must have been the quickest refuelling that that port had ever performed—every soldier who could find sufficient space on deck to allow him to breathe was there watching. Was it going to be right hand down or left hand down ? We went right and sailed into the Red Sea ; we were relieved but thoughtful.

The Red Sea at the best of times is inclined to be stuffy. I relied on the ship's doctor for all my information—apparently this trip was going to be as good as any previous one from the temperature point of view—it brought forth a wonderful crop of stories, of previous convoys and of the number of people who had collapsed and had failed to reach the other end. I was very dubious at the time whether I should follow suit, when to the delight of everybody our old ship began to move a little faster. It was fascinating—nobody on board had any idea this old ship had such a reserve of energy ; accompanied by the most appalling noises from the engine-room we moved forward with ever-increasing speed and, praise God, the breeze, what was left of it, after passing through the officers' sun-deck, reached my company doing gun drill on an ancient 2-pounder at the back of the ship. This had only one meaning for us and especially to the riflemen, who excelled themselves at this time with classical remarks that will go down in history—our armoured brigade was likely to be used in the near future and with that thought in our mind we set to work. The average number of conferences and discussions reached unprecedented heights. Conferences on a brigade level, attended by the Brigadier, became a daily event, and those for company commanders took place practically every hour and were entirely dependent on the floor space. I was always accused of talking more than anybody else, which was a gross libel but quite amusing. Kenneth Hicks,[1] took all this in his stride and was, as usual, to be found on the sun-deck during the hours of daylight coping with the vast organization of P.R.I. and making adequate preparation for messing when we landed.

At last, after a record run through that sea which lives up to its name, we reached Port Tewfik. Of what subsequently happened I have a very vague recollection—I can remember meeting Kyrle Simond[2] as we dropped anchor, and being told to get my company ready to disembark in half an hour. I left Kyrle Simond with Stephen Trappes-Lomax,[3] who was querying one or two points, and retired to my temporary office to think it all over again. I was suffering at the time from gippi-tummy, assisted by the purgative action of the ship's porridge. I was right; by the time I was ready again and Stephen had checked all his points the order was cancelled, and eventually after many other warnings and cancellations we went ashore in lighters in the pitch darkness to the strain of the ship's signature tune, played by Hawkins and Everett.

My first impressions of Egyptian soil were not good.

We reached Quassasin the next day after a traditional journey in cattle-trucks. I was convinced that this sort of thing only happened in France in the last war, but it certainly happened to us. Hugh Gough[4] said it was part of our education and very nearly had to walk for making such a remark. After a few days at Quassasin we all moved to Tahag and had the terrifying experience of being transported there by Palestinian drivers.

The date was 12th July and we had been in the country five days when things began to happen; excitement prevailed. My own company was to move to Cairo to re-form as an anti-tank company, and the rest of the Battalion was to re-equip immediately.

That we were ready on time was very largely due to the terrific efforts of John Baines[5] at Brigade and to Cherub Angel and Kyrle Simond. Everyone worked like Trojans and the result was good.

---
[1] Second-in-Command until 25th November, 1942 when he left to command a Recce Regiment.
[2] Adjutant until 25th October, 1942.
[3] Commanded "D", Lloyd's Company.
[4] Padre until the fall of Tunis, May, 1943.
[5] Staff Captain, 23rd Armoured Brigade.
[6] R. L. Angel, M.M., Q.M.

"C" Company[7] reached Cairo on 14th July and set to work to train as anti-tank gunners. Luckily we had had the great advantage, whilst at sea, of being able to instruct all the officers and a substantial number of N.C.Os. on the mechanism of the gun, so we were able to complete the four weeks' course in twelve days. One of the instructors at the school at Almaza was Hiliary Magnus,[8] who was well able to combine a sense of humour and power of description with his knowledge of the 2-pounder anti-tank gun.

On 18th July the Colonel[9] came over to see us with the news that the Battalion was moving up to near Burg el Arab in a few days. There was little doubt then in my mind that we should not be able to join him—a very great disappointment to us all but the equipment and situation did not permit it. The Battalion moved from Tahag on 18th July forward towards Alamein. Alamein in those days meant very little to any of us, but we were very soon to realize just how important it was.

"C." Company left Cairo on 24th July to join the Battalion, and if their move was anything like ours it was to say the least of it, unorthodox.

The situation on 21st July was critical, probably the most critical day of the war. The only hope was to delay the enemy's advance along the coast road and south of it.

I am not going to attempt to describe the battle that took place on Ruweisat Ridge on 23rd July because I was not there and my knowledge is second-hand.

It was with this intention that the 23rd Armoured Brigade joined the battle near El Ruweisat. Judged by territorial gains and vehicle casualties the attack was not a success, but it did achieve the object of delaying the enemy and making him still more tired. To those who had trained in that Brigade for the previous two years and who fought in the action it was almost a tragedy, such a little appeared to have been gained at the time; but that is one of the most outstanding features of this war, one never realizes during a battle what the reactions of the opposite side are, and in this case the Hun was too tired to go on. As far as the Battalion was concerned two companies, "A" and "B" under Wilfrid Suter and John Francis, respectively, worked under command of the Colonel, and "D" Company, under Stephen Trappes-Lomax, was under command of the Royal Tank Regiment, working with the Australians farther north.

The results, as I have said, were not conspicuous, but what was far more important was the fact that the Battalion, after several weeks at sea, could within a few days of landing in a foreign country, fight a major action. It was proof enough of its efficiency.

"C" Company, the anti-tank company, was ready to move from Cairo on 23rd July; that we were so ready was as much a miracle as

---
[7] "C" Anti-Tank Company.
[8] Formerly Adjutant Battalion.
[9] Lieut.-Colonel G. H. Hunt O.B.E.

anything else, the terrific energy of everybody assisted by our former divisional commander at G.H.Q., produced the results and within a few hours of collecting our guns we moved up the road past Mena, where a few days before we had spent some pleasant, though rather hot, afternoons with Hiliary Magnus siting anti-tank guns around the Pyramids and in easy range of Mena House.

All was well until we reached Burg el Arab, we were well ahead of schedule ; in fact we were four hours ahead of time and found the liaison officer, Keith Egleston at the appointed place where we turned off that wonderful road and took to the sand. Then our troubles started. Looking back on it I can never but be amazed that we arrived anywhere except in the German lines. The friendliness of everybody was truly amazing, the ease and grace with which they misdirected you down tracks that had ceased to exist, to H.Q. that had moved days before or had never been at that particular point ! Such was our introduction to the desert, and now in 1943 quite an amusing one, but then it was shattering. Keith, I am certain, kept us sane, at least he kept me sane ; the more involved we became the more it amused him, and in the end one could but laugh.

By the evening of 25th July it was rumoured that we were near the Battalion. This apparently was a rumour started by Larry Fyffe, who said he had seen a truck-load of riflemen go past and he thought he recognized them as some men in one of the other companies. Personally, I think most riflemen look alike, and thought that this was slender evidence, but then the C.S.M. solved the problem, they could not be ours they were not wearing their hats !

Late that night I found the Battalion coming out of their positions. I remember it well as I had for the previous four hours been indulging in a little private " swanning," namely, wandering about, in my scout car and finally came across the Battalion just in time, a little farther west and I should have been in the bag.

When eventually I rejoined my company the next day I found that the general opinion was that I was probably in the bag or, otherwise not available, and Stanley Tibbetts had taken over command—we very soon changed places and motored up to join the Battalion.

There had been a few casualties, Peter Coryton killed, John Ford and Dennis Bowers wounded. There were a few casualties amongst the riflemen, but we had lost a lot of trucks, which was serious. Fortunately we had a few days grace to do some urgent repairs and take stock of ourselves, and so at the end of July we moved north to the coast, a few miles east of El Alamein.

South of El Alamein was the Alamein Box ; the word Box was then on 29th July, rather going out of fashion but it had a few days to live, in which time the Battalion assisted in the digging and general construction of the positions. We struck a particularly hard streak of rock; within a few hours I was wondering whether I was so lucky to be commanding the anti-tank company. The sequence of events in siting a defensive position is all clearly laid down in the text-books, but what is never mentioned is the all-important fact of divergent views of senior officers and the consequent changing positions with the net result that much soil has been moved but much time wasted. All the same I learned quite a lot from the riflemen during those few days; their views on Egypt and the Western Desert were crystal clear and were always delightfully to the point.

Having constructed a truly magnificent position in the Alamein Box we handed it over to another unit and moved south. We left the 23rd Armoured Brigade with regret. Under our Brigadier we had trained in England for many months and had become a highly efficient force based on sound understanding between all units.

We joined the 7th Motor Brigade early in August. This Brigade was more than a name to us; we had heard such a lot about it and so many friends of ours were in it, and the prospect for the future seemed good. Our teething troubles, however, were many and rather prolonged, but eventually they were overcome.

Stephen and John Francis went with their companies and some anti-tank guns to the forward columns, and the remaining two companies, " A " and " C " with Battalion H.Q. moved to the east of Himeimat. Here we met a company of the 60th Rifles under John Hope, and a battery of the R.H.A. with whom we were going to work for the next few weeks.

It was a fascinating piece of desert, in most places firm sand ideal for driving, very few flies compared with Himeimat, farther west, and above all no mines.

August was a month of many changes in the desert. The Prime Minister came and went, units were changed and moved, and finally by the third week in August the stage was set for Rommel's attack.

The Battalion re-formed, and was now in reserve, north of Deir el Ragil, as unpleasant a piece of desert as could be found anywhere. " C " Battery, R.H.A., under Jack Lomas, arrived to support us— his face betrayed his anxiety ; after all his training in the desert, he was to support a Territorial battalion fresh from England ! In a few weeks' time he was to alter his opinion a great deal and " C " Battery supported the Battalion until the fall of Tunis, first under Jack Lomas, then under Paul Hobbs.

Early in September Rommel attacked through our minefields around Himeimat and began moving east. Slowly we moved back, the Huns, following, being actively engaged from land and air the whole time. This was the first time we had seen the Royal Air Force in strength and it was a good sight.

One night during this battle Kenneth and I went to dinner with General Renton. In spite of Jack Wintour's idea as to the location of H.Q. we arrived in time. Jackie was a wonderful man with a compass; as far as he was concerned there were four cardinal points— North, South, East and West ; and anything in between was a touch of East or a touch of West, but he never got lost for long, even when looking for prime ministers in the desert ! An excellent dinner, including desert snails in butter, and good news of the battle made a very delightful evening. About 10 o'clock we started for home, only a few miles away, both of us certain we knew the way. After a very short time it was obvious that we were " swanning " in the truest sense of the word, and then Kenneth said he felt ill !

Having dealt with the snails and rechecked our hopeless position we moved forward again—into a slit trench, and there we stopped with the front wheels of the Jeep pointing in different directions. When we awoke the next morning we were a few hundreds from the Battalion, but with a damaged Jeep to explain to the Colonel. Somehow or other Henry Beckwith managed to get the wheels straight and all was well.

A few days later we moved west again and then a magic message from Vic. Turner on the blower as to the amount of loot in his area, and we were well forward " covering our losses " and replacing damaged equipment from the battlefield.

During our searches for enemy equipment I came across a German staff car in excellent order, which we took back to our lines and camouflaged. Very carefully, every evening when we leaguered, it came in last and made an early getaway in the morning. Unfortunately, one morning it would not start and the Colonel saw it. He was very nice about it, but I lost it—it went as far forward as Tmimi, in the November run.

The German attack was a complete failure, and the next move was obvious to all of us, but before that could happen a lot of work had to be done, so, in the middle of September, we moved north to the coast near Burg el Arab and started to get clear again. Those few days outside Alexandria were wonderful, and they were not all outside. Hew Butler broke all records in the French cake-shop; never have I witnessed such a display. Unfortunately Keith Egleston could not compete as he was just beginning to turn yellow with jaundice— very sad after all the time he had waited ! But still he had managed to get into Alexandria on some pretext or other on an average once a week.

After an inspection by the Army Commander, the 7th Motor Brigade moved into the desert, west of the Cairo—Alexandria road, for a few days, and then we moved to join the 1st Armoured Division at Khatatba.

It was now decided that an interchange of officers between ourselves and the Regular Battalion of the Regiment in the Division should take place. Eddie Gibbons, Godfrey Carter, Jim West, and John Fish came to us, and Peter Shepherd-Cross, John Ward, Jim Norman and Bill Salt relieved them. This exchange of officers was undoubtedly a sound move, and we were all to realize in a very short time how fortunate we had been. Eddie Gibbons and John Fish went to " B " Company and Godfrey Carter and Jim West came to " C " Company.

Khatatba is within easy reach of the Delta and that is its only attribute. Our time there was spent, as far as I can remember, in sending leave parties off to Cairo and then attempting to find sufficient men for regimental duties—and the sandstorms were quite up to standard. Starting at 11 o'clock in the morning with a gentle duststorm, by 2 o'clock it was difficult to breathe let alone see to do any work, but with any luck by 5 o'clock things were back to normal for Khatatba.

Fortunately, early in October we moved to a slightly better place, Bir Victoria, and then training started in earnest. We had been told the role of the 1st Armoured Division at a memorable introductory talk by General Briggs at Khatatba and now we were to practise this particular manœuvre of passing through minefields protected by a Minefield Task Force ; we practised it by day and by night, and then did it all over again to make certain that those who had been on leave and had just returned really understood it all. It was certainly sound training and with a purpose, and what is more, it really achieved its object of making certain that every single officer and man did understand his own particular job, and when a few weeks later it was tested, it worked.

By 18th October all ranks had had leave ; all the equipment had arrived ; we had had quite the worst khamsin on record, during which the Mess collapsed and Godfrey got lost ; and we were ready to move. The Regular Battalion of the Regiment acting as Minefield Task Force had slipped away a few days before, and on 20th October the remainder of 7th Motor Brigade followed, reaching El Imayid without many incidents. The Battalion arrived at the appointed place on the track a few miles east of El Imayid at approximately 0200 hours, on 23rd October, and were well asleep by the time Brigade H.Q. arrived and claimed our ground. In vain did we protest, but we had to move—I remember Kenneth coming round to company commanders and very nicely but firmly saying one mile west—please and quickly !

The Battle of El Alamein was to start at 2100 hours on the 23rd, so said our message to all ranks from the Army Commander, which was read out to the troops in the afternoon. The rest of the day was spent in receiving and giving orders, and, speaking personally, trying to understand the hieroglyphics on the maps with which we had all been issued. Finally at 2000 hours we moved into position, ready to move forward later at night. It was whilst we were waiting, prior to moving to the start of Sun Track, that a lone aeroplane dropped a small bomb near Kenneth which all added to the general standard of good humour prevailing at the time.

At about midnight the Brigadier told us to move to the start of Sun Track and to move steadily along, keeping in line with the other units on Moon and Star Tracks. By first light we had reached Springbok Road, where we stopped for breakfast and watched the first batch of prisoners coming west and the wonderful sight of Bostons in close formation going overhead in a continuous, ceaseless procession. Battalion H.Q. was at the junction of Springbok Road and Sun Track, and there we spent most of the day (October 24th) trying to get some news which was accurate. The scarcity of news throughout the battle was a great handicap ; rumours are quite amusing in their right place, and nobody is better at producing them than the average rifleman, but they are a confounded nuisance in a battle, when accurate and up-to-date news is of first-rate importance.

And so we spent the day of the 24th. Most of the anti-tank guns were attached to the motor companies, so I had time enough to visit Brigade H.Q. on Moon Track. One of Jim West's guns was giving trouble and it was decided that it should be tested by firing a round. I asked Mike Edwardes, who said, " Good heavens, no : we can't have guns firing around here ! " But the Brigadier said it would be all right as long as we didn't hurt anybody, which always struck me as rather delightful.

We moved at 1700 hours along Sun Track across the Qattara Road towards the minefields. The noise and the dust were disconcerting, but I have recollections of seeing riflemen and Military Police at the gaps in the minefields, all the time wondering where on earth we were, and that apparently went for everybody else. Opinions apparently differed as to our position and which gap we were to use, but Jim Norman apparently knew which one, so through we went, and then things started to happen.

It was still dark about 0400 hours on the 25th when we passed through the gap and came up alongside a battalion of Australians in the middle of a counter-attack, much to their indignation. There was neither room nor time to argue over the relative niceties of the ground we stood on—there was a gap between 51st Highland Division on the left and the 9th Australian Division on the right and we took it. The Colonel, who was to the best of my knowledge the only person who knew our exact position and was right, allotted our company positions, " D " right, " B " centre, " A " left, with remainder of " C " in reserve, and we started to dig in. Two months before, in the Alamein Box, we had struck rock and we struck it again. The riflemen said it was the same old rock. It probably was ; it certainly broke the same number of picks and bruised the same number of arms. But before we had had sappers and dynamite, and now we only had a very little time before it would be light. The rifleman is always best in a difficult position, and by sheer hard work the majority of weapons were in reasonable firing positions by the time it was light.

Carriers had gone forward from the motor companies and had come under heavy fire ; they returned bringing some prisoners and a few wounded. It was now just light and we were able to see what the ground was like ; it was nothing like what I had visualized, but then the shelling started in earnest and one's thoughts were on other things. The shelling was heavy and accurate, most of it being directed against our vehicles, which were very conspicuous. However, after a short time things seemed to sort themselves out, and everybody set to improving their positions and getting below ground.

During the morning the motor companies had plenty of work, particularly the mortars and machine-guns. By first-rate observation the machine-guns of " A " " B " and " D " Companies fired with great effect. " A " Company's under Philip Flower, who was unfortunately killed, and later under Sergt. Jones, were magnificent and must have done a great deal of damage as well as being a most heartening sight. Mike Bird, " B " Company, and Peter Lockwood-Wingate, " D " Company, kept their machine-guns firing with terrific zest and effect. By noon we had had a number of casualties, including Philip Flower killed, and Kyrle Simond, our adjutant, and Peter Lockwood-Wingate, Tim Dewhurst and Jim West wounded. The R.A.P. run by John Almond, our M.O., was just by the gap in the minefield, a very noisy place but a very efficient one. Casualties were moved from there with great speed. Unfortunately, Hugh Gough, our padre, had been wounded on the way up to the R.A.P. so they were rather short, but he returned to us some months later, before the action beyond El Hamma, but that is another story.

After very heavy shelling for some hours the first wave of Bostons came over and it was a heartening sight, and they came again and again and one could realize the greatness of our strength. My Company H.Q., near Battalion H.Q., was in a former German signal centre, recently vacated, but it was not for some time after we had been there that my driver discovered that they had not all gone. One wounded German must have been there for several days judging by his condition, and the others were likely to remain, so we decided to move house, which was quite the wrong moment to do so judging by the din upstairs. My signal sergeant, Sergt. Brooke, representative of all riflemen, and superbly inquisitive, was rewarded for his diligence by finding a German operation order and signal code which was well received by the " I " Branch.

Visiting the other companies was as unwelcome as it was difficult, but I left with their curses for troubling to come over, but knowing that they were satisfied with the position of the guns attached to them, and when later in the afternoon the tank attack came in, they were justified.

They appeared suddenly from behind a ridge with the dust blowing in front of them, a mixture of M. 13's and Mark III's. The majority of them came up against Jack Salt's guns, but a gun under Sergt. Allen, in Jim West's platoon, did great work. Larry Fyffe was in the unenviable position of receiving the " overs," but several well-aimed long shots were very effective. On top of all this, the riflemen in the motor companies were keeping up a continuous and accurate barrage of small-arms fire which had the desired effect of making the tanks close their lids, and it also caught the crews baling out. Frank White, " D " Company, was quite first-class at this, and not many got away from his area.

It was all over in a very short time, and then came the difficult task of counting the birds. Many claimants, enthusiastic riflemen, for this was their first victory with the 6-pounder, and equally positive Australians ; the net result was that fourteen tanks were knocked out and destroyed by the Battalion and an unknown number damaged.

It was not possible to realize the full extent of our tanks' actions. Shermans were cruising around us most of the time, and in the evening the Bays put in a strong attack on our left flank but it was difficult to see the result.

The next day was spent improving positions in the intervals between German shelling and some rather questionable bursts from our own side.

Cherub Angel and Hugh Miall ran our echelon superbly ; never were we better served, the sight of the " Q " trucks coming unconcernedly through the minefields was good.

Our bit of ground was developing into a built-up area, everybody seemed to take a fancy to it ; for the life of me I cannot see why, but at times the congestion on the ground was alarming, and all unnecessary visitors were asked to move. So when on the morning of the 27th, the K.R.R.C. motored through the Battalion and sat down in our midst and started to brew up it was too much. But as they said where could they go ? So they stayed and somehow there was room.

Some German tanks, to our north, were causing trouble, and Larry Fyffe was very worried about them. In the midst of an argument as to their make and design I was called away to explain the mystery of a burning Churchill tank just in front of us. The mystery was soon solved, but not before all and sundry had been accused of shooting it. An excellent piece of work was done by John Fish and some riflemen in " B " Company in rescuing the crew. Meanwhile, the tanks to our north were invitingly advancing at 1,200 yards, I admired Larry's patience in withholding his fire, and soon they turned and went back.

By the 29th it was decided that we should go back to the coast for a rest and refit. We had heard rumours of a very successful action by a battalion to our south, but had no idea who it was, and when after an uneventful journey we reached the coast, we heard the most excellent news of Vic. Turner's Battalion.

A most astounding victory that had far-reaching results, it acted as a stimulus to us all for a still greater effort.

Weeks later Vic. Turner, in a letter said, " We were all very excited by the success of the Battalion on the 25th and it goaded us to success," which was characteristically generous of him.

After a period of rest north of the coast-road near Alamein, during which time company commanders and others worked as hard as ever, we all moved east to Sidney Road, ready to move back along Sun Track ; after six days we were back where we started, but much had happened in that time and we were able to see more clearly what the position was. A substantial advance had been made, but the enemy was still very strong with little sign of cracking.

The plan for the second stage of the battle was the same as before —to move forward along the tracks Sun, Moon, Star and Diamond to Tel el Eisa, and " debouch " through the minefields seven miles east of Tel el Eisa station. Our reinforcements arrived. Dennis Bowers, back after his wounds in July, and George Russell who came back to me, in magnificent form, also a new officer Freddie Hicks.

We moved forward just before midnight and reached Tel el Eisa without any untoward incidents and then along Diamond Track, which by this time was like most desert tracks, a rough wavy bottom which shook any vehicle to pieces and covered with several feet of the finest powdered sand. We were going over ground that had recently been won and arrived at our position beyond the minefield to find, as usual, others in possession. The 10th Hussars were fighting just east of the Rahmad Track which was our objective and showed no signs of moving—the position we eventually occupied was a few thousand yards east of the Rahmad Track ; units were even more congested here than in the former position, anti-tank guns appeared from all over the place and started digging in. There was very heavy shelling, in which George Russell was unfortunately killed and Freddie Hicks wounded. In the evening the Motor Brigade carried out a night attack on the Sidi Rahmad Track, immediately to our east.

Patrol reports from various sources were inclined to be optimistic, apparently, as they said it was not very strongly held. The Brigade was to attack with the three battalions, and on reaching the Track the R.B. on the right and the K.R.R.C., left, were to move forward a further two thousand yards.

It was decided at a conference at headquarters, earlier in the evening, to move forward with two companies " D " and " B " leaving the anti-tank company and " A " Company under the Second-in-Command ; on reaching the objective the anti-tank guns were to come forward on the success signal. After the most painful and heartbreaking delays in getting transport and ammunition up from the vehicle park, " D " and " B " Companies were ready to move at 2100 hours. Off we went on a compass bearing in extended line, desultory shelling going on but nothing much else, until in a very short time Stephen said he thought we were there. The colonel decided that we should go on a little farther to make certain, and then it all happened, just like 5th November. The Hun had withheld his fire until the very last minute and cover was very scarce. A truly uncomfortable position at first but was eased by the speed at which " D " Company went for them. Bill Brownlow and Frank White led their platoons in with great effect, supported by Mike Bird with his machine-guns on the left. Stephen Trappes-Lomax appeared for a second and then went forward to find out what was happening, because suddenly it had become very quiet until anybody moved and then everything seemed to open up. Stephen disappeared and we did not see him until the next day. In the midst of it all Godfrey, thinking he had seen the success signal, was moving slowly forward with the anti-tank company, quite the last thing that was required. They drove slowly along in open formation and when in the midst of the firing they were induced to go back the company's counter-march was a credit, they moved off with wonderful speed.

When the Motor Brigade, less the K.R.R.C., withdrew that evening not very much had been gained, at least so it appeared to us, but unknown to us the enemy was severely shaken and had begun to thin out. "D" Company had had many casualties; Ivan Cosby wounded but still game; early the next morning very few had returned, but slowly throughout the day they came in and by the evening Stephen had well over half his company back. They had fought a most gallant action and it was a pity that the success of it was not more apparent.

It was obvious now that the end was in sight—the big tank battle was in progress at Tel el Aqqaqir and plans for the chase were in progress. Unfortunately the Battalion, less one company and eight anti-tank guns, was ordered to move back and refit whilst the rest of the Brigade got ready to move west ; " B " Company under Eddie Gibbons (John Francis had been wounded a few days before and unfortunately had had to go back), and myself with Jack Salt and Larry Fyffe joined Vic. Turner's Battalion. It was very sad that the Battalion had to go back at this stage, but they were rather thin on the ground, particularly " D " Company. I said good-bye to them as they moved off down Boomerang Track, wondering when and where we should meet again. It was Sidi Barrani several weeks later.

My time with Vic. Turner's Battalion, when I commanded " S " Company, was one of the most pleasant memories I have of the desert. The chase was on and Tom Pearson led it with characteristic energy, Alamein to Aqqaqir to Daba and then by night across the desert to Bir Khalda. A remarkable move full of amusing incidents which can be told later and in more detail. The pursuit was beginning to slow down by the time we had reached Bir Khalda and then to everyone's dismay the weather broke and our much needed petrol and food got stuck on the Fuka escarpment.

The Armoured Division was from now on to play only a secondary role in the pursuit, and I went back to the battlefield to look for the Brigadier's caravan and other stray vehicles.

Walking over the whole battlefield a few days later in mid-November I was able to appreciate more clearly what had been achieved and how great our success had been.

The Battalion joined the Brigade at Mersa Matruh, where I rejoined. All were in good order with new vehicles and an armoured car per company which until you rode in it seemed to be a great acquisition. My own Daimler scout car had benefited with a few days' rest and a few spare parts from Galal aerodrome, and the future from many points of view seemed good ; and so we arrived at Buq-Buq ; thence we went down the Sofafi track to Bir Sheferzen—quite the worst track in the desert, and I for one was made to realize the limitations of an armoured car. With patience and suffering we reached El Adem and then on the road again to Gazala and Martuba.

We arrived at Martuba at the end of November and prepared to stay. The speed with which houses and other permanent dwellings appeared was astounding, and once again we were able to visit the other companies. To our very great regret the Colonel left us after commanding for over a year. We regretted his going especially at this stage of the campaign after having led us through the most difficult period. Kenneth, who had had to go to hospital for a short time with a septic wound, arrived back only to be posted away. And so Kenneth who had been with us first as Adjutant and then as Second-in-Command went back to Cairo, later to command a Recce. Regiment, and all of us were sorry at his going. We came to realize in the next few weeks how much we missed him, with his quite unique ways of doing things, and what a terrific help he had been to all of us. Cherub Angel, our wonderful quartermaster, also left us. After six months in the desert he was as fit as the rest of us and not a little older, but unfortunately one night at Sidi Rezegh he strained himself pulling vehicles out of the mud and he had to go sick.

The magnificent service rendered by Cherub to the Battalion, and to the whole Territorial Army, was an example of service and one that can well be copied. We missed him a lot, as was natural.

Our new Colonel arrived to command, and in a few days the Motor Brigade moved with all impedimenta (our other Battalion with livestock) back to Tmimi. Possibly a unique move; Norman Odgers, our new Adjutant, always maintained that it was a classic. Certainly very few people will ever forget it and will admit that it was an experience not to be repeated. Unfortunately we were to have several others of a similar kind in the future. When we did reach Tmimi several days later we were told to prepare to stay there for some time. Accordingly, permanent dwellings, some of which can be seen to this day and possibly will be used by many generations of Arabs to come, were erected and in a short space of time we were all well installed.

The Colonel had terrific energy and enthusiasm, and this was soon being displayed to the full. By Christmas-time the Battalion was looking as spick and span as it did for the King's inspection at East Grinstead, and the result of weeks cleaning was as revealing as it was good.

Christmas Day, 1942, was a very memorable day. It was the last fine day for several weeks to come and everyone was in terrific spirits.

After a ceremonial church parade at which decorations won at El Alamein were presented, the Regular Battalion came over to us for a party, and a most unusual party it was.

And here at the end of 1942 is a very suitable place to close. Much had been accomplished in the six months that the Battalion had been in the desert, and by the end of the year its name was well known. Many changes had taken place, many splendid officers and men had been killed or wounded, and few of the original Territorial officers were still serving, but the spirit was the same as ever, and in 1943, the Battalion was to do great things, but that story can be told by someone else.

THE 7th BATTALION IN THE MIDDLE EAST

By LIEUT.-COLONEL D. L. DARLING, D.S.O., M.C.

THE Battalion ended the first phase of the Alamein campaign at Martuba in the eastern foothills of Jebbel el Ahkder.

At the beginning of December, 1942, we all said " Good-bye," with the deepest regret, to Hunt, who left us to go as Chief Instructor to the M.E.T.C. He was succeeded by Darling, who came from G2 10 Corps.

Little happened at Martuba except continuous and constant downpours of rain which increased in intensity when we were ordered to move to Divisional concentration area at Tmimi.

Instead of doing the forty miles journey along the main tarmac coast road, the Brigade moved across a desert track with ourselves bringing up the rear. The next three days were spent in pulling, pushing, unditching and generally using every form of physical and mechanical persuasion to move the Battalion forty miles from Martuba to Tmimi.

At Tmimi our first worries were whether Carlisle, who had been sent back with Sergt. Butteris to Cairo to buy Christmas fare for everybody, would arrive back in time. The days seemed to pass with no news of Managing Director " Oxo," and even the riflemen were heard to remark that they would transfer their allegiance to " Bovril " (when nothing stronger was available) if the firm of " Oxo " failed them this Christmas. However, Carlisle and Butteris duly arrived with mountains of Christmas food and drink and we are still firm supporters of " Oxo " versus " Bovril."

Christmas Day dawned bright and clear and a Brigade Parade Service was held at which medals won by members of the Brigade at the battle of Alamein were presented by Major General R. Briggs, the Divisional Commander.

After the Parade Service all officers and sergeants of the 2nd Battalion were entertained by us, and by 1400 hours, when an inter-

7th BATTALION

Inspection by General Sir H. M. Wilson

The Army Commander's Inspection

battalion football match started, certainly among the higher ranks, the peak of Christmas Day celebrations had been reached. The riflemen's Christmas Dinner took place in the evening and seemed to be a greater success than the officers' celebrations held previously. The whole Battalion was entertained by the 2nd R.B. on New Year's Day with football, boxing, and a Motor Gymkhana Meeting. At one moment it looked as if the Motor Gymkhana Meeting might have to be cancelled, as a rather tiresome gentlemen known as the G.H.Q. Maintenance Inspector made his unwelcome appearance in the early hours of the morning. However, all was well as Odgers, the Adjutant, with his renowned tact, reminded the Unit Maintenance Inspector that he was a Scotsman and, therefore, he would be breaking all laws of civilisation to carry out inspection of our vehicles on Hogmanay.

Platoon and Company training continued throughout January, which was only marred by an unfortunate accident in which Tibbetts and one rifleman were wounded, and two riflemen killed.

The month's activities concluded with an inspection by the Corps Commander.

Little happened in February apart from normal training, except for a triangular Athletic Meeting run by the Battalion who threw out an open challenge to 2nd R.B. and 1st/60th, the final placings being ourselves first, our Regular Battalion second, and a Battalion 60th Rifles third. Fredericks and White, the E.M.E. and B.T.A., astonished everybody by producing on the day of the meeting a most magnificent cup known as the Chechiban Chalice, made entirely by the L.D.A. which would have done credit to Asprey's shop window in Bond Street. They further enhanced their reputation as general contractors by supplying from scrap a bath-house which supplied enough hot water to bath the whole Battalion twice a week—no mean achievement in the middle of the Western Desert. The only complaint the riflemen had was that the water was more often than not too hot.

At the end of the month we were delighted to be told that we were on the move again, and on 23rd February the carriers moved by transporter to Tripoli.

On 1st March we were inspected by the C.-in-C., General Sir Henry Maitland Wilson, G.B.E., K.C.B., D.S.O., A.D.C., who had flown specially to Brigade H.Q. in order to inspect the two Battalions of the Regiment in the Brigade. The inspection went off extremely well, which was remarkable considering the fact that the C.O. only learnt over a glass of port at dinner at Brigade the night before from Pearson, that they intended to " double past " and " advance in review order." This in spite of a firm gentleman's agreement not to carry out either of these drill manœuvres.

The next day we started the long and uneventful trek to Tunisia, arriving on the 15th and taking over the same night 3,000 yards of front from the Scots Guards at Medinine. It was a lovely reverse slope position covered with green corn and fig trees which Rommel had attacked a week previously in an attempt to disrupt the 8th Army's L. of Cs. and base installations. Our only regret was that he had not waited for our arrival before he attacked. Our ten days' stay at Medinine was entirely employed in active harassing carrier patrols by day, and fighting patrols by night, in order to maintain as many troops in the Mahatma hills on our front as possible, and prevent them from being withdrawn to reinforce the main enemy positions on the Mareth Line. General Montgomery visited the Battalion whilst we were at Medinine and spent an hour and a half going round the Company positions and talking with the riflemen.

On 24th March we moved farther north and took over on the left of a Guards Brigade who had been much weakened by their abortive attack on the " Horse-shoe " feature.

Meanwhile, the 8th Army's first attack on the Mareth Line had failed, and it had been decided to exploit the success gained by the New Zealand Division in their outflanking movement towards El Hamma. The 27th March was spent in handing over our position successively to an Indian Battalion of an Indian Division, the Coldstream Guards, the Grenadier Guards, and then finally, as we were pulling out and thought our responsibilities had really ended, reconnaissance parties from our other Regular Battalion arrived with the startling information that they too were to take over our positions. We made apologies to Stevens, the C.O., for being so rude as to leave the estate without being able to show him around the best covers, but suggested he might find anything from a guardsman to an Indian soldier who would be delighted to show him which way the foxes usually ran !

As we were the last unit in the Division to be relieved (in theory at least) of our commitments opposite the Mareth Line, we brought up the tail of the Division in the long, long trek across the desert to join the N.Z.D. in the " left hook " towards El Hamma. Although we left our Mareth position at 9 o'clock on the night of the 27th, we crossed our start line, only four miles away at Medinine, eight hours late owing to traffic congestion in front. At one moment it seemed likely that the dawn would break before our tail, which would have been in full view of German O.Ps., was clear of the Mareth position.

After a non-stop drive of some 160 miles across the most awful going, the Motor Brigade concentrated at 1400 hours on 29th March ready to pass through the N.Z. Division whose attack was due to commence at 1600 hours that afternoon. The New Zealanders supported by an Armoured Brigade, were 100 per cent. successful in their attack and punched a clear hole through the German infantry. 21st Panzer Division, through which the whole Armoured Division, with the armour leading, were successfully passed through in the early hours of the night. Dawn on 30th March found us about five miles short of El Hamma, which the Germans, who had recovered from their initial surprise, were defending strongly with rearguard anti-tank screens. The enemy were pushed out of El Hamma on the 30th March, and retired to the hills about six miles north of the town. On the evening of 30th March, we, as the leading Battalion of the 7th Motor Brigade, moved through El Hamma in order to be able to continue the advance on 31st March.

At first light on 31st March, we were ordered to send forward carrier patrols to find suitable routes for wheels and of regaining contact with the enemy. No contact was made, but one suitable route over difficult country which wheels could traverse was duly found by Gibbons, O.C. " D " Company, who unfortunately lost his life on a mine whilst carrying out this task. The position at midday on the 31st was that the 1st Armoured Division was deployed around El Hamma on the extreme left of the 8th Army, which had now reached the main Wadi Akrit positions. On our immediate front the enemy were holding the last line of hills which guarded the entrance to the main Tunisian plain. These hills formed the right flank of the enemy Wadi Akrit positions. At 1400 hours the Commander of the Motor Brigade ordered the C.Os. of his three Motor Battalions to attempt to force a passage by one of the four possible routes through these hills on our front that night, in order that the remainder of the Armoured Division could be passed through at first light, and thus turn the right flank of the Wadi Akrit positions. Our task was the most westerly pass between Dj el Beida and Dj Hadoudi.

After a seven mile night march, although " A " Company went slightly astray, the pass was captured, largely as a result of a very fine sword charge by " D " Company led by Becher. As dawn broke at 0530 hours on 1st April, everybody had high hopes that the 2nd Armoured Brigade would exploit our success with the minimum of delay. However, the golden opportunity was let slip, and we grimly held on to our positions from 0530 hours until 1000 hours under direct observation from the hills around us of enemy artillery and mortar O.Ps., who lost no time in making life extremely uncomfortable. To add insult to injury, the medium regiment which should have been in call at first light had moved out of call during the night, and the two R.H.A. O.P. officers informed the C.O. at 0900 hours, in response to his somewhat irate demand for artillery support that their guns were out of range. By the time the leading armoured regiment arrived the position was hopeless, and we were withdrawn, much the worse for wear and very bitter that so much wasted effort, which could have paid a wonderful dividend had its initial success been taken advantage of, had been utterly wasted.

The first four days of April were spent in reserve around El Hamma, and with the arrival of new drafts, the Battalion was reorganized up to full fighting strength less one platoon of anti-tank guns. Carlisle took over " A " Company, Beckwith with Dewhurst as Second-in-Command went to " B " Company, Fyffe with Bird as Second-in-Command commanded " C " Company, Becher with

Eeles as Second-in-Command commanded " D " Company, White combined the duties of O.C. H.Q. Company, and B.T.A. and Brooke took over Adjutant.

Officer reinforcements were Street from the Devon Regiment as Second-in-Command (since the beginning of December, the Battalion had had no Second-in-Command), Brigstocke, Pemberton, Burton, Nicholls, Vatcher, while Shepherd-Cross returned later at Bouthadi from a Regular Battalion, and took over " A " Company from Carlisle who returned to H.Q. Company.

While reorganizing, a bombing attack killed three Riflemen and a stray shell wounded R.S.M. Worboys, who had to be evacuated. It is worthy of record that the Battalion, in spite of the loss during this brief period of three Company Commanders, the Adjutant, Signals Officer, the R.S.M. and a proportionate number of key W.Os. and N.C.Os., did not lose one little bit of its fighting efficiency or dash—a very great tribute to regimental tradition and the morale of the Battalion.

During the first week of April the 8th Army attacked and drove the enemy out of the Wadi Akrit positions, and from the 5th to the 8th we were constantly on the move chasing Rommel's rearguard across country, finally arriving at the delightful little Tunisian town of Bouthadi, where we were welcomed with open arms by the French and Arab inhabitants.

A period of stalemate with the enemy moving back on to the Enfidaville Line now set in on the 8th Army front. Fredericks and White seemed to travel miles over the country visiting farms, ostensibly to buy eggs, but in reality, we found out when they began to receive invitations out to dinner, to improve the Anglo-French entente with the local inhabitants. The only unfortunate incident in a very enjoyable four days at Bouthadi was a visit from the Luftwaffe in the bright moonlight with a heavy concentration of butterfly bombs on our particular olive grove which luckily proved more frightening than lethal. Street and the Colonel, who had both slept through the first attack, were seen making remarkably quick time for the same slit trench neck and neck when the second packet started dropping, while Fyffe was heard reasoning severely with Bird after the latter had landed squarely on Fyffe's middle in the bottom of a slit trench.

Our brief stay at Bouthadi was ended by the unexpected news that the Division was to move via Sbeitla and Le Kef to join the 1st Army. We started at 2000 hours and by breakfast on 14th April had done nearl 150 miles during the night—very fast going on indifferent roads for a night march. Although the move was supposed to be highly secret, we were welcomed by the inhabitants of Le Kef with banners stretched across the street saying " Welcome to the 8th Army." While bivouaced in the neighbourhood of Le Kef we made our first contact with another Territorial Battalion of the Regiment and we were visited by General Sir Harold Alexander, Commander

18th Army Group, who spent an hour going round the Battalion talking to riflemen.

The 1st Army plan seemed to be an attack in the Goubellat Plain which was to be exploited by two Armoured Divisions. We, therefore, held ourselves in readiness to play our part with the 1st Armoured Division to which we belonged. The attack, however, was not a success, and the Armoured Division was left in Goubellat Plain with the role of containing as much enemy armour as possible, while the 1st Army regrouped to make a main effort to capture Tunis and Bizerta farther north in the direction of Medjez el Bab. On Easter Day, after Hugh Gough had held an early service in the high cornfields around Bouarada, we moved to the north of the Goubellat Plain and took over from the 26th Armoured Brigade in undulating country overlooked by Jebbel bou Kournine. That night, in order to improve our positions, " D " Company made a successful night attack over 2,000 yards to Argoub el Megas. This feature was at the apex of a triangle, the right side being formed by a lake or Chott, and the left by broken tank-proof country and the base by ourselves less " D " Company. Its particular advantage lay in the fact that it gave our armour more scope and room to move. Argoub el Megas was a small ridge with " D " Company firmly holding our side of the slope and German infantry and tanks holding the other side of the hill, with the ridge itself a happy hunting ground of artillery and mortar O.Ps., and snipers of both sides. While going out to visit " D " Company at first light on Easter Monday in his Jeep, the C.O. was considerably startled to run practically head on into a German Mark IV Special proceeding in the opposite direction. It was rather like the Pekinese passing an Alsatian in Hyde Park with his nose high in the air and hoping he had not been seen, which luckily was the case. On arriving at "D " Company, suitable arrangements were made to deal with the Mark IV Special on its return from his reconnoitring mission. It was knocked out at 1,100 yards with the third shot by one of Egleston's anti-tank guns, after which we all breathed more freely. One other Mark III Special, which had the audacity to poke its nose over the Argoub el Megas crest during the course of the morning, was faithfully dealt with the same way. It was sufficient to persuade the remaining German tanks to keep well their side of the boundary.

Owing to our success on Easter night, we were ordered to carry out a further night attack on the " White House " feature on Easter Monday night, a further advance of some 2,000 yards over unreconnoitred country. This attack failed as the only route by which anti-tank guns could have reached the position for consolidation by first light was strongly guarded by German tanks, including " Tigers." On meeting these, our two leading anti-tank guns immediately got into action at 200 yards range and exchanged shot for shot with the " Tigers " every time a flare was put up, in an attempt to clear the route, but unfortunately the six-pounder shots failed to penetrate the front armour of the " Tigers " and both six-pounders, after being most gallantly handled, were knocked out by direct hits. Previous to the attack, the Argoub el Megas position had been handed over to a Regular Battalion of the 60th, and, when it was found impossible to get anti-tank guns forward, the Battalion was ordered to withdraw back through 1st/60th and come into Brigade reserve.

Next day Commander 9 Corps, while commiserating with us on our lack of success with six-pounders versus " Tiger " tanks, suggested that we might have used a Piat mortar, the existence of which all of us were in complete ignorance. We immediately asked him to show us this " new " weapon, and a knocked-out " Tiger " tank was duly found on which the Piat was to demonstrate its great killing abilities. Unfortunately the Piat mortar on this occasion did little else except set the surrounding corn on fire and wound the Corps Commander so severely that he had to be evacuated to hospital. Our first introduction to the Piat mortar was, therefore, not a success, although somebody was heard to say, perhaps rather unkindly, that they were obviously good for promotion.

The chief bugbear of the area was the 1,500 feet Jebbel Kournine which, rising perpendicularly out of the cornfields, gave the enemy most wonderful observation of all our dispositions for miles around. All movement received prompt attention from enemy artillery, and, after three previous unsuccessful attempts to dislodge the enemy from the top of Kournine by other units, 2nd R.B. were asked to make a final attempt to capture this feature. This attempt unfortunately also proved unsuccessful, after which the enemy were left in undisputed possession of this very annoying mountain fastness.

On 30th April, we again took over the Argoub el Megas position from the Battalion of the 60th, and we were busily engaged in containing as many troops on our immediate front as was possible with all the aggressive ruses we could conjure up. Probably the two things that stuck in our minds at this period were the very lonely feeling one had at last light when the armoured regiment, who took up hull down positions with us by day, pulled out to their safe leaguer area in rear, and the invariable mortar and artillery fire which greeted their noisy arrival at first light next morning. Our casualties during this period were confined to sniping and mortars, with the exception of Beckwith who was killed while out on patrol with Rogers, who was taken prisoner on the same venture. Sergt. Perrin, " D " Company Mortar Sergeant, was unluckily killed while endeavouring to worm his way forward to get a better view of some enemy tanks, after he had already dropped one of his bombs neatly down the cupola of a Mark III Special. That night the enemy made one attempt to penetrate our position with infantry with little success, and left two prisoners of war of the Hermann Goering Division in our hands.

On 4th May we were relieved from the Argoub el Megas position by 2nd R.B., just prior to the main 9th Corps attack through Medjez el Bab which resulted in the capture of Tunis and Bizerta.

The 1st Armoured Division, having carried out its task of containing the greater part of the enemy armour in the Goubellat Plain prior to this attack, now chased the remaining enemy towards Creteville and Cape Bon peninsula.

After the capture of Tunis, it seemed possible that the remainder of the German forces, of which the Hermann Goering Division and the 10th Panzer Division (which had recently arrived from Russia) were on our immediate front, would make a last stand to defend the circle of hills running from Hamman Lif through Creteville to Enfidaville, which guarded the entrance to the Cape Bon peninsula. This proved to be correct, and our armour came up against strong opposition in the narrow Creteville Pass. The Motor Brigade's task was to dislodge the enemy O.Ps. and establish our own O.Ps. on the high ground overlooking the Creteville Pass. We were given the task of clearing the whole of the right flank of the Creteville Pass, in order that the armour might pass through to the Cape Bon peninsula.

May 10th-12th provided some excellent hunting in the high hills and woods overlooking the pass. The achievement of "A" Company under Shepherd-Cross in scaling Jebbel Resas and evicting 300 Hermann Goering Panzer Grenadiers and the complete O.P. was particularly noteworthy. "A" "B" and "D" Companies were all engaged on this task, while "C" Company formed an anti-tank screen in readiness to deal with a possible last savage rabbit effort by twelve enemy tanks who were disputing our passage through the pass. The Tunisian campaign ended on 12th May with Battalion H.Q. firmly established in a large French wine distillery in the middle of the Creteville Pass, engaged in counting up the prisoners (80 per cent. being German from the 10th Panzer and Hermann Goering Divisions) who had been sent in by the three motor companies. When the hills had been cleared the Companies came down and concentrated around Battalion H.Q., and with over a million gallons of wine in the Distillery, no time was lost in celebrating the Tunisian victory by all ranks in a right and fitting manner.

After a very enjoyable three days at the Distillery the Battalion moved to Brigade concentration area in Hamman Lif about twelve miles from Tunis. Leave parties were sent into Tunis, which appeared to revert to normal in a remarkably short time, although the Germans had cleared the shops of everything they could lay hands on.

While at Tunis we lost our Padre, Hugh Gough, who went to Division on promotion. He had been with us since pre-war Territorial days and was extremely popular with officers and men alike. His departure left an irreplaceable gap in the Battalion.

On the 16th a Regimental dinner took place in Tunis which was attended by 64 officers from the four Battalions of the Regiment who had taken part in the Tunisian campaign. This had been preceded by an Allied Victory March through Tunis in which the Battalion was represented by two officers and 20 men.

In the last week of May we returned to Tripoli and set up our summer quarters in the farm colonies round Suani Ben Adem.

At Suani we said good-bye with the very greatest regret to Brigadier Bosvile, who had commanded the 7th Motor Brigade ever since we had been in it. All our fighting, except our initial effort in July, 1942, had taken place under his direction. We could not have found a better or more inspiring huntsman anywhere.

Dewhurst took over Adjutant from Brooke, who went to Brigade as G3. Shortly afterwards a farewell inspection parade was held by the Divisional Commander, Major-General Briggs.

In the middle of June we were inspected by H.M. The King during his visit to North Africa, and the Battalion was extremely lucky after this inspection to be detailed for internal security duties in Tripoli, while H.M. The King inspected other formations in that town. The riflemen were thus able to see H.M. at close quarters twice during the week. While we were at Suani Ben Adem, Mott-Radclyffe literally dropped in without any warning from the skies and, after we had made certain that his visit was not designed to canvass votes for the next Windsor bye-election, he was duly taken on strength as Second-in-Command " A " Company, much to the annoyance of " A " Branch, G.H.Q., who just could not understand how anybody could arrive in the Middle East except through the normal channels. For a considerable time they refused to recognize his existence in their domain either physically or on paper.

At the beginning of July the Battalion moved to join the 8th Armoured Brigade at Homs, only to return on detachment to Tripoli to take over guard duties from 2nd R.B., who were returning to join another Armoured Brigade in the Delta.

Carlisle left us at Tripoli to go to Civil Affairs and Trappes-Lomax returned with a new draft of officers consisting of Persse, Bowring, Downing, Whiter, Thrift, Lowrison, Eastwood, Battey, and Ostime —the last six returning to us as officers after completing an O.C.T.U. course. We returned to our Armoured Brigade at Homs at the end of August in time for the Brigade race meeting, in which there were races for officers, N.C.Os. and the local inhabitants. The scale of the meeting may be judged by the fact that the Tote handled over £10,000 during the afternoon.

Street left us at the end of the month to join the British Mission to Marshal Tito. During his brief stay with us we really felt we had changed the colour of his buttons completely.

Our last memory of Homs was a Brigade Rifle Meeting, where we maintained the shooting tradition of the Regiment by sweeping the board in all events.

In September we moved back to the Delta in two parties, half by road and half by sea, and arrived at Beni-Yusef at the end of the month. The road party, with its assorted collection of battle-worn

British vehicles and captured German transport, looked more like Bertram Mills's Circus on tour than anything else. The fact that we all arrived safely at the other end of the 1,500 miles march did great credit to the ingenuity of the M.T. staff.

At the beginning of October Sinclair joined as Second-in-Command from a Staff appointment at G.H.Q. Trappes-Lomax left to a Staff appointment, Mott-Radclyffe taking over " B " Company, and R.Q.M.S. Selby left to take up a Q.M. appointment in the Regiment.

In the middle of the month we were greatly honoured by an informal visit from the Foreign Secretary, Mr. Anthony Eden, who spent over an hour going round the lines talking to the riflemen. He seemed almost as delighted to be with a Rifle Battalion as we were to see him.

On the 1st November the C.-in-C., General Sir Henry Maitland Wilson, carried out a ceremonial inspection of the Battalion, which, with the presence of the Cairo Area Band, which was largely composed of Bandsmen from 2nd R.B. and the 1st/60th, had quite a pre-war peace-time atmosphere. The C.-in-C. visited the Sergeants' Mess after the inspection, and lunched in the Officers' Mess before returning.

In the second week of November Sinclair left us to take over command of the 2nd Battalion of the Regiment and was succeeded as Second-in-Command by Southby.

About this time it became obvious that great things were going to happen in the Mena area, and the Battalion was greatly honoured by being chosen as part of the force responsible for guard and defensive duties during the Mena Conferences.

Two troops of Household Cavalry were put under our command, and for the next month we were extremely busy looking after the Delegates at the Mena Conferences. Possibly one of the most amusing stories of the Conferences was the discomfort suffered by a certain very important personage, who found (*a*) bed bugs, (*b*) no hot water, (*c*) broken-down sanitary arrangements, (*d*) a bed which collapsed in the villa which he had been allotted. A riflemen with true Cockney wit, on being told of the above calamity, remarked, " Cor lummee ! It's a ruddy shame these politicians having to come and rough it out at Mena."

Mena House itself reverted to its pre-war peace-time scale of food and drink with H.M. Government as the willing hosts. It was impossible to pay for anything and some of us at least felt that we got a little back on our income tax.

After the Conferences we remained at Mena over Christmas, being visited by a Yugo-slav Mission, from Marshal Tito, who lunched in the Mess.

In spite of the proximity of the lights of Cairo, some very strenuous company training was done in the enclosed Delta country without anyone catching Bel Hartza from the innumerable canals and irrigation ditches.

Christmas Day was celebrated in tremendous style, starting in the morning, after the usual church services, with an N.C.Os. football match against the riflemen, followed by a Donkey Race Meeting, which was professionally organized by Persse, Christmas dinner at which the whole Battalion sat down in one dining-hall, and finally a party given by the Officers for the Sergeants' Mess, which started at 4.30 p.m., and ended at 9 p.m.—without doubt one of the most exacting and enjoyable days of our African tour.

At the beginning of January we moved to Ataka, south of Suez, to form part of a force which had concentrated there for a special task. At this time we were officially informed that we were part of the 9th Armoured Brigade, and during our stay at Ataka we made tremendous friends with the Warwickshire Yeomanry who were also part of this special force. We had periods of intensive training with them, during which they appeared to have unlimited track mileage and ammunition to expend. In the first week in March we did a three-day scheme with live ammunition across almost virgin desert to Helwan from Beir Odib, some fifty miles south of Suez, with the Warwick Yeomanry. From Helwan, after a week at Mena—where we lost Southby, who went to command another Battalion of the Regiment—we moved to Burg el Arab, which gave us an opportunity of re-visiting the Alamein battlefields.

Whilst there we carried out exercise "April Fool" on the 1st April. This consisted of (*a*) getting Bird married off in the morning, (*b*) playing Gezira cricket in the afternoon, and (*c*) giving a regimental dance with the 2nd Battalion in the evening. The combined cricket side from the 2nd Battalion and ourselves failed to defeat Gezira, and the match was perhaps notable for the number of runs which our opening bowler, Sinclair, of the 2nd R.B., had knocked off him in his first two overs. We were informed by the old gentlemen who had been watching Gezira cricket for years that it was a record which would stand for all time !

At Burg el Arab our preparations to proceed overseas were interfered with by the unfortunate mutiny in the Greek Brigade, situated right alongside the Battalion, and in the Greek Navy in Alexandria Harbour. During the second week in April the Battalion was busily employed in the unenviable task of containing the Greek Brigade. We were glad to be able to hand over our duties to 2nd R.B. and to proceed with our preparations to go overseas.

At the end of April we found ourselves as part of our Brigade on the same troopship as 2nd R.B., saying "Good-bye" to Egypt—the end of a very definite phase in our life during this war.

THE 8th BATTALION IN NORTH-WEST EUROPE

THE account of our activities in 1944 really begins on 6th June—" D " day—as the previous months, although eventful and strenuous, were of little significance compared with those which followed.

" D " day found us at Aldershot and by 13th June we were in a concentration area in Normandy prepared for our first battle. Ten days later we were heavily involved in the attack over the River Odon west of Caen. Companies were under command of their respective Armoured Regiments and after heavy fighting, in which many casualties were sustained, succeeded in reaching their objective. Unfortunately, the threat of a counter-attack to the right flank of the bridge-head was considered so severe that the whole Brigade was withdrawn the next night. This was a disappointing ending to our first battle, particularly as the hill in question was not regained until the final break-out in August.

Among our casualties were Mick McCrea and Kenneth MacKenzie, both wounded, and Michael Lane, who subsequently died of his wounds.

A period of reorganization followed when we attempted to learn a lesson or two from our first battle. During this interim period the Colonel left us, and his place was taken by Colonel J. A. Hunter from the 60th. Major John Dickinson, also 60th, joined us and took over " H " Company. Noel Bell took over " G " Company, and was promoted Major. By the 16th July we had recovered from our earlier battle, although we were still short of men. This enabled us to take part in the battle for the high ground south-east of Caen on 18th July.

Companies were again under command of Armoured Regiments, and we headed the advance under cover of an intense air bombardment and heavy artillery barrage. The day was marked by heavy fighting on the slopes of the high ground north of Bourgebus and Bras and, in spite of fairly heavy casualties, prisoners and a considerable quantity of equipment were taken.

We spent an uncomfortable night and the next day Companies reverted to command of the Battalion and we were ordered to attack Bras and Huberts Folie in conjunction with the 3rd Royal Tanks and Fife and Forfar Yeomanry. This attack was highly successful, and by night-fall we had captured both places—handed them over to the Infantry Brigade and pulled back to our positions of the night before.

During these two days the Battalion had captured nearly 600 prisoners and a considerable quantity of equipment, including 27 Nebelwerfers.

We then moved back over the River Orne and reorganized north-west of Caen. John Dickinson left us and John Straker took over command of " H " Company. We also received a few reinforcements, but nothing like as many as we wanted to make us up to strength.

News of the American break-through in the west was a tremendous fillip to morale, and we all felt that our hard and unspectacular fighting around Caen was paying a dividend after all. We had not long to wait before we too were swept up in the advance, and the 31st July found us clear of the village of St. Martin Debesances south of Caumont, right through the enemy defences. Le Beny Bocage was captured on the 1st August by 3rd Royal Tanks and " G " Company and twenty-four hours later we were ten miles to the south-west and moving fast.

The village of Bas Perier was the limit of our advance at this time as we came up against the Panther tanks of the 9th S.S. Panzer Division, and we took up a defensive position as a Battalion with the 23rd Hussars. This was a most unsatisfactory position as our left flank was in the air and remained so for the next week. Heavy fighting ensued in this area and the road behind us was cut by the enemy for thirty-six hours. During this time Michael Willcox, our M.O., and Jeff Taylor, our Padre, did most excellent work in the R.A.P. with about 40 casualties who could not be evacuated, and both were subsequently awarded the Military Cross.

An Infantry Battalion from another Division subsequently opened up communications to us and relieved us. We then sat in a supporting position behind where we had little contact with the enemy, but were heavily shelled day and night for five days.

A welcome relief by a Guards Battalion gave us a much-needed rest. By this time, 10th August, the Battalion was nearly 300 men short, and since the Caumont break-through on 31st July we had lost John Priestley, who was killed, John Straker, Philip Sedgwick, Eric Yetman, Peter Morley, John Elgood, and David Stileman, who were wounded. Luckily for us we found a complete Company from 60th Rifles waiting for us. Peter Bradford who commanded it took over " H " Company, and one platoon went to each Motor Company and the Support Company. This welcome addition of first-class material brought us into fine shape for the hectic and exciting days that were to follow.

On the 12th the advance continued, and from this time until we reached the Seine the Battalion worked as an armoured infantry group with the 23rd Hussars. The 15th found us at Vassy, and it appeared that the enemy were withdrawing slowly. From there on, the advance speeded up and apart from a few rear-guard actions there is little to record except that we advanced about eight or nine miles a day. Demolitions were frequent and mines were found, but no determined enemy opposition was encountered. On 20th August the now famous Falaise pocket had been closed and we pushed on to squeeze in the southern side of it. The rapidity of our advance and the enemy disorganization was such that Donald Sudlow's platoon in " G " Company captured Lieut.-General Kurt Badinski, Commander of the German 276th Infantry Division, and his complete staff, near Bailleul.

There is little to record from there onwards until the 28th, when we reached the River Seine at Vernon, and prepared to cross over and break out of the bridge-head which had already been established on the other side. Our objective was Amiens, with a still more remote one of Antwerp, and at this time both seemed a long way off.

However, we made a distance of eighteen miles the first day against disorganized opposition, and after another day of much the same sort of thing it was decided to try to push on to Amiens during the night. In spite of driving rain, this operation was successfully carried out and at 6 o'clock in the morning of the 31st August " H " Company, under command of the 23rd Hussars, and " G " Company, under the 3rd Royal Tanks, entered Amiens. Surprise was complete and the main bridge over the River Somme was captured intact. A considerable number of prisoners were captured including General Eberbach, Commander of the German Seventh Army.

During the day a good bridge-head was secured over the River Somme, and we all had a good night's rest about seven miles beyond Amiens. Our casualties during this period were extremely light. Mick McCrea returned to us just before we crossed the Seine and was unlucky to be wounded again shortly afterwards.

By this time the Guards Armoured Division had come up on our right and captured Arras, which we by-passed to the left. A short advance on 2nd September took us to the coal-mining area of Lens and Loos, and that evening " E " Company (Major A. P. Rowan) had a successful small battle near Hulloch destroying two anti-tank guns.

The anniversary of the outbreak of War was a fitting day on which to enter Belgium, and at 11 o'clock " H " Company and the 23rd Hussars reported that they had crossed the frontier. Only the enthusiasm of the Belgian people held us up, and it was their presence rather than that of the enemy which prevented the Brigade from reaching Antwerp that night.

However, we covered eighty-five miles during the day and nightfall found us north of Brussels at the same time as it was captured by the Guards. Early next morning " G " and " H " Companies with 3rd Royal Tanks and 23rd Hussars advanced to Antwerp. Progress was not so fast as on the 3rd, but by the end of the day the city and the docks had been occupied.

Our reception in Antwerp surpassed all expectations and it was with the greatest difficulty that the enthusiastic Belgians could be persuaded to allow us to get on with our proper business. One of the more amusing incidents was when " G " Company's mortars had an excellent shoot on some Germans the far side of the River Scheldt. The mortar observation post was on the top storey of an hotel and the route to and from it was by the hotel lift.

The defence of Antwerp was taken over from us by our Infantry Brigade and Companies concentrated with their Armoured Regiments south of Antwerp. Attempts were made to recondition our vehicles after our four hundred and fifty mile advance from the other side of the Seine, but we were not entirely free from operational commitments. Odd parties of enemy continued to appear, and one morning " H " Company (Capt. H. R. Townshend) captured thirty.

Our stay near Antwerp was all too short and on the 7th our battered vehicles were off again towards the Dutch frontier and Eindhoven. The Guards had already secured a bridge-head over the Albert Canal, and our operations of the next fortnight on the Guards' right flank were all designed to secure a good jumping off place for the Arnhem operation.

Once again the Battalion was grouped with 23rd Hussars and the 10th found us fighting a really hard battle against an enemy parachute Battalion at Helchteren. Tom Bird, who had arrived on 9th of September as Second-in-Command instead of Jack Risdon, was severely wounded early in the day, and " H " Company, who were leading suffered severe casualties from mortars. However, they succeeded in advancing some 2,000 yards. " F " Company (Major D. F. Cunliffe, M.C.), were put in round the right flank supported by a squadron of the Hussars and succeeded in loosening the defences considerably. A much wider movement round the left flank by " G " Company and their squadron cut the enemy's escape road farther to the east and the battle was virtually over.

By the end of the day we had captured well over two hundred prisoners and judging by the number of enemy corpses, must have killed quite as many. Our casualties were not light. Donald Howarth, and Robin Ellis were killed, Tom Bird, John Straker, and Angus Dixon were wounded. Sergt. Read and eight other riflemen were killed and we had nineteen other ranks wounded. But the result was highly successful and we advanced some ten miles the next day with only slight opposition.

The next few days saw us near Peer while the Arnhem operation began, and as soon as a bridge had been secured on the right of the Guards over the Escaut Canal we moved north-east so as to protect their right flank. The days were uneventful except for the 21st September when we had an encounter with the 107th Panzer Brigade at Gerwen. This Brigade was attempting to cut the Guards' centre line north of Eindhoven, and they were frustrated by the action of 23rd Hussars and " F " Company initially, and then by " G " Company, who made a valiant attempt to secure the village of Gerwen but were prevented from doing so by the fading light. But the enemy had had enough and departed during the night.

On this day another part of the Division had secured a bridgehead over the Bois de Duc Canal at Zomeren, and we and the Hussars thereupon retraced our steps and crossed over this bridge, being directed on Deurne. The 23rd was a day of unpleasant fighting with " G " Company mostly in the lead. Our most serious loss on this day was our Padre, Jeff Taylor, who had been with us since Normandy, and whose personality and quiet courage had made a tremendous impression on all ranks. The village of Vlierden, south of Deurne caused a great deal of trouble, and it was necessary to organize a Battalion attack supported by the Hussars on the morning of the 24th before we could clear it. " H " Company and " F " Company were both involved and the village yielded a total of seventy prisoners and an anti-tank gun. Our casualties were not heavy—eight all told including Jeffery Coryton, who was wounded by a Bazooka. Opposition after this was slight and we reached Deurne without further incident.

The Division pushed on rapidly from here and reached the River Meuse at Boxmeer the following day, but the Battalion was not involved and we settled down to three weeks of patrolling just north of Deurne. This quiet period was of immense value as we absorbed considerable reinforcements and overhauled our vehicles. We were also able to cement our already strong liaison with 23rd Hussars as each Motor Company lived and worked with their respective Squadrons throughout this period.

From the middle of October until just before Christmas we were involved in the attacks towards Venlo through the appalling marshy country of South Holland. Long periods of holding an extended front in face of heavy mortaring and shelling, and an extremely active enemy took their toll, and by about the 16th December we were ready for a rest.

On the 17th the complete Brigade was withdrawn for a rest and refit, and we were lucky enough to go with them. We all prepared for a good Christmas and an intensive period of training, but once again we were unlucky and the 21st found us packed up again and off at high speed to the Ardennes to take part in the defence of the River Meuse. This highly successful period in the most delightful country really belongs to 1945 as we were still battling down there on the 16th of January. It will therefore be dealt with in our next letter.

THE FIRST WITHDRAWAL IN CYRENAICA, 1941.

THE 9th BATTALION.

BY LIEUT.-COLONEL E. A. SHIPTON, O.B.E., M.C.

THE following is a brief account of the action of 9th Battalion The Rifle Brigade, during the first withdrawal in Cyrenaica, Libya, 31st March—12th April, 1941.

The Battalion landed at Port Said, 31st December, 1940. For some five weeks it was stationed near Ismailia while being reorganized after the voyage out, and while the vehicles were issued with the necessary desert equipment—sand-tracks, additional water carriers, etc.

At the end of this period the Battalion went into the Western Desert, some two weeks being spent in policing a large area round Cyrene in Cyrenaica—that is, keeping the peace between the Italian smallholders and the Arabs, who had flocked back immediately the Italian army had been driven from the area. A further two or three weeks was spent in a similar role in and around Benghazi.

The Battalion then took up positions at Mersa Brega, some one hundred and fifty miles south of Benghazi. It had not been in this region for more than a matter of days, when, from the aggressive patrolling on the part of the enemy, it became obvious that he meant to attack. It was known that in addition to Italian divisions, there was one German armoured division, and a good proportion of a second German armoured division on our immediate front.

The higher command realized that we could not hold such a force and, should he attack, we were ordered to withdraw, delaying him as long as we could.

The Battalion formed part of the support group of an armoured division, which also included a company of the Free French, one regiment, Royal Horse Artillery, one battery anti-tank artillery, one machine-gun company, two light anti-aircraft guns and a detachment of the field ambulance. Our right flank rested on the sea at Mersa Brega ; on our left was a gap of five miles and then a comparatively weak and ill-equipped armoured brigade ; although comparatively few were engaged in enemy action during the withdrawal, so great were the mechanical breakdowns that most of the vehicles had to be abandoned, or destroyed, as they withdrew, and but few reached Tobruk, after a withdrawal of over four hundred miles in eight days.

The next troops behind us were the Australians in the Benghazi area, to our rear. It should be added that the greater part of the 2nd Armoured Division had been sent to Greece.

CYRENAICA, 1941 (9TH BATTALION)

March 31*st*, 1941.—As was anticipated, the enemy attacked our position at Mersa Brega with armoured cars, tanks and motor-cycle combinations soon after 0800 hours on the morning of 31st March, and our carrier patrols, which were operating about a mile and a half in front of our advance company (" C ") on Cemetery Hill, on the main Tripoli road, some two miles south of Mersa Brega, were, after a stiff fight, during which most valuable information was sent back, forced to withdraw into the company locality on the above-mentioned Cemetery Hill.

This locality was held by " C " Company until about 1015 hours, when orders were given for the position to be vacated, except for one rifle platoon and the carriers of the company, who were ordered to hold on as long as possible and then come in ; the rest of the company was pulled into battalion reserve.

In spite of very heavy dive-bombing the platoon and carriers hung on to Cemetery Hill for about half an hour longer, and were then compelled to withdraw.

Some fifteen enemy tanks, with two motor-cycle combinations, then passed over Cemetery Hill, and came to a halt just in front of our main position held by " A " Company. " B " Company was on the left and echeloned back behind " A " Company. The forward defended localities of both companies were covered, for the most part, by marshy salt pans (mostly impassable to tanks) and mined. The widely-separated flanks of our position, however, could not be adequately protected.

The enemy tanks remained out of range of our anti-tank guns, but were engaged by indirect fire by the R.H.A., and save for one or two derelict ones, withdrew behind Cemetery Hill at about 1200 hours. About this time, this high ground was occupied by enemy infantry and guns, which caused us considerable trouble by firing on our main positions.

At about 1430 hours that afternoon " A " Company's positions were again heavily dive-bombed simultaneously by sixteen German planes, causing casualties and the loss of five vehicles.

At about 1630 hours in the afternoon four enemy tanks and one company of infantry moved up the coast and attacked our right flank resting on the sandhills on the coast at Mersa Brega. Here were two sections of " A " Company and one detached platoon of " C " Company that had been echeloned back to form a flank. They were supported by a machine-gun section of the Northumberland Fusiliers. This little force fought magnificently, and repulsed the attack with heavy loss to the enemy, and continued to hold this position till dusk, the remainder of " C " Company being moved up again from reserve during the afternoon to cover this flank. At 1700 hours the Battalion front was again very heavily bombed.

At 1930 hours our right flank was again attacked by twelve tanks and strong infantry forces. The tanks engaged our positions with guns and machine-gun fire. Our anti-tank guns replied with some success, but by 2045 hours enemy tanks and infantry were infiltrating through our main positions, and were soon well to our rear. It was now getting dark and " A " Company was then extricated with the loss of about one platoon and a further four vehicles ; all abandoned vehicles being rendered unserviceable before they were left. " B " Company had been withdrawn previously, and " C " Company on the right flank was got away save for one platoon. " D " Company was not in action that day. It was digging a reserve position in rear at Agedabia.

The way " A " and " C " Companies held off these very heavy attacks on our right flank, until dark, was a magnificent piece of work, they were constantly attacked by tanks and greatly superior numbers of infantry. It must be remembered, too, that this was the first time these troops had ever been in action.

That night the line was stabilized on an intermediate reserve position some twenty-five miles in rear.

April 1st.—" A " and " C " Companies had suffered rather heavily on the previous day ; " B " Company was intact, and " D " Company had been brought up into position. Twice during the day the positions were very heavily dive-bombed and machine-gunned by two squadrons of Messerschmitts. Casualties were, happily, light, but several more trucks were lost.

The enemy's ground forces made no attempt to attack our positions that day.

April 2nd.—At dawn on 2nd April, our scout platoons located one enemy armoured unit some three miles in front of our position, and checked the enemy from tapping along our front to find the weak spots.

Once again the scout platoons were very well handled.

Wireless worked excellently, and much most valuable information was passed back. They were later driven in, but not before they had given warning of a strong force of German infantry debussing astride the main road that ran through our position.

At 1030 hours the above-mentioned enemy infantry attacked, escorted by tanks. The Battalion was ordered by Support Group to withdraw, and commenced thinning out. However, eight enemy tanks were round our right flank, and cut off the previously reconnoitred route of withdrawal of " B " Company. The vehicles of " B " Company were soon in difficulties, for they endeavoured to withdraw across some treacherous salt-pans in their rear. The company commander made valiant efforts to extricate them, but unhappily only some half-dozen men of the whole company managed to get clear.

Other enemy A.F.Vs. had in the meantime come round the other flank ; but in spite of this, all the rest of the Battalion was safely withdrawn, except for the complete scout platoon of "C " Company, which had become too heavily engaged with the enemy A.F.Vs. to be able to disengage. This gallant action by the carriers of " C " Company undoubtedly contributed greatly towards the extrication of the remainder of the Battalion—no easy matter in daylight and in contact with an armoured enemy.

The Battalion, now much weakened, withdrew some thirty miles and at once deployed in positions about one mile north of Agedabia, and was again in action.

Between three and four that afternoon a strong artillery concentration was put down, followed by a heavy attack by enemy A.F.Vs. and infantry. Enemy tanks were soon through almost to our artillery positions. A counter-attack was put in by a squadron of our tanks, and the Battalion and gunners were withdrawn, with very few further casualties, to Antelat, to the north, where that night was spent, undisturbed by the enemy.

April 3rd-4th.—Leaving Antelat on the morning of 3rd April, the whole of the Support Group moved northward in desert formation to Sceleidima, which was reached about mid-day. The Battalion was then ordered to hold the line of the escarpment from Sidi Brahim in the north to Sceleidima in the south. The ground was very broken and hilly, and positions for the companies were very difficult to find. They were, however, quickly occupied, but wireless touch was soon lost with H.Q. Support Group, who had moved considerably farther north. It was, however, re-established in the early hours of the following morning, but reception was extremely bad and much interrupted. The Battalion was on the move most of that night and about midnight came under the command of the Armoured Brigade, with whom it moved on the following morning thirty miles due east across the desert to Msus. There was great difficulty in getting orders to " A " Company, which was several miles away. Wireless contact was, however, eventually re-established, and that company followed on and caught up the rest of the Battalion at Msus. Food stores and a petrol dump here were reported to have been blown up and the wells destroyed, but it was happily found possible to refuel a large number of the vehicles, and after considerable difficulty to get water from the wells—vital in view of the proposed trek northwards across the desert the next day.

April 5th.—On 5th April the Battalion again moved in desert formation with the Armoured Brigade from Msus to Ghedir-ess-Sciomar, some forty miles to the north. Near here the Battalion laagered for the night, and then rejoined the support group.

April 6th.—On the afternoon of 6th April, the Battalion and one troop, R.H.A. (anti-tank) acted as rear-guard to the Support Group at Bu Gassel. There was, however, no enemy interference. Dusk fell about 8 p.m. and the Battalion withdrew north-eastward to Maraua (on the main Tobruk—Benghazi road) where it refuelled, and was ordered to drive on through the night and, if possible, to arrive south-east of Derna, a further eighty miles, by dawn on the 7th. This was the third night running that the drivers had been on the move all night as well as all day.

April 7th.—The Battalion passed through Derna at about 0800 hours on the 7th. " C " Company and " H.Q. " Company were leading, and as they breasted the very steep, long hill, with many hairpin bends, at the eastern exit to the town and approached the Derna aerodrome, they were ambushed by tanks supported by anti-tank guns that had apparently cut across the desert from the west. Happily, some guns of the R.H.A. (anti-tank) were present, also two Bofors light anti-aircraft guns, and these managed to account for some sixteen enemy A.F.Vs. The company sergeant-major, " C " Company, also collected all possible anti-tank rifles and silenced several enemy guns. Four of our cruiser tanks then arrived and gave valuable aid in clearing up the situation. However, practically speaking, all that had remained of " C " Company was lost here, also some two-thirds of battalion headquarters and headquarter company. Four officers were killed in this engagement.

The remainder of the Battalion reached Tobruk about 2200 hours that night. In the eight days' withdrawal (some 400 miles) it had lost 16 officers, some 350 men, 42 carriers out of 44, and nearly 150 other vehicles out of some 200. Fortunately, many of the casualties are prisoners of war.

April 8th.—The next morning that portion of the personnel for which transport could be found was formed into a mobile column. It was only possible to make up a small and very incomplete battalion headquarters, with no signal communication of any kind, and one composite motor company. The remainder of the personnel, for whom no transport could be found, was left as a dismounted party to assist in the defence of Tobruk. About a month later, this party was evacuated by sea from Tobruk to the Nile Delta, where the Battalion started to reorganize.

The mobile column so formed was based some eighteen miles east of Tobruk, and had, with other columns recently arrived from Egypt, the role of delaying the enemy endeavour to invest Tobruk.

April 11th.—On the 11th April, Tobruk was finally surrounded by strong forces of the enemy, and the mobile column was withdrawn, as previously planned, eastward another twenty miles to the aerodrome at Gambut. A day or two later it again withdrew eastward through Sollum, held Halfaya Pass for two or three nights, and then moved another ten miles east to Buq-Buq, where it stayed until 22nd April, when it proceeded south and inland to Safafi up on the escarpment. Here a good deal of patrolling was done, but no contact made with the enemy, and on the 27th the Battalion moved northwards again to Samalus. The column remained here for an uneventful fortnight, and was then pulled back to the neighbourhood of Cairo to reorganize and refit.

The account of the operations by the Commander in the summing up concludes with the following reference to the Battalion :—

" The brunt of the fighting fell on the Battalion, who were very well handled by their Colonel throughout. They proved the very high state of training they had reached and I cannot speak too highly of the work carried out by their scout platoons, it is most unfortunate that these should have suffered so severely. The spirit and cheerfulness at all times shown by all ranks of the Battalion was a tonic to all who saw them engaged."

TWO YEARS IN BRIEF 1941—1942.

THE 9th BATTALION.

BY CAPTAIN F. J. M. SCHUSTER
AND
CAPTAIN E. N. SARGEANT

THE Battalion docked at Port Said on the afternoon of 31st December, 1940, after a long but pleasant journey round the Cape. The general hope was that we should be allowed to pass New Year's Eve on board as the ship we were on was being used as a troopship for the first time and was still full of luxuries. But that was not to be—we disembarked that night—a cold, dark moonless night and one which introduced us at once into the customs and manners of the country; for in spite of the lateness of the hour beggars besieged us every yard of our one-mile march to the siding, and the special train was over two hours late. We saw the New Year in, drinking the last of the ship's champagne, comforted by the news given us that afternoon " that the high pundits in G.H.Q., Cairo, were certain the war would be over by August."

The next morning we arrived at a camp—then just being built—to discover that the chief beggar and pesterer of the previous night had now turned into our engine driver. There, too, we had our first view of the landscape which was to become only too familiar—just barren desert.

The next six weeks were spent training energetically in the new type of open campaigning—desert warfare—and trying hard to forget the many lessons we had learned in England where roads exist and where the words " tank obstacle " have a meaning. Here bad dust storms were encountered and there were many amusing experiences of getting stuck in sand-drifts and being temporarily lost as we found our desert feet.

In the middle of February (1941) the Battalion set out for a secret destination, but with the rumour that we were going to spend a quiet and comfortable summer policing the recently occupied parts of Cyrenaica, so to our future regret a large part of our heavy baggage accompanied us. For the first month it looked as if, for once, rumour was going to be right ; a very pleasant month was spent at Cyrene with various officers appointed military governors of districts and having great fun administering jurisdiction over the natives and crawling Wops : then on to Benghazi with police and guard duties for another three weeks. Here we lived like kings, in abandoned luxury flats, with plenty of wine and food to be had for the bartering of very minute quantities of issue tea and sugar. Several sheep were " unavoidably " involved in traffic accidents, but as the local shepherds only claimed five piastres (1s.) compensation for each animal, the damage to individual pockets and regimental funds was not great. The bathing too was excellent and we all felt that really wars were not too bad things when we were transported to, and given a living in, a lovely spot by the sea whereas in peace time we would have paid a small fortune for this Mediterranean holiday—but it was not to last for long.

In the middle of March we moved down to Mersa Brega to take over the forward positions. It was during the drive down that a certain officer, who was well known for his sleeping propensities, was lost in the desert for the night. Having visited his Company H.Q. to receive orders to move at first light he tried to return to his platoon, but failed to find it. The next morning the scout platoon commander having driven some two miles on his way saw what he took to be a valise in the distance—he drove up only to find the missing officer curled up and quite happily asleep in his red windcheater—but in future he always took a compass when visiting at night. We found the forward positions very lightly held as the majority of troops had been withdrawn to go to Greece and other theatres. So our first campaign started. On 31st March the forward patrol of armoured cars came hurtling back to our lines with the story that German tanks were on their tails. And they were. That was the beginning of a nightmarish ten days and nights in which without any air support and anything to fall back on in the rear, with practically no supplies and very little communications to higher formations, we were shoved, pushed and finally hurled back over a vast area. In Tobruk the remnants were collected together, for by that time we had lost many of our officers and men and an even greater percentage of our transport through ground and air attack and even in some instances lack of petrol. One composite company was formed with all the available transport to go out on mobile column work and the remainder were left behind to form part of the Tobruk garrison.

Memories of that retreat are vague, but I shall never forget the riflemen offering round a tin of bully—" The most expensive meal you've ever eaten, cost £20,000 to cook "—he had just picked it out of a blazing cruiser tank.

Nor an A.A. sergeant in charge of a Bofors gun, who loathed the Germans more than anybody I have ever met and showed it to them in no mean manner whenever they came in the air or on the ground, and brought his gun back, minus one wheel, making his crew lean " out board " to keep it on an even keel.

Two Years in Brief (9th Battalion)

By mid-May we had all been relieved and were back in the Delta faced with the serious task of re-forming—the remnant from Tobruk rejoining us there having been brought out by destroyer. Another battalion was very generous in sending us several officers and N.C.Os. to help us in this task.

Training went on in earnest for the next three and a half months although the proximity of Cairo added delights to the evenings and week-ends. In mid-September we moved up once more into the desert, being passed out as "desert worthy" on the way up, and joined a Guards brigade.

Till the start of the November battle we were engaged mainly in column and patrol work and were undoubtedly the cause of many of those communiques—"Libya—nothing to report besides normal patrol activity"—which those engaged used to think rather an understatement. At the commencement of the battle our brigade was held, more or less, in reserve, primarily to go off on a long "cutting off" trek when the opportunity came, and secondarily to meet any emergency. Actually the emergencies always came up—we never got off on our trek! On one of these, known at the time as "The November Gold Rush" we were shown a spectacle which was a sight for sore eyes. The Germans were threatening our supply line with a large armoured column and we were sent back to the wire to deal with it. It did not appear a pleasant task as we were up against some fifty tanks and we had no armour. However, on arrival, a couple of squadrons of R.A.F. bombers roared over and dropped their load on the advancing enemy column. It stopped them for a short time, but after licking their wounds they got going again; another roar in the sky—this time coming from the other way—over came fifty Stukas— "Now it's our turn," we thought. But no: the Stukas circled round and went back over their own troops, into a dive, down one by one— each picking his own little target. This time he was really hurt but he was given no rest, for back came our own bombers—and then, having had enough, off he went.

Roughly at the same time the truck of a little camouflage officer, attached to us, broke down at dusk whilst we were on the move. He put it right and drove after us attaching himself to what he thought was our column and meandered along behind it for some way, when he halted he was horrified to hear German being spoken all round— but in the darkness he managed to slip away without anybody apparently noticing, and he rejoined us during the next day.

And so the advance went on day by day. Several prisoners were taken; this was all right when they were in batches and could be dealt with—but there were occasions when they were rather a nuisance. One Company Commander, faced with a recalcitrant German and temporarily without anybody to keep a good eye on him, thought the best solution would be to order him to take off his boots (the desert was very stony just there)! He had forgotten, however, that the prisoner had previously stated he had been marching and fighting for five days without any rest and a hasty counter order had to be given as the statement was apparently true. As a rule the riflemen used to get on much too well with prisoners of war.

From November, 1941, onwards we always had superiority in the air and this was of very great assistance, especially when making long pincer marches. On one of these when we were escorting a large supply of petrol up to the tanks which had made a swoop right up behind the enemy lines and were sitting there hoping to catch him as he came back, three 109's flew low overhead and started performing aerobatics just above us. It was all very nice and friendly and they provided excellent target practice for everybody ; one was hit and crash landed—nearby—the other two flying off straight away : the pilot climbed out and came over incensed and shaking his fist in fury, still firmly convinced we were friendly, and got the shock of his life. The other two brought back a few Stukas but fortunately without much damage.

By the end of December we had once again reached the neighbourhood of Mersa Brega—and there we sat till the end of January—sat is perhaps not the correct word, for operations were extremely mobile and frequently resulted in long rushes one way or the other—when we were relieved by another battalion of the Regiment. We laagered alongside each other for the night and a great time was had by all. It was on this night that one company commander, who prided himself on being an old " desert rat " and never getting lost, was unable to find our laager on returning and spent the night out wandering ! On relief we went back some one hundred miles and sat down to rest and re-equip for a week or two ; the first day the order was given to off-load all trucks. The battalion pessimist remarked that would surely lead to a move ; it did. A considerable noise was shortly heard, which was taken to be field firing, but it proved to be a large enemy tank column. So began the Msus Stakes. We were hastily reorganized into a column with a horse gunner regiment and a Yeomanry anti-tank regiment and had an interesting, and at times amusing, withdrawal knowing very little of what was happening or why. A riflemen, seeing some natives watching the retreating vehicles, shouted out, "What's up, mate ? Waiting for a number 15 Bus ? "

So we eventually settled down in the Gazala line—where we stayed with very little activity until the end of April, when we were sent down to the sea at Buq-Buq to continue the short rest which had been so rudely broken in January. And here the Guards Brigade organization was magnificent ; on arrival tents had already been drawn and issued for messes, an unlimited supply of beer was laid on and a special leave train from Matruh had been arranged. In fact a very good time was had by all for about a fortnight. Then we were hauled back to be in time for the May battle. During this the whole Battalion had a series of lucky escapes, in fact many friends thought that everybody had been put in the bag on several occasions. At first,

Two Years in Brief (9th Battalion)

near Hacheim, we were hotly pursued by a large number of tanks ; luckily a dust storm was blowing and a safe and speedy if somewhat ignominious getaway was made by all. Next we were put in a " box " at Tamar, some eight miles north-west of Knightsbridge ; we sat there very comfortable for a few days—only to be ordered to our annoyance into Tobruk :—the box was completely over-run the next day. In Tobruk we once again settled ourselves in comfortably, especially Battalion H.Q. who found and used an old Wop dugout and were extremely indignant on a change of plans being ordered. Tobruk was invested within six hours of our leaving and fell in another forty-eight hours. From then on we fought rear-guards all the way back to Alamein—finally reaching the line and planting ourselves down in the middle of it without knowing it was there. There were certain difficulties at this time including a complete lack of maps, of any scale, for the last few days. It was during one of these rear-guards that a scout platoon was covering the getaway of a battery of horse gunners who had swept into action as if at Olympia and remained firing over open sights at the advancing tanks till they were only some 700 yards away. A herd of camels looked after by natives nearby, who also thought it was time to make an exit in the same direction, overhauled the carriers, which never very fast in the desert were by then very old, all having completed over two thousand miles.

In the words of the platoon commander—" I didn't mind much when the camels going fast shot past me ; I didn't really worry when a Wog galloped past us on a donkey—but I did begin to get a little anxious and think the carriers weren't much good when a Wog passed me on his own two feet ! ". However, by clever use of ground he managed to get them all out safely.

We remained in varying parts of the Alamein line till the middle of August, 1942, when the authorities apparently felt the same as we did—" that after nearly eleven months unbroken in the desert it was time to have a spell down Cairo way." And, with the exception of one unfortunate company, which was attached to another battalion, back to Mena we went—for about three weeks we were told.

As we hit the road near Alexandria the majority of trucks drove on a smooth surface for the first time since the previous September— having in the meanwhile completed some ten thousand miles over all kinds of going—and one could almost hear the sighs of relief as the convoy sped towards the luxuries.

The first few days were spent in getting clean, eating and drawing stores, getting more clean and so on. A large farewell party was given in Shepheard's on the Regimental Birthday ; finally everybody had to be rounded up later that same night, the Battalion being called out to be ready for action—Rommel had attacked and Cairo was threatened.

TUNISIAN TURNTABLE

By Lieut.-Colonel R. A. Fyffe, D.S.O., M.C.

The following is a Record of the part played by the 10th Battalion The Rifle Brigade in the Tunisian Campaign.

1. The Bou Arada Vale.

The Battalion, less " B " Company, landed at Bone on 7th December 1942, after a completely uneventful voyage, the latter part of which was in weather suitable for a peace-time cruise. The only jarring element had been provided by a naval officer who, coming aboard at Algiers, prophesied continual air attack as far as, and at, Bone. It had therefore been with some pleasure that we noticed an anti-aircraft cruiser accompanying us out of Algiers harbour, but any confidence which she inspired was immediately liquidated when she turned due west ; we continued due east.

Bone, had in point of fact, been heavily bombed, but the arrival of a squadron of " Beaufighters " had reduced the attacks to a fairly light scale, usually twice nightly, at dark and just before dawn. We were billeted in a tobacco factory, and few will forget the feeling of claustrophobia brought about by the fact that the troops had to sleep so closely packed that it was virtually impossible to step between them, the thick smoke-laden atmosphere, and the huge glass roof through which the flak could be seen climbing skywards towards diving raiders.

For this reason, towards the end of our stay, we moved the Battalion out every evening to bivouac on the sand-dunes, and converted air raids from an unpleasant experience into an entertaining spectacle.

By 19th December our vehicles had arrived, with the exception of " D " Company's carriers, which had been sunk complete. Sergeant O'Brien, who was with them, fortunately survived, drifting ashore on a raft. From Gibraltar he went to Bone in H.M.S. " Dido," but by the time he arrived the Battalion had left, and he was sent back to Gibraltar in a mine-sweeper as he had no equipment and was therefore suspect to the military mind ! Undeterred, however, he stowed away, and after hiding during the voyage he landed in Algiers whence he hitch-hiked five hundred miles to rejoin the Battalion near Bou Arada : a good effort.

On 19th December the Battalion started to drive eastwards, and arrived at Testour after two days and one night of hurry through rear areas, full of rumours resulting from the repulse of Blade Force, owing to the arrival of German tanks in considerable numbers. This force was an armoured regimental group, consisting of the 17th/21st Lancers, " B " Company, R.B. and a battery of R.H.A., which had landed at the end of November and had nearly reached Tunis before being forced to withdraw in the face of strong opposition and German air superiority.

Of Testour, the predominant memory is that of continuous and torrential rain in an olive grove, with mud above one's knees and talk of an attack scheduled for Christmas Day, which was, however, cancelled owing to the weather, so we moved on Christmas Eve to a drier area at Sidi Ayed, about twenty miles to the southward.

From this harbour our active participation in the campaign began in the shape of two patrols provided by " C " Company, which went out on Christmas night, headed respectively by Sturgess and Pawson. The former's patrol had an encounter with an enemy party and one of the riflemen was wounded—our first casualty.

At this time a battalion of Spahis was holding the Bou Arada area, their number including a " type formidable "—one Sergeant Henriot who lived in " No Man's Land " in a derelict farm and spent his days shooting chickens for the pot with a service rifle and his nights marauding amongst French farms, obtaining news from their owners, and interrogating Arabs.

This great man had discovered that German armoured cars came daily to a certain farm, so an ambush was arranged for their benefit consisting of Pawson's platoon in the farm itself and Winter's platoon as a mine-laying " stop " to trap the cars were they to pass the farm. As this was our first innings of any size there was great competition to play, and a numerically strong officers' team was fielded, consisting of the Platoon Commanders concerned, Welman, who was I.O. and one other officer. Sergeant Henriot also joined in, accompanied by two braves—or " commandos " as he liked to call them. The whole party motored out into " No Man's Land " about eight miles and with tremendous silence disembarked, having sent Henriot ahead as an advanced guard. This task he had accomplished to no small tune, having advised the farmer to leave with his family, and in consequence every light in the house was blazing, the farmer's children were crying, the sliding door of the garage was being opened with a roaring rattle which would have awakened the dead, and the car was noisily being cranked amid loud expostulations, eventually being pushed into life by the " commandos " who gave a rousing cheer as it finally disappeared, lamps blazing, into the night ! When cautioned about this noise, Henriot merely remarked that the farmer constantly went out at night so the disturbance would not cause any suspicion ! The English part of the force then went silently to action stations : the French retired into the farm, cooked themselves an excellent meal and went to bed in the farmer's beds.

A bitterly cold night was passed by all (except the French) and when morning came it brought no sign of armoured cars. However, at about 1000 hours a motor-cycle combination came up the road with three Germans aboard and was about to turn into the farm when two Arabs began riding towards it gesticulating. Obviously they were blowing the gaff, so just as the Huns ran to their motor-cycle to get away, Pawson, Welman and the two other officers, who were watching from a vantage point on a roof some one hundred yards away from them, assembled their available fire-power—one Bren and two Tommy guns—and carried out an officers' shoot at the now rapidly retreating enemy. Two of the Germans were killed, but the motor-cycle and its driver got away. A well-expressed fire-order from Welman then directed a hail of bullets on the Arabs, one of whom galloped into dead ground, while the other was wounded. On the whole it may be said that the officers' shooting promised well for future King George competitions, especially on " snap " practice carried out by Welman on the Arab whose behind bobbed up and down as he crawled along a ditch.

The French were for shooting this " salot " out of hand, and while the remainder of the force retired to a rendezvous with the trucks, insisted on interrogating him on an open slope in full view of an enemy armoured car which had now materialized. So ended an amusing event, and a salutary lesson in inter-allied co-operation.

On 30th December the Battalion suffered a slight reverse, as the Colonel and Nicholl lost their drivers, one Humber, and a scout-car, the drivers concerned electing to brew up rather than keep watch while their officers were away. One driver was killed when two German eight-wheelers arrived to join in the lunch party, and the other was put into his scout-car to form part of a mournful procession which, in full view of the bereaved officers motored in convoy back to Hunland. Only a dead body and some derelict " steak and kidney pud " remained as a warning to those who might put the observation of a brew before that of enemy movements !

31st December was another melancholy day. Welman had somehow attached himself to Henriot's " équipe " and for some nights had enjoyed the life of a guerilla in their company. On this particular night he had been with Henley, the adjutant, to hatch some deep plot for future excursions *chez* Henriot over a well-cooked " pea-hen à la commando " when the scout-car in which they were travelling ran on to a French mine. The driver was killed, Henley was luckily thrown off the top of the car and only badly cut. but Welman's foot received the whole weight of the overturned car and he had to go to hospital for amputation, and thence to England. It was the very worst luck that Welman, who was so tremendously energetic and doing such a lot for the Battalion, should have had to retire from the campaign upon which he was already making his mark in no uncertain manner.

At the beginning of January, 1943, the Battalion moved to the Bou Arada area, companies being installed near various farms, the aspect of which several officers and men, " C " Company especially, will remember for many a long day ! Let it not be thought, however, that life was entirely devoted to high living : all companies took their share in nightly patrols which searched farms and laid ambushes for the enemy, whose own patrolling was pretty energetic. Many of our parties had exciting encounters and these patrols were of the highest value in teaching leadership, and field-craft in a way which luckily proved inexpensive, though the distances involved and the country covered called for skill and high physical qualities in those who hunted in the Bou Arada Vale.

At this time an observation post, known as Two-Tree Hill, was manned at first light daily by the Derbyshire Yeomanry. This hill dominated Hunland and so it was inevitable that the Germans should in due course ambush the Yeomanry troop. This occurred on 10th January, and the enemy began to install themselves on a ridge, the ownership of which conferred complete domination of Bou Arada and its surrounding communications.

Accordingly " A " Company was sent, with one squadron of the 17th/21st Lancers, to prevent any such intrusion. This they did, meeting opposition to the strength of about two companies, and at nightfall " C " Company was sent to help them to consolidate on the high ground north of Bou Arada. The remnants of the Germans put up a certain amount of resistance, but during the night they retired. They still, however, remained on Two-Tree Hill and on the following day " D " Company, supported by one squadron 17th/21st Lancers, attacked this position. Reconnaissance had shown no signs of the enemy, but as soon as the riflemen were near the objective very heavy machine-gun and mortar fire was opened on them from well-concealed reverse-slope positions, and they were pinned to the ground. Only by first-class co-operation on the part of the tanks were they able to retire, and their comparatively light losses were cheap payment for a sharp lesson in enemy methods of concealment and clever siting of automatic weapons. In this action, Littlejohn was wounded and unfortunately for the Battalion had to be evacuated to England.

It should be noted that the company rode on the back of the tanks until they came under fire. This meant that the Commander was unable to issue orders, as control was already extremely difficult to maintain owing to the dispersal of his platoon commanders.

Two-Tree Hill was attacked by forces of varying sizes three times after this during the campaign, but was never taken, being evacuated by the Germans at the end of April when they became outflanked by the British attack up the Goubellat Plain to Kournine.

Besides Two-Tree Hill another post was manned daily on some high ground about three miles east of Bou Arada, called the Argóub, and in order to forestall any enemy attempt to " jump " this feature two platoons of " C " Company were sent on to it on 17th January. One of their carriers was blown up on a French mine on the way, and here it should be explained that these mines were laid in two minefields across the main Bou Arada—Pont du Fahs road, both fields being supervised by jet-black Senegalese who spoke neither English nor French. The drill was to flash a signal (moves being always by night) when approaching, whereupon the guardian would pick up the mines. Consequently, what with the black men being so black that they were almost invisible in the dark and no means of conversation save grunts à la "Sauders of the River," accidents were liable to occur in even the best regulated units !

The two " C " Company platoons were reinforced on the 18th by the remainder of " C " Company and by " B " Company, who arrived on the Argoub just before first light, the remainder of the Battalion remaining in the Bou Arada area.

Amongst the officers of " B " Company was Wilson who had attempted to instil keenness about observation into his platoon by the offer of a lavish financial reward to the rifleman who could first produce a piece of worthwhile information. He was not surprised, therefore, when a panting rifleman announced to him that he had seen a large number of German tanks approaching. Taking this story " cum grano " Wilson reluctantly left his first light brew-up to confirm the news, and to his personal surprise and financial loss found it to be undoubtedly true !

A German tank battalion, followed by infantry and self-propelled guns, came nose to tail down the very road which half an hour before had been used by the two companies of somewhat dozy riflemen, passing about half a mile away from where they were now speedily digging in, as it appeared that the enemy might attack the Argoub in order to protect their flank.

There followed a battle for which the two companies on the Argoub had a dress-circle seat, though " A " Company, who were in front of Bou Arada, enjoyed the front row of the stalls ! The enemy attacked the village but were repelled by extremely heavy artillery fire, and after a ding-dong fight, lasting all day, retired when eight of their tanks became bogged and six more were destroyed.

This was our first sight of German tank tactics, and the feelings of " B " and " C " Companies, two miles behind the enemy tanks, and unable to intervene in a purely tank versus gun battle, can well be imagined !

When the Germans retired a troop of the Lothians' Valentines followed them up, but became easy victims to a Mark III armed with a long 75 mm. gun, and this gave us a preview of the way in which our armoured regiments were entirely outmatched in tanks.

At dusk, Pawson laid some mines across the road down which German vehicles were now passing, and a jeep containing two huns blew up with a most gratifying roar—unfortunately our only contribution to what was a most interesting battle. If the enemy had captured Bou Arada the extremely attenuated British line would have been forced to withdraw (had a withdrawal been possible, which is doubtful), about fifteen miles, and the southern flank of the British position at Medjez would have been left entirely open. " B " and " C " Companies would, of course, have inevitably fallen into the bag.

The next day the remainder of the Battalion came on to the Argoub. The enemy shelled ".D " Company and Battalion H.Q. areas during the morning, and Elkington was killed. He had been Second-in-Command of " D " Company since April, 1942, and, young as he was, had shown marked ability and an endless power of taking pains in that position ; he was very greatly missed by his men, for whom he had done so much, and by all who knew him.

On 21st January " B " Company returned to the main Battalion area, " C " Company remaining alone on the Argoub, well dug in and well wired. Patrolling was carried out each night, and during one such sortie Pawson, having ascended a tree to pass the time when watching for enemy movements, found himself looking at only too short a range upon a German section who had silently approached and were digging in ! Pawson therefore lowered himself to the ground, getting his lanyard entwined in the tree while doing so, and began to crawl away. He had hardly turned the corner of a cactus hedge, when he found himself face to face with another enemy section ! Changing direction again he once more encountered digging Huns, and indeed was crawling about in the middle of a German platoon area. So he shouldered his Tommy-gun and marched straight between two sections at what he afterwards described as a most riflemanlike pace !

A few days previously Gunn had joined and the following night took out a patrol with the object of scuppering an enemy post, but unfortunately he and his whole party disappeared after a good deal of firing had been heard. We were all very relieved, therefore, to hear some weeks later that he and his riflemen companions were prisoners of war in Italy.

On 27th January the Battalion rejoined " C " Company on the Argoub, and two days later was relieved by a parachute battalion, going back to Bou Arada. However, having got in at 0430 hours we were ordered immediately to take over a position from the London Irish Rifles who were on the other side of the Bou Arada valley ; this we did at 0530 hours, coming under command of the Irish Brigade.

On 3rd February we were relieved by the same London Irish battalion and returned whence we came, only to have to move our harbour two nights running owing to the arrival of a regiment of 5·5's who wanted our areas.

The game of general post might have been expected to have run its full course by this time, but military exponents of this sport know no moderation, and on 6th February the Battalion, less " B " Company, once more made its way to the Argoub where we relieved a battalion of the Guards.

A Parachute Battalion was now on our right, and amidst gales and icy rain the old routine of patrolling started again, enlivened by friendly competition with the parachutists whose personal loads (one man carried a 3-inch mortar continually) made us appreciate our trucks more than ever.

During this period most of the 6th Armoured Division had gone southwards to the Maktar area where it was rumoured that the Americans were receiving a rough handling from the Germans, having lost about eighty tanks. Accordingly the Battalion, less " C " Company, was rushed to Maktar and thence Sbiba, together with the Guards Brigade, as the enemy had attacked through the Faid Pass and were preparing to push north-west. " C " Company, plus the anti-tank platoon, remained at Bou Arada until 17th February when it joined the Battalion, just north of Thala, unfortunately having had to leave the anti-tank platoon behind.

II. Thala

Immediately " C " Company rejoined the Battalion on 19th February, the Colonel was ordered to take a small composite force south to the Kasserine Pass. This force was to consist of one squadron Lothians and Border Horse, R.B. Tac. H.Q., " C " Company R.B., one artillery battery 25-pounders, one troop of anti-tank guns and one section field ambulance : its object was to repulse the enemy who were reported to be infiltrating round the flanks of the Americans holding the pass. The force reached its destination at 0400 hours on 20th February and the Colonel went to make contact with General Stark, the American Commander. The latter appeared to be a little out of touch with the situation, but spoke of a U.S. battalion being on the north-east side of the road and another astride the road in the pass. He said that a liaison officer would report to the Colonel at 0800 hours to show him the exact layout of the American units. This officer failed to materialize, so the Colonel and the author mounted a scout-car to see for themselves what was going on. American ambulances were driving up into the pass at intervals, but all we could find were a few U.S. infantry crouching in a wadi, who knew nothing about anything. We therefore drove from crest to crest, halting behind each and having a good look before going on again. During this process one of the American ambulances passed us, and on peering over the next crest we saw it being taken over by some Germans ! " C " Company scout platoon under Fairweather was therefore sent out to make contact with the enemy, which they did, losing two carriers to anti-tank fire. The tank squadron was then used to maintain contact and to help forward a U.S. Armoured Battalion which was to attack into the foothills of the pass. It was obvious that any Americans who might have been in the pass had long ago disappeared, except for those south of it. The U.S. battalion made some headway but towards evening a general American retirement began on both sides of the road. This was brought about by the appearance of German tanks accompanied by S.P. guns. These

Tunisian Turntable (10th Battalion) 117

tanks were Mark III's and IV's and more than a match for the Lothians' Valentines and Crusaders, the latter gradually being knocked out, although most gallantly and skilfully fought. The S.P. guns also did great damage, all the officers of the 25-pounder battery being killed.

The Yeomanry squadron, realizing that the main object was to keep the enemy from breaking through before dark, fought to the bitter end, gradually being forced to retire on to " C " Company who were dug-in with the anti-tank guns ; as darkness fell the last Valentine was set on fire. The Lothians' squadron had fought a most gallant action which had a great influence upon subsequent events, by gaining time for the remainder of the Brigade to be concentrated.

The force now withdrew to a ridge about four miles nearer Thala, having lost one anti-tank gun and the whole Lothians' squadron, but being reinforced by four American-manned Grant tanks. An anti-tank defence was organized and the enemy was awaited.

At about 0200 hours on 21st February enemy tanks began to fire tracer in the direction of the Grants. As soon as these replied, giving their position away, they were all four set on fire by the German tanks, which then advanced, being engaged by anti-tank fire. The anti-tank gunners shot as best they could but the Germans lay back behind the glare of the burning Grants where they could not be seen, but could see, so that they knocked out all the anti-tank guns one by one.

The force again withdrew, pursued by enemy tank fire, and as dawn broke passed through the 17th/21st Lancers and the main body of the Lothians who were preparing to fight a tank battle. This they did during the afternoon, once again being completely out-tanked, only keeping the Germans off by most gallant efforts.

In the meantime the Leicestershire Regiment was digging in on high ground south of Thala and the Colonel's force had been withdrawn behind them. Here " C " Company was joined by " B," " D " Company remaining in reserve north of Thala. " A " Company had been sent already to Sbiba in case a break-through occurred there.

Towards the evening of 21st February, the battered Lothians and the 17th/21st began to come into harbour near the Battalion in the dark, when suddenly some tanks following behind them opened up on " B " and " C " Companies. They were enemy, who had passed through the Leicesters and had motored right into our positions. One of them, passing near to a rifleman of No. 12 Platoon who was digging his slit trench was invited by the digger to " keep away from my . . . trench, you're knocking it in." The rifleman received a revolver bullet past his ear for his pains. The German tanks shot about the place, their commanders meantime shouting "Hands up—come out : surrender to the Panzers " in good English. The situation was not particularly easy to unravel as nobody knew which were our tanks and which German in the dark and the confusion, but in the end a gunner scored a direct hit on a Mark III setting it on fire. This made recognition easier, and it was not long before nine enemy tanks were ablaze and their daring attempt at a night break-through was thwarted. No German infantry appeared near our area, although they did establish themselves in the Leicesters' neighbourhood, and throughout the night there was confused firing and alarms of various types, as information was nil.

At dawn on 22nd February the Lothians made a sortie towards Leicester Ridge, but suffered heavy tank losses. The enemy began to make reconnaissances with his tanks, during which process there was a good deal of anti-tank and artillery fire on both sides, some of the Germans being engaged over open sights by 25-pounders, together with some American " tank destroyer " S.P. guns which had arrived.

This went on all the morning and the programme was occasionally varied by enemy dive-bombing and ground-strafing attacks, and the unwelcome dropping into our lines of American-fired shells, our allies seeming to have rather a penchant for the delivery of " shorts."

Towards the afternoon, the enemy were reported forming up for an attack ; this news coinciding with the shelling and bombing usually associated with German offensive action, and we felt a bit small without our anti-tank guns, and with only twelve tanks of the 17th/21st and about six of the Lothians left in the whole Brigade. Nothing materialized, however, and the next day reconnaissance showed no enemy on Leicester Ridge, so " C " Company occupied it, being reinforced by a battalion of the Coldstream Guards during the night.

On 24th February a regimental group consisting of " C " Company, the R.B., and the 16th/5th Lancers, together with supporting arms, moved down the road towards the Kasserine Pass to try and regain contact with the enemy, who had mined their line of withdrawal most thoroughly. Progress was therefore slow, and as the 16th/5th had only just arrived from re-equipping with Sherman tanks (thereby missing the battle) it was not thought worth while to endanger these new tanks by taking risks with the enemy minefields. On 25th February the Guards Brigade re-took the Kasserine Pass, and the Battalion went to Ebn Ksour to rest.

This was not to be for long, and on 28th February we were ordered to move to Medjez, there to warrant once again our nick-name of " the Plumbers " (or stoppers of holes). A German attack was expected, but nothing occurred, and after a week orders arrived for the Battalion to go to the Argoub. No sooner had we motored five miles, than a hectic brigade-major caught up the column to say that one company had to be left behind, so " C " Company was given the honour of carrying out that very much maligned manœuvre, the counter-march.

The Battalion finally concentrated west of Le Kef on 17th March, leaving the Argoub for good, and rejoining the armoured regiments who were refitting.

So ended the game of general post, and with the arrival of the

Shermans there also departed the inferiority in equipment which had cost the Brigade so much.

We were not sorry to see either of these go, but we were extremely sad to learn that Brigadier Dunphie was to leave us. For the next few weeks training was the order of the day.

III. FONDOUK

4th April saw the Brigade moving southward over very dusty roads to the Maktar area, and on 6th April the advance was continued by night to a leaguer just west of Jebltrozza. The following day the Brigade attacked the Fondouk Pass. This pass was a narrow gateway into the plains of Kairouan, and was dominated on both sides by very steep ranges of hills which were the key to the successful passage of the ground below.

The plan therefore was for the Guards Brigade and an American division to capture the north and south sides of the pass respectively, after which the 6th Armoured Division would go through.

All went well to the north, but the Americans started late and failed to reach their objective, with the result that the pass was still overlooked by the enemy, and heavy enemy fire was brought down upon the approaches to it.

The situation was aggravated by news that the German 10th Panzer Division was retiring hurriedly northward, hard pressed by the 8th Army and was about to present a very vulnerable flank to us —and if only we could get through the barrier separating us from the plains to the east.

26th Armoured Brigade was therefore then ordered to force the pass and in leading this attempt the 17th/21st suffered heavy losses on a minefield which was covered by anti-tank guns. " C " Company, who were allotted to them, came under intense fire, and the situation was unpleasant, until towards evening the 16th/5th found a way round the left flank, and turned the enemy's anti-tank screen.

They were greatly helped in this by the action of " A " Company's scout platoon, two sections of which knocked out the crews of four enemy anti-tank guns which were holding up the tanks. These guns were sited on two steep hillocks which could only be approached over completely open country. The carrier sections motored across this ground under cover of fire from the Shermans' 75's and Besas, then dismounted and, led by Toms, charged the guns on one of the hillocks, killing, or capturing, their crews. From this position they then brought heavy Bren fire to bear on the other hill, killing, or driving away, the remaining guns' crews. The 16th/5th Lancers were thus enabled to resume their advance.

The other two armoured regiments were passed through this gap, but it was not until the R.E. had worked all night clearing a lane through the minefield that wheels and artillery were able to follow the armour. Valuable time had therefore been lost during a day, during which the Battalion had been forced to sit under shell-fire, which was all the more annoying owing to the feeling of frustration at being unable to press on towards the retreating 10th Panzer Division.

During this day also Dust was killed when his platoon was heavily shelled, and his death deprived us of an officer who had done extremely well during the early days when he had carried out some first-class patrols and whose complete imperturbability was an invaluable asset.

On 8th April, the whole Brigade formed up in " box " for the first time, and we headed north-east towards Kairouan over dead flat country covered with a profusion of the most beautiful wild flowers. Various small pockets of enemy were encountered, but they readily surrendered, especially members of a penal battalion whose officers had decamped with all their available transport ! Towards evening the Lothians had quite a good tank battle with remnants of the 10th Panzer Division, destroying fourteen tanks and a number of soft vehicles.

The advance was resumed next day, but just as we were starting " A " Company and the 16th/5th were dive-bombed and Toms was killed. His death was indeed a loss to the Battalion, in which he had proved himself an outstanding scout platoon commander as well as a very delightful personality.

During the afternoon our armour ran up against a strongly defended enemy position in the foothills of the range which runs round the side north of the Kairouan plain, and " D " Company, now reorganized as the support company, was moved on to some high ground to form a defensive right flank for the Brigade. The tanks found that they could not penetrate the enemy's localities, which contained about twenty anti-tank guns, a battalion of infantry, and a battalion of tanks, including some "Tigers," so at dark we leaguered in the hills to the west, after a remarkably hazardous journey across the open plain—a demonstration of amateur star-cum-compass navigation which would have given any of the 8th Army battalions the willies !

One of " D " Company's scout-cars went the wrong way, passed two " Tigers " on the road, recognized them, turned round, and repassed them flat out, pursued by shots from the rather affronted Mark VI's !

Next day we advanced to Spibkha where we were heavily divebombed, losing several trucks in the process. Far the most serious loss, however, was the anti-tank gun platoon's pig ! This animal had grown with the platoon from a little squealer into a rather fine large porker and whenever the guns were employed the pig went too. Hitherto it had survived all the menaces of war, but on this occasion, when the 8th Army units took over from us, he was nowhere to be found. A reconnaissance sweep was made, but all efforts failed, and perhaps he now roams the Kairouan plains, or more likely he was taken on the strength of the 8th Army !

The Battalion was withdrawn and on 17th April went into a concentration area north of Bou Arada. The next few days saw a great reunion of riflemen, as the 7th Motor Brigade had come to Le Krib, and visits between Battalion and 7th Motor Brigade H.Q. were the main daily event, incidentally proving to all concerned that Rifle Brigade officers still maintain their sartorial uniqueness!

IV. KOURNINE

This concentration of the 1st and 6th Armoured Divisions was in preparation for the next attack, which took place on 23rd April. Supported by three regiments of artillery, infantry advanced across the Bou Arada—Goubellat road, followed by the Armoured Brigade moving "one up." There were a fair number of mines about, but on the first day we advanced as far as the high ground north of Sugar Lake, a salt lake which lies about five miles north-west of Pont du Fahs, and during 23rd and 24th April there was heavy armoured fighting, the Germans having reinforced this sector with anti-tank guns and artillery. During an exceptionally heavy bout of shelling Sturgess was killed, and in him we lost an officer whose courage, enthusiasm and forthrightness of character were an example to everyone of what a rifleman should be. He was a fine leader, and his platoon reflected his personality in its high standards and by its devotion to its Commander.

On 25th April an Armoured Brigade (1st Armoured Division) passed through us, but could make no headway and a deadlock was reached. The situation at this time must have been almost unique, as three Battalions of the Regiment were deployed within a few thousand yards of each other, Brigadier Bosvile, and his staff of riflemen, being right in the midst of this Rifle Brigade "benefit."

The dominating feature throughout this battle was a hill called Kournine, a two-humped mountain on the top of which the enemy was very strongly installed and which provided a first-class look-out. A patrol from "B" Company reached the top of this hill, but saw no enemy and reported it clear. This, however, cannot have been a true bill, and it seems likely that the enemy realized that the patrol was only a small one, and lay low.

The Brigade was withdrawn on 27th April, leaving the 1st Armoured Division to continue what had now become a completely static battle, enemy anti-tank guns and tanks definitely dominating the attempts of our armour to advance.

This battle had not involved the Battalion to any great extent, beyond the usual commitments of companies in protecting by night the armoured regiments to which they were allotted, and the formation of a defensive flank to the south by "D" Company. It had been one in which the companies had all been exposed to a good deal of shell-fire and bombing with not much to show for their pains in the way of a chance to take offensive action. One of the only entertaining incidents was an indirect shoot by Hedges' mortar platoon, on some tanks which were ensconced behind a ridge in such a position that our Shermans could not safely cross it. After firing a large number of bombs the mortars scored a direct hit and the enemy were persuaded to withdraw, a successful conclusion to this rather novel employment of the 3-inch mortars as " tank-disturbers."

Soon after we left the field of battle Brigadier Bosvile temporarily took over command of the 1st Armoured Division, and the Colonel did the same with the 7th Motor Brigade. These commands, however, reverted to normal after only a few days, and the C.O. was shortly back with us again after a pleasant interlude at the Motor Brigade H.Q. which he described as being delightfully well equipped with every convenience, and possessing a first-rate *maître d'hôtel* in the shape of Sturt, whose catering efforts were nothing if not remarkable. He also reported the cellar as being noteworthy !

V. The Final Round

Once again preparations were made for a big attack, and this time it was to be a knock-out. The 7th Armoured Division and the 4th Indian Division came round from the 8th Army to our concentration area south of Medjez, and we were able to meet many old friends in consequence.

On 6th May the 4th Indian Division, the 1st and 78th Divisions attacked the hills east of Medjez, supported by six hundred guns. The first two formations were successful and we were able to start advancing towards our first objective, the village of Massicault.

The Royal Air Force had said that such would be their air superiority that we need take no camouflage or dispersal precautions, and they were as good as their word, for during the next six days we saw only six enemy aircraft, these being a small formation which attacked us on the first day of the battle.

Surprisingly little resistance was encountered, only a few 88's and tanks—and soon we were passing derelict enemy guns and positions and in the evening reached the main Tunis road—a great joy to drive upon after months of bad roads and bumping across country.

We harboured that night some two miles beyond Massicault. The next day it became evident that the enemy were on the run. The companies had great fun routing small parties of Huns out of farms where they tried to hold out after the Shermans had passed them, and on our left the 7th Armoured Division was known to be making good progress, passing to the north of Tunis. Our armoured regiments bumped a fairly heavy anti-tank screen in the outskirts of the city, so we bore away south-eastward to cut Tunis off from Cape Bon and the south.

By now Italian and German prisoners were coming in pretty frequently and mushrooms of smoke above Tunis told of enemy demolitions. Towards evening we heard that the Derbyshire Yeomanry and the 11th Hussars had entered the town after a close race, and loud cheers went up from everyone on receipt of this news. The night of 7th May was spent near Mornagnia. The country now was highly cultivated and covered with prosperous looking farms standing amongst vineyards which had a most deliciously soft and seductive smell. We saw many German dumps, mostly of rations, M.T. parks evidently hastily abandoned, and on one track a series of hastily scribbled sheets of paper stuck up on trees, bearing the name of a German unit and pointing towards Cape Bon.

The Brigade's task was to cut the base of this Cape so that the enemy could not retire into it, and Arabs reported that many Germans had already gone in that direction driving herds of cattle before them.

It was therefore almost certain that the enemy would make the town of Hamman Lif into a strong-point, as this town lies on the shore of the Gulf of Tunis in a narrow gap between a range of steep mountains and the sea, the width of the gap being about half a mile. This town protects the Cape Bon entrance from the north.

The armoured regiments were checked by heavy anti-tank fire on reaching the outskirts of the town, and " B " Company was ordered to try and " winkle " these guns. They advanced into the town, but were shelled and came under accurate sniping and machine-gun fire. Frewen was killed whilst leading his platoon amongst the houses. He had not been with the Battalion long, but had already shown himself to be a first-rate officer, and, with his quiet unassuming manner, a delightful character. He had hoped to remain in the Regiment after the war, and this fact, together with his intense enthusiasm for anything to do with the Regiment, made his death a particularly great loss.

The company could make no headway, and there was a pause while the Guards Brigade were being brought forward to do the job. However, before they could arrive the Lothians forced their way down the seashore and through the town after a heavy artillery concentration had been fired into it, and by a magnificent effort they broke through anti-tank defences which a German general afterwards said he thought could hold out almost indefinitely.

The remainder of the Brigade poured through, amidst great rejoicing by the inhabitants, the French appearing to be sincere—the Arabs opportunists to a man ! The Bey of Tunis was winkled out of his blue and white painted palace and his highly decorative but completely ruritanian guard laid down their 1914 muskets. Certain officers of the Battalion accepted the hospitality of the local hotelier to the tune of some excellent brandy and a lot of hand-shaking, while a German heavy gun vainly tried to reach the village with its ponderous shells which fell shorter and shorter as the barrel wore out !

This was on 9th May, and the next day the Division cut the southern end of Cape Bon, reaching Hammamet that evening. Prisoners of war were now coming in by the thousand and there was

I

little organized resistance, such as there was being easily dealt with by the Shermans' 75's and the motor companies. The carrier platoons of the companies had been kept busy during this final phase reconnoitring through the many olive groves for the armoured regiments, and proved themselves indispensable under these particular conditions where tanks were rather like elephants forcing their way through jungle.

Only one enemy block remained now—the German 90th Light Division and the Italian Ariete and Young Fascist Divisions who were sandwiched between the 6th Armoured Division and the 8th Army in the Enfidaville area. It was known that Graf von Sponeck, their Commander, had expressed his intention of fighting to the end, so the Brigadier, not wishing to lose tanks unnecessarily, advanced slowly southward to increase the " squeeze " on the surrounded enemy. On 11th May efforts were made to find a prisoner who would take a note to Sponeck demanding surrender, but none would face his wrath.

On 12th May bombers from the 8th Army gave the enemy a heavy pounding, the whole hillside sprouted white flags like mushrooms, and white verey lights rose in great numbers from the enemy positions. The Brigade I.O. heard that von Sponeck had ordered the cease fire an hour before, and went to fetch him in. He surrendered to General Freyberg and General Keightley at about 6 p.m., immaculately dressed in green uniform and greatcoat with scarlet facings and lining. Colonel Holbeck, the Commander of the 155th Regiment, also came in.

The stream of prisoners was endless: they came on foot and crowded into vehicles. We had all talked of Sponeck and the chances of his surrender for days, but when he did arrive a rifleman approached one of the officers of the Battalion and asked what the German's name was. When told " General von Sponeck " the rifleman merely said " Never 'eard of 'im, Sir," and turned away to his evening " brew-up.". It had been such an amazing week that many of us wondered whether perhaps the rifleman wasn't right after all.

VI. Conclusion

The final enemy surrender was six months exactly since we left Scotland. The Battalion had fought on every single part of the Tunisian front save one, the most northerly, where the mountains are covered by cork forests and the country is not suitable for vehicles. We had passed through all those phases which seem to be an indispensable part of every British campaign—the " penny packet " phase when both sides were weak, but we had to dance to the Germans' tune owing to his shorter communications, the inferiority phase, when we were defeated through the lack of adequate tanks: and then the arrival of the Shermans and a regiment of self-propelled 105's, bringing with them first a return of confidence and then victory—swift and resounding, made more certain by complete air superiority.

We had learned the lessons of hard experience in many different types of country and variations of weather, against an enemy who gave of his best and of his worst, from crack formations such as the German 10th Panzer Division down to the Italian San Marco Marines, whose exact role nobody could ever comprehend, least of all themselves.

The Battalion took its full share of duty : sometimes—in fact, nearly always—unspectacular, but we hope well done. Our losses from first to last were mercifully small :

Killed	Officers, 5	Other Ranks, 41
Wounded	,, 6	152
Prisoners of War	,, 1	38

So now we wait for the next adventure ; over the evening brew-up our camp-chair strategists make their plans, and we are looking northward—to Rome, perhaps Paris, maybe Berlin, but always in the end to the Old Kent Road.

10th BATTALION RIFLE BRIGADE
12th MARCH, 1944—19th MARCH, 1945

BY MAJOR N. C. SELWAY
AND
MAJOR J. F. LONSDALE, D.S.O.

THE main party of the Battalion left Robertville, for Italy, on 12th March. An advance party under Bobbie Selway preceded us, and the rear party, who were to take the vehicles over, remained to conduct a hectic rear-guard action against Arab looting parties. We embarked at Bone, from the same dock on which we had first set foot on African soil fifteen months earlier, and for all of us except the unfortunate few who sailed in LCTs, the trip was uneventful.

We disembarked at Naples on 14th March, going ashore over an upturned Italian hospital ship which had been scuttled by the Germans when they abandoned the port, and marching six miles to a temporary camp, where for two days the cookhouses were besieged by half-starved civilians, until we were able to get away to the Divisional concentration area at Piedimonte d'Alife. During the three weeks which followed, Dick Southby arrived to take command of the Battalion, we trained hard during the day, and the raids on Naples and the eruption of Vesuvius provided a nightly firework display.

On 7th April we moved up to take over a section of the line south of Cassino from a parachute battalion, and were there for ten days. Little was known about the ground between our positions and the river, and we spent the first few nights lifting mines and reconnoitring routes down to the bank opposite San Angelo in Teodice. " C " Company, however, successfully ambushed an enemy patrol causing casualties and capturing three prisoners. By day there was no movement, and the time passed quietly apart from periodical artillery and Neibelwerfer stonks. During this period we lost Angus McNaughton, wounded in the leg by a schumine whilst on patrol. On 17th April we were relieved by the 8th Indian Division, who were to make the assault, and returned to Piedimonte, where intensive training became the order of the day.

The 8th Army had by now moved across from the Adriatic, and before long details of the plan were made known.

13 Corps were to attack straight up the Liri Valley, whilst the Poles and French cleared the high ground on either side.

The Armoured Brigade were to be used in support of the infantry divisions, and, until the Division could concentrate, any break-through would be exploited by an armoured reconnaissance group formed from the Derbyshire Yeomanry, and the Battalion.

It was considered probable that the enemy would fight one big action south of Rome, and that the city would fall within four weeks. This proved an accurate forecast, as the reserves were all committed in the Liri Valley, and the city was entered in twenty-four days.

The Germans made no secret of the fact that they regarded Highway 6 through Cassino as the road to Rome, and, in spite of sweeping claims elsewhere, the battle for the city was fought and won in the shadow of Monastery Hill.

Before the 8th Army could break out of the valley, the 1st Parachute Division, the 15th Panzer Grenadier, the 90th Panzer Grenadier, the 26th Panzer, and several other good infantry divisions as well, would have to be killed, captured or destroyed.

The rest of the month, during which Dick Fyffe left us to Command a R.W.K. battalion in the 78th Division, was spent in preparing for the big attack.

On 11th May the assault began with a barrage from a thousand guns, and the crossing by the infantry of the Rapido.

D+2 found the Battalion preparing to enter the bridge-head, which was now a meagre 800 yards deep.

At this stage " A," " B " and " C " Companies were commanded by Lonsdale, Goschen, and R. Fairweather respectively, Support Company by Booth, and " H.Q." Company by Blacker. Wilson was Adjutant, and Selway Second-in-Command.

The scout platoons were the first to cross, and for two more days were all that could take part in the battle ; although R.S.M. Crocker succeeded in blowing himself up, whilst guiding a certain "parker" to its resting-place.

It was by now apparent that the Germans were determined to fight it out, and news was received of the repulse of the Poles from the Monastery.

Fierce fighting continued in the bridge-head, and the Derbyshire Yeomanry, pushing forward slowly with the scout platoons, soon began to find the Sherman tank a liability in close country. During the fighting on the 16th, Duncan Gray was wounded. At length, after heavy casualties to the leading squadron, the Battalion was ordered forward to deal with a strongly held position, Pt. 83, which commanded the road to Aquina. No reconnaissance was possible, and orders had to be given from the map. The Battalion attacked with " A " and " B " Companies : both scout platoons went ahead and obtained valuable information, the enemy proving to be in considerably greater strength than had been anticipated.

The Canadian Corps were now entering the bridge-head, and the Indians withdrawing. The narrow twisting lanes were choked with transport, and the bridges still under fire. " A " Company were unlucky as they crossed, and Gray and one or two more were wounded.

However, by last light the motor companies were forming up and the best being made of a confused situation. John Bodley of " A " Company, wounded later, had done some splendid work with his carriers (for which he was awarded the M.C.), and had confirmed the belief that the Germans remained in force.

As darkness fell Lonsdale on the right, and Goschen led their companies forward in a gallant attempt to reach their objectives. Westnedge, of " B " Company, was killed at the head of his platoon, and both companies suffered losses. Forced to withdraw for the remainder of the night, a fresh plan was made, and then, with considerable artillery support, the position was successfully occupied the following morning. A devastating concentration caught the Germans as they left their trenches, and the resultant chaos was indescribable.

The enemy were now on the run, although snipers and bazooka men in the close country prevented any speedy exploitation. The following night, under cover of an unpleasantly sharp air-raid, Cassino, and the Monastery itself were evacuated, and the Battalion, pressing on up the valley, mopped up parties of the enemy from various divisions, a sure sign that things were now going well.

By 18th May, two days later, the tanks of the reconnaissance group, probing the Hitler Line at Aquino had reported that there were signs that the line was not held in strength.

Accordingly, at first light the following day, while the whole world watched and waited, two scout sections under Stewart-Wilson went forward with the hazardous mission of finding out where the Germans were.

It did not take them long. As the mists lifted in Aquino, a half-track and gun were revealed, getting into position, and a sharp fight ensued. Both enemy vehicles were destroyed, but all the carriers were hit or set on fire.

After some early successes, which included the destruction of an enemy S.P. gun, the platoon was held up and finally extricated itself with difficulty. Ralph Stewart-Wilson was missing for several hours ; his carrier having been knocked out ; he was forced to take cover in a slit trench, which on closer inspection proved to be a .German latrine. He returned with valuable information. A brigade of the 78th Division then took over the task of clearing the town, and we went back for four days rest.

On 25th May we passed through the Adolf Hitler Line, using the gap made by the Canadians, and came up on their right with orders to seize a crossing over the Melfa and advance on Arce. The leading tanks found a bridge intact and succeeded in crossing, but a tank having been knocked out so that it completely blocked the bridge, " B " Company were unable to cross owing to accurate small-arms fire, which caused several casualties, including Roger Parker, who was wounded. During the night both we and the enemy were bombed by German planes, causing a remarkable display of protesting light signals from the far bank. We occupied our time recceing along the river-bank for a crossing : at first light an attempt to cross drew fire, but an hour later Victor Hannay waded over to find that the only enemy remaining were a few deserters. The Battalion established itself on the far bank and the 1st Guards Brigade passed through us.

We rested for forty-eight hours and had some delightful swimming in the river, then moved up on the left of the Guards Brigade who were attacking Monte Piccolo and Monte Grande. In the early morning of the 29th the enemy began to fall back and the Lothians passed through us across Route 6 and entered Arce. The same evening we were ordered to cross the river and capture Fontana Liri.

Information that the bridge was intact proved to be false, and as the river was too deep to ford, a long detour had to be made. At last light the enemy withdrew, and the following morning the 10th Indian Division took over from us in the town, after an unpleasant night during which we suffered a number of casualties. " A " Company, in particular, suffered heavily. One of the platoons, on occupying a house, exploded a device which killed several men, and Bomford gallantly rushing in to render what aid he could was himself killed. Dale, Second-in-Command of " B " Company, was another who was wounded during the night.

Then we moved back to south of Arce to join the 2nd and 7th Battalions, and the 61st Brigade was formed.

On 3rd June we caught up with the rest of the Division at Alatri and the following day became the leading infantry behind the 16th/5th and 17th/21st Lancers. By evening we were north of Serrone, having covered twenty-five miles and left behind a good deal of scattered opposition. During the night " A " and " C " Companies marched four miles across country to occupy Monte Morrone and at first light the armour continued up the main road. During the day news came that Rome had fallen, and we drove hard throughout the night through Cave, and the outskirts of Rome to south of Mentana, where we were halted by an artillery and M.G. screen. On the 7th we entered Mentana and Monterotondo, and the 1st Guards Brigade took over the lead. During the next nine days we received reinforcements, reorganized and followed the advance through Narni and Todi. On the 18th we resumed the lead with orders to seize the high ground east and north-east of Perugia and cut the main Perugia—Arezzo road. This was accomplished by "A" and " B " Companies, after a night compass march in pouring rain and very poor visibility. The enemy were taken by surprise, and " B " Company destroyed a Mark IV tank and several enemy vehicles. From our positions we were able to overlook Perugia, and the Guards went in and captured it.

On 21st June we relieved 2nd R.B. astride the road in the Mount Rentella area, " C " and " D " Companies establishing themselves on Rentella with "A" Company north of the road 1,000 yards short of Corciano. " A " Company were ordered to capture Corciano that night, but found the monastery on the hill between them and the town to be strongly held. They cleared it after a sharp fight, but were unable to continue to Corciano before daylight, so consolidated in their position. The following day Rentella was heavily counter-attacked by the enemy who succeeded in recapturing the summit, after hand-to-hand fighting resulting in heavy casualties to both sides. "D" Company Commander, Ian Blacker, and Pat Wilding were among those killed in a very gallant attempt to hold their position. However, our O.Ps. were now able to observe the reverse slopes of the hill—heavy artillery and mortar fire forced the Germans to abandon their position and " B " Company re-occupied it. Meanwhile, " A " Company had been conducting an all-day fire fight with the enemy in Corciano, and at one time were under fire on three sides and at very short range, from two tanks and an S.P. gun. Fortunately the monastery was very strongly built. After dark, Mike Atkin Berry led a patrol into the town, found the enemy just pulling out and captured five of the stragglers. By first light the company was dug in 800 yards north of the town, from there the whole of the reverse slope of Rentella could be engaged, and the position was firm.

We remained in the same positions for the next few days and sent day leave-parties into Perugia, where three cinemas, two canteens and an Officers' Club were already running, although the town was still under artillery fire. The 8th Indian Division then relieved us, we harboured for three days south of Lake Trasimeno, and on 3rd July moved up to the western side of the lake to take over from the 78th Division north of Castiglione del Lago. The Battalion then became part of a 16th/5th Lancers Regimental Group with orders to advance on Arrezo. On 5th July, despite demolitions and torrential rain, an advance of eleven miles was made, and Castiglioni Fiorentino was entered without opposition, but increasingly heavy and accurate shelling on the leading squadron and " A " Company, who were with them, proved that the enemy had O.Ps. on the hills east of the road. A patrol along the road found enemy astride it, barring the way to the town, and by the evening of the 5th " B " Company were held up just below the summit of Monte Maggio, with " C " Company similarly placed on Monte Rentella. Both positions were strongly held, and " B " Company's attack had cost them a number of casualties, including Eddie Clark (killed), and Charles Morpeth (wounded). " A " Company relieved " B " on Mount Maggio, and 7th R.B. passed through to put in a two-company attack. They captured the hill and held it for twenty-four hours before losing it to a strong counter-attack. On the night of 9th and 10th we were relieved by the 1st K.R.R.C. and the 1st Guards Brigade, and the Brigade went into reserve for a week, which included three very pleasant days spent camping at Trasimeno.

On the 15th the Guards Brigade and New Zealanders attacked to clear the hills covering Arrezo. After twenty-four hours the enemy fell back and " B " Company with the 16th/5th Lancers entered the town and raced for the main road bridge over the Arno, whilst " A " Company with the Lothians followed them through, directed at the Buriano bridge. This was captured intact, but the Arno bridge went up when " B " Company were within 100 yards of it, a great disappointment as it enabled the enemy to recover and take up new positions.

For the next fortnight we pushed westwards along the north bank of the Arno, leap-frogging with the 7th Battalion whilst the 2nd Battalion protected our right flank. " C " and " A " Companies made a night attack on a ridge north of S. Giovanni Valdarno and captured it, only to find at first light that enemy paratroops were still holding another ridge to their rear—the two forces being dug in back to back. There seemed to be some difference of opinion as to who had cut off who, and hard fighting continued all day until the arrival of a troop of 17th/21st Lancers helped to persuade the enemy to disperse and withdraw. Four days later the Brigade attacked the Paula Line with 7th R.B. on the left and ourselves on the right— " A " and " B " Companies up. The position was an extremely difficult one to attack—an open approach, devoid of cover and heavily mined, leading to a precipitous sandstone cliff, with spandau positions in caves half-way up, which could only be reached by tunnels from the rear. Fortunately the enemy was fairly thin on the ground : even so progress was only possible by night. After three days of fighting in intense heat, and having suffered a number of casualties, which included John Bodley killed, and Paul Morgan wounded, on mines, and which reduced both leading companies to fifty strong, we were through and occupied Vaggio, where the Guards took over the advance.

For the next ten days we were in the S. Agata-Cancelli area, protecting the right flank of the advance and sending long range patrols on to the Prato Magna. We resumed the lead again at Pontassieve and alternated with 7th R.B. in that task through Rufina to Scopeti and Rata. Only rear-guards were opposing us, but there were a number of sharp clashes, and small scale night attacks and we lost both Duncan Gray and Jimmie Stevens during this period. Dick Fyffe returned to the Battalion to take over from Bobbie Selway, who had been commanding whilst the Colonel was in hospital.

On 16th August we again took over the lead astride the Dicomano-San Godenzo road. " C " Company occupied S. Godenzo, " B " captured Poggio Erbolini and " D " finally established themselves on the highest point of the Muraglione Pass, against scattered opposition and occasional harassing fire.

After a few days rest at Dicomano, whilst the Divisional sappers repaired the blows on the pass in record time, we joined the rest of the Brigade north of San Benedetto on 27th August. Then followed a miserable week of continuous rain spent sitting in reserve along the road, as it was impossible to get off it. Finally we returned to Dicomano, but were called up again on 8th September, to attack Portico with the 17th/21st Lancers. However, a blown bridge in the town prevented the armour from getting through, and the enemy held out with great determination, although " D " Company held positions overlooking him to the west of the road. Finally the Armoured Brigade took over, and the 61st Brigade went to join the 1st Guards Brigade in the mountains north of Castel del Rio.

There we remained for the rest of the winter, the Brigade working two battalions up so that we had a fortnight in the line followed by a week in reserve at Grassina on the outskirts of Florence. Until the first week in December we made slow but steady progress, attacking in turn a series of parallel ridges running east to west. During this period the standard of patrolling reached a very high level, and we dominated " No Man's Land " to such an extent that scarcely a night passed without the enemy losing men, and few of his patrols returned to their own lines unscathed. In one patrolling period of three weeks the Brigade inflicted sixty-nine confirmed casualties on the enemy for the loss of four wounded, the Battalion's share of this being twenty without loss in one week. Finally we were brought to a standstill by the Veno del Gesso and Tossignano. On 14th December, " B " and " D " Companies had a hard night's fighting in an unsuccessful attempt to relieve 2nd R.B. in Tossignano—after that the line became static.

On 7th December, whilst the Battalion was resting at Grassina we had the great honour of being inspected by Field-Marshal Sir Maitland Wilson and Lieut-General Sir R. Eastwood. A few days later Teddy Goschen and Ken Dale left us to take up staff appointments. Christmas was celebrated in the line, but our Christmas parties the following week lost nothing in enjoyment through being a few days late. The officers' dance, excellently organized at Villa Capponi by Teddy Voules, was a great success too, had it not been marred by the tragic car accident afterwards which resulted in the death of Ken Dale.

We finished the winter on Mount Penzola, where the Folgore Group finally relieved us on 2nd March.

Throughout five months of mountain warfare the Company Administrative Staffs did splendid work in getting supplies to the forward troops, under extremely difficult conditions and usually at night, as by day the mule-tracks were under enemy observation.

After a week of social activities we left Florence on 9th March for our training area at Cattolica. There the reorganization began immediately, and at midnight on 19th March, 10th R.B. ceased to exist, and became 2nd R.B. For many of us it was a sad day, but we take our new name knowing well the great traditions and record which are now entrusted to us to uphold.

2ND RIFLE BRIGADE
63/3/A
1st *April*, 1945

The following letter has been received by the Commanding Officer from Field-Marshal The Hon. Sir Harold Alexander, G.C.B., C.S.I., D.S.O., M.C., A.D.C., written in his own hand.

I regret so much that your distinguished Battalion has to be disbanded.

As an old Regimental officer myself, I well know what a blow this will be to your chaps and what disappointment it will cause. But there is one reason only for this decision and that is a shortage of man-power, which is not surprising in the 6th year of the war.

Your Battalion has a very fine record and I shall always be proud I had them under my Command and very grateful for the distinguished part they played in the great victories we won in Tunisia and Italy.

Yours sincerely,

H. R. ALEXANDER

MAESEYCK, 1945

Field-Marshal Sir Bernard Montgomery, General Sir J. T. Burnett-Stuart and the Commander, 9th U.S. Army

THE
RIFLE BRIGADE
1939—1945

Volume 2

Contents

	PAGE
1ST BATTALION, B.L.A., 1945 ..	1
FRENCHMEN AND BELGIANS WITH THE 1ST BATTALION	19
THE APENNINES TO THE ALPS, 1945 (2ND BATTALION). BY MAJOR A. J. WILSON, M.C. ..	21
7TH BATTALION: ITALY—AUSTRIA—EGYPT, MAY, 1944, TO SEPTEMBER, 1945. BY LIEUT.-COLONEL V. STREET, D.S.O., O.B.E., M.C., AND MAJOR T. L. DEWHURST, M.C. ..	28
8TH BATTALION ..	44
MILITARY HONOURS AND AWARDS ..	55

Illustrations

	PAGE
FIELD-MARSHAL SIR BERNARD MONTGOMERY, GENERAL SIR J. T. BURNETT-STUART AND THE COMMANDER, 9TH U.S. ARMY:—	*Frontispiece*
1ST BATTALION: "C" COMPANY AT NEUSTADT ..	16
1ST BATTALION: CHRISTMAS, 1945 ..	16
7TH BATTALION, 1945: TOSSIGNANO ..	30
LIEUTENANT-GENERAL SIR RICHARD L. McCREERY, K.C.B., K.B.E., D.S.O., M.C., AND GENERAL MARK W. CLARK ..	38

1st BATTALION THE RIFLE BRIGADE, B.L.A.
1945

The New Year opened with the Battalion still holding a wide front from Nieustadt, on the Dutch-German border, to Holtum, about five miles north of Sittard. The cold was still intense and there was over a foot of snow lying on the ground. Skating on the canal was a popular recreation, but hardly compensated for the fact that the troops of the forward companies, of whom 50 per cent. had to stand-to all night, found life pretty bleak with night temperatures of up to 26 degrees below zero. Most of them, fortunately, had positions in barns or outhouses, heavily loopholed, and sandbagged the buildings. The less fortunate ones soon learnt to build cover for their slit trenches.

With the New Year, too, came United Kingdom leave. This was arranged on the ballot system, with the one obvious provision that all key men couldn't be away at the same time. At times it caused difficulties, but these were gladly accepted in such a welcome cause. Those people whose names didn't come out of the hat in the first few weeks at least had the compensation of having a less spine-chilling train journey to Calais than the earlier ones.

On 3rd January we all moved back for a short rest to Geleen, a small mining town south of Sittard. The Battalion managed to make itself comfortable and, in spite of having to reconnoitre no fewer than three possible counter-attack roles, there was just enough time for each company to have its own dance. In spite of a certain lack of beauty in the female partners, all these dances were very successful. The officers, too, gave a large party to officers of the Division; surprisingly, some of the Christmas champagne stocks still existed, which was fortunate, for our wine merchant in Maastricht had been arrested by the Americans as a collaborator, but unfortunately not before we had paid our bill.

On 9th January we returned to take up our jobs at Nieustadt and Holtum again until the battle of the Roer Salient began. A new arrival about this time was Keith Egleston, who joined the Battalion and went as Second-in-Command to " A " Company, where he arrived just in time to take over command temporarily from Christopher Milner, whose name was one of the early ones out of the leave hat.

XII Corps, to which we belonged, had been given the task of clearing the enemy from the triangle formed by the Rivers Roer, Wurm and Meuse, and the 7th Armoured Division remained on the left of the Corps for the operation. The Divisional plan was for the 131st Brigade to attack northwards and secure Echt, Schilberg and Susteren. The 8th Armoured Brigade, who were placed under command in the initial stages, were then to go through and swing right, thereby loosening up the enemy and assisting the 52nd Division on the right to advance northwards. Our own Brigade, the 22nd Armoured, would then break through northwards to Montfort and St. Odilienberg.

Our own job during the first stages was to cover the bridging by Churchill bridgelayers of two small streams south of the Vloed Beek on the main Sittard—Schilberg road. In the evening of 16th January the covering parties from " I " Company (Peter Luke) moved out. Extra time had been allowed for unforeseen contingencies, which was just as well, as a German patrol moving about near one of the bridging sites had to be brushed aside and it was found that a German standing patrol was established in a house commanding the second site and so they had to be blasted out, too. The bridges were finally completed half an hour before first light. In addition, we were to seize the main crossing over the Vloed Beek if it were possible; in fact, shortly after daylight we discovered that the enemy had left and the Sappers were already beginning to build a Bailey bridge. By 1000 hrs. " I " Company were relieved of the local protection of the bridges and were ordered to try to link up with the 2nd Devons, who were in the Susteren area; in doing this, a platoon of " I " Company under Peter Mitchell took seventeen prisoners from a single house. We were then left to garrison Nieustadt and look after the three bridges; during this period Peter Bickersteth was wounded doing a very good night patrol across the Vloed Beek. Meanwhile, the 8th Armoured Brigade had got on well on the right, but the 131st Brigade, who had the 1st Royal Tanks under command, being severely handicapped by a sharp thaw, had had stiff fighting and fairly heavy casualties, and although Schilberg and Echt were in our hands St. Joost, which lay only just off the proposed Brigade centre line, was not.

A plan was made for " I " Company to attack the village with a squadron of 8th Hussars and a troop of Crocodiles in close support; the village was reported to be held by only a company of Germans.

After a delay caused by the Crocodiles not arriving to time, the attack went in at 1500 hrs. and within fifteen minutes seventeen prisoners had been taken from Para Regiment Hubner. By 1630 hrs. " I " Company had advanced about 300 yards in bitter house-to-house fighting and it became apparent that the prisoners' story of St. Joost's being held in battalion, not company, strength with supporting S.Ps. was only too true. Paddy Boden, who was commanding while Colonel Victor was on leave, decided that we had bitten off more than one company could chew, and " I " Company were ordered to make themselves firm where they were. Forty-three prisoners had been taken and at least 20 others of the enemy were killed; against this " I " Company had had 3 killed and 23 wounded, including one Platoon Sergeant killed and all the other Platoon Sergeants wounded. Peter Luke and Peter Apsey received immediate M.Cs. for their part in the battle, in which " I " Company fought with great dash.

During the night two company attacks by the Durham Light Infantry failed to make any further progress, nor did a battalion attack by the same unit the following morning. Meanwhile, " I " Company were relieved by " C " Company, who remained in position till the 9th D.L.I. had finally cleared St. Joost during the afternoon. Towards evening " A " Company, commanded by Keith Egleston while Chris Milner was on leave, was put under command of the 9th D.L.I. with orders to exploit to the northern end of the village. By midnight they were firmly established, having taken more prisoners and captured an S.P. gun intact. The following morning, 22nd January, the 5th Dragoon Guards, with " C " Company under command, set out for Montfort: a group consisting of a troop of the 5th Dragoon Guards and the Scout Platoon and a Mortar Platoon from " C " Company managed to reach Aandenburg, just north of Montfort, where they spent a hectic twenty-four hours, the enemy reacting most strongly to this intrusion.

Against repeated counter-attacks they held their ground and, though suffering some casualties they inflicted many more until they were relieved by the 2nd Devons the following day. " C " Company was at this time being commanded by Dawson Bates, as Eric Sargeant was sick. In the meantime, a column, including " I " Company, advancing on Montfort from the south, were held up by another blown bridge, but by 24th January Montfort was entered and the Battalion took over the defence, less " A " Company, who had been placed under command of the 2nd Devons and who now went back to Echt for a short rest.

The following day the troops on our right flank advanced to the high ground on the west bank of the Roer and the Battalion was ordered to move up to cover the gap of 4,000 yards between the flanks. It was, of course, not possible to cover the ground completely, but by last light " C " Company on the right and " A " Company on the left were in position. The next day, 26th January, an attempt was made by a squadron of the 5th Dragoon Guards with Ben Remnant's Scout Platoon of " I " Company to enter St. Odilienberg, but they were held up by mines and it was while lifting these that Ben Remnant was fatally wounded by a sniper; he was a very great loss. During 27th January the Devons cleared St. Odilienberg and we were ordered to establish a patrol base in or near the town. At last light " A " Company were moved up to the southern end of the town and were kept busy lifting mines and rounding up odd prisoners from the cellars. After the Germans had put in a strong fighting patrol one night which obtained a direct hit with a panzerfaust on a section position, killing one man and subjecting the remainder to severe shock, it was decided that in view of the commanding position it held overlooking the far bank of the River Roer we must defend the place properly and not just use it as a patrol base as originally ordered; accordingly, a second company was moved up. During the next ten days or so things were quiet and companies relieved each other every forty-eight hours. That ended the battle of the Roer Salient as far as we were concerned and everyone was most complimentary about the hard fighting the Battalion had done.

Up to the time that we entered St. Odilienberg the weather had continued to be intensely cold. Each company had to spend at least two nights completely in the open, and on two occasions it was not even possible to get greatcoats to them, but it was surprising how well everyone stood up to this rigorous climate.

Not long after the Battalion's entry into St. Odilienberg the thaw set in and it became a battle with the mud which at one time became impassable to all vehicles except Weasels.* On one particular

---

* A Weasel is a small amphibious tracked vehicle with very wide tracks. Four Weasels were loaned to the Battalion for the Roer operations.

morning the Colonel was reduced to riding up at stand-to on a cart-horse.

We had been promised that we should be relieved by 8th February, but the take-over of one armoured division by another was clearly not practicable with the roads in the condition that they were. However, on 13th February we moved back to Maeseyck just inside the Belgian border across the Meuse, and after a week's rest training programmes were again the order of the day. " A " and " I " Companies were in a not very clean Belgian barracks, with " B " and " C " Companies billeted close by. There was no delay in organizing dances, there was plenty of beer in the town, and, though there were few other entertainments on the spot, the Divisional Concert Party put on a nightly show which was generally considered far better than the indifferent E.N.S.A. shows which were on in the neighbourhood. During the first week we were under command of the Americans and were visited by Mickey Rooney, who gave an admirable " Jeep Show " which was much appreciated.

After the battles between the Rivers Maas and Roer the 1st Battalion came back on 15th February, 1945, for a very welcome rest to Maeseyck, a small Belgian town on the west bank of the Maas. Battalion Headquarters, " A " and " I " Companies were in a barracks and " B " and " C " Companies in billets on the outskirts of the town. It was here that we had expected to spend several weeks before the crossing of the Rhine, but sure enough at the beginning of March came the oh, too familiar order to prepare to move to a new area on the morning of 7th March. About the same time we received the very welcome news that our Colonel Commandant was flying out to pay us a farewell visit, but unfortunately on the very day that we were scheduled to move. His visit was strictly unofficial and the " old boy net " had to be brought into action to postpone the Battalion move until the afternoon in order that the General might have the morning to go round the Battalion.

The programme started in the barracks with " A " Company (Chris Milner) on parade and then an inspection of " I " Company (Peter Luke) vehicles, which seemed quite naked when one thought of the Odilienburg mud with which they were covered only a week or two before. This was followed by a walk round some of H.Q. Company barrack rooms—a reminder of Tidworth days—after which we went down to the town to look at "C" Company's billets. In the absence of Eric Sergeant, who had recently had an argument with a tree in his jeep, David Clive was commanding this Company. They were mostly living in cottages along the main road and the Belgian families were very excited by the inspecting *cortège*. The last item on the programme before lunch was "B" Company (John Witt) cookhouse and dining-hall, which was in part of a large nunnery the other side of the town. The cookhouse staff had laid on a magnificent show. The numerous tins of bully and M. and V. from the Company reserve rations stacked neatly on a large table made as fine a display as is to be seen in any Co-op. stores. We were pressed to an inevitable "brew" by the cooks, who were resplendent in white coats and aprons, which two weeks before had been snow suits, and then returned for lunch to Tac. Mess, which was in a rather second-rate café opposite the barracks. The Mess staff, however, rose to the occasion and produced a very good lunch, to which came Brigadier Tony Wingfield, Commanding the 22nd Armoured Brigade, and all the Company Commanders. Such are the exigencies of war that, lunch over, the Battalion was allowed to put off the move no longer.

After some frantic last-minute loading of vehicles we moved off on the road to Zomeren, a very rural little village on the north side of the Dutch-Belgian border. The General had to go back that afternoon, but on the way Colonel Victor took him to a point on the route and for the last time as our Colonel Commandant General Sir John Burnett-Stuart saw the Battalion march past. It must have been a very sad moment for him and it certainly was for all of us. We were all very honoured that he should come out to Europe in the middle of a campaign to say good-bye to his Battalion, but as no one could have been more welcome than he was we all hope that now the black days of war are over our Colonel Commandant of 1936-45 will pay us another unofficial visit.

Our next and final resting place before the Rhine crossing was the unattractive village of Zomeren, a few miles south of Eindhoven. We feel that the less said about that spot the better, but owing to accidents and sickness there had to be a good deal of reshuffling of appointments amongst the officers. Bill Jepson-Turner, having had a rest at home and got married, returned to "C" Company; Paddy Boden was to take over from Colonel Victor, or so rumour had it, and rumour seemed to have got it right for once, for John Witt was to be seen poring over P.R.I. ledgers, and David Clive went to " B " Company. Peter Luke, after a very successful tour with " I " Company, went home for a rest and was replaced by Alan Parker, who had handed over Adjutant to David Burnett-Stuart at Maeseyck. Christopher Milner remained in charge of " A " Company.

The 24th of March found the Battalion enjoying a period of the best weather we had experienced for a long time. Speculation was rife over the probable date of the Rhine crossing. Quite early the roar of engines overhead brought everyone running out of their houses: there could be no doubt that the balloon was going up, and excitement was intense! Many got their cameras out to take a snap of the massed aircraft as they passed, and it was astonishing, when the negatives were developed later, how many complete blanks there were! All those who had watched a similar sight before Arnhem proclaimed this to be superior in every respect.

Then began a wearisome move through traffic congestions and bottlenecks. On the 25th we reached our forming-up area between the Meuse and the Rhine, having crossed the German frontier for the first time, fully prepared to deal with saboteurs and a hostile population. The complete absence of these came almost as a disappointment to many and in fact was a phenomenon which was to hold good, with one or two exceptions, throughout the coming campaign.

We crossed the Rhine on 27th March and on the following day drove out of the bridgehead: the hunt was on! Motor companies had been " farmed out " to their respective armoured regiments and had to deal with woods and villages defended by German infantry armed with Spandaus and bazookas. Each obstacle demanded a rapid appreciation and fire plan, followed by an energetic assault by the motor platoons and tanks: there was little rest for anyone. Losses were light when compared with those of the enemy, but it was the loss of the individual leaders which was hard to bear. Peter Apsey was seriously wounded during this period and, to the deep regret of all, died soon after being evacuated.

Opposition throughout was fiercest on the northern flank and it was north that we turned to cut the communications of the German para armies. Chris Milner and " A " Company had a particularly successful fight in Stadtlohn with the odds heavily against them; " C " Company fought through Ramsdorf, and, in order to get past road blocks, blew up houses for the tanks to roll over; " I " Company waged a spirited battle between Ahaus and Ochtrupp, where, tragically, Mike Robinson was killed when his carrier ran over a mine. The devastation wrought by the R.A.F. in towns and villages had to be seen to be believed, and in many cases was a serious hindrance to our advance. Finally we reached the Ems near Rheine.

On the far bank of the Dortmund—Ems Canal came our first serious brush with enemy training establishments, hurriedly thrown in to stem the tide. This particular unit consisted of some thousands of officer cadets from Hanover: they were well dug in on the high ground around Ibbenburen. It became clear that these steep, wooded hills were unsuitable for armour, and we were not sorry to be ordered to get our whips out again and flog on to the Weser.

It was now for the first time that we felt that we were right through the opposition and, instead of ruined towns and deeply cratered streets piled high with rubble, we passed through villages whose inhabitants had not yet had the meaning of war brought home to them. The German Air Force gave " I " Company one most unhappy afternoon and made us realize how unpleasant life must be for the enemy with our planes taking a constant toll. We reached the Weser without undue trouble, but only in time to see the bridge at Hoya blow up.

Bridges to the north of Hoya were found to be strongly held and the Battalion joined in another movement northwards, designed to cut the enemy escape route through Bremen. Here again the motor companies had some stiff battling. " A " Company had a good party clearing Bassum, and " I " Company passed through Syke and captured Barrien. It was just north of this latter village that Peter Mitchell was killed, fighting like a lion in an attack on a strongly defended wood: his loss was a terrible blow to all. Later, an enemy counter-threat developed to the west of Syke, and for a time it appeared as if we might have to deal with an enemy tank attack; but this was seen off without trouble. As a result the enemy resorted to anti-tank raids by small parties of specially trained N.C.Os. armed with bazookas: one of these parties gave " C " Company an exciting chase across three miles of country before it was finally put in the bag. The time came now for the scene to shift to Nienburg, preparatory to crossing the Weser and Aller. At this stage Victor Paley, who had been with us since June, 1943, left to join the VIII Corps and Paddy Boden took over the Battalion.

The Battalion crossed the Aller at Rethem on 16th April. " A " and " C " Companies were with their armoured regiments, directed on Luneburg, while the remainder guarded the left flank of the Brigade. There was, as usual, a lot of village and wood clearing to be done, but the enemy was more willing than before to surrender. Opposition came principally from marines and yet another training establishment, this time sapper cadets, who were woefully skilful in destroying bridges. But, although we were shelled fairly heavily near the river, once through the defended localities we met only the odd self-propelled gun and the inevitable Spandaus and bazookas: owing to the absence of enemy mortars, motor platoons, supported by tanks, were able to deal with quite large bodies of hostile infantry. " A " Company cleared Walsrode and captured its bridge intact, although it had been prepared for demolition. The following day they reached Fallingbostel, where a prisoner-of-war camp was liberated: among the prisoners were five taken from this Battalion at Calais and one from the 9th Rifle Brigade at Derna in 1941; needless to say, they were all delighted to see us! It was soon after this that George Burder was killed, another more than tragic event. This was an area that contained also concentration camps, of which Belsen was one, and scenes of atrocities such as Schneverdingen, where a trainload of political prisoners, whose train had been derailed by the R.A.F., were machine-gunned and slaughtered by their S.S. guards. Later on some officers, including John Witt, were to visit Belsen and to come away with horror and disgust on their faces.

The advance continued towards Hamburg and the Elbe. Our two Wasp flame-throwers had, at this stage, their first operational "squirt" —and very effective they proved. All were keen to reach the Bremen—Hamburg autobahn; partly out of mere curiosity and partly out of desire to test their captured cars; but some days were to elapse before we could drive without fear of ambush through the thick woods which flanked the autobahn on either side. " A " Company had a sticky but highly successful party in Daersdorf, and this movement culminated in our arrival on the high ground overlooking Hamburg. Harburg and the bridges across the Elbe were strongly held and the time came for a considerable regrouping.

The Battalion was given the task again of protecting the left flank of the Brigade and of preventing straggling parties of Germans from approaching Hamburg. We were told that we should stay for several days: consequently it came as no surprise when we were told to move almost immediately to capture Buxtehude; it has long been an accepted joke among the riflemen that the longer one is told originally to stay in an area the less time one actually spends there! We moved on 20th April to a forming-up area and a detailed plan was made that evening to capture the town. The following morning all were lined up with their fingers on the trigger when news reached us that the town had surrendered: a highly gratifying anti-climax! The important naval equipment, which we had been ordered to capture consisted largely of one stout German admiral and his " personal " staff of four hundred exceptionally unattractive Wrens. But to make up for this unwanted booty the barracks in which they were living turned out to be modern and comfortable: Battalion Headquarters were not slow to take full advantage of this. Little did some realize what an unmitigated nuisance the Wrens were to become and how difficult it would be to dispose of them! We spent some twelve days quite comfortably at Buxtehude, during which time we amused ourselves by blowing up various bridges to cut enemy communications and, with considerably less enthusiasm, by giving protection to a series of tanks which got inexplicably but quite inextricably bogged. From Buxtehude, too, the gunners, though limited in ammunition, shot with great excitement but doubtful success at ships sailing the Elbe and trains steaming along the far bank. The period at Buxtehude was also marked by a revival of social activity amongst the officers of the Brigade. Remaining stocks of champagne were consumed at a party given at Battalion Headquarters to all officers of the Battalion and a few old friends from Brigade Headquarters and 5th R.H.A. An expedition made by the C.O. and Bill Jepson-Turner to dine with the 1st Royal Tanks nearly ended in disaster when, on the return journey, an over-enthusiastic sentry (not a Rifleman) fired a burst of Sten at the car, puncturing the spare tyre, front tyre and the back of the front seat in which they were both sitting. Fortunately this incident ended with nothing worse than four sore feet caused by a six-mile walk home as a result of a petrol stoppage!

Meanwhile, it was becoming increasingly evident that the Germans had " had it "; and rumours of a complete collapse were rife. But no one could foresee how the end would come, and we could only wait with impatience. Even the civilians were accepting this as a fact and were spreading fresh stories themselves that the war was over, their chief emotion being one of relief. It came as no surprise, therefore, when we learned that Hamburg had surrendered. The Battalion was allotted some German officers for liaison and guide duties, and on the afternoon of 3rd May, with mixed emotions the Battalion, less " A " Company, led the Brigade into Hamburg; " A " Company alone, who were with the 8th Hussars, crossed the Elbe that day. The devastation on both sides of the Elbe was unbelievable, and it is incredible how human beings could survive such a bombardment: there could be no doubt that here relief was the one overriding feeling.

On 4th May it was confirmed officially that all German forces in North-West Europe had surrendered unconditionally. On that day, too, we drove through Hamburg to fresh billets in Pinneberg. There was news that we were bound for Denmark, and complete sets of maps were issued. The prospect of being in a friendly country again was viewed by all with enthusiasm, for, although we had not been actively hindered by the German civilians during our advance, we had missed deeply the welcoming smiles and cheers of Frenchmen, Belgians and Dutchmen. So it came as a great disappointment to learn that this scheme had been cancelled.

Thus ended for the Battalion a highly successful campaign. At times there had been fighting as bitter as in Normandy a year ago; at times resistance had crumbled and unmistakable signs of the future collapse had appeared. We had inflicted on the enemy casualties out of all proportion to our own, but our losses, though not large in number, were most grievous in quality: the kind one can never afford. The full realization of this tempered our joy and gratitude at the end.

VE Day, 8th May, found the Battalion once more on the move to an area north of the Kiel Canal with Battalion Headquarters in Bunsoh. This area, though reasonably pleasant, was poor consolation for the delights of Denmark which had been the one-time dazzling prospect before us. Bunsoh, to which we were to return later, was chiefly notable for the re-forming of the echelons under direct Battalion command, together with the beginning of the " charades " of " Peninsula C."

"Peninsula C," it should be explained, was one of the areas in Schleswig-Holstein chosen for the collecting of the disarmed German forces and from which they were to be dispersed to essential work as required.

Celebrations on VE Night did not reach any tremendous heights: perhaps because it had been celebrated in advance during the previous few days and perhaps because supplies of the necessary pyrotechnics were exhausted!

Paradoxically, it seemed strange, at night time, to see houses with lights blazing and no necessity for black-out and to be able to drive with full headlights on vehicles without any worry.

The Battalion settled down in the Bunsoh area with a view to some maintenance and relaxation, with fairly reasonable commitments in the way of road patrols and bridge guards. About this time it was amazing how many people found that they had long-lost friends or relations in Denmark, the seeking of whom simply necessitated personal liaison. Major-General Dewing, father of Nick Dewing (" I " Company), was head of the British Military Mission to Denmark in Copenhagen, and " I " Company, to a man, considered that the Company should at once be dispatched as his personal bodyguard.

Several duties as liberators were performed, notably the liberation of Esjberg by Dawson Bates (" C " Company) and Charles Steer (" I " Company): their success was immediately repeated by their respective Company Commanders, Bill Jepson-Turner and Alan Parker.

The " peace " was rudely shattered on 12th May by orders to move. The object of this exercise was to take up " stop positions " to seal up " Peninsula C " in the area of Eddelak. This was the first of several moves which embraced several of the more rural districts of South-West Schleswig-Holstein. During the course of this enforced motor tour we took in the area of Tensbuttel and finally came to rest at Bunsoh once again, remaining there until 29th May.

We began to suspect that these moves were the brain children of G Ops Branch of higher formations trying to justify their jobs and to make work for themselves. However, it became apparent that the scheme was to enlarge " Peninsula C " to accommodate more Germans than had at first been estimated. Also becoming more and more apparent was the fact that local Military Government for the Battalion area was the Battalion's responsibility in liaison with Brigade and the

Divisional Civilian Military Government Detachment. It was at Tensbuttel that John Baker (I.O.) produced his first Battalion Military Government sign bearing the legend

MILITARREGIERUNG
WERKTAGE 0930—1130
SONTAGS GESCHLOSSEN

This proved the panacea of all ills for the inquiring Germans who were shown the sign, then propelled sharply in the general direction of the "Militarregierung." John Baker and his Intelligence staff, assisted by our German-speaking Dutch and Belgian interpreters, were kept very busy, not only meting out local justice and deciding whether a farmer could go from X to Y to see if his cows were O.K., but moving displaced persons out of each new area we took over. This was a task in itself: try to imagine assembling 350 Russians at an R.V. at a given time and without the help of anyone who could speak Russian. Add to this the question of transport and the lack of enthusiasm of some Russians at the prospect of returning to Mother Russia.

Life for the companies followed the pattern to which they had settled down: routine patrols, guards and the occasional wild-goose chase in search of some usually mythical local or high Nazi official. Where possible football pitches were marked out and inter-company and inter-platoon matches played. These activities, of course, marked the advent of a spell of brilliant weather. Fortunately, too, there were quite a few streams and lakes available for swimming.

On 26th May Dick Jepson-Turner brought the Battalion Band, under Mr. West, to visit us, having first been to the 8th Battalion. Concerts were given, usually in rural surroundings, in company areas. These were much appreciated, being the first form of local entertainment in the Battalion area. On 28th May an Officers' Band Night was held to which were invited Brigadier Paley, Colonel Robin Hastings, Colonel Charles Liddell and officers of the 8th Rifle Brigade. A very good party ensued and one at which an experiment to make time stand still proved eminently successful!

The Battalion moved on 29th May to the Hademarschen area to take up, as it later proved, its final " stop line " positions of " Peninsula C," to wit, the south bank of the Kiel Canal. Here at last the boundary was clearly defined and presented less difficulty in supervision. One German had enterprisingly built himself a raft and was busily engaged one night in getting himself across the canal in the " I " Company area, only to receive two Sten bullets for his trouble. The recovery of the bodies of several other unsuccessful " crossers " was one of the other uncongenial tasks to be performed.

" A " Company were lucky in having a motor-boat with which to patrol their stretch of canal. The riflemen proved very adaptable and took easily to this new means of transport. No excuse, however, could be found to make the motor-boat a permanent and official addition to the vehicle establishment of the motor battalion.

Keith Egleston (" A " Company) was able to give tea parties in the " Ascot Sunday " style on the canal. The one to which " Riccy " Greville, of the 8th Rifle Brigade, was invited proved most unfortunate in that the arrival of tea coincided with the breaking down of the engine, an enormous cloudburst and the arrival of what appeared to be a huge liner going through the canal.

Divisional Headquarters having come to rest in Itzehoe meant that more films and E.N.S.A. shows were available and we were able to send trucks in each evening to these shows. In addition, we had fairly frequent visits from an Army kinematographic section, who gave film shows in the village hall of Hademarschen. Football (even despite the warm weather) and swimming were still the main forms of recreation. The final of the Battalion Platoon Knock-out Football Competition resulted in " B " Company H.Q. beating H.Q. Company Signals. P.T. was introduced, and one period, on a company basis, had to be incorporated in the day's activities.

The Battalion were invited, in mid-June, to provide a company to set up and run a Brigade rest camp at Glückstadt: this, of course, led to rumour and counter-rumour that the whole Battalion was going as well. Accordingly, on 15th June, " A " Company left Hademarschen to start the " Stag at Ease," as the rest camp was to be called, and the following day reconnaissance parties for the Battalion visited Glückstadt. After many false starts, the remainder of the Battalion did move to Glückstadt on 23rd June, taking over the area of the 1st Royal Tank Regiment. This move coincided with the departure of a portion of " C " Company to VIII Corps Headquarters at Plön, to take over the duties of G.O.C.'s guard for the period of a week.

Once established in Glückstadt it seemed apparent that we were to stay there for some time: indeed, apart from one tentative move to either the Brunsbuttel or Wilster area, nothing was to disturb us. Meanwhile, Major-General L. O. Lyne, C.B., D.S.O., the Divisional Commander, had gone to Berlin to take over his appointment as British Representative on the Allied Military Government Council. He had the 11th Hussars and the 131st Infantry Brigade from the Division as a nucleus of his garrison troops in the British sector, with the armoured and gunner regiments of the Division each doing a turn of duty. The armoured regiments were, by now, being re-equipped with Comet tanks to replace the Cromwell.

With a longish stay in view, a regular pattern was evolved: training programmes, duty company roster to cope with the various guards, including Battalion quarter guard, drill courses for junior N.C.Os. and potential N.C.Os. The Battalion, it should be remembered, although now all in the same town, was not yet centralized; companies still had their own area radiating from Battalion Headquarters. Central messing for the men under company arrangements was commenced, together with Sergeants' Messes, recreation rooms and canteens. A programme of football, cricket, basketball and water polo, to culminate in a Victor Ludorum, was begun, and at the same time training was started for the Athletics Championship to be held on the Regimental Birthday.

During July and August the Battalion entertained, on 25th July, Field-Marshal Sir Henry Maitland Wilson, who was attending the Potsdam Conference, and on 11th August Major-General The Viscount Bridgeman. Eric Sergeant returned to the Battalion to take over Second-in-Command in place of John Witt, who had been posted to the 9th Rifle Brigade.

VJ Day was celebrated quietly as a Battalion holiday. This sudden finish to the war had brought relief to many, not least to those with the symbol " F.E.1 " after their age and service release group number.

The Regimental Birthday was the usual holiday, with a sports meeting in the afternoon and swimming and water polo after tea, and a fun fair running during the tea interval. A concert in the evening was followed by a dance. The weather helped to make the day a great success by producing one fine day in a spell of miserable weather.

" A " Company were the winners of the Sports, with H.Q. Company as runners-up. The final of the Water-Polo Knock-out Competition was played off between very shivering teams from " I " and H.Q. Companies, with " I " Company the eventual winners.

The main topic, with the advent of September, for those who had been with the Battalion since it went to the Middle East in September, 1941, was " Python " and " Lilop." Obviously the majority of those affected were in early age and service release groups as well, so that the Battalion would not enjoy a great deal more of their services.

With this in view, a Battalion College has been formed by Colonel Paddy Boden, under the " headmastership " of Chris Milner, the object being to give those of early release groups and others who wished it an opportunity of brushing up various subjects before their return to civilian life. A general education course was run (history, geography, English and elementary mathematics) as well as other practical subjects, such as woodwork, automobile engineering, electricity, plumbing, book-keeping and accounts.

The normal round of duties during this period was interspersed with various other duties, such as guards on ships passing through the Kiel Canal. One of these ships was seen heading smartly out of the Elbe Estuary, having failed to call at Cuxhaven, and fetched up at a Scottish port. The guard were later proved blameless despite the suspicion of this as a new method of getting a quick week-end leave at home. One party went off to Copenhagen as guards at L. of C. Headquarters, and others to instruct the Danish Army in various subjects. All the Copenhagen parties seemed reluctant to return and were enthusiastic about their self-imposed secondary role of furthering inter-Allied friendship.

Rumours and speculations were rife during early October about the future of the Division and the Battalion. These were finally cleared up when the Divisional Commander addressed the Battalion on 16th October on the current affairs of the Division. The main outcome of this was that only men of Age and Service Group 32 and over were to remain with the Division: anyone in this category who had done more than two and a half years' foreign service on 1st November, 1945, were also ineligible to remain. The Battalion was to draw all available " eligibles " from the 8th Rifle Brigade, who were to receive our " ineligibles." This exercise became known as " Re-sort " and " Re-org," and the remainder of October and November was devoted to it.

1st BATTALION

"C" Company at Nieustadt

1st BATTALION, CHRISTMAS, 1945

During this period Bill Jepson-Turner was posted to the 8th King's Royal Rifle Corps and Dawson Bates took over command of "C" Company. Walter Carpenter, our Medical Officer since Homs, returned from a prolonged "Lilop" to find that he had been posted to the 4th Armoured Brigade. The "rascally medico," as Brigadier Victor Paley was wont to call him, had succeeded in becoming a member of the Rifle Brigade Club.

On 28th November Brigadier Tony Wingfield paid his farewell visit to the Battalion prior to handing over command of the 22nd Armoured Brigade to Brigadier H. Scott, who had been Second-in-Command of the Brigade in Italy.

In December it was confirmed that the naval party which was occupying the nearby barracks with "A" Company were moving out and plans were made for the remainder of the Battalion to move in after Christmas.

Alan Parker ("I" Company) had, during November, injured his back playing Rugby and as a result of this was invalided to England. On 5th December Rodney Russell arrived to command "I" Company. His journey was something of an epic, and signals were received almost hourly in the latter stages. These were mainly misleading and out of date, saying that Major Russell was at "X," R.H.U., when, in fact, he was somewhere entirely different.

December proved to be a month of changes. Major-General L. O. Lyne gave his final address to officers of the Division on the 10th of the month, and a few days later command was assumed by Major-General G. P. B. Roberts, who had commanded the 22nd Armoured Brigade in the desert.

On 12th December Colonel Dick Poole arrived preparatory to taking over command of the Battalion from Colonel Paddy Boden, who was going to the 11th Armoured Division as G.S.O.1. Command, in fact, passed to Colonel Dick Poole on 17th December.

Christmas, 1945, was noteworthy in that it was the first one for over four years that the men were able, as companies, to sit down to Christmas dinner together. The usual football match between Officers and Sergeants was played, with the result, as always, wrapt in mystery. The Sergeants, led by R.S.M. Stacey and Sergt. Brown, D.C.M. ("C" Company), who looked very seductive "glamour girls," claimed a win. "B" Company's Sergeants' arrival was most spectacular, in the "glee boys'" style, in a farm cart, complete with piano and barrel of beer. They dispensed both beer and songs during the game. Other entertainments in the form of concerts and dances were given. " B " Company also put on an excellent production of " Cinderella," which was brought very much up to date. Norman Griffiths (" B " Company), having gone home on " Python," was unfortunate in missing the impression of him given by Rfn. Lucas.

The move into the barracks to join " A " Company, each company having a given day to move, and the settling in, brought us to the end of 1945. The period between VE Day and the New Year had been one of change-over from war time to peace time. The transition, despite difficulties as to personnel, had been effected comparatively smoothly and the New Year was started with the Battalion almost completely re-formed.

Most of the men who had been with the Battalion at the end of the war were now awaiting demobilization either with the 8th Rifle Brigade or a home establishment in England. Those who had been exchanged between the 1st Rifle Brigade and the 8th Rifle Brigade and vice versa were able, by mutual arrangement, to revisit their old battalions weekly, and many football matches between battalions and companies were played and one found it difficult to realize that the old faces now playing for the 8th Rifle Brigade were not still 1st Rifle Brigade.

FRENCHMEN AND BELGIANS WITH THE 1st BATTALION

[*Both Cope's History of the Regiment and Costello's " Adventures of a Soldier" record how a number of Spaniards were enlisted into the Regiment in 1813 and how they " made excellent Riflemen and were distinguished for their bravery." As will be seen from the following account from the 1st Battalion, history has once more repeated itself with Frenchmen and Belgians instead of Spaniards*]

FOR nearly ten months volunteers from France and Belgium served with the 1st Battalion. The majority of them joined in early September at Mazingarbe, a mining village between Bethune and Lens, when the Battalion, less " A " Company, together with the 1st Royal Tanks, was grounded for a few days after its fighting round Lillers and Bethune, whilst all the available petrol went to part of the rest of the Division in its dash to Ghent. They came at a time when the Battalion was under strength and so were particularly welcome, and many close friendships were soon made with the Riflemen. It is probable that the Battalion was one of the very rare units of the Second Army who had an appreciable number of men of another nation serving in their ranks.

The first Frenchman to join was Yves Dumy, who was recruited by Charles Steer, then commanding a motor platoon in " I " Company. He was immediately nicknamed " Ifs and Buts " by the Riflemen. Noel Paniez was, perhaps inevitably, called "Christmas Basket," which gave pleasure to all. By 7th September the numbers had risen to seventeen, divided more or less evenly between " C " and " I " Companies, and scattered among the various platoons and sections, where their local knowledge of languages was found to be very useful. Practically none of them spoke any English at all. A few days later we were joined by a Belgian, Dennis Vanoystaeyen, who spoke perfect English and whose brother also came in November.

At first when they joined they wore rather nondescript uniform, composed usually of a battle-dress blouse and civilian trousers with a pair of German jackboots to complete the picture. Alan Parker, the Adjutant, was rather taken aback when inspecting some men one day to find one of the parade wearing check trousers. It was a very broad check and was visible a good way off. " Frenchman," whispered the R.S.M. before the Adjutant could place the man in durance vile. Later, however, they were all issued with Army kit and went about looking extremely smart, most of them with a large " France " written on their shoulders for all to see.

Giving them leave to go home was quite easy and they seemed never to have any trouble lorry-hopping to their destination, nor in getting back to us, even though we had moved, as on one occasion, seventy miles across the front, even though they spoke little or no English and in spite of the uncertainty and erratic way of their travelling when we were on the Dutch-German border. They always seemed to get back about the right time, usually loaded with parcels of cakes and presents for their friends.

Their pay was a very much more difficult matter. The British Treasury was obviously not going to take on any extra commitments if it could be avoided, and for a long time they existed with the support of company funds and the P.R.I.; their brother-Riflemen always kept them supplied with cigarettes. After more than two months of haggling and rude letters, and after several visits from the French Army Liaison Staff, who naturally pointed out how much easier it would be if they transferred across to the French Army, it was finally possible to get them paid by the French authorities on French Army rates of pay, which worked out almost the same as ours. Moreover, their time with us was allowed to count as part of their French Army service.

We were all very sad when two of their number were killed in action. They also had their share of wounded, and it is pleasant to hear that they are all making a good recovery. Gilbert Cleret was even evacuated to England, which must have made hay with the hospital records.

They fought very well, and very rapidly fell into our way of doing things, and two of them were awarded the Croix de Guerre on the report of them sent to the French Army authorities by the Commanding Officer.

All these men have gone now, some to their homes and some to the French Army, where we hope they will earn added distinction, and, in particular, that Negroni will speedily realize his ambition to become an officer. We will not easily forget them. They showed the spirit of resistance at its best.

THE APENNINES TO THE ALPS, 1945
(THE 2ND BATTALION)

By Major A. J. Wilson, M.C.

MARCH, 1945, found the Battalion reorganizing and training at Cattolica on the Adriatic coast. Life was on a suburban and semi-detached basis in groups of villas by the sea, but it was comfortable none the less and nice to be cheek-by-jowl for a change with the other battalions of the Brigade. Everybody worked hard in lovely weather, and the thunder of exploding 2-inch mortar bombs seemed never to cease. Only Worsley, wrestling with war establishments and scales of transport, must occasionally have longed to exchange the warlike atmosphere of a " rest period " for the comparative calm of the battlefield.

Once again all the preliminaries to a battle took place—each company commander produced as if by magic the names of countless people who were excellent soldiers but perhaps not quite suitable for whatever they were doing, and the Colonel, who by now knew us all only too well, produced his invariable series of Solomon-like judgments to keep everybody happy. We were delighted during this period to welcome Palmer as Second-in-Command, and some of us felt that we really knew what we were fighting for, when it was discovered that twenty-four hours before arriving in Cattolica he had been having supper in the Berkeley.

We moved to a concentration area on 8th April, greatly encouraged by the fact that the Battalion was to operate with the Lothian and Border Horse, in whose ability and gallantry we had learned to have the greatest confidence. This feeling of confidence was greatly increased by the start of the battle on the Senio, which was heralded by an air bombardment and a barrage of greater intensity than those at Cassino. Even Mr. Crocker, the R.S.M., was impressed. News came through of encouraging advances by the infantry divisions, and Cowan, the Intelligence Officer, reported daily that formation after formation of the enemy opposed to us had been eliminated. But still the 6th British Armoured Division was not employed. We moved farther forward to a concentration area close behind the Senio, and some of us, whose reading of the map was less good than our reading of the battle, even established a bridgehead over the river. " B " Company officers and N.C.Os., led by their commander and his walking-stick, held a T.E.W.T. on the banks of the river itself, while Lonsdale's force, more camouflaged than others, brought back memories of the Liri Valley with the reappearance of their camouflage smocks. Eventually, however, the gap, for which the Army Commander had been so patiently waiting, was seen to be finally yawning in front of the V Corps at Argenta. The 6th British Armoured Division would pass through and destroy the enemy south of the Po crossings.

The Battalion moved forward, confident and not a little excited, on 19th April to help deliver the knock-out blow. " A " and " B " Companies, each under command of the corresponding squadron of the Lothians, were to attempt to secure a crossing of the Po di Primaro south of the little village of St. Nicolo Ferrarese. For the first time in Italy squadrons and companies manœuvred in the North African manner, relatively unfettered by the going. Unhappy Germans waved white flags or were engaged by the guns and Brownings of the Lothians' tanks. Towards nightfall and about a mile and a half short of the obstacle resistance stiffened, " B " Squadron of the Lothians losing four tanks to a well-sited anti-tank gun. Up came the motor companies to protect the regimental " laager " and strong fighting patrols from " A " and " B " Companies were soon going forward. Parker (" B " Company) reached the river, but found it strongly held by a company of infantry thickened up by a troop of tanks. Our artillery harassed the bridges in an unsuccessful attempt to prevent the enemy from blowing them, but in vain.

It was accordingly decided that " A " Company with " A " Squadron should secure the village of St. Nicolo, after which " B " Company and " B " Squadron should pass through and exploit the bridgehead which had been secured by " A " Company. Lonsdale's operations were effected with success, and the village was cleared in fine style, despite considerable shelling and the remarkable antics of a German colour-sergeant, who attempted to escape the vigilant " A " Company Bren gunners by driving off in a sepoy's cart. " B " Squadron passed through and made some progress on the far side of the

Po di Primaro against stiff opposition and very considerable shelling. This phase was notable for a special action by Mitchell's platoon of " B " Company, who indicated targets to the tanks with rather more than exercise precision. Towards nightfall " B " Squadron lost further tanks, and it was decided to hold on to the bridgehead for the night and bring " C " Company up into the village to join " A " Company. A counter-attack seemed likely that night, but never materialized.

Next morning brought the news of a successful advance by the remainder of the Division on the left flank, and No. 2 Lothians Regimental Group was accordingly ordered, somewhat to its chagrin, to hand over its hard-won gains to the 8th Indian Division and return to the main body of the Division. If decisive success had not been obtained at St. Nicolo, it is perhaps justifiable to maintain that we had contributed greatly to successes elsewhere by drawing much of the enemy armour and artillery away from the 16th and 17th Lancers, whose advance farther south we were now to exploit. For these efforts during the St. Nicolo operations Mitchell (" B " Company) was awarded the M.C., and Cpls. Hegarty (" A " Company) and Clay (" B " Company) the M.M. No praise can be too high for the Lothians during these difficult operations. " B " Squadron in particular bore considerable tank losses with fortitude and yet continued aggressive and anxious to engage the enemy.

The remainder of the 21st was spent in regrouping and quick reorganization before starting at first light on the 22nd to move up behind the other armoured regiments. As we moved up we saw encouraging evidence of German disorganization in the shape of abandoned guns and other material, while prisoners escorted by grinning riflemen of the other battalions became more frequent. At each successive conference the intention paragraph of the Colonel's orders became more optimistic, and even the professional cynics and pessimists, like the Quartermaster, caught something of the prevailing enthusiasm. Final orders were for No. 2 Lothians Group to secure the bridge over the Panaro at Bondeno, about four miles south of the River Po itself, thus sealing one of the few exits of the rapidly closing trap between the Po and the Apennines. The brunt of this operation in the early stages was borne by " C " Company and " C " Squadron, who advanced first through close country against determined opposition from two Mark VI tanks and the inevitable Wagnerian characters armed with bazookas. " C " Squadron lost eleven tanks, but succeeded in getting one tank over the bridge before it was blown up by its defending Germans. " A " Company meanwhile had cleared a village east of Bondeno against lighter opposition, while " B " Company in a rival effort to reach the Bondeno bridge before " C " Company had some spirited entertainment shooting up rapidly disappearing Germans on a conveniently placed embankment.

The Colonel decided to hold the Bondeno bridge by means of three company groups, each supported by tanks, in an effort to prevent any further German traffic escaping north over the Panaro. This regrouping was achieved after some skilful motoring in the dark by about midnight on 22nd/23rd April, and the Battalion settled down to await developments.

On Lonsdale's " A " Company front these materialized in the shape of a Mark IV tank, an 88-mm. gun and some infantry at 0400 hrs. The Mark IV was destroyed after a splendid example of fire discipline in the best tiger-hunting tradition by Goodrich of the Lothians. Our own 6-pdrs. also claimed a hit. The infantry, saluted by a *feu de joie* from everybody, vanished into the mist. On " B " Company's front near the Bondeno bridge itself the opposition advanced in style in broad daylight to dig themselves in within 100 yards of our platoons, who were in houses on the other side of the river. Stewart-Wilson, firing his 3-inch mortars at a range of 250 yards with a quarter charge, helped " B " Company and the snipers to disillusion the enemy, who after an uncomfortable two hours retired in some disorder. " C " Company's efforts were restricted to the lucrative occupation of shooting up enemy lorries who were routed by their provost with monotonous regularity in the direction of the cavalier-like figure of Fairweather.

During the late morning the Lothians sallied forth from the Bondeno perimeter and reached the Po itself, refuelling on its banks and in full view of the enemy with their customary *sang froid*. Altogether, it was a good day, marred only the next night by the news that Palmer had been unluckily wounded by a shell from an enemy S.P. gun which crossed the Po and fired about fifty shells at scattered targets in the Battalion area.

On the 24th we were relieved by the New Zealanders and retired four or five miles into harbour to get some much-needed sleep. Alas !

it was to mark the end of our extremely pleasant and fruitful association with the Lothians, for orders came through that we were to cross the Po by the New Zealand Division bridge on the 26th and operate on their right flank up to the Adige in a more or less independent role. It is quite impossible to state in words the sum of our debt to the Lothians, who had fought magnificently and with outstanding skill and dash. To their Colonel's quick planning and thinking, and to the brilliant execution of his plans by the whole regiment, can be attributed a tremendous amount of the success achieved by the regimental group.

Over the River Po we went on the 27th, crossing by pontoon bridge, and there followed a series of quick moves to concentration areas of one sort or another before we received final orders regarding our role of protecting the flank of the New Zealand Division as they formed up to cross the Adige. Our task was to move forward on their right and, if possible, to reach the Adige itself at Lusia. It was hoped that this move would cut off a further number of Germans between the Rivers Po and Adige. After " A " Company had cleared Saguedo " B " Company moved forward five miles on foot in darkness to Cavanazza, where a sharp battle took place and Mitchell's platoon were heavily counter-attacked and for a time isolated by about seventy enemy. They contrived to hold out until first light, when a successful attack by the remainder of " B " Company, well supported by a troop of tanks from the 7th Hussars and Stewart-Wilson's invaluable mortars, cleared the village. Several unskilful and not very determined attempts by the enemy to infiltrate back into the village were repulsed with the aid of a Wasp flame-thrower, and later that afternoon the Battalion were relieved by the 1st Welch Regiment.

Back in harbour we found Martin waiting to join us as Second-in-Command, and after an all-too-short night's rest we moved forward over the Adige to continue our role of right-flank protection to the New Zealanders. By now events were moving quickly and the 29th was a day of fast motoring and surrendering Germans. Monselice, about fifteen miles south of Padua, was entered in triumph, a New Zealand tank with a bulldozer leading the advance, while immediately behind followed a section of the 2nd Rifle Brigade carriers and then the bulldog figure of General Freyberg in his jeep. The Battalion followed up the Germans for three or four miles beyond the town, but were then called off the chase, not altogether to our sorrow, for all companies were by now extremely tired and in need of a night's rest.

The night of 30th April/1st May found the Battalion in harbour still near Monselice, and supremely confident in the fact that no move was likely for at least two days. It caused little surprise, therefore, to everybody that we were on the road at 0200 hrs. bound for Padua, Treviso and all stations north. It speaks well for the standard of training of the 61st Brigade that the whole Brigade column, despite having received no warning of the impending move, was able to be on the road in the right order and moving at the correct speed and density within an hour of getting its orders.

A night of alarms and excursions followed, and many officers displayed a perhaps natural lack of knowledge of the intimate geography of Padua—even the resourceful Worsley on the Battalion net could offer only the coldest of comfort in the shape of an instruction to " follow the others "! However, the patron saint of Rifle Brigade motoring, as so often in the past, somehow ensured that at first light everybody was on the right road and going along happily behind the 27th Lancers, who reached Treviso without opposition.

Just north of Treviso some of us were fortunate enough to catch an action picture of the 7th Rifle Brigade Headquarters, led by their Colonel, advancing to the attack. The speed at which Colonel Douglas's half-track was moving gave us a good idea of the tempo at which operations were now proceeding. Our part in them on the night of 1st/2nd May was unspectacular, though Fairweather had occasion to use his moustache and diplomatic talents in the village of Coregliano, but on 2nd May a rapid advance by " A " Company and " C " Squadron of the 27th Lancers towards Belluno led to the surrender of the German 65th Infantry Division, complete with commander, to the Battalion.

The next day, 3rd May, further operations by " A " Company and a successful diplomatic mission by the Colonel to the opposing Corps headquarters were followed by the surrender of a further 6,000 of the enemy, including the complete divisional artillery of the 715th Infantry Division, who had sharpened us to some purpose in the past winter at Fontanelice. The scene as the mass surrender took place was incredible and almost embarrassing. A steady stream of men, armoured cars and field artillery drove towards us, and we felt extremely thin on the ground. At this stage we finally received confirmation of the news that Vichtinghoff had surrendered his Army Group to Field-Marshal Alexander at Caserta, which was welcome news, though for the next five days or so it was not greatly to affect the role of the Battalion.

On 4th May, after an overnight move to an area west of Udine, the Battalion was ordered to make for Austria at full speed by way of the Isonzo Valley and the Predil Pass. Force was not to be used except in self-defence, but every effort was to be made to get the road opened as soon as possible. " B " Company moved first, and spent the night with the 1st Welch Regiment at Plezzo, where they were joined the next day by the rest of the Battalion.

The next few days were spent in patrolling, bridge building and, above all, in parleying. The Colonel, accompanied by a company commander and the R.S.M., visited the opposing divisional headquarters in the best Balkan tradition of blindfolded envoys, while the Germans employed a circus of negotiators to visit Battalion Headquarters at Mittle Brett. This was led by a parachutist, who might well have been Rex Harrison imitating a Nazi. Martin's fluent German was much in demand, while Mr. Crocker became an expert at organizing the reception of envoys. Mention should also be made of the efforts of Parker, who walked every inch of the way from Plezzo to Cave del Predil (sixteen miles and up 4,000 feet) in his capacity as advanced director of parleys, and of Pontifex, who took the Scout Platoon on an effort to find a rival way into Austria by way of Yugoslavia, only to find their way blocked by four feet of snow.

Finally, agreement was reached and one of the company commanders who had gone forward on foot to Tarvisio returned with the Commander of the German 97th Corps, who was empowered to arrange for the final surrender of the whole of Army Group S.E.

The Battalion moved forward for the night of 7th/8th May to Tarvisio, and on 8th May entered Austria, the Scout Platoon being the first troops of the Eighth Army to cross the frontiers of the Greater German Reich. The war in Europe, and for many of us our Odyssey, was over.

7TH BATTALION LETTER
ITALY—AUSTRIA—EGYPT: MAY, 1944, TO SEPTEMBER, 1945

By Lieut.-Colonel V. Street, D.S.O., O.B.E., M.C., and
Major T. L. Dewhurst, M.C.

Arrival in Italy

Setting sail from Alexandria in two convoys, the Battalion landed in Italy at the beginning of May, and concentrated a few miles north of Taranto. Almost immediately the Battalion was ordered into the line some fifteen miles east of Mt. Cassino, so, saying farewell to our good friends the 9th Armoured Brigade, with whom we had trained for so long, we moved off into the battle area.

We came under command of the 2nd Independent Parachute Brigade, who were holding a mountain line whilst the bulk of the Eighth Army regrouped for the coming battles for Cassino and the Hitler Line. Three or four days were spent at Filignano reconnoitring the ground we were to take over and learning the art of loading mules. While at Filignano General Freyberg, our Divisional Commander at the time, paid the Battalion a visit.

Formation of the 61st Brigade

On the evening of 18th May, just as we were preparing to move into the line, the whole operation was cancelled and we moved back to concentrate with the 9th Armoured Brigade again ready to reinforce the major attack which had developed two days earlier against Cassino. This plan, too, was changed a few days later, and we moved to Villa Volturno, just north of Capua. Here we had the task of acting as the nucleus around which the 61st Infantry Brigade formed. Brigadier Gore, who was to command the Brigade, had not yet arrived, so the task of collecting together the Brigade Staff and ancillary units fell to the Commanding Officer, Colonel Darling.

At this time the Battalion was reorganized slightly. Motor companies went on to an R.A.S.C. 3-tonner basis. " D " Company was re-formed as a motor company under Bill Becher, who shortly afterwards went home, his place being taken by Norman Odgers. One hundred Ulster Riflemen from a disbanded A.A. regiment arrived as reinforcements.

THE ADVANCE UP ITALY

On 29th May the Battalion set off, following the 2nd Rifle Brigade, to join up with the 10th Rifle Brigade, who were awaiting our arrival with the remainder of the 6th Armoured Division near Aquino. Here Hugh Meldrum arrived as Second-in-Command.

At Alatri we went into action again for the first time for just over a year—we were to remain in action with hardly a break for more than twelve months and until the end of the war. With " A " Company leading under Peter Shepherd-Cross, supported by a squadron of the 17th/21st Lancers from the 26th Armoured Brigade, we advanced through Alatri against a rearguard of scattered infantry and a few guns. Opposition was light, and four guns and some forty prisoners were taken. We had few casualties, but unfortunately among them were Larry Lowrison and Scruffy Downing.

Thereafter the Division was given the task of protecting the right flank of the main Eighth Army thrust towards Rome. It was at this time that we ran into unexpected trouble near Cantelupo. While preparing to move through the 1st Guards Brigade, the Battalion leaguer was subjected to intense and accurate shelling from 88-mm. and 75-mm. guns. We had a number of casualties, including Cpl. Cann—the Battalion photographer, an original member of the Battalion—and Sergt. Conus, our Intelligence Sergeant, killed, while Peter Shepherd-Cross and the Signal Officer, Sandy Brigstocke, were wounded. Dick Adams took over " A " Company and Tom Liddell came a few days later from the 2nd Rifle Brigade to take over Signal Officer.

And so the chase continued. Leaving Rome, to our regret, ten miles to our left flank, we advanced, leaving the plain behind, up the west bank of the Tiber into hilly country. Our first serious obstacle was a demolition a mile short of Narni. With herculean efforts and the aid of our R.H.A. Sherman O.P., the majority of our vehicles were hauled across and the Battalion moved in to liberate the first town which looked worthy of liberation. From here " B " Company, under Charles Mott-Radcliffe, was sent forward with all haste to secure the bridges at Terni, but he was unfortunately just too late to prevent their demolition. In the meantime, " A " and " C " Companies were disposed on the heights overlooking the town, while Adjutant Tim Dewhurst and Intelligence Officer Peter Bowring received an address of welcome from the inebriated leader of the local partisans.

At Narni we paused for a few days while the Sappers bridged the demolition with a Bailey, later to be called (after the C.O.) "Bombhead R.B." From there we were directed to Todi and so on towards Perugia, where the 1st Guards Brigade were given the task of clearing the town with the 2nd Rifle Brigade established on the hills overlooking the Trasimene—Arezzo road. The Battalion was given the task of clearing Mt. Melba, an important feature dominating the countryside.

In pouring rain at 2200 hrs. we set out on a three-mile approach march to Mt. Melba. " A " Company took the first objective without opposition. " B " Company then pushed on to clear some houses half-way up the feature, taking some prisoners in doing so. " C " and " D " Companies then fought their way over the most difficult ground to the top and by dawn were established there. " A " Company followed up and relieved " D " Company. It was an unpleasant position to hold and well registered by the enemy. It was not long before the first counter-attack came in on " C " Company and was repulsed, and two further counter-attacks in considerable strength developed against " C " Company during the day, but were fought off, heavy casualties being inflicted. In one of these attacks the enemy penetrated as far as Company Headquarters, and were beaten off by Company Commander Larry Fyffe personally. He was subsequently awarded a bar to his M.C.

Intense and accurate mortar and shell fire took a heavy toll, particularly amongst officers, as did the many mines which were scattered about. Johnnie Persse, Cripps, Whitehead and Bob Wright were all killed. Many casualties were saved by Geoffrey Hirst, our Medical Officer, who was later awarded the M.C.

Two days later the C.O., while out with a reconnaissance party from the Guards to prepare a clearing-up operation, was hit in the shoulder by a large shell splinter. To those of the Battalion who had seen Colonel Darling in the desert at El Hamma, at Argoub el Megas, and leading the Battalion up Italy, he seemed to bear a charmed life and we had come to believe that nothing could touch him. As someone later remarked, it was a great day for the Germans, for at last

TOSSIGNANO

7th BATTALION, 1945

Major T. L. Dewhurst, M.C.   Lt.-Col. D. L. Darling, D.S.O., M.C.   Capt. D. A. McI. Kemp.

after five years of war they had produced a weapon that would penetrate Darling! Further trouble was to follow, for Norman Odgers and his C.S.M., Lewis, were both seriously wounded.

Hugh Meldrum took over the Battalion temporarily, and owing to casualties "D" Company was once more reorganized as a support company. A few days later Dick Fyffe, who had been commanding a battalion of the Royal West Kents, came to command the Battalion.

With the enemy pulling back again, the situation had become more stabilized and life was peaceful, apart from the odd shell and butterfly bombing raids at night. Soon the chase was resumed into the mountains approaching the Gothic Line.

Acting as flank protection of the infantry division advancing on our left, the 6th Armoured Division advanced through Castiglione del Lago and Cortona towards Arezzo. The approaches to this town were found to be strongly defended, and on 2nd July we successfully attacked the dominating feature of Mt. Maggio, but unfortunately Harry Whiter was killed and Maurice Ostime wounded.

A strong counter-attack during the day was held, but during the following night, which was particularly dark, the enemy succeeded in infiltrating into some of our forward positions and forced "A" and "C" Companies to pull back in order to avoid being overrun. After two hours of confused fighting in the dark the situation was stabilized. At dawn a number of men were found to be missing, some of whom were known to have been wounded. Stretcher-bearers were therefore sent out in pairs under the Red Cross flag and succeeded in accounting for all but two. One pair of stretcher-bearers walked into a German Spandau post, where after exchanging cigarettes they were told that the missing two had been taken prisoner the night before. Surprisingly enough, the Germans then allowed the two stretcher-bearers to return to our lines.

Soon after this the Battalion was relieved, and the Guards Brigade put in an attack, clearing the two ridges in front of Arezzo. We then successfully seized the bridge north-west of the town and gained the far bank of the Arno. This crossing was not, however, held as meanwhile the 26th Armoured Brigade had found a crossing near Laterina which was easier to exploit.

The chase continued through close and difficult country short of Faella, where the enemy made a short stand. In the course of the fighting here Charles Callistan, who had come from the 2nd Rifle Brigade, was killed. Eventually the enemy was forced back and the Battalion entered Faella.

In Faella we rested for some days—our first rest since the advance had started at the beginning of May. It was a small and clean little village, and the hospitality of its inhabitants was overwhelming. For months afterwards any Rifleman from the Battalion who was in the neighbourhood would look in on the village and would be sure of a warm welcome.

About this time Charles Mott-Radcliffe left to take up his duties as the Honourable and Gallant Member for Windsor, his place as Company Commander of " B " Company being temporarily taken by Bill Brownlow and later by Dick Adams. Ted Eeles had succeeded Norman Odgers in " C " Company, while Peter Shepherd-Cross and John Brooke had " A " and H.Q. Companies respectively.

After a few days in Faella we relieved the 2nd Rifle Brigade, who were holding some hamlets to the north around St. Donato. Here our activity was confined to extensive but extremely successful patrolling. We were fortunate enough to be back resting at Faella once again for the Regimental Birthday, which was the occasion for a great celebration by both Riflemen and civilians, with a dance on the village green, a beauty contest, side-shows and so forth. About this time we bade farewell to the 4th R.H.A., who had supported us so well ever since our first battle in Italy.

By the beginning of September the Battalion was established near Consuma, guarding with the Derby Yeomanry the right flank of the Division. Here Douglas Darling came to command once more, having fully recovered from his wound, and Dick Fyffe left to command the 10th Rifle Brigade. Peter Shepherd-Cross had left a few days before as an instructor to the C.M.T.C., his place as Commander of " A " Company being taken by Tim Dewhurst. Mike Bird had become Adjutant.

We were not long at Consuma before being pulled out and re-directed up Route 67 towards Dicomano and the main defences of the Gothic Line. The weather changed suddenly, torrential rain and storms making the country impassable. Houses for shelter became as important as topographical features in any tactical plan. We relieved the 10th Rifle Brigade near Rufina and set about clearing the area around. This having been done, after a short pause we went through the 10th Rifle Brigade and the 1st Guards Brigade to tackle the great St. Benedetto Pass. It was on this pass that the 6th Armoured Division had been directed in an attempt to link up with the main forces of the Eighth Army driving towards Forli.

The village of St. Benedetto was occupied at the foot of the pass, and " B " Company pushed on up the road until held up by the demolitions. " C " Company was then pushed round the left flank to assault Mt. Freddo, a dominating feature. This they succeeded in doing on a bitterly cold night in a heavy storm. As a result, the head of the pass was cleared and the advance continued down towards Bocconi, where accurate shelling and another blown bridge prevented any further forward movement on that route. " A " Company, with a platoon of " B " Company, supported by a troop of tanks and a Divisional artillery concentration, then did an outflanking movement through the Mt. Freddo positions and cleared the demolition, thus enabling the Engineers to get busy on building a bridge. Just after this was completed and the road opened for a further advance, the Battalion was pulled back to the Dicomano area to rest.

THE WINTER LINE IN ITALY

At the beginning of October the 6th Armoured Division was redirected on Imola, taking over a sector from an American division. It was hoped that the Eighth Army advancing up the coast would shortly reach the town and thus enable the 6th Armoured Division to debouch on to the plain. The main feature of the area taken over by the 6th Armoured Division was a ridge running from the Santerno up to Mt. Taverna and away to Battaglia. The 1st Guards Brigade were on the right, while the 10th Rifle Brigade held the left of this line.

Towards the end of October we moved up into the Divisional sector, Bill Brownlow having just taken over as Adjutant. On 26th October " B " Company pushed forward towards Orsara, a small ruined church on a feature which commanded ground between the 61st Brigade and the 1st Guards Brigade. By nightfall one platoon was astride a small ridge leading up to Orsara, and the following night " A " Company was pushed through with the intention of taking Mt. Taverna, the next dominating feature. Difficult going and a pitch-dark night made the move forward extremely slow, and by dawn only the intermediate objective on the lower slopes of Mt. Taverna was reached. Here the Company dug in preparatory to assault as soon as darkness fell. Accurate and intense mortaring of the Company, which was completely overlooked, caused so many casualties that the attack had to be called off and the Company drawn back.

It was clear that no further advance would be possible until Mt. Penzola, a feature on our left flank which dominated the whole area, had been cleared. The 1st Guards Brigade had been moved round to this flank and prepared to assault the peak. Meanwhile, our activity was confined to aggressive and highly successful patrolling. The Germans on several occasions attempted to retake Orsara, but on each occasion were beaten off with casualties. Monteloro was another of our posts which came in for attention, and one night a strong German fighting patrol attempted to break in, but were severely handled by Ted Eakins and fled, leaving several casualties and weapons behind.

At the beginning of November Hugh Meldrum left to go home, and Vivian Street returned as Second-in-Command after an absence of fifteen months, the greater part of which he had spent in the Balkans. About this time a battalion rest area was established at Passignano and Morocco, south of Florence, off the Siena road. Here we left all our heavy kit, our anti-tank guns and carriers, and sundry other things not required in the line. Every three weeks or so throughout the winter we would be withdrawn back into this area for a week's rest and refit, and we soon came to regard it as our home.

At the end of November just before the Guards' attack on Mt. Penzola was due, Larry Fyffe with " C " Company moved forward into Fontanelice, which was found to be heavily mined and booby-trapped. Penzola was taken a few days later and the whole Battalion moved into the Fontanelice area, forward positions being established along a ridge on the other side of the village. Preparations were then made for the capture of Tossignano, a large village perched on one of the last remaining features before Imola and the open plain. This village appeared to frown down on practically the whole Brigade sector, although Fontanelice itself could not be observed from it.

The Battalion's role in the Tossignano operation was to put in a diversionary attack from the left in order to draw the enemy's attention that way. The 2nd Rifle Brigade was then to put in the main attack from the centre and right. Accordingly, on the night of 12th/13th December "B" Company advanced and occupied the hamlets of Cogalina and Montecchio while " C " Company moved up the road to Borgo Tossignano. This phase was carried out in silence and was completely successful. Bob Earley, with a strong fighting patrol then moved out towards Tossignano. As was expected and intended, this move made the Germans think an attack was coming in on their right flank and down came his D.Fs. Bob Earley, under very intense fire, continued his advance slowly, and at the same time the R.E. started work on the demolitions between Borgo Tossignano and Fontanelice. This again drew considerable fire. This enabled the 2nd Rifle Brigade to form up on our right and assault Tossignano in the early hours of the morning.

The following evening the 10th Rifle Brigade moved up and relieved us and we moved back into our Florence rest area, taking no further part in the battle for Tossignano. Whilst out resting we received the news that the Tossignano operation had failed, and that we were to move back and take the place at an early date. Christmas Day was accordingly celebrated two days early and we moved off immediately afterwards back into the Fontanelice area. Immediately we got back into the line we started planning the assault on Tossignano. The plan was made in the greatest detail, models and photographs were carefully studied, and company commanders flew over the town on reconnaissance flights. We were issued with flamethrowers for the first time. Every contingency was catered for and by 28th December we were ready and confident that we should be successful. On that day the operation was postponed for a week; later it was postponed a further few days, and finally called off altogether, as it was decided that the Eighth Army on our right would not be able to carry out an offensive for some three months or more owing to a shortage of shells, and the Tossignano operation had therefore lost its point. Although it was a relief to us that we were not required to undertake this operation which would have undoubtedly involved heavy casualties, we all felt some disappointment that we were not to have the opportunity to avenge the 2nd Rifle Brigade.

With the attack on Tossignano definitely called off, we settled down to three more months of holding our winter line. Snow had come at the end of December, and this reduced our activity to patrolling and ambushes. Bill Raynor and Oliver Montgomery both gained the Military Cross for their work on these patrols during the winter. Regular periods resting back in our Florence rest area relieved the monotony of our life. We shall all remember those long drives back over the pass along appalling roads through snow and ice, but they were well worth while even though our period out of the line was never more than a few days. The Regiment's villa in Florence became a memorable institution. Here an officer could for four or five days live in pre-war comfort in the most delightful surroundings, waited on hand and foot. There is no doubt that we all owe Ted Voules a debt of gratitude for all he did to make that villa the outstanding success that it was.

At the end of February the Brigade was relieved by the Italian Folgore Group and we moved back into our Florence rest area to sort ourselves out prior to moving over to the Adriatic coast. It is noteworthy that during the whole of the winter while holding the winter line the Battalion did not lose a single prisoner either out on patrol or to an enemy raiding party, in spite of frequent and determined efforts on the latter's part to obtain one.

On 6th March, while in our rest area, Vivian Street was married in Florence. The wedding and the dance to celebrate the occasion on the night before were attended by nearly every officer in the Brigade.

From the Florence area we moved over to Cattolica, a little fishing village on the Adriatic, where we settled down to a few weeks' intensive training for the final battle. As a result of the amalgamation of the 2nd and 10th Rifle Brigade, we received a number of much-needed reinforcements. Geoffrey Meyrick, Harry Huntsman and Robin Hone joined us from the 2nd Rifle Brigade. Peter Shepherd-Cross returned and took over " C " Company from Larry Fyffe, who took his place at the C.M.T.C. A feature of our stay at Cattolica was the sailing races, which we organized in fishing-boats on Saturday and Sunday afternoons and which were enjoyed by officers and riflemen alike. Before we left Cattolica the Eighth Army Commander, General McCreery, paid us a visit.

The Spring Offensive in Italy

Early in April, as the final offensive opened, we moved into the Divisional concentration area near Forlimpopoli. Here the Division was in Army reserve waiting for the opportunity to break through on either of the attacking Corps' fronts. After one change of leaguer area, the Division was finally launched through the Argenta Gap on 18th April and directed on the Po west of Ferrara. We were grouped with the 17th/21st Lancers in Divisional reserve and so did not move on the first day of the break-through. The second day we moved up on the left of the other two groups who had been held up, and we advanced with our left flank on the Reno.

" C " Company had set off first with the 17th/21st Lancers, travelling on the tanks of the latter's reserve squadron. By the evening Segni had been reached, and owing to an impassable ditch and strong anti-tank defence no further advance was possible that night. To assist the 17th/21st Lancers forward, " A " Company was therefore moved up early next morning, travelling on two Arks, carriers and M.10's, for the nature of the country and the many enemy snipers left behind made forward movement of " soft " wheeled vehicles impossible at that time. In the late afternoon, after the remainder of the Battalion had moved to within a mile or so of Segni, the 17th/21st Lancers, with " A " and " C " Companies, attacked and with Sapper assistance crossed the anti-tank obstacle and got through the narrow gap into open country beyond. This action at Segni was the decisive factor on the 6th Armoured Division's front, for the whole Division was quickly passed through the gap the 17th/21st Lancers and ourselves had made, and broke through into the enemy rear.

After the Segni obstacle had been successfully overcome, the 17th/21st Lancers headed as fast as possible for Poggio Renatico, followed by " A " Company travelling on every available carrier. After various skirmishes *en route*, Poggio Renatico was reached as darkness fell and was found to be held. It was clear, however, that the enemy was in confusion, for numbers of stragglers, vehicles and horses were rounded up as the town was approached. It was too dark to attempt to clear the town, so the group stopped on the outskirts, blocking the exits to south and east.

At dawn the following day " A " Company started to clear the town, and after a few hours had successfully overcome all opposition, taking a considerable number of prisoners and capturing much equipment and several vehicles. This operation was not accomplished without " A " Company suffering several casualties. For his part in this and the operations of the previous few days, Tim Dewhurst, who commanded " A " Company, was awarded the Military Cross.

" B " Company moved up into Poggio Renatico that night, and in the early hours of the morning one of our patrols contacted the New Zealanders advancing from the south to the Reno.

The next morning we were relieved and set off again with the 17th/21st Lancers to St. Agostino. Not far from here contact was made with tanks of an American armoured division advancing from the south, which made it clear that enemy resistance south of the Po was now virtually at an end. We then moved into an area about ten miles south of Ferrara, where we sorted ourselves out ready for the move forward over the Po.

After a two-day rest we found ourselves moving again at short notice, for the Guards Brigade and the New Zealanders had crossed the Po almost unopposed and had advanced up to the Adige, again almost unopposed. We moved hard after them, crossed the Adige and halted at Casa Odo between the Adige and Padua, against which the New Zealanders, with General Freyberg in the lead, were advancing with all speed.

After one night at Caso Odo news came through that the pursuit would be taken up by other formations and that the 6th Armoured Division would move north no farther. For us it seemed, therefore, the war was over and we started settling down for a prolonged stay. Our rest was, however, short-lived, for that very night we were ordered to move as fast as possible on Udine with the 27th Lancers. So began the last phase of the pursuit which carried us with hardly a pause into Austria.

Passing through Padua at dead of night, we made for Treviso, where contact was made with an American combat force which had come in from the left flank. Pushing on, we made for the Piave, only to find the bridges completely destroyed and no possible way round. At this time we were leading the Eighth Army in their advance on Austria, and it seemed for a few minutes that these demolitions would deprive us of our hard-won position and enable some other unit far behind to draw ahead by making use of the more northerly route,

[*Official War Office Photo*]

LIEUT.-GENERAL SIR RICHARD L. McCREERY, K.C.B., K.B.E., D.S.O., M.C., AND GENERAL MARK W. CLARK

with a Guard of Honour provided by 7th Bn. The Rifle Brigade at Klagenfurt, June, 1945

whose bridges were believed to be intact. The Colonel was not to be outdone so easily, so, waving on the American combat team who had been jostling us for the lead for the past half an hour, we turned about and flew with all speed back to Treviso and thence back on to the northerly route before anyone had realized what had happened.

With a squadron of the 27th Lancers we swept on over the Piave and headed for the next great river, the Tagliamento. Our advance had now become a triumphal procession, for every man, woman and child in the villages and hamlets we passed through lined our way, cheering and singing and showering us with flowers. As each new village was passed the church bells rang out to warn the next one of our approach. And thus on we went in perfect spring weather with a feeling of victory in the air.

Just short of St. Vito, near the Tagliamento, once more we contacted the scattered remnants of the German Army. Darkness was falling, so no action was possible, but at dawn we pursued them past St. Vito, and in a short skirmish on the Tagliamento we captured several hundreds of prisoners and a number of tanks.

By this time we were many miles ahead of our nearest rivals, although we had news of the New Zealanders speeding along the coast heading for Trieste. We had lost all contact with Division and Brigade, so there was nothing for it but to push on into Udine. Using the causeway, we crossed the Tagliamento and sailed down the highway into Udine at a steady 40 m.p.h. The scene as we arrived in this great town cannot adequately be described in words. Some 20,000 people had gathered to welcome us with cheers and flowers and wine. In addition, several hundred partisans armed to the teeth saluted our entry with repeated volleys from their weapons. Slowly we made our way through the dense and clamorous crowds and gained the farther exits of the town, establishing blocks to the north, east and south.

Shortly after our arrival in Udine contact was made with a small party of German tanks to the north of the town. These appeared to wish to surrender, but when James Keith moved forward on foot to meet the leading tank commander, a German officer in the tank shot and seriously wounded him with a pistol. A general skirmish then ensued, during which several Riflemen were wounded, one of whom died later. Geoffrey Merrick soon afterwards brought his anti-tank guns into action and knocked out one tank, the remainder having disappeared in the failing light. It was not, however, until the following day that James Keith and his party were recaptured. This was to be the last of many tanks knocked out by the Battalion during the war.

Our stay in Udine was short-lived, for twenty-four hours later found us heading east again to stop Chetnik and Tito forces from further fighting and at the same time to prevent, by peaceful persuasion, Tito's men from advancing west of Goriza, which they had already occupied. Contact was made with the Chetniks at Cormons and they soon agreed that the Chetnik forces of some twenty thousand would withdraw through us into a concentration area near Palmanova. As was expected, it was not possible to obtain the agreement of the Tito forces not to advance farther west, and as we were not allowed to use force the only course open to us was to physically block the roads and thus delay their forward movement while the Chetnik forces pulled back behind us. This we were successful in doing, and Tito's forces reached Cormons only a few minutes after the last Chetniks had been evacuated.

The 1st Guards Brigade then relieved us at Cormons and this enabled us to move back to Udine and north up towards the Tarvisio Pass. The 2nd Rifle Brigade and the 1st King's Royal Rifle Corps were advancing up the two roads to Tarvisio on the right and left respectively. We followed behind the 1st King's Royal Rifle Corps, who, like the 2nd Rifle Brigade, were being repeatedly held up by demolitions.

VE Day found us at Chiusaforte and soon after midnight we moved through the 1st King's Royal Rifle Corps and up into Tarvisio preparatory to crossing the frontier into Austria soon after dawn. We breakfasted that morning at the top of the pass and then moved forward to the frontier. At about 8 a.m. the German commander surrendered the frontier to the Divisional Commander, the frontier gate went up, and the Battalion, with two squadrons of the 27th Lancers, moved forward into Austria at the head of the 6th Armoured Division and the Eighth Army.

The Battalion was directed on Klagenfurt, where we had orders to secure all public buildings and utilities before the arrival of Tito's forces from the south. Through lovely country we sped past Villach and on into Klagenfurt, being greeted as we went by several thousand released prisoners of war and crowds of apparently friendly Austrians.

The Occupation of Austria

By midday Battalion Headquarters was established in the old Nazi Party headquarters in Klagenfurt, and guards were placed on all public utilities and all roads into the town blocked. Not long afterwards Tito's forces started arriving on the outskirts of the town, their intention being to set up a government in Klagenfurt, which is the capital of Carinthia, to which they laid claim. After some discussion they were allowed in, and for the next few weeks the town was jointly occupied by ourselves and them—a situation fraught with difficulties, but which happily gave rise to no incidents between ourselves and the Tito forces, although at times our Riflemen were sorely tried.

Our first task was to round up what was left of the German Army and disarm them; at the same time, we had to cope with the tens of thousands of refugees arriving from every direction.

Three days after we had been in occupation news was received that the German Balkan Army Group, consisting of some hundred thousand men of every nationality—Germans, Cossacks, quisling Yugoslavs and so forth—was advancing from Yugoslavia to surrender to the British. Tito's forces, however, without reference to us, decided that they would accept the surrender of this army and disarm them themselves, so they accordingly established a road block on the Drava bridge some five miles south of our road block on the southern outskirts of Klagenfurt. At dawn the following day news came through that Tito's forces were in difficulties, so the C.O. and Vivian Street hurried down to the Drava and came in at the tail-end of a battle, with the Germans firmly in control of the Drava bridge and the Tito forces taken to the hills, leaving their two tanks " brewing up " on the roadside. After considerable negotiations between the Tito and German commanders and the C.O., it was agreed that we should take the surrender of the Army Group. Accordingly for four long days the German Balkan Army trekked out of Yugoslavia through the 7th Rifle Brigade, and so into concentration camps.

The battle between Tito's men and the Germans on the Drava bridge was really for us the last shots of the war. Soon afterwards Tito's forces withdrew back into Yugoslavia and we were able to settle down to happier pursuits in addition to our occupational duties.

From among the many captured animals we gradually built up a

Battalion stable of some seventy horses. A mounted troop of Riflemen was formed and the Battalion played an active part in the many race meetings, horse shows and gymkhanas that were organized. The 6th Armoured Division ran a race meeting once a fortnight which was always well patronized by the Riflemen. The C.O. was one of the judges, and Murray Hunter clerk of the scales. Vivian Street, Bill Brownlow and Tom Liddell were the chief stable jockeys. L./Cpl. Jenkins, a professional jockey before the war, was in charge of the horses in training and got them extremely fit, considering the short time he had to do it in.

A good Battalion football team was built up and won the 6th Armoured Divisional Knock-out Competition. At the time of writing (February, 1946) our team is still undefeated after over fifty games.

Boating, swimming, fishing, cricket, mountaineering, athletics and, later, " fratting " were all indulged in—in fact, there was practically no sport which was not undertaken during those four months in Austria.

In July Douglas Darling left the Battalion. He had taken over command soon after Alamein and had led the Battalion across Africa to Tunis and thence up Italy into Austria, with only one short break when he was wounded. A total of two and a half years in command of the same battalion is a war-time record that few can have beaten. Vivian Street, who had in May gone to command the 2nd Rifle Brigade, returned to command the Battalion. Soon afterwards Dick Richardson left on leave and George Worboys took his place as Quartermaster. R.S.M. Hemp came to the Battalion as R.S.M.

In August, soon after we had moved to a new area round Kuhnsdort and Eisenkeppel and had started settling down for the winter, we received orders to move to Egypt at seven days' notice. " C " Company, under Jim Lonsdale, who had come from the 2nd Rifle Brigade to replace Peter Shepherd-Cross, was hastily recalled from Ulm, where we had been running a staging camp on the Eighth Army route to Calais. We took farewell of our many friends in the 6th Armoured Division and on 20th August set off on our journey back to Egypt. It was a sad day for us all, for we were, after three years, leaving the Eighth Army with whom we had travelled from Alamein to Austria. On the day we left we received the following telegram from Lieutenant-General Sir R. L. McCreery, Commander of the Eighth Army:

" Please convey to all ranks under your command my congratulations on the distinguished record of your Battalion during the three years you have served with the Eighth Army. Good luck to you all."

Our Divisional Commander, Major-General H. Murray, wrote to us as follows:

" Together for fifteen months the 7th Bn. The Rifle Brigade and the 6th Armoured Division have made history. We had few breaks from the time the 61st Brigade was formed and the war in Italy finally concluded. The physical and mental demands made on all ranks during the last twelve months of the war were tremendous. This period was probably the most exacting of the whole war. It included the long chase up half the length of Italy during the heat of the summer, then a break-out battle with armour, and a final pursuit of 200 miles at high speed into Austria. Only units and regiments of exceptional fighting qualities could have conducted such widely different operations successfully. The share of the 7th Battalion was a lion's share—a battalion the 6th Armoured could ill afford to lose. We shall have happy memories of the association and hope that the time will come when it will be renewed."

THE RETURN TO EGYPT

At the beginning of September we reached Egypt after a long and unpleasant journey. It was almost exactly three years from the day when we had arrived in that country from England. It was an extremely hot day, and as we moved into one of the well-known transit camps on the Canal we thought back on the mountains of Austria and were not amused.

THE 8TH BATTALION LETTER
1945

THE story of our activities during 1945 opens on Christmas Eve, 1944, and finds the Battalion, having moved in a great hurry on 20th December from Poperinghe, where the Brigade was resting and refitting, stretched out along the Meuse from Namur to Givet, a front of some sixty miles.

Here with companies under command of armoured regiments, " F " Company and the Fife and Forfar Yeomanry at Namur, " G " Company and the 3rd Royal Tank Regiment at Dinant, and " H " Company and the 23rd Hussars at Givet, the Brigade was holding the bridges over the Meuse, and awaiting the arrival of the spearhead of Rundstedt's offensive. Battalion Headquarters and Brigade Headquarters were at Mettet, while " E " Company was in support of all three companies.

In the evening the advanced elements of the 2nd Panzer Division arrived opposite Dinant and some shells fell in the town. The next day, Christmas Day, regimental groups moved forward from the river, and " G " Company attacked the village of Foy Notre Dame and took thirty prisoners. This was the high tide of the German offensive. The 2nd Panzer Division was in a pretty poor way, having suffered heavy casualties and being out of petrol. During the day " G " Company continued mopping-up operations, captured forty-two more prisoners and found quantities of equipment and columns of abandoned M.T. without petrol.

During the remaining days of 1944 the Brigade, still in regimental groups, moved slowly forward east of the Meuse as the Germans went back and consolidated their position in the " bulge." The New Year found the Brigade under command of the 6th Airborne Division, who had been hastily brought over from England, facing the enemy who were occupying the village of Bure. The task of the Brigade was to protect the flanks of the Division and form a firm base for them. On 3rd January " F " Company, with the 2nd Fife and Forfar Yeomanry, moved to an exposed position on Chapel Hill to support the infantry attack on Bure. The attack was successful, though costly, a number of self-propelled guns were knocked out by our tanks, and " F " Company dug in as well as they could in the snow-covered rocky ground of Chapel Hill.

During the next few days the position stagnated and the 6th Airborne Division could make no further headway. They remained where they were, holding the line for the next ten days until they were pinched out by attacking formations from the flanks. Meanwhile, " F " and " H " Companies relieved each other on the unenviable position on Chapel Hill. Farther behind with " G " Company, " E " Company and Battalion Headquarters, boar hunts and stag hunts were organized in the snow. Colonel Hunter went out once or twice with the local " sportsmen," but, although there was great excitement and much noise, no pig were killed. Eventually Donald Sudlow and Eric Yetman met an enormous boar whilst on a walk and killed it by emptying their pistols into its body. Its magnificent head subsequently adorned the bonnet of one of " G " Company's half-tracks for many months.

On 14th/15th January, 1945, the Battalion moved to Bree, on the Belgian-Dutch frontier, for a well-earned rest and refit. It had been on the go practically continuously since D Day. We were rather disappointed that we could not join the rest of the Brigade at Ypres, but made plans for enjoying a belated Christmas at Bree. The journey there was quite adventurous, as the roads were packed with snow and ice, and the carriers made such heavy weather of it that eventually each one had to be taken on tow by a half-track. When we arrived we were billeted in private houses and schools. Christmas was celebrated on 21st January in conventional manner, and the C.O. visited the company dining-halls and promised us all a victory Christmas in 1945. On the 22nd the Commander-in-Chief visited the Division and presented decorations and certificates.

After the Christmas celebrations we started a large programme of maintenance which was badly needed, and of training our reinforcements. Besides this, many parties and dances were arranged, and liaison with the local population was good. We all enjoyed our stay at Bree, where we remained until 10th February, despite many rumoured moves, and the departure of advance parties on one occasion. Leave to England was in full swing at this time, and the Battalion sent six officers and 133 other ranks during January.

On 11th February the Battalion moved to Panningen, meeting

again our friends of the 6th Airborne Division and being under command of the 5th Parachute Brigade. The Division was holding a long front of the Maas, having relieved formations that were to take part in the battle of the Reichswald Forest, shortly to begin. On the 13th a rugger match was organized against Headquarters, 5th Parachute Brigade, in which the Battalion suffered defeat but not so severely as was expected. The same day preparations were made to relieve the 13th Parachute Battalion. This was, however, cancelled the next day, and the Battalion moved to Roosendaal in Western Holland, coming under command of the First Canadian Army. At this time the 29th Armoured Brigade was still training and drawing its new tanks, Comets, at Ypres and the 4th Armoured Brigade had taken its place in the Division. The Battalion was thus on its own and was being put in wherever the need for an extra infantry battalion was felt.

During our stay at Roosendaal we saw for the first time the V1's as they winged their way over, bound for Antwerp, and the nights were made hideous by the barrage put up from the flak guns. Here, too, our interrupted training was resumed, and a great many oysters from the beds at Bergen-op-Zoom were eaten. The price in money was expensive, but, paid for in cigarettes, we could afford to have them for dinner nearly every night.

On 24th February the Battalion moved via Tilburg to Megen, and on the 25th the Battalion, less " H " Company, relieved the 18th Canadian Armoured Car Regiment holding a long front on the River Waal west of Nijmegen.

Positions were taken up with " F " Company on the right and " G " Company in the centre, and " E " Company holding the left of the line. As very little was known of the enemy on the other side of the river, an extensive programme of harassing, sniping and observation across the river by day and night was initiated. One of the great problems in this position was the maintenance of the soft-earth roads, which quickly gave way in wet weather under the unaccustomed traffic and which would soon have been impassable, making it impossible to supply the forward companies. An army of Dutch civilians was employed by the Battalion on this work, and we left the roads, in spite of heavy rain, better than they were to begin with. We were very much cut off from the world here, as the River Maas ran close behind Battalion Headquarters and the rations came up over a ferry from the other side. On several occasions, in order to save the roads, the "Admiral," Capt. H. R. Townshend, made long voyages down the river in a "duck" and landed with the supplies and "N.A.A.F.I." opposite Battalion Headquarters.

Meanwhile, " H " Company had joined Brockforce on Nijmegen Bridge, with two platoons of " E " Company under command. Their job was to protect this vital link with our bridgehead over the Waal, with special emphasis on the destruction of " frogmen " or logs of wood to which were attached explosive charges, or any other thing the Germans might float down the river. A great deal of ammunition was expended on various bits of flotsam.

Life in this sector was fairly quiet, sporadic machine-gunning and mortar fire on the forward companies and the incessant flight overhead of buzz-bombs being the only manifestation of the enemy. On 5th March the G.O.C. 49th Division visited the Battalion and it was decided to arrange a company raid over the river. A suspected enemy post was decided on. On the 8th and 9th " F " Company sent reconnaissance patrols across the river. These were carried out successfully, no mean feat in a flat-bottomed boat, but no signs of the enemy were found. It was then obvious that they were not holding the banks of the river, but were farther back on the winter " bund." A further patrol was sent across on the 10th, again by " F " Company, but they were unfortunately swept down-stream by the current and landed opposite the town of Tiel. Here they were met by fire at point-blank range, and Phillip Sedgewick was killed and Tubby Mason wounded. Sergt. Elkington brought the party back. Next day orders were received for the Battalion to move to Diest to rejoin the 29th Armoured Brigade. Thus we lost one of our best platoon commanders; his grave was found near Tiel after the war was over.

On 13th March the Battalion arrived in its new area. We were scattered in little villages between Diest and Louvain, each company joining up with its own armoured regiment. It was very pleasant to get back to our own Brigade and to meet our friends again. Here we started training with regiments, and it was with great excitement that we saw their new and powerful-looking Comets, and, although they had, we were told, already revealed some weaknesses, they were a great improvement on the Shermans, which had earned the nickname of " Ronsons," for obvious reasons. This cheered us greatly, for it was obvious that we were getting ready for what was to be the final battle of the war. Here also daily leave parties to Brussels were run, and everybody enjoyed the hospitality of that most hospitable of cities. On 17th March General Dempsey, G.O.C. Second Army, Major-General Roberts, G.O.C. 11th Armoured Division, Brigadier Harvey, Commanding the 29th Armoured Brigade, and Brigadier Churcher, of the 159th Infantry Brigade, met at Battalion Headquarters. It was clear that big things were afoot. That day also Lieut.-Colonel V. B. Turner, V.C., and Major L. I. T. Whitaker visited the Battalion.

During this time we had noticed a great increase in air activity: swarms of planes went over us daily for the Rhine, and we also saw the great fleet of Dakotas and gliders go over bearing the 6th Airborne Division to their successful landing over the Rhine. We wished them luck, and on the 28th ourselves received the order to march. The Brigade started in the early hours of the morning and, motoring all day, reached the Rhine at Wesel at about 4 p.m. We crossed straight away with really very little traffic difficulty. It was a tremendous thrill to be across the Rhine, and everybody felt that here really was the last big obstacle crossed. We leaguered that night close to Wesel, companies with their usual armoured regiments. Wesel itself had to be seen to be believed. It was quite literally reduced to dust, with a few gaunt skeletons of buildings rising out of the ruins. The next day no move forward was made, owing to the fact that the original attack had been so successful that the roads were now blocked with transport trying to get forward. The news was excellent, and we were given our centre line or " Charlie Love " right up to the Elbe.

The next day, 30th March, we started towards Horstmaar on two roads, with " F " Company and the Fife and Forfar Yeomanry on the left, and " G " Company and the 3rd Royal Tank Regiment on the right. It soon became apparent that it was going to be quite a sticky business on the left, as the tanks were frequently being held up by snipers and the odd Boche armed with two or three bazookas or panzerfausts. " F " Company got tired after dismounting and clearing several villages and woods, so in the afternoon " H " Company and the 23rd Hussars took over and they too found advancing a very slow business. Meanwhile, " G " Company and the 3rd Royal Tank Regiment pushed on well and reached Horstmaar that night. They left a good deal behind them, however, and " E " Company had a busy day mopping up. They captured about 175 prisoners. That night it was decided to regroup the Division, giving an infantry battalion to each armoured regiment. The 29th Armoured Brigade therefore consisted of two groups, the 3rd Royal Tank Regiment and the 4th King's Shropshire Light Infantry group and the 23rd Hussars and the 8th Rifle Brigade or the Harding-Hunter group. On the 31st the 3rd Royal Tank Regiment group was in front and we merely moved up behind, crossing the Ems by night and remaining near a place called Sinnigen all day. Here " H " Company had a bit of a battle, with " C " Squadron of the 23rd Hussars in support. They attacked an 88-mm. flak site that had been shelling the road behind us, destroyed the guns and took about 250 prisoners.

Perhaps I should explain here that when the Battalion worked with the 23rd Hussars companies were permanently affiliated to squadrons and worked together throughout the period. " A " Squadron and " G " Company, " B " Squadron and " F " Company, and " C " Squadron and " H " Company were always paired like that, with " E " Company giving support where it was required, or blocking roads, collecting prisoners or protecting flanks. Colonels Harding and Hunter had joint headquarters from where the battle was controlled, sometimes by one and sometimes by the other, depending whether it was primarily a tank or an infantry battle. This battle group was an impressive size on the road, taking up some five miles of space, but the W/T communications were so good that control was fairly easy.

On 2nd April we moved across the Dortmund—Ems Canal, the crossing of which had been forced by the 159th Infantry Brigade, who had a very sticky time there. We moved through the 3rd Royal Tank Regiment group and took the lead. With " F " and " B " leading, we passed through a very narrow gorge and moved on until we came to the village of Tecklenburg. Here we met considerable opposition and " B " Squadron halted while " F " Company systematically cleared the village. This took some time, as the defence was determined, the core of it being an N.C.Os.' training school from Hanover, helped by local Volksturm. This was the only place where the Volksturm gave us any trouble at all. Meanwhile, in the gorge behind us a few stout Boche had crept up and shot up our " A " Echelon, " brewing up," among other soft vehicles, the C.O.'s caravan. The Boche were eventually chased off by " E " Company. " F " Company finished clearing the village by dark, not without some casualties, and Tubby Mason was unfortunately killed here whilst directing the fire of a tank standing on the back. The state of the village after the battle would, we hoped, discourage further efforts by the Volksturm.

During the night we moved on again behind the 3rd Royal Tank Regiment and in the early morning crossed over a bridge secured by them. We passed through with " G " Company and " B " Squadron in the lead, bypassing Osnabruck to the north. Here " G " Company had a small battle and destroyed two 88-mm. guns. " F " Company then took the lead again, and we raced for the Ems—Weser Canal at full speed. The bridges had been reported intact and we were determined to get them. After a few brushes with stray Boche, " F " Company reached the bridges at 2000 hrs. that night, and in spite of a feeble effort to blow them up, the group had no fewer than five bridges intact by nightfall.

On 4th April we followed all day behind the 3rd Royal Tank Regiment group and leaguered that night near Essern. We took the lead the next morning and by 1000 hrs. were in Stolzenau, on the Weser, but found the bridge blown. " H " Company made a successful assault crossing and established a bridgehead, followed shortly by " G " Company, who extended it northwards. A small bridgehead was thus secured. During this time, " F " Company had cleared the town. " H " Company had several casualties during their attack and their Second-in-Command, Phillip May, was killed, a great loss to the Battalion. In the evening the Germans put every aeroplane they could scrape up and get into the air against us, scoring a few casualties in the town. At this time the weather was bad and the enemy planes attacked us without much interference during the next forty-eight hours, causing heavy casualties to the Sappers and seriously interfering with the building of the bridge.

The night passed quietly, but at 0800 hrs. the enemy put in a determined counter-attack about a battalion strong. This was dealt with. The shelling of " G " Battery, 13th R.H.A., which was our own particular battery, caused very heavy casualties to the enemy. All day the bridge area and the town were heavily shelled by the enemy and very little progress was made with the building of the bridge. In the afternoon a Commando battalion was put over to try to enlarge the bridgehead, but the opposition was too heavy and they joined up with " H "

Company and waited. During the fighting a section of " H " Company was overrun and Lieut. T. K. Swanwick was killed. That night two more battalions of Commandos were put over to take over the bridgehead. During the relief there was a further attack on " H " Company and in the fighting several Riflemen were killed. Everyone was back across the river early on the 7th and the Battalion moved back to reorganize. This action cost us 50 casualties.

On the next day the Division moved across a bridge at Petershagen built by the 6th Airborne Division, who were to the south of us. We moved on all day with no fighting. On the 9th, with " G " Company and " B " Squadron again leading, we set off for the River Aller, the next obstacle. No opposition was met until the village of Steimbke was reached. In this village we met the remnants of the S.S. troops that had attacked the bridgehead at Stolzenau and it took the remainder of the day for " G " and " H " Companies to clear it. They had the support of " G " Battery and two squadrons of Comets, and Steimbke paid for its resistance by being flattened. The local population appeared from all sorts of holes and cellars after the battle. Eric Yetman was wounded and subsequently died, and thus we lost another first-class platoon commander. Meanwhile, " F " Company and " B " Squadron had bypassed the village and swanned on to reach the Leine at Nordrebber, where the bridge was blown. The total of prisoners taken during the day was about 180.

We remained in this area for four days and on the 14th moved forward through the 159th Brigade and crossed the Aller. On the 15th we swanned northwards through Winsen, past Belsen, which had been declared " open " territory by the orders of Himmler himself, and finished up at Bornstorf. On the 16th we tried to advance northwards. All three companies were soon involved in quite heavy battles, " F " Company having a sharp one at Reinigen, where some casualties were caused by mines, David Fyffe being killed by one. The 3rd Royal Tank Regiment, however, broke through on the right and we turned and followed them, passed through them and went on some twenty miles to Wreidel. Throughout the day we picked up British prisoners of war who had been making forced marches in front of us, and they were in a pretty poor state.

On the 17th we moved on again and " G " Company had quite a battle at a cross-roads. Two of " A " Squadron tanks were " brewed up " at short range by an 88-mm. and one carrier was also destroyed. " Limejuice " (the code word for rocket-firing Typhoons) was called, after which " G " Company cleared up the situation. On the right " H " Company and " C " Squadron were having considerable difficulty at the village of Barum, which was quite strongly held and had no convenient approach. They withdrew to reorganize, and all available artillery, including the mediums, mortars and tanks, were turned on to the village. Meanwhile, " F " Company and " B " Squadron, who had bypassed the village and got round behind, were having a good shoot at transport in the south, beetling back to the Elbe bridges. They were also shooting-up Barum from the rear. By this time " H " Company was ready, and a heavy concentration of H.E. and smoke was put down; even Regimental H.Q. tanks joined in the shooting from a flank, which rather disturbed the control of the battle.

" H " Company and the tanks of " C " Squadron rushed the village and soon had it cleared, leaving it a burning rubbish heap. They took 250 prisoners and destroyed three 88-mm., four 20-mm. and one 37-mm. guns in a model operation, and casualties in the final attack were nil.

It was clear now that the enemy were getting away over the Elbe as quickly as possible, and the next day we pushed on again, bypassing Luneburg to the south-east, to the approaches of an obstacle almost as formidable as the Rhine. Dull explosions and columns of white smoke in the sky told their story of bridges blown up. " G " Company reached Neetze that night just short of the river. At last light they engaged some vehicles hidden in a wood; this turned out to be M. Belli's famous Continental Circus and the message came back over the air: " Two lions brewed up, two bears escaping, two elephants and circus staff captured."

On the 19th we moved back to Westergellersen to await the crossing of the Elbe. We stayed here, maintaining our vehicles hard and generally cleaning up and resting. Colonel Hunter caught a grayling of between 3 and 4 lb. in the local stream. On the 26th we moved up to the Elbe at Winsen and held a bit of the line. On the 30th we returned to rejoin the 23rd Hussars.

At 1630 hrs. that evening we moved forward for our last battle, but progress was very slow owing to jammed traffic on the bridge that had now been built. The 15th Scottish Division had a good bridgehead and in the early hours of the morning we pushed through their forward elements at Schwarzenbeck. Just beyond, " G " Company and " A " Squadron met two Tiger tanks; one of our tanks was knocked out and the Tigers were engaged in the dark. At first light " G " Company attacked the place and cleared it, taking sixty prisoners. " H " Company had moved westwards, but were held up a short way on, where there was quite heavy shelling. " F " Company then started moving up the main road, but were held up by mines; progress was slow and casualties were caused.

Meanwhile, the Fife and Forfar Yeomanry had broken through and the advance again gained impetus. " H " Company was left behind to clear up the centre line: they attacked and cleared the village of Kankeiau and then moved on. That night the remainder of the Battalion, having swung northwards off the main road, spent the hours of darkness in a bog.

The 2nd of April saw us moving really fast, with the Fife and Forfar Yeomanry in front directed on Lubeck and ourselves north of that town. When we arrived, everything was in confusion. There were thousands of disorganized Germans fleeing from the Russians, who came quite quietly; there was no resistance to speak of, and prisoners were flowing in far too quickly to count. The Battalion had between 3,000 and 4,000 that evening. On the 3rd " F " Company reached the Baltic at Travemunde, where they found large columns of Germans fleeing from the east, and took about 20,000 prisoners. " H " Company moved to Neustadt, where they found shiploads of refugees who were practically starving. In the evening the group concentrated at Niendorf, where we waited several days and finally celebrated VE Day. A tremendous firework display was hastily organized, and the sky was lit up for miles around with bonfires, tracer bullets of every calibre and Very lights. A good many people were lit up too, but in spite of this no casualties occurred.

On 11th May the Battalion moved to Schleswig, where after a lot of cleaning had been done by forced German labour we quickly settled down into the magnificent building Schloss Gottorf. It was not very comfortable, but there were great advantages in all being together. The summer was spent very pleasantly. The Battalion was allotted five boats from the yacht club and soon a tremendous keenness grew up and a great many people learned to handle a boat. There was bathing in the lake; athletics and cricket were in full swing. Everyone enjoyed this summer to the full after nearly a year's continuous fighting.

On 27th June Lieut.-Colonel Hunter, D.S.O., M.B.E., M.C., left the Battalion, having commanded it since shortly after D Day, and we were all very sorry to see him go. He was succeeded in command by Major C. H. Liddell, M.C. In the autumn releases from the Army started and we lost some more old friends and later on had to send most of our younger soldiers to the 1st Battalion. Now with releases from the Army going ever faster, we are very much below strength and look like being disbanded within a month or two. This, then, must be the last letter that we shall write to you. With all best wishes,

MILITARY HONOURS AND AWARDS

LIEUT. R. B. ADAMS, *3rd April*, 1945: Croix de Guerre with Silver Star.

MAJOR A. W. ALLEN (1st Battalion), *20th September*, 1945: D.S.O.
For gallant and distinguished service in the defence of Calais in May, 1940.

A./SERGT. R. V. ALLEN, *14th January*, 1943: M.M.
At El Wiskha on 25th October, 1942. In the early morning of 25th October, No. 11 Platoon, with its four anti-tank guns, was placed in position guarding the right flank of the Battalion. At 0600 hrs. the platoon commander was killed and three of the guns were moved to another area.

Sergt. Allen's detachment was therefore on its own, directly supporting "B" Company. A tank attack by some twenty enemy tanks started at 1430 hrs. and was directed straight at "C" Company's forward guns. They were immediately engaged by this particular gun. Four Mark XIIIs. were definitely hit and, temporarily, the gun ran out of ammunition. By this time the shell fire was extremely heavy and it was almost impossible to stand up without getting hit. Sergt. Allen, however, immediately started restocking with ammunition until he found that his gun had been put out of action by shell fire. Sergt. Allen, by his coolness and care, kept his gun in action throughout four days under heavy shell fire, machine-gun fire and sniping, and throughout the duration of the attack.

He was responsible for the destruction of at least four tanks. He showed considerable leadership and set an example to his men.

RFN. A. M. ANDREWS, *11th April*, 1946: M.M.

CAPT. (QRMR.) R. L. ANGEL, M.M., *H.M. Birthday Honours List*, 1942: M.B.E.

RFN. S. E. ALLRIDGE (2nd Battalion), *24th April*, 1945: M.M.
For courage and initiative during the attack on Tossignano. At 0600 hrs. on 14th December, 1944, Rfn. Allridge was ordered to seize a house on the southern side of Tossignano to relieve pressure on " C " Company, 2nd Rifle Brigade, who were being counter-attacked in the western end of the village. The entry into the house was forced and the platoon established on the ground floor, which consisted of one room. Rfn. Allridge took up a difficult and exposed fire position where he remained for some two hours, in spite of grenade and small-arms fire, assisting in repelling all attacks until finally the platoon was forced to withdraw down the hill when the ceiling was blown down and the room set on fire with petrol. Rfn. Allridge remained behind with his platoon commander and L./Cpl. Dyer to cover the withdrawal. He spotted a German shooting with a rifle from the next-door house, whereupon he advanced in full

view, shot away the rifle and silenced the fire from the house by shooting into all windows which overlooked his platoon's line of withdrawal. On reaching the cover of some rocks at the foot of the hill he continued to expose himself, engaging with his T.M.C. a Spandau which was firing at his platoon, until he was seriously wounded in the arm.

Rfn. Allridge's courage and coolness in a difficult situation did much to inspire the other members of his platoon.

LIEUT. P. C. APSEY (1st Battalion), 24*th April*, 1945: M.C.

On 21st January, 1945, in a company attack on the village Saint Joost, Lieut. Apsey commanded the left-hand leading platoon. The village was strongly held by a battalion of the Parachute Regiment Hubner. Throughout the action, which lasted several hours, Lieut. Apsey set an inspiring example to his platoon. Despite the heavy machine-gun and shell fire, he went fearlessly from section to section encouraging his men, and whenever a section was held up he exposed himself to strong enemy fire by going to the section and leading it forward himself. He attacked every enemy position at the front of his men, engaging the enemy with grenades and fire from his Sten gun. By his splendid example and complete disregard for his own safety, Lieut. Apsey led his platoon forward on to their objective, capturing many prisoners and inflicting heavy casualties on the enemy.

CAPT. (T./MAJOR) W. J. APSEY (1st Battalion), 27*th January*, 1944: M.C.

This officer was commanding "I" Company during the attack on Cardito on 3rd October, 1943. He maintained throughout complete control by a display of coolness and initiative. Having formed up his company on the start line he followed the leading platoon in a carrier and was in continuous communication with the attacking platoons.

He personally located and pointed out the enemy machine-gun posts which were holding up the advance, and engaged one with fire from his carrier.

Arriving on the objective, he organized the consolidation and street clearing which resulted in the successful conduct of this operation, in which a small force defeated a far larger German one.

Throughout the entire engagement he showed the greatest coolness and judgment, and the success of this operation was in no small part due to his admirable conduct and display of leadership throughout.

LIEUT. M. I. ATKIN-BERRY (10th Battalion), 7*th December*, 1944: M.C.

For outstanding leadership and devotion to duty during the period 21st to 23rd June, 1944, in the attack on Corgiano.

On the night of 21st/22nd June Lieut. Atkin-Berry was ordered to attack and clear a large house, known to be occupied by the enemy, which was well defended and in a commanding position on a hill. By skilful disposition of his platoon, backed up by intrepid and determined personal leadership, and in spite of very heavy mortar and machine-gun fire, Lieut. Atkin-Berry successfully forced an entrance and cleared the house, killing a number of Germans and taking prisoners.

The house's capture was vital both to the next phase of our own operations and to the enemy. Throughout the day, 22nd June, the position was subjected to intense shelling and mortaring, and was attacked on three occasions by tanks and self-propelled guns at short range. As a result of the fine leadership and cool example of Lieut. Atkin-Berry, all attacks were beaten off and the morale of the platoon maintained at a high pitch.

On the night of 22nd/23rd June, Lieut. Atkin-Berry led a fighting patrol into the town of Corgiano itself. This involved scaling the walls of the town by ladders. Fire was continuous during the attempt, but Lieut. Atkin-Berry successfully reached his objective, surprised the enemy and captured five prisoners. As a result, the enemy withdrew from this stronghold, which might otherwise have required a battalion to clear.

Throughout the period Lieut. Atkin-Berry set an outstanding example of personal disregard of danger and sound judgment and conspicuous leadership which was an inspiration to his platoon and to his company.

SERGT. L. M. BAILEY (10th Battalion), *7th December*, 1944: M.M.

On the night of 16th May, 1944, in the Gustav Line south of Piumarola, Sergt. Bailey's platoon was met by cross-fire at short range from three enemy machine guns. His platoon commander was killed and the platoon became divided.

Under heavy fire Sergt. Bailey moved in the open from section to section, rallied the men who were pinned to the ground and in scanty cover, and then laid out and supervised the occupation of a defensive position. Dusk was falling by the time this was completed, and the enemy had the exact range and the location of the platoon by direct and fixed-line fire. Sergt. Bailey nevertheless led a section out successively to right and left of his position, worked his way even closer to the enemy and by deliberately drawing enemy fire, in some cases at a range of only twenty yards, caused the enemy to disclose his dispositions in detail.

Having discovered by this means that the enemy were in much greater strength than was calculated, Sergt. Bailey received orders to withdraw his platoon under cover of darkness. Still harassed by concentrated fire, Sergt. Bailey went from section to section, gave orders for withdrawal and, after he had waited to see every man clear and on his way back to a covered R.V., finally led the platoon back over difficult and unknown country to rejoin his company. Mortaring and shelling were continuous during this operation in addition to machine-gun fire.

During the following three days Sergt. Bailey has continually shown outstanding qualities of leadership and has been largely responsible for maintaining the high standard of morale in his platoon, in spite of severe shelling, mortaring and sniping.

MAJOR J. N. BAINES, *25th November*, 1943: M.B.E.

During the period immediately prior to the Battle of El Alamein this officer was Staff Captain to the Brigade, and when the D.A.A. and Q.M.G. had to be evacuated on account of sickness the greater part of the primary "Q" work had to be carried out by Major Baines.

Thanks to his untiring energy, tact and devotion to duty, the administrative arrangements of the Brigade worked without a hitch.

Major Baines became D.A.Q.M.G. of the Brigade, and in spite of the fact that the units of the Brigade were often dispersed over very wide areas during the advance from El Alamein to Enfidaville, there was never once a shortage of ammunition or commodities of any nature.

This reflects great credit on the work of Major Baines, and is deserving of the highest praise.

LIEUT. J. R. BAKER (1st Battalion), 13*th March*, 1945: M.C.

On 22nd August, 1944, Lieut. Baker was commanding a mortar platoon which was in support of " C " Squadron, 1st Royal Tanks. His orders were to mop up enemy positions that were overrun by the tanks.

It was not long before two tanks had been knocked out by bazookas and Lieut. Baker was then ordered to lead the advance astride the main road.

The enemy was in position in strength and the whole time this officer was under heavy small-arms and mortar fire. Despite this, he led his platoon forward to deal with a numerically superior enemy in the woods and houses. By his gallant example and skilful handling of the platoon the task was successfully completed. Showing complete disregard for his own safety, he continually encouraged the platoon with such success that more than once the platoon got to grips with the enemy and hand-to-hand fighting took place. Heavy casualties were inflicted on the enemy and over thirty prisoners were taken.

SERGT. A. BALDOCK, 15*th June*, 1943: M.M.

On 9th April, 1943, this N.C.O. commanded a section of the scout platoon which was given the task of attempting to get round the left flank of the position at the Fondouk Gap and bring small-arms fire to bear on enemy anti-tank weapons whilst the Regiment attacked frontally.

Though unsuccessful in achieving this purpose, he led his section throughout with great coolness and courage in the face of heavy fire, and his section was instrumental in bringing the fire of tanks on to a concentrated enemy anti-tank position, thereby destroying the gun.

SERGT. G. W. BALDWIN (8th Battalion), 2*nd August*, 1945: M.M.

On 17th April, 1945, Sergt. Baldwin was commanding a carrier section leading the advance with a troop of tanks. The vanguard was approaching the cross-roads north of Barum, on the Uelzen—Luneberg road, when enemy A.T. guns, which were well concealed in the wood, opened fire at a range of 200 yards and destroyed the two leading tanks. The remaining tanks and the carriers withdrew under cover of smoke, leaving Sergt. Baldwin and his crew and six wounded men in the open 200 yards from the enemy position. The Germans opened fire on Sergt. Baldwin and his party with a 20-mm. gun and damaged his carrier. Sergt. Baldwin helped the wounded to get under cover into a shallow ditch and then lay down beside his carrier, which was completely exposed. He observed the enemy and reported back the exact position of the enemy guns on the wireless. He was then ordered to try to get the wounded men back along the ditch. He administered first aid and sent four of the men back down the ditch; the remaining two were too badly wounded to move. Sergt. Baldwin remained with these two men and continued to act as an observation post for the field and medium guns, which were now shelling the enemy position. Sergt. Baldwin's own position was uncomfortably close for medium guns. When our guns had ceased firing and he could be of no further use as an observation post, Sergt. Baldwin lifted the two badly wounded men on to the carrier and drove them away to safety. There was no means of telling whether the enemy guns had been destroyed or not, and the whole road was exposed to their fire.

Sergt. Baldwin's coolness and courage during this action were an example to all, and there is no doubt that his accurate observation and corrections from a very exposed position were a tremendous factor in the subsequent overrunning of the enemy position with the capture of three 88-mm. and two 20-mm. guns as well as some prisoners.

LIEUT. (T./CAPT.) H. C. BARING, 13*th August,* 1942: M.C.

On the night of 14th/15th June the Battalion, less one company, with two batteries of R.H.A. and attendant light A.A., etc., was cut off by an enemy force between it and the Acroma Gap in the minefield.

It was necessary in order to extricate this force to proceed northwards to the gap in the main Tobruk—Gazala road. This included descending the Acroma escarpment, which is generally considered to be impassable to wheels except on the tarmac roads, none of which could be used owing to the enemy and to our own minefields.

By 0200 hrs. the force had accomplished the descent of half of the escarpment, but there remained the last part, which was precipitous and completely impassable. Capt. Baring, who was adjutant of his Battalion, made a reconnaissance and found a spot which, though apparently impassable, was slightly less so than the rest, and he led the force down it with the result that the whole force less one carrier, which was hit by enemy shell fire during the descent, reached the main road intact, and by 0645 hrs. was concentrated on the Acroma—Tobruk road in accordance with its orders.

Capt. Baring showed the greatest coolness and resource, and by his action brought through two-thirds of the supporting arms of the Armoured Brigade which otherwise could not have failed to be destroyed.

13*th December,* 1945: M.B.E.

For outstanding zeal and devotion to duty as Brigade Major of the 61st Infantry Brigade since its formation in the spring of 1944, and throughout the whole of the Italian campaign, with special mention during the period 20th April to 2nd May, 1945. During this period Major Baring has shown himself to be a Staff officer of outstanding efficiency and to have a capacity for work when in dire need of sleep far in excess of the normal officer of his rank and age.

As a direct result of this officer's efforts, the orders, march tables and abnormal number of forward brigade moves when wireless communication was often impossible were carried out by all units under command without a single hitch. Most of these moves were of a priority nature, and had any of them failed the whole of the successful dash which carried the Brigade over the Austrian border into Klagenfurt would surely have failed, as the time factor in every phase was the dominating one.

During the whole of the Italian campaign this officer's endurance and capacity for hard work have been an inspiration to the whole Brigade staff.

MAJOR H. A. BARKER, *30th December*, 1941 : O.B.E.

This officer served as D.A.Q.M.G., H.Q., Alexandria Area, from November, 1939. In the early days of this period a vast increase in responsibilities was occasioned by the rapid growth of the command and the increasing activity on the Western Front, with no corresponding increase in establishment.

For the first year, therefore, responsibilities far in excess of those normally borne by an officer of his rank were accepted by this officer in an exemplary manner.

MAJOR J. L. BARLOW, *24th August*, 1944 : M.B.E.

CPL. J. W. C. BARNETT, *28th January*, 1943 : M.M.

On 26th/27th October, 1942, Cpl. Barnett was layer of a 6-pounder anti-tank gun on the Snipe position. This gun was continuously engaged during the night and following day, accounting for fifteen German tanks, set alight and destroyed.

At about 1200 hrs. the gun became very short of ammunition. To reach the other sections of his troop, of which both guns had been knocked out and which still had some ammunition, he crawled 300 yards under heavy machine-gun fire from a body of enemy tanks.

He dragged two boxes back to his gun before these tanks could develop their attack at 1300 hrs., thus making it possible to continue resistance.

He then went to fetch more. His courage was of the highest order.

CPL. (A./SERGT.) R. W. BARRATT (1st Battalion), *27th January*, 1944 : M.M.

This N.C.O. throughout the action of the attack by "I" Company at Cardito on 3rd October, 1943, displayed conspicuous gallantry and leadership. When his platoon was pressed by heavy machine-gun fire he was commanding a section.

He immediately took the initiative and, crawling forward to the post which was holding up the attack, he destroyed it single-handed with hand grenades and T.S.M.C. fire, killing three enemy and silencing the gun. Later, after the objective had been reached and the fighting for the possession of the streets was in progress, he maintained this outstanding degree of leadership, personally clearing two houses containing snipers who were preventing consolidation being effected.

On his own initiative he worked round and killed two snipers on housetops. Finally, after the street fighting had ceased, he brought in one enemy prisoner.

This N.C.O.'s untiring devotion to duty, fearless display of courage and initiative were an outstanding example to members of his section.

31st August, 1944: Bar to M.M.

Throughout the period of operations west of Villers Bocage covering 10th to 14th June, 1944, this N.C.O. commanded the mortar section with the greatest bravery and skill.

On the morning of 14th June strong enemy patrols were within 400 yards of the company front. They were making the greatest use of hedges and cornfields and observation on them was difficult.

A./Sergt. Barrett went forward with a 38 set until able to observe. Under machine-gun fire and being sniped at from three different positions, he directed the fire of his mortars with great accuracy and effect. The patrol was completely disorganized and withdrew. A./Sergt. Barrett followed them up and with his second rapid fire either killed or wounded the whole patrol except six, who surrendered to one of our tanks.

His coolness, complete disregard of personal safety, and enthusiasm were a great example to all ranks.

SERGT. T. J. BARRETT, *22nd July,* 1943: M.M.

Sergt. Barrett was in command of two 6-pounder anti-tank guns which accompanied the leading company when the Battalion were ordered to capture the White House north of Argoubel Regas on the night of 26th/27th April, 1943.

After proceeding 1,000 yards, the Battalion came to a narrow defile guarded by six Mark VI German tanks, which were protected by at least one company of German infantry.

While the remainder of the Battalion endeavoured to deal with the German infantry Sergt. Barrett immediately got his guns into action and exchanged shot for shot with the German tanks at short range, hitting them repeatedly.

He continued to fight his guns until they were both knocked out by 88-mm. H.E. fired from the German tanks.

After his guns were no longer able to fire, Sergt. Barrett, although wounded severely in the right side, made two attempts to salvage the then damaged guns in Bantams. On each occasion the Bantams received direct hits and were set on fire under him when on the point of towing the damaged guns out of action.

On the second occasion Sergt. Barrett was wounded again and was evacuated unconscious.

Throughout the action, which was fought under greatly superior enemy fire at point-blank range, Sergt. Barrett by his personal courage and devotion to duty did everything in his power, until he was rendered unconscious, to inflict the maximum damage and casualties on the enemy.

L./CPL. J. BARTON (8th Battalion), *12th July,* 1945: M.M.

On the night of the 6th/7th April, 1945, the platoon in which L./Cpl. Barton commanded a section was holding part of the battalion bridgehead over the River Weser. L./Cpl. Barton's section was in a forward position and his main task was to give warning of any enemy counter-attack. Throughout the night the position was mortared and shelled and casualties were also sustained from sniping. By his cheerfulness and example L./Cpl. Barton kept his section together and in excellent spirits. At about 0400 hrs. an enemy counter-attack was launched and L./Cpl. Barton's section post was attacked. As instructed, L./Cpl. Barton ordered his section to withdraw to the main position and give the alarm. While this withdrawal was taking place, L./Cpl. Barton remained by himself in the forward position and engaged the enemy with an L.M.G. The L.M.G. was smashed by a panzerfaust, but L./Cpl. Barton continued to engage the enemy with a rifle and did not return to the main position until the alarm had been given and the defensive fire brought down. On returning to his section, L./Cpl. Barton continued to engage the enemy with all weapons until the attack was finally broken up and beaten off. Throughout this action the enemy was heavily engaging the position with mortar fire and airbursts from 88-mm. guns.

L./Cpl. Barton's conduct throughout was a fine example and inspiration to all. There is no doubt that his gallantry and coolness under very difficult circumstances were largely responsible for the enemy attack being beaten off.

LIEUT. C. C. BASS, 13th September, 1945: M.C.

For services whilst a prisoner of war.

T./CAPT. D. W. BASSET, 14th January, 1943: M.C.

Capt. Basset is a motor-company commander. On 23rd October, 1942, and the two subsequent days, he commanded the gap, making parties on Sun Route. The sappers placed under his command, supported by a troop of Crusaders and his own carrier platoon, forced a way through six enemy minefields in the face of considerable local resistance and enabled the Bays' regimental group to deploy on 24th October.

His courage and determination were outstanding during this action.

On the 26th and 27th Capt. Basset commanded his company on the Snipe position, 866295, with two troops of 6-pounder anti-tank guns under command. Capt. Basset's position was on the northern flank and was attacked by enemy tanks once by night and four times by day. All these attacks were repelled.

He personally supervised the fire of his machine guns, which killed four enemy snipers.

He went round his company under intense fire, encouraging sections that had suffered casualties and reorganized his line after successive attacks so that it might withstand the next one as firmly as possible; after nightfall he supervised the evacuation of wounded and withdrew the company safely when orders to do so were received.

He held his section of the front, which was exposed to heavy shell fire, always rallying his men by his determined bearing despite considerable casualties, and he repelled repeated and heavy attacks.

The anti-tank troops placed under his command accounted for twenty-seven enemy tanks burnt with others hit and guns and lorries destroyed.

His courage and devotion to duty were of the highest order and an example to all ranks.

LIEUT. (A./MAJOR) R. T. BASSET, 1st April, 1941 : M.C.

This officer was commanding a company shadowing enemy columns and by his bold handling of patrols under bombing and machine-gun fire he obtained valuable information from enemy territory. On 22nd/23rd October his company was detailed to guide another unit to the start line which he was also to secure. By a detailed reconnaissance of the position within fifty yards of the enemy he brought the unit to within 100 yards of the enemy unseen. He has consistently set a courageous personal example.

12th February, 1942: Bar to M.C.

Major Basset was commanding a company of the Rifle Brigade in a mixed column on the eastern flank of the Sidi Rezegh position. During 21st and 22nd November, five German tank attacks were made on this position, and the brunt of these attacks fell on the column to which Major Basset belonged.

His cool bearing and leadership were an outstanding feature in the turning back of these sustained tank attacks, and, although wounded, he continued to carry out his duty, encouraging his men, and set a fine example which undoubtedly played a decisive part in those days.

Although severe casualties were sustained by all units in this column, the enemy tanks never broke through.

LIEUT. J. D. BATES, 22nd July, 1943 : M.C.

Lieut. Dawson Bates was in command of No. 12 Platoon, "C" Company, when his company was employed in the attack on Djebel Saikra on 27th March, 1943.

Showing a complete disregard of danger, and under heavy and accurate artillery fire, he led his platoon through two minefields with such dash and determination that the heavily defended enemy localities were forced to surrender and their occupants killed or captured.

Shortly afterwards he heard that his company commander was killed; he at once assumed command, directed the furtherance of the attack and organized a consolidation of the objective after it had been captured.

He was first in his platoon to reach the objective, and his courage and coolness in arranging the consolidation, under continuous heavy fire, were beyond all praise.

His action set a fine example of leadership and determination to all his brother-officers and men.

A./MAJOR G. N. BELL (8th Battalion), 13th March, 1945 : M.C.

This officer commanded " G " Company, 8th Rifle Brigade, which was under command of the 3rd Royal Tank Regiment in the advance from the Seine to Antwerp. On 31st August, 1944, before light, after an approach march by night, " G " Company, supported by the leading squadron of the 3rd Royal Tank Regiment, entered Amiens. Information from local sources indicated that there were many German troops in the town, but, acting in the boldest manner, A./Major Bell led " G " Company, supported by a squadron, and forced their way through the town, caused many casualties to the enemy and reached the River Somme.

On 3rd September, 1944, " G " Company, again co-operating with the leading squadron of the 3rd Royal Tank Regiment on the approach and entry to the town of Antwerp, A./Major Bell supported the leading squadron of tanks at Boom, on the outskirts of Antwerp, where a bridge was discovered that had not been destroyed, and again at the fighting at the actual entrance to the town the company closely followed the leading tanks into the harbour and there assisted in destroying much enemy equipment, capturing several hundred prisoners, and safeguarding the port installations.

In both the instances quoted A./Major Bell has displayed the greatest powers of leadership at all times. Under enemy fire A./Major Bell has shown great initiative and determination, and the co-operation between motor infantry and tanks which has been the cause of these successes has been largely due to the zeal and determination shown by A./Major Bell.

RFN. F. BENNETT (8th Battalion), *1st March*, 1945: M.M.

At Helchteren on 10th September, 1944, " H " Company, 8th Rifle Brigade, was engaged in an attack on a strong enemy position. Rfn. Bennett's platoon was heavily mortared and sustained many casualties. Rfn. Bennett was ordered by his section commander to try to get observation on the enemy. He immediately went into a house and observed from an upper window. The house was at the time under mortar fire and the upper windows were receiving considerable attention from machine guns and snipers. In spite of this, Rfn. Bennett remained at his observation post for over an hour, reporting valuable information which ultimately contributed to the destruction of the enemy's position.

Rfn. Bennett's conduct and his complete disregard of danger throughout this action were a fine example to the rest of the men of his platoon.

CPL. A. J. BERRY, *18th February*, 1943: M.M.

Cpl. Berry has for the past eighteen months been signal operator in a carrier platoon and throughout the summer campaign of 1941, the Sidi Rezegh battle and the campaign of 1942. He has set a fine example by continuing to transmit messages even when under heavy fire from ground and air.

On 25th June, near Bir Thalata, his carrier was hit and knocked out. Though under fire, he transferred his set to another carrier and re-established communication. Again, on 3rd August, 1942, at the western end of Dierel Alinda, when the carrier patrol of which he was a member was acting as O.P. escort, the R.H.A. O.P. officer went forward and was wounded. Cpl. Berry ran forward under fire and carried the officer back to his carrier, which was behind a ridge.

His consistent courage and devotion to duty have contributed largely to the high standard of signal communication in the Battalion and set an inspiring example to all ranks.

2/LIEUT. P. B. BIDDELL, *5th November*, 1942: M.C.

For conspicuous gallantry and devotion to duty. On 31st August, 1942, when commanding his platoon at 42938782 at 1830 hrs. he was attacked by about thirty German tanks.

He ordered his platoon to hold their fire till the enemy was within 300 yards, when he opened fire and destroyed five tanks.

He continued to fight with his platoon, although slightly wounded, until overrun, but he remained in his position till after the attack and recovered two guns and all the platoon transport. There is no doubt that his courage and leadership saved his platoon from destruction, and thus enabled them to remain in action.

7th January, 1943: Bar to M.C.

Throughout the attack by "I" Company on Cardito on 3rd October, 1943, this officer displayed conspicuous qualities of leadership and command. It was entirely due to him that the momentum of the attack was maintained throughout the advance.

Moving well in front of his leading section, by his coolness, bravery and ability to sum up the situation he directed three independent attacks on enemy posts which were impeding the advance. He personally silenced the last one with T.S.M.G. fire. Later in the street fighting he accounted for two snipers.

His personal conduct, coolness and complete disregard of his personal safety were an outstanding example to all.

LIEUT. T. A. BIRD, *9th May*, 1941: M.C.

For conspicuous gallantry and leadership on 22nd January, during an attack on Tobruk, 2/Lieut. Bird led a carrier platoon to test the northern defences. Meeting very heavy defensive fire, he withdrew his platoon without loss and after two hours advanced again; on this occasion the fire was decreasing and was silenced by the guns supporting his attack.

His platoon penetrated the minefields and wire and moved forward to enemy strong-points at Ras el Medauuar which were still engaging the patrols of the neighbouring company, which was pinned by fire. Working his carrier around the flank, he completely surrounded the strong enemy position, protected by mines and booby traps, and forced it surrender.

The position contained, in addition to infantry, nine 105-mm. guns, as well as machine guns, and had up till then completely held up the advance on this flank.

This officer showed considerable bravery and initiative in taking on such very superior numbers and handled a difficult situation with skill and coolness and the loss of only one carrier.

14th January, 1943: D.S.O.

Major Bird was company commander of the 6-pounder anti-tank company of the Rifle Brigade in the Snipe position on 26th and 27th October, 1942. He was put in command of the anti-tank defences of the position by the Commanding Officer and sited and co-ordinated the fire of fifteen guns of the Rifle Brigade and six guns of the Anti-Tank Regiment. The position was immediately counter-attacked during the night and five separate tank attacks were made the next day; all these were repulsed.

Major Bird paid no heed to his own safety, but went from gun to gun giving encouragement and when necessary taking the place of wounded men in gun crews.

He went round after each attack, finding out what guns had been damaged and redistributing them and their ammunition to each section as he thought best.

All this he did under intense fire, never showing the least concern, but proving himself an inspiration to all ranks.

Major Bird was finally wounded in the head at about 1400 hrs., but carried on until the effects of concussion and the hot sun knocked him out just before last light.

His company accounted for fifty-seven tanks burnt, besides others hit and guns and lorries destroyed. He was always at the critical point performing many duties, directing the fire of a gun whose No. 1 was wounded, loading another of which all the crew but one had been wounded, fetching ammunition and cheering his men.

His courage and leadership gave all ranks confidence and enabled them to beat the enemy off and withdraw in good order when orders to do so were received.

24th September, 1942 : Bar to M.C.

On the night of 25th/26th July, 1942, this officer commanded a fighting patrol to the north of Gebel Kalakh.

He led his patrol across 2,700 yards of open ground in brilliant moonlight, the last half under heavy machine-gun fire.

At about 100 yards short of the objective a wire fence was encountered, which he negotiated under intense fire, and then took his patrol in with great gallantry and determination, overrunning three enemy posts and capturing two officers and fifteen other ranks, including the entire crew of an anti-tank gun; other casualties were also inflicted.

In spite of heavy small-arms and mortar fire from positions sited in depth and on either flank, he withdrew his patrol without casualties.

The success of this patrol which identified in the southern sector an enemy division previously reported in the north; was almost entirely due to the careful preparation and courageous leadership of its commander, to his unwavering determination to attack and capture a heavily defended position and to inflict casualties on the enemy.

L./CPL. E. W. BISHOP, *9th September,* 1941 : M.M.

L./Cpl. Bishop was awarded the Military Medal, being taken prisoner by the Italians. In the withdrawal he escaped and, helped by Arabs, sometimes disguised as one, walked from Agedabia back to Tobruk, where he arrived about six weeks later.

L./SERGT. J. W. BLACKMAN, 20*th September*, 1945: M.M.
For gallantry and distinguished service in the defence of Calais, May, 1940.

LIEUT.-COLONEL N. R. BLOCKLEY, 24*th August*, 1944: O.B.E.
Lieut.-Colonel Blockley commanded the Reconnaissance Regiment of the 5th Division throughout the campaign in Sicily and Italy with marked success. During the more fluid phase of the fighting and especially during the fast drive through Southern Italy, the dash and efficiency with which the Regiment was handled by Lieut.-Colonel Blockley were the chief factor which enabled us to gain information, to anticipate the enemy at obstacles, to work round his flanks and to keep touch with neighbouring formations. Lieut.-Colonel Blockley was quite untiring in his efforts, was undeterred by enemy fire and never brooked, for long, delay caused by rough country or bad demolitions. I consider that the efficient handling by Lieut.-Colonel Blockley of this Regiment was a major factor in the successful operations carried out by the Division.

CPL. C. H. BLUNDEN, 2*nd October*, 1942 (Dieppe operations): M.M.
Cpl. Blundell was the section leader in Capt. Webb's troop, which played a conspicuous part in the final assault on the battery. Cpl. Blundell set a high standard of leadership and showed a great example in house-to-house and hand-to-hand fighting through the battery buildings.
He was wounded, but refused to receive medical attention and continued to destroy the enemy until there were no Germans left alive.

LIEUT. (T./MAJOR) P. A. D. BODEN, 9*th September*, 1942: M.C.
This officer has commanded a company with conspicuous ability throughout the campaign, for two months of which his company was in almost continual contact with the enemy whilst operating on column detached from the Battalion. Three different column commanders have spoken most highly of Major Boden's coolness in emergency, quickness of appreciation and skilful co-operation.
On 26th January, 1942, Major Boden had been operating on column for some two days in the Antelat area when the orders to withdraw were received.
By his calm and skilful handling of his company the column was enabled to withdraw from a confused situation without loss, whilst knocking out an enemy gun and other vehicles.
Again, on 22nd February, 1942, this officer was second-in-command of a small column in the Charruba area which was suddenly attacked from two sides by a superior enemy force. In the resulting confusion the column commander and also the R.H.A. troop leader were taken prisoner, but Major Boden at once took control of the situation, collected two of the 25-pounder guns, got them into action and organized the orderly extraction of the remainder of the column without further loss and knocked out an enemy armoured car and an enemy gun in the process.

CAPT. J. E. C. BODLEY (10th Battalion), 27*th October*, 1944: M.C.

In the late afternoon of 16th May, 1944, during the attack on the Gustav Line south of Piumarola, this officer was ordered to take his scout platoon forward to seize a hill vital to both ourselves and the enemy, pending the arrival on foot of the rest of the company. Information was that enemy opposition was negligible. Six hundred yards from the objective the platoon came under extremely heavy fire from their right flank, an area which had been believed to be in our own hands when Lieut. Bodley received his orders.

In spite of this, Lieut. Bodley pushed forward by the most bold and skilful handling of his platoon, and succeeded in getting one section on to his objective. They there came under intense machine-gun and mortar fire from enemy on the reverse slope. Casualties were suffered, but Lieut. Bodley persevered in an attempt to work round the flank to a position from which he could observe the enemy on the reverse slope. During this flanking movement his own and one other carrier became bogged. Realizing that the enemy were in considerably greater strength than had been expected, Lieut. Bodley ordered his platoon to withdraw into cover, but himself remained with his bogged carriers in a position overlooked by the enemy at a range of about 100 yards.

He remained in this exposed position for half an hour, collecting information about enemy dispositions and weapons. This information he calmly reported back on the wireless, which he was by now operating by himself. When dusk fell Lieut. Bodley called a section of his platoon forward, extricated his carriers from under the noses of the enemy and rejoined his company.

Throughout the action this officer displayed the very highest standards of leadership, determination and cool judgment under heavy short-range fire. He successfully extricated his platoon intact from an extremely difficult position, and by his complete disregard for his own personal safety obtained information without which a successful attack the following morning could never have been made.

MAJOR J. T. BORTHWICK, 29*th March*, 1945: M.B.E.

As G.3 at the formation of this Division in October, 1942, and G2 since, this officer has done excellent work under varying and frequently novel conditions. He has twice acted as G.1 for periods of several weeks during the present campaign, including the period of the break-out from Normandy, when many different and unprecedented problems were presented by the speed of the advance, the transportation difficulties involved in its peculiar equipments, the wide dispersion of the Division, and the many different formations with which it was operating, often simultaneously. The co-ordination of maintenance, movement, regrouping and tactical allotment would have taxed the most experienced G.S.O. Major Borthwick grappled with them successfully and admirably. He is always cool and alert and it was largely due to his efforts that the direction and reshuffling of the various contingents of the Division were kept under control, and the varying teams of equipments made available to successive formations as and when required; a quick and efficient officer whose valuable services merit reward.

MAJOR (T./LIEUT.-COLONEL) T. J. B. BOSVILE, 13*th August,* 1942: D.S.O.
From 27th May to 10th June Lieut.-Colonel Bosvile has commanded his unit in action. From 2nd June to date he has had immediate command of two battery guns.

In the area north and slightly west of Knightsbridge he has been largely responsible by his skilful direction for the relief of pressure on the Guards Brigade box.

In particular, on 8th, 9th and 10th June, by his utter determination to take offensive action, the patrols which he has organized and directed have been responsible for the withdrawal of thirty tanks, the destruction of ammunition lorries, the disposal of enemy sentries and the recovery of a Grant tank within 200 yards of the enemy.

Throughout this and all actions he has shown a complete disregard for danger and by his visits to patrols, to anti-tank guns and to battery positions under fire, has encouraged all ranks to resist to the utmost. His command, his control and his complete disregard of fatigue have been an example of fortitude to all ranks.

28*th January,* 1943: Bar to D.S.O.

Throughout the operations at El Alamein and in the Snipe, Woodcock and Tel el Aqqaqir positions, from 23rd October to 4th November, 1942, this officer commanded and conducted the successful operations of the 7th Motor Brigade.

His constant desire to be aggressive, his anxiety to maintain the offensive, his quick decisions and his calm and considered judgment were largely responsible for the destruction of over sixty tanks and a large number of enemy personnel.

In conditions of extreme hardship and frequently under heavy shell fire, his energy, firm determination and complete disregard of safety were an inspiration and an example to those who served under him and to all who saw him.

11*th July,* 1945: C.B.E.

8*th November,* 1945: American Legion of Merit—Degree of Officer.

Brigadier Thomas J. B. Bosvile, British Army. As Deputy Assistant Chief of Staff, G.1, Supreme Headquarters, Allied Expeditionary Force, from May, 1944, to May, 1945, throughout the planning stage and subsequent to D Day, played a vital role in the functions of the G.I. Division. Working with an integrated staff, he was responsible for the co-ordination of all high-level staff matters with his American counterpart, a task which he accomplished in an exemplary manner. He was instrumental in developing the plans and establishing the Allied Expeditionary Force Club in Paris and the Allied Expeditionary Force Programme. His ability, efforts and devotion to duty reflect high credit upon himself and the British Army.

SERGT. G. C. BRADBURY, 5*th November,* 1942: M.M.

On 31st August, 1942, at 1815 hrs., his gun position was attacked by some twenty tanks. He held his fire until they were at very close range and hit two with three shots.

His platoon was overrun, but he removed the mechanism from his gun and withdrew his team, helping one man who was wounded.

After dark he returned to the scene of the action and succeeded in recovering his gun. A German patrol arrived on the scene during this operation, but was driven off by fire.

Through his gallantry and leadership his gun remained in action throughout.

CPL. P. H. BRADSHAW, *27th September,* 1940: M.M.

For services in Norway.

LIEUT. E. BRAIN, *27th July,* 1944 (Burma): M.C.

He was operating forward of his column as a fighting patrol at 0001 hrs. on the night of 18th/19th April when he was informed by the local Nagas that a Jap patrol had arrived at Sakhalu, M.Z. 90, and was staying the night.

He set off immediately with his platoon, led one section and arrived at Sakhalu at 0500 hrs. In the words of his report, "Arrived 0500 hrs., gave battle 0501 hrs." One of his men who was wounded in the subsequent battle reports that a sentry spotted them when about twenty yards from the inspection bungalow. The sentry was shot when about to give the alarm. Lieut. Brain led the three sections into the bungalow. He personally disposed of the Jap officer and one other. In the meantime a Jap light machine gun opened up from an outhouse and gave considerable trouble. The Jap patrol was undoubtedly well trained and tough, and throughout the action Lieut. Brain behaved in a gallant manner, and through his cool-headedness and initiative fought a very successful action.

The Jap casualties were thirteen killed, two wounded and three taken prisoner.

RFN. H. BRAYSHAW, *16th December,* 1941: G.M.

During the morning of 8th May, 1941, Rfn. Brayshaw showed a complete disregard for his personal safety by entering a building, which was burning and in a state of collapse, to rescue a comrade.

In a cellar in this building Rfn. Brayshaw saw his comrade trapped, and in danger of drowning in the slowly rising water from fire pumps. The water was nearly boiling. Rfn. Brayshaw was lowered head-first by a rope ten feet into the cellar, where, standing in four feet of water, he released his comrade and tied the rope around him. He then waited in the cellar, surrounded by falling burning debris, until his comrade was safe. He was then pulled out himself. Rfn. Brayshaw was engaged on fire-watching at the time of the incident.

SERGT. R. A. BRETT, *14th October,* 1940: M.M.

Sergt. Brett was commander of a section of guns at Snipe on 27th October, 1942; he fought his gun with outstanding courage, accounting for one Mark III destroyed and sharing in the destruction of five other German tanks. Throughout the day he held an exposed position which was continually shelled.

In the evening attack, after he had set on fire an enemy tank, his gun was hit by shell fire and knocked out; he rendered it useless to the enemy and got his crew, including one wounded, away safely.

During the operation he led his section with great dash and was himself wounded at Tel el Aqqaqir.

During his service in the Western Desert Sergt. Brett distinguished himself by a series of gallant and successful actions.

He was recommended for actions at Asida in May, 1942, when he knocked out a German armoured car and a troop carrier, and at Bir Tacata in June, 1942, where he saved a burning portee under fire.

His spirit and example, which typify the unshakable morale of the men under his command, have inspired many others both within and outside the Battalion.

RFN. R. BRIDGER, 9*th September*, 1942 : M.M.

For consistent courage and good work throughout the period, and in particular on 22nd November, 1941, when the carrier platoon of his company attacked an enemy position south of Sidi Rezegh aerodrome.

When a carrier was disabled by Breda fire from close range, this rifleman went forward in a 15-cwt. truck and despite heavy small-arms fire at 500 yards' range succeeded in towing the carrier to safety.

Later, on 22nd November, 1941, on Sidi Rezegh aerodrome, they again went forward in a 15-cwt. truck under heavy fire from a force of twenty-five enemy tanks and rescued the crew of a cruiser tank which had been disabled by enemy fire.

MAJOR-GENERAL THE VISCOUNT BRIDGEMAN, M.C.

1*st July*, 1940 : D.S.O.

1*st January*, 1944 : Companion of the Order of the Bath.

L./CPL. G. H. BROWN, 25*th April*, 1941 : D.C.M.

This N.C.O. accompanied Lieut. C. H. Liddell on two reconnaissance patrols on the nights of 2nd/3rd December and 7th/8th December, 1940. He and another N.C.O. crawled right up to the enemy defence, which had sentries posted about fifty yards apart. He got through these and scaled the wall of the defence to get inside the camp. He then crept back again and was thus able to bring very valuable information about the size and strength of the defences and location of anti-tank mines.

Again on the night of the 7th/8th he managed to crawl up to another side of the camp and got up very close. He was able to report a gap in the defences closed by night by enemy tanks, which was of the greatest value.

These two patrols took a very long time and required endless patience, skill and courage in eluding the watchfulness of the sentries.

MAJOR E. J. A. H. BRUSH (1st Battalion), 20*th September*, 1945 : D.S.O.

For gallant and distinguished service in the defence of Calais in May, 1940.

18*th April*, 1946 : O.B.E.

SERGT. G. BUDIBENT, *5th October*, 1944: M.M.

On the night of 29th/30th June, 1942, Sergt. Budibent with four carriers formed part of a small force ordered to intercept and harass the enemy moving down the road to El Daba. He so skilfully disposed his carriers that when day dawned he was able to bring most effective fire from short range to bear on the enemy column, which consisted of guns and lorried infantry. As a result of the engagement, fifteen enemy vehicles were knocked out, one two-man tank captured and twenty prisoners taken, who were rounded up by Sergt. Budibent under fire.

By his example and spirit this N.C.O. "set the pace" for this successful action, whilst on many occasions during the campaign he has shown himself to be a resourceful and fearless leader.

LIEUT. G. C. BURDER (1st Battalion), *1st March*, 1945: M.C.

This officer was commanding a force of two mortar platoons with a troop of tanks holding the village of Geffen on the night of 10th/11th October, 1944.

After artillery preparation, a battalion of infantry supported by artillery and mortar fire twice attacked this force. During the confused close-quarter fighting he constantly visited his section posts, encouraging and directing the fire of his men, and himself engaging the enemy with small-arms fire and grenades.

His quick appreciation and disregard for personal safety prevented enemy infiltration on several occasions. Throughout he maintained personal liaison with the troop of tanks and the platoon on his left, despite having to make these journeys under heavy fire of all descriptions. His example under fire has always been of the highest order, and on this occasion he excelled and his conduct undoubtedly saved his platoon from being overrun.

LIEUT.-COLONEL P. G. R. BURFORD, T.D., *8th November*, 1945: American Legion of Merit—Bronze Medal.

RFN. S. H. BURNHOPE, *14th January*, 1942: M.M.

This rifleman is the company medical orderly. During the night of 26th/27th October the Battalion attacked and consolidated an enemy position called Snipe, 866295.

During the following twenty-four hours the Battalion was in continuous action against about a hundred enemy tanks and was under incessant mortar, shell and machine-gun fire.

Many riflemen were wounded during this period. Rfn. Burnhope ran to all of them, however exposed the position, and administered first aid to them under heavy fire, showing complete disregard of his personal safety and the utmost bravery.

He attended a mortally wounded officer and while this officer was still living he sat with him in an extremely exposed positon to enemy fire until the officer eventually died. At all times during this extremely severe operation Rfn. Burnhope fulfilled his duty beyond praise, many lives undoubtedly being saved by his prompt and courageous action.

C.S.M. G. BUTCHER (10th Battalion), 19th April, 1945: M.M.

For conspicuous devotion to duty, personal courage and unflagging determination and cheerfulness in action during the period 11th May to 24th August, 1944.

C.S.M. Butcher has throughout proved himself to be a tower of strength to his company, exposing himself to the heaviest and most accurate fire without the slightest hesitation, and rallying and encouraging the men under the most difficult conditions of weather and enemy action. C.S.M. Butcher has, time after time, been worth an extra platoon to his company and to the battalion.

His complete disregard of danger, in spite of having been wounded on two occasions, and great personal endurance and outstanding powers of leadership have been throughout an inspiration to all with whom he has served.

L./CPL. H. G. CABLE (1st Battalion), 12th April, 1945: M.M.

In a company attack on Saint Joost on 21st January, 1945, L./Cpl. Cable was commanding a section in the leading platoon. After the first two houses had been taken from the enemy one of the supporting tanks was fired at by a panzerfaust from a slit trench in the garden. The shot missed and a moment later another German brought a panzerfaust to the aim from a neighbouring slit trench. Seeing this, L./Cpl. Cable quickly ran forward and threw a grenade into the trench from ten yards away, killing the occupants of the trench. Almost at once an enemy section in a concrete emplacement opened fire on another section of the platoon which was working its way forward on the left, killing the section commander. L./Cpl. Cable seized a Piat and entered a house, firing two bombs from the window at twenty yards' range. His fire killed one of the enemy and the remainder surrendered.

L./Cpl. Cable's individual bravery enabled the platoon to advance to its first objective.

L./CPL. H. E. J. CANN, 14th October, 1943: M.M.

This N.C.O. is a medical orderly. In the Battle of El Alamein he was constantly exposing himself to heavy fire in order to attend to the sick and wounded.

Throughout the period 23rd October, 1942, to 31st March, 1943, L./Cpl. Cann has shown great devotion to duty, and by his personal initiative, especially in dealing with men blown up on mines, has undoubtedly saved the lives of many men.

A./CPL. D. CARLTON (10th Battalion), 7th December, 1944: M.M.

For conspicuous gallantry and devotion to duty at Monte Rentella. On 21st/22nd June, 1944, Cpl. Carlton was signal corporal of a company which was ordered to seize the feature to the north of Monte Rentella.

On approaching the objective, the company came under heavy machine-gun fire. Cpl. Carlton, however, carrying a heavy load of vital signal equipment, followed his company commander into the assault, and on reaching the position calmly set about establishing communications.

Small-arms, mortar and shell fire was intense and any movement in the open was almost suicidal. Cpl. Carlton, however, volunteered to carry a message down 800 yards of exposed hillside to the reserve company, with whom it had been found impossible to make contact by any other means.

This task accomplished, he immediately set out up the hill again, still under intense fire, and showing an example of personal courage and devotion to duty which was an inspiration to all who witnessed it.

By the time he approached it, however, the company position had been overrun. Cpl. Carlton, however, although a signaller by trade, gathered together the men in the vicinity, organized them as a section and, still under heavy fire, successfully conducted a fighting withdrawal to the reserve company area.

Cpl. Carlton's complete disregard of his own safety and fine qualities of leadership and initiative in a crisis are worthy of the highest commendation and have set a magnificent example to all ranks of the Battalion.

RFN. R. G. CAVEY, 22nd July, 1943: M.M.

On 26th March, 1943, whilst Rfn. Cavey was acting as wireless telegraph operator on the platoon H.Q. carrier at Djebel Saikra his vehicle came under heavy fire and was disabled. His platoon commander was ordered to go to Battalion H.Q.

Rfn. Cavey went forward himself on foot under heavy fire and was able to obtain complete information as to the enemy position on the flank of Djebel Saikra. He then returned to his carrier, continued to operate his set and pass the information.

He proceeded forward on foot, still under fire, and returned at least three times to his carrier to pass further information, which later proved of great importance in the final successful attack on the Djebel Saikra feature.

His devotion to duty and disregard of personal safety were a fine example of coolness and bravery to all the other operators in the Battalion.

MAJOR W. M. CHAPMAN-WALKER, 6th January, 1944: M.B.E.

COLONEL CHICHESTER-CONSTABLE, D.S.O.

24th October, 1940: Bar to D.S.O.

RFN. D. A. CHARD, 14th January, 1943: D.C.M.

During an action on 26th/27th October on the Snipe position Rfn. Chard was No. 3 on a 6-pounder anti-tank gun.

In the first attack at night his No. 1 was wounded, but he still continued to engage the enemy. At night he allowed the enemy tanks to approach to 200 yards, firing their machine guns at his gun, before he opened fire. He hit one, which caught fire, and so damaged the other that its guns were silenced and it was immobile.

During the whole of the action his gun was under heavy machine-gun fire from the rear.

At first light he attended to the wounded whilst he was himself still under fire.

When the position was attacked by infantry he manned a Bren gun and caused casualties to the enemy.

In the last tank attack, in the evening at about 1700 hrs., he turned his gun completely round from south-east to north-west and then held his fire till three enemy tanks had approached. Two of them caught fire and the third was damaged. Owing to shortage of ammunition, he was unable to set the third tank on fire.

During the action his crew were killed by fire from these tanks, but he still continued to fire his gun. He was responsible for the destruction of ten enemy tanks, and by coolness and courage was an inspiration to his platoon in very critical circumstances.

CPL. S. C. CLARK, *9th May*, 1941 : M.M.

On 21st January, west of Tobruk, this N.C.O. was in command of a carrier forming part of a patrol which had withdrawn after heavy shelling. On seeing that another carrier had broken down, within view of the enemy position, he volunteered to go and retrieve it. He moved out, rectified the petrol stoppage and returned to the carrier, being under heavy shell fire the whole time.

On 22nd January this N.C.O. volunteered to take his carrier along the exposed flank of the patrol across the open so as to draw enemy fire while the remainder of the patrol advanced unobserved. He carried out his role with great skill and coolness, drawing heavy anti-tank and small-arms fire. This enabled the remainder of the patrol to reach within a hundred yards of the enemy's position and capture it.

LIEUT.-COLONEL E. N. CLARKE, 1*st July*, 1940 : O.B.E.; 23*rd May*, 1946 : C.B.E.

L./CPL. R. E. CLARKE, 1*st June*, 1943 : M.M.

When the pass between Dj Zemlet el Beida and Dj Hadoudi, north of El Hamma was attacked in the early hours of 31st March, 1943, "C" Company, of which he was medical orderly, for four hours held a position which was continuously under heavy fire at close range.

Throughout this period L./Cpl. Clarke, with complete disregard of his personal safety, continued to move about in the open, tending the wounded and supervising their evacuation.

By his bravery and devotion to duty in rendering prompt medical attention, this N.C.O. undoubtedly saved the lives of many wounded.

CPL. A. D. CLAY (2nd Battalion), 23*rd August*, 1945 : M.M.

Cpl. Clay is signal corporal of " B " Company, 2nd Bn. The Rifle Brigade. On 26th April, 1945, " B " Squadron, 2nd Lothian and Border Horse, and " B " Company, 2nd Rifle Brigade, were ordered to cross the River Po Morte at S. Nicolo Ferrarese and to establish a bridgehead on the west bank of the river. The crossing was held by the enemy with infantry, supported by tanks and S.P. guns, while S. Nicolo Ferrarese itself, through which it was necessary to pass in order to get across the river, was heavily shelled and mortared throughout the day. Cpl. Clay travelled with a No. 48 set in a Honey tank. This wireless set was the only link which the motor company commander had with his platoons, and its successful operation was therefore vital to the success of the infantry crossing. After a short period it became evident that the set could not be operated satisfactorily from inside the Honey, since the operation of the high-powered set in the tank inevitably jammed the transmission of the smaller set which was being operated by Cpl. Clay. Accordingly, without hesitation and acting entirely on his own initiative, this N.C.O. placed his set in an exposed position on the outside of the tank, where it was not affected by jamming. Despite continued heavy shelling and mortaring, in addition to fire from enemy tanks, Cpl. Clay continued to operate his set from this exposed position for a period of four hours, during which time he passed countless messages having an important bearing on the conduct of the operation.

It was entirely due to the determination and initiative displayed by this N.C.O. that communication was maintained during a critical phase of the operation, and his coolness, skill and utter disregard of his own safety during this period were worthy of the highest praise.

SERGT. C. V. CALISTAN, 13*th August*, 1942: M.M.

For conspicuous gallantry and devotion to duty at Bir Hacheim, and on 8th June, 1942. Sergt. Calistan commanded one of a section of guns supporting carriers in an attack on an enemy O.P. and anti-tank-gun position.

His guns came under considerable anti-tank supporting gun fire almost at once, but by his good fire orders made possible by his determination to observe his fire, he scored two direct hits on one of the guns and disabled it. When observation became difficult owing to blast, he left his vehicle and observed from a flank, where he was engaged by machine-gun fire. His vehicle was twice hit by anti-tank fire, but was kept in action.

On a later occasion he was again with the carriers when they went in against a concentration of enemy vehicles protected by anti-tank and machine guns; he kept his gun well forward in the action, destroying an anti-tank gun and a staff car.

At the end of the engagement he was wounded by a shell while sitting high up on his vehicle directing the fire of his gun.

Throughout these two actions he was a magnificent example to his crew and carried out his duty as No. 1 with complete disregard for his own safety.

14*th January*, 1943: D.C.M.

Sergt. Calistan was sergeant commander of a section of 6-pounder anti-tank guns, sited on the west flank of the Snipe position, on 26th/27th October, 1942. Sergt. Calistan's troop was engaged by enemy tanks both during the night and the following morning; by midday on 27th October all the other guns in his troop had been knocked out, and all the other members of his own gun crew but himself wounded and incapacitated; also the troop was almost out of ammunition.

At about 1300 hrs. fifteen German tanks attacked his section. The

Commanding Officer arrived at his position and acted as loader while he laid the gun and acted as No. 1.

With the greatest courage and coolness he waited until the tanks were some 300 yards away, and hit and set nine of them on fire. He then had no more ammunition left.

Unperturbed, he waited while his troop commander fetched more ammunition and when it arrived he hit three more enemy tanks in as many shots and so broke and repelled the enemy attack.

He continued to operate his gun for the rest of the day; after dark he received orders to close on to company headquarters and withdrew with the rest of his company. He set off to walk the quarter of a mile back under heavy machine-gun fire from three German tanks, carrying one of the wounded members of his crew; the wounded man was hit and killed in his arms. He immediately returned to his troop position to fetch the last remaining wounded men, whom he brought safely back, still under intense and accurate fire.

Throughout the action the quality of his determination was such that when the last point of human endurance and ability to continue to fight had been reached Sergt. Calistan took a new lease of courage. This he communicated to all around him and with their help he saved the day, so enabling his Battalion to withdraw safely from a critical position after inflicting losses on the enemy of fifty-seven tanks burnt.

During this action his superb gallantry was outstanding among many courageous acts performed.

L./SERGT. M. W. CARTER (2nd Battalion), 28*th June*, 1945: M.M.

For conspicuous courage and devotion to duty during the period 1st September to 31st December, 1944. This N.C.O. has carried out numerous reconnaissances and fighting patrols, in which he has done more than his duty and shown conspicuous courage and initiative.

In particular, during operations against the Gothic Line at Monte Peschiena he took part in three night patrols between 18th and 23rd September, 1944, to locate and destroy the enemy, who were dug in on a feature some 200 yards from his company's locality. On one of these patrols his patrol commander and two men were pinned to the ground by two Spandaus firing at ten yards' range. Sergt. Carter seized a Bren gun and, completely disregarding the enemy fire and grenades being thrown, took up a position to the flank and silenced the enemy, thereby enabling his patrol commander to rejoin his patrol. Sergt. Carter continued to fire and forced the surrender of three of the Germans opposing him.

On two subsequent patrols, one more German was taken prisoner, two were killed and two wounded. This N.C.O. was, by his skill and determination, to a considerable degree responsible for the success of these patrols; also he subsequently enabled his company to occupy the dominating feature successfully.

The actions of this N.C.O. and his fine leadership have been a constant inspiration to his platoon.

COLONEL F. O. CAVE, O.B.E., M.C. : Order of the Nile (3rd Class).

16*th April*, 1942: O.B.E.

He commands the Equatorial Corps, S.D.F., which is now withdrawing to the Sudan after a long spell of severe and periodical operations in the area Boma-Maji, some twelve hundred miles from H.Q. at Khartoum. Throughout this period and particularly in the later stages he has shown the greatest initiative and resource, and he has improvised and maintained a line of communication to supply his forward troops, at a distance of over three hundred miles from riverhead to Juba, with the minimum of guidance and assistance from H.Q., having previously organized the expansion of his corps to more than double its previous strength. It is entirely due to his devotion to duty and readiness to accept responsibility that his corps has been able to operate in that remote area.

CAPT. (T./MAJOR) D. F. CUNLIFFE (9th Battalion), 19*th October*, 1944: M.C.

On 18th July, 1944, Major Cunliffe's company ("F") was advancing south-west from La Prieure. After crossing the road near Le Mesnil-Frementel, Major Cunliffe put his company into the thick hedges and trees from which fire had been coming and from which some of our tanks had been destroyed. Owing to the speed and determination with which Major Cunliffe acted, this operation was completely successful and four 88-mm. guns and six nebelwerfers as well as a considerable number of prisoners were captured.

On 19th July the Battalion was detailed to attack the village of Bras, behind our tanks. Major Cunliffe's company was leading and in spite of heavy mortar fire he led them with great dash and determination into the village.

The operation was completely successful and over 300 S.S. prisoners were captured.

SERGT. E. CUNNINGHAM, 23*rd April*, 1942: M.M.

For conspicuous leadership and courage on 12th December, 1941, when the carrier platoon of which he was platoon sergeant made an attack on a strongly held enemy position south-west of Gazala.

Despite being wounded in the shoulder, he went forward under heavy Breda and machine-gun fire to cover the rest of the platoon while they were refilling with ammunition.

His courage and example were largely responsible for the capture of a hundred prisoners and for inflicting heavy losses on the enemy in men and vehicles.

CPL. R. CUNNINGHAM, 22*nd July*, 1943: M.M.

Cpl. Cunningham, while advancing up Djebel Saikra during an attack at dawn on 27th March, 1943, saw an enemy machine-gun post firing from a position higher up the hill.

All his section having become casualties, he attacked the post single-handed and with the aid of hand grenades captured the whole post, killing one, wounding two and taking prisoner three of the enemy.

After the objective had been gained Cpl. Cunningham was ordered to take back a wounded man from the top of the hill. This he did under heavy fire and through two unmarked minefields.

His was a fine example of section leading and he was throughout a source of great inspiration to all ranks.

COLONEL W. P. S. CURTIS, 11*th October*, 1945 : O.B.E.

This officer arrived at Antwerp in January, 1945, to find that he was placed in command of a disorganized Civil Affairs detachment and that relations with the civil authorities were strained.

Within three months, through his untiring efforts, his inspiration to all under his command and his personal dealings with the civil authorities, he now commands an organized, efficient and forceful detachment, and the relationship between the military and civil authorities is of the utmost cordiality.

SERGT. J. COOPER (8th Battalion), 29*th March*, 1945 : M.M.

Sergt. Cooper has commanded a carrier section from August to October, 1944, during the advance from Caumont to Antwerp and then on to Deurne. On many occasions during the advance Sergt. Cooper's section has led the advance.

At Putanges on 18th August Sergt. Cooper made a reconnaissance of the River Orne with great skill and coolness and, in spite of the presence of two Panther tanks, returned with very useful information. Again, west of Arras, on 1st September, information was received that a column of enemy horse-drawn artillery and transport was moving down the road from west to east. Sergt. Cooper immediately moved forward with all speed and, cutting the road, succeeded in causing such confusion among the enemy that the tanks were able to come up and finish them off. A large number of prisoners were taken.

During the whole advance Sergt. Cooper's section destroyed many enemy vehicles and took a considerable number of prisoners.

Sergt. Cooper showed himself at all times to be a gallant and resolute leader who was always quick to take the smallest opportunity to inflict damage on the enemy and to speed up the advance. His coolness and skill have been an inspiration to all those who have served with him.

CPL. R. A. COOPER (2nd Battalion), 19*th April*, 1945 : M.M.

' For conspicuous gallantry during the period 1st May to 31st August, 1944. During this period the coolness in action and the eagerness shown by this N.C.O. to destroy the enemy have been exemplary. He has invariably volunteered for tasks when it has not been the turn for duty of his own carrier section.

On 24th July, in operations in the Terrannova area, this N.C.O. was ordered to carry out a patrol to locate enemy O.Ps. which were bringing down accurate artillery fire on an R.E. party attempting to repair the road. The country was extremely difficult and close, and Cpl. Cooper came upon an enemy patrol at extremely short range. The enemy opened fire on him, but fortunately missed at twenty yards' range. Quite undeterred, this N.C.O. remained in the area until he had pin-pointed all the enemy positions. His information was of the greatest value and enabled our own artillery to silence these enemy O.Ps.

The example shown by this N.C.O. in contact with the enemy has always been of the highest order and has served as an encouragement to all those working with him.

SERGT. A. V. COAD, *22nd July*, 1943 : D.C.M.

At 0530 hrs. on 9th May, 1943, Sergt. Coad's platoon was ordered to advance into Hamman Lif. His platoon officer and two other ranks were seriously wounded.

In spite of heavy mortar and small-arms fire and continual sniping, he, with the aid of Cpl. Steggles, succeeded in taking the three wounded men in consecutive journeys to a place of safety. He went back a third time and brought back the officer to a safe place where he could receive medical attention. Sergt. Coad then returned into the battle and assumed command of the platoon and remained in position until ordered to withdraw.

Later in the same morning, at 0830 hrs., the company went forward to the attack.

Sergt. Coad was commanding the platoon when the company was pinned down by heavy fire. His platoon suffered more casualties and the platoon on his left had their officer killed and the sergeant wounded. On seeing this, Sergt. Coad immediately took charge of both platoons and succeeded in getting all the wounded back to a place of safety.

He rallied and encouraged the men who remained and carried out an organized and successful withdrawal of both platoons, stage by stage, when ordered.

In this action Sergt. Coad displayed the highest quality of leadership and by his coolness and courage and complete disregard of his own personal safety undoubtedly saved the lives of many men in a critical situation.

RFN. R. COATES (7th Battalion), *7th January*, 1944 : M.M.

During the night of 8th/9th July, in Monte Castiglion Maggio, the company to which Rfn. Coates belonged was strongly counter-attacked. Rfn. Coates's left hand was all but severed from his arm by a burst of Spandau fire. He did not inform his section commander that he had been hit, and as his position had been overrun he was ordered to retire.

Seeing L./Cpl. Gadson wounded and unable to walk, Rfn. Coates half-lifted him and half-dragged him down the hill, a distance of about 600 yards, across very steep and broken country, to the shelter of a deep wadi.

Throughout this time a heavy artillery concentration was being fired on the hill, as it was thought that all our troops were clear. This did not, however, deter Rfn. Coates from sticking to his wounded comrade, and he rallied the remainder of his section by joking and talking cheerfully as though he were completely unhurt.

It was not until he had put L./Cpl. Gadson in a position of safety and had made sure that the remainder of his section were present and unharmed that he mentioned his own and extremely serious wound.

By his devotion to duty and self-control Rfn. Coates saved L./Cpl. Gadson from falling into the hands of the enemy and set an example to his section which was of the highest order.

RFN. E. COCKBURN, 1st June, 1943: M.M.

Rfn. Cockburn was a member of the company ordered to capture the pass north of El Hamma between Dj Zemlet el Beida and Dj Hadoudi before first light on 31st March, 1943.

Soon after the advance began the company came under heavy fire and he was wounded in the shoulder and leg. In spite of these injuries, and before the order to charge had been given, Rfn. Cockburn dashed forward alone, and single-handed captured a gun position. He remained fighting with the company until it was ordered to withdraw at 1030 hrs.

L./CPL. M. CONLIN, 25th November, 1943: M.M.

L./Cpl. Conlin was a section commander in a motor platoon. During all operations from 18th February to 31st May, particularly at Djebel Saikra (Medenine), and at Djebel Kournine (Tunisia), he set an outstanding example of bravery and devotion to duty.

During an attack on the night of 29th/30th April his platoon commander was severely wounded and the platoon was pinned by heavy machine-gun fire and grenades at thirty yards' range.

When the platoon received orders to withdraw two hours later L./Cpl. Conlin refused to leave his officer and attempted to carry him down the precipitous slope, but was heavily fired upon; he then lay on his back and rolled his officer on top of himself, while another helper dragged him down the hill by his legs. He succeeded in moving fifty yards, but again came under heavy fire.

He remained with his officer, in spite of repeated orders to withdraw, and it was not until it was nearly light and his dying officer gave him a final order to leave him that L./Cpl. Conlin withdrew, knowing that it was not humanly possible for anything more to be done.

CPL. P. J. CONLON, 9th May, 1941: D.C.M.

For conspicuous gallantry and devotion to duty at Sidi Saleh on 6th February. This N.C.O. was platoon sergeant of a platoon whose area had been penetrated by an enemy medium tank and was being surrounded by enemy infantry. Although the other section was forced to withdraw by heavy enemy fire, he protected the anti-tank guns on the right of the position by engaging the advancing infantry with light machine-gun fire.

He subsequently went forward under fire, rescued two wounded men and brought them and the section truck back to safety, the remainder of the section having been killed or wounded.

CPL. E. W. COPE, 14th January, 1943: M.M.

This N.C.O. was No. 3 of a 6-pounder anti-tank gun in the Snipe position on 26th and 27th October, 1942. Throughout the action, under continuous and intense shell and machine-gun fire, he engaged enemy tanks whenever they appeared in his sights at a suitable range.

A shell landed behind his gun, killing the loader and injuring the No. 4. Cpl. Cope attended to the injuries of the wounded man and then continued to fire the gun with his troop sergeant, who was acting as No. 1. Finally, Cpl. Cope was himself wounded and could not continue to fire the gun.

He crawled away with his troop sergeant and helped to fetch a new crew to the gun. Under the direction of his No. 1, he fired with coolness and skill, helping to set on fire five tanks and knocking out two guns.

He never flinched in his duty, and his courage was outstanding.

2/LIEUT. J. F. COPE, 9th September, 1941: M.C.

On the night before El Agheila fell into enemy hands, 2/Lieut. Cope, with a section of his platoon, had been out on patrol some two to three miles south-west of El Agheila, on withdrawing at dawn to the King's Dragoon Guards H.Q., then some miles north-east of El Agheila. 2/Lieut. Cope left his patrolling section outside the fort at El Agheila and himself went inside to see whether one of his other sections had returned.

Our troops usually held the fort by day but evacuated it by night. On entering, 2/Lieut. Cope heard voices which he at first took to be English but later found to be Italian. He went inside to investigate, when fire was suddenly opened upon him by a party of Italians, who tried to capture him. 2/Lieut. Cope opened fire and saw two fall and was able to make good his escape, picking up the section he had left outside the fort and withdrawing under a hail of light-automatic and small-arms fire.

The recommendation in this case was initiated by the O.C. King's Dragoon Guards, under whose orders 2/Lieut. Cope was operating with his platoon. .

CPL. F. O. C. COWARD (1st Battalion), 12th July, 1945: M.M.

On the evening of 1st April, 1945, Cpl. Coward was leading a section in a platoon attack on a wood. He led his men with great dash, but while rounding up some prisoners heavy fire was opened from a nearby house. Cpl. Coward got his men into cover, but while doing so was hit in the throat by a bullet. With three others he crept into a shelter which was occupied by a German officer. The whole area was completely open and was raked by Spandau fire. Cpl. Coward then collapsed and the three other men in the shelter believed he was dead. Under a smoke screen they got away. Cpl. Coward came to and, being menaced by the officer, shot him and crawled from the shelter. He observed a German with an automatic weapon following his three comrades and, though in great pain, he managed to shoot him and crawled across the open ground under heavy enemy fire until he was observed and picked up.

Cpl. Coward's splendid courage when in great pain and his sense of duty undoubtedly saved the lives of three of his comrades.

SERGT. T. V. A. COWHEY, 12th February, 1942: D.C.M.

At Sidi Rezegh on 22nd November, this N.C.O. was platoon sergeant of the carrier platoon of his company.

During the afternoon, when the main German attack was made on the aerodrome with sixty tanks, he displayed qualities of the highest courage and initiative. When many of our own tanks had been overrun and his platoon was under intense fire from the enemy tanks at a range of less than 1,000 yards, he moved out into the open and assisted in getting away wounded R.A.C. personnel.

Later, when a further German attack, supported by infantry and anti-tank guns, was made west of the aerodrome, he moved his carriers boldly out to within 1,000 yards of the enemy tanks, engaged the infantry and inflicted heavy casualties on them.

Throughout the day his fine spirit and courage were an example to the rest of his platoon.

LIEUT. G. CORYTON (8th Battalion), 13th March, 1945: M.C.

On 10th September, 1944, Lieut. Coryton was commanding a platoon in the leading company of the battalion to which he belonged when attacking Helchteren. Early in the battle two of Lieut. Coryton's sections were completely destroyed by enemy mortar fire, but he immediately reorganized the remainder of his platoon and pressed forward to his objective. Lieut. Coryton was then given command of another platoon whose commander and platoon sergeant were both casualties. He quickly formed the whole party into one full-strength platoon and began clearing a line of houses which were strongly held by the enemy. Enemy mortar fire was intense and heavy casualties were suffered, but such was Lieut. Coryton's determination and calm leadership that the whole operation was completely successful and large numbers of the enemy were killed.

Throughout the nine hours' heavy fighting against an enemy who refused to surrender, Lieut. Coryton showed a complete disregard for his safety and had such control over the situation that he was an inspiration to the whole company.

LIEUT.-COLONEL G. COX, 13th December, 1945: O.B.E.

For service rendered as Senior Staff Officer for Physical Training in the Central Mediterranean Force since June, 1944. He was also Secretary of the Central Mediterranean Army Sports Control Board and one of the British Army representatives of the Allied Sports Control Board.

The healthy and efficient state of P.T. and sports organization in this theatre is due very largely to this officer's work.

CAPT. G. A. COZENS, 13*th December*, 1945: M.B.E.

For service as D.A.P.M., 207 Sub-Area, during operations in April and May, 1945.

This officer's efforts and tact contributed greatly to the extremely high standard of discipline maintained by the British troops throughout, which was a very large factor in ensuring that harmonious relations with the local Yugoslavs were maintained to the very end.

Prior to this date this officer carried out similar duties with this sub-area at Piræus, Greece, H.Q., which was frequently subjected to fire from all weapons from small arms up to 105-mm. guns.

R.S.M. T. CROCKER (10th Battalion), 28*th June*, 1945: M.B.E.

R.S.M. Crocker has been R.S.M. of the 10th Battalion for three and a half years. During this period he has proved himself time and again to be a leader and organizer of the highest quality, and his influence upon the Battalion has always been of the most inestimable value.

He is a trainer and disciplinarian of the best type and the fact that his standard of service and devotion to duty have been inculcated into the N.C.Os. throughout the Battalion has been most noticeably reflected in the unit's fighting capacity and morale.

His qualities have been particularly marked during the last six months when the Battalion has been dependent almost entirely upon mule maintenance. The task of organizing this maintenance was given to R.S.M. Crocker, and it is due to his unceasing devotion to duty and outstanding organizing ability that at no time has any sub-unit lacked any ammunition, stores or foodstuffs where it has been humanly possible to provide them, no matter what the conditions of weather or enemy interference may have been.

R.S.M. Crocker's past services have included participation in the first Benghazi campaign, 1940-41, as C.S.M. of a company of the 2nd Battalion, service under the P.R. Branch of the War Office, lecturing and broadcasting on the campaign, and service in the Tunisian and Italian campaigns as R.S.M. of the 10th Battalion.

He showed notable gallantry in the Liri Valley battle, controlling transport and personnel continually moving amongst the vehicles under shell fire, and ensuring that they were parked in positions which he had personally reconnoitred and which gave the maximum of concealment. While guiding a vehicle into such a position he was wounded in the face by a mine explosion.

R.S.M. Crocker has sixteen years and ten months' service and his magnificent influence upon all with whom he has come in contact during that period cannot be over-estimated.

LIEUT. (T./MAJOR) D. L. DARLING, 8*th July*, 1941: M.C.

For conspicuous good work throughout the whole period 15th November, 1940, to 17th February, 1941, and in particular during the action at Sidi Saleh on 6th/7th February, 1941, when this officer was commanding a company on a three-and-a-half-mile front.

Though repeatedly attacked by medium tanks and infantry, by day and night, on at least one occasion supported by artillery, all attempts to penetrate the position were stopped.

This officer's consistent visits to his company locations under fire and his resource and initiative in handling his anti-tank guns were evidently responsible for the success with which the vastly superior enemy forces, both tank and infantry, were contained and destroyed.

13th August, 1942: Bar to M.C.

On the night of 28th/29th June Major Darling was in charge of Corps H.Q. convoy when it was ordered to make a break-out from the Mersa Matruh area through the enemy forces which encompassed it.

Owing to traffic congestion, the column became disintegrated and Major Darling did much not only to keep the Corps transport together but also to organize other stragglers who were continuously encountered.

From 0130 hrs. on 29th June to about 1200 hrs. on 30th June Major Darling and the vehicles following him were under almost continuous fire.

His coolness under fire, his unflinching determination and his skill in leadership and navigation were responsible for getting the convoy through with only one casualty.

At about 1030 hrs. on the morning of 30th June Major Darling was fired on by a British 2-pounder anti-tank gun at close range. He believed that British troops had mistaken him for the enemy, and got out of his vehicle to investigate.

He was at once called upon by a German to surrender, but immediately pulled out his revolver and killed his assailant.

He then called upon some of his companions to assist and succeeded in leading the party so that all the crew of the gun were killed except one, and he was taken prisoner.

Major Darling, with assistance, set fire to the gun and portee, as he was unable to rescue it.

By his prompt action Major Darling undoubtedly saved many lives and the vehicles in the convoy.

19th August, 1943: D.S.O.

For conspicuous courage and outstanding leadership on the night of 26th/27th April, 1943. He led his Battalion in an advance over the Argoub el Meghs feature of the Goubellat track.

One route only was practical for any vehicles and anti-tank guns, and this was found to be securely defended by German infantry with more than one Mark VI tank.

Colonel Darling brought forward two of his 6-pounder guns and engaged these tanks, but the shot would not penetrate, though the range was not above 150 yards.

The guns and some carriers were then set on fire by the tanks, and it was clear that there was no way of getting anti-tank guns forward to the infantry.

Colonel Darling therefore ordered his Battalion to withdraw and by magnificent leadership extracted them with comparatively small loss from a situation which would have become completely untenable in the daylight owing to the absence of anti-tank defence.

Throughout he set a superb example of courage and determination which has been an inspiration to his whole Battalion.

23rd August, 1945: Bar to D.S.O.

For outstanding leadership and devotion to duty while in support of the 17th/21st Lancers during the 26th Armoured Brigade's break-out to Poggio Renatico between 20th and 22nd April, and again in the 61st Infantry Brigade's pursuit from Monselice to Udine, 30th April and 1st May.

In just over twenty-four hours Lieut.-Colonel Darling led his force with such determination and drive that he covered a distance of over 100 miles and, although attacked by enemy tanks, he knocked out three of them, besides overcoming pockets of resistance and taking over 1,000 prisoners.

There is no doubt that as a direct result of this officer's action the vital nerve centre of North-East Italy fell into our hands, thereby virtually ending the campaign in that important sector. This officer's complete disregard for his own personal safety has always been an inspiration to the troops under his command.

CPL. H. DAVEY (10th Battalion), *7th December*, 1944: M.M.

For conspicuous gallantry and devotion to duty on 22nd June, 1944. Cpl. Davey was N.C.O. in charge of stretcher-bearers in a forward position. Severe shelling, mortaring and machine-gunning were being experienced and casualties were considerable.

In spite of the intense fire throughout the day, Cpl. Davey showed complete disregard of his personal safety and went repeatedly out to exposed positions to bring in wounded, tending them under fire and finally helping to carry them down a mile of exposed and accurately registered road to the nearest point to which it was possible to bring an ambulance.

Cpl. Davey's bravery and coolness were an inspiration to all who saw him, while his organizing ability and devotion to duty undoubtedly saved the lives of many seriously wounded men who otherwise would not have received medical attention until too late.

MAJOR J. E. DAVIES, *24th August*, 1944: M.B.E.

CPL. D. DEBELL, *27th April*, 1944: M.M.

For services while a prisoner of war.

MAJOR T. L. D. DEWHURST (7th Battalion), *23rd August*, 1945: M.C.

Major Dewhurst commanded a composite company of the 7th Bn. The Rifle Brigade which accompanied the 17th/21st Lancers group in a thirty-mile break-through from Segni to Poggio Renatica on 21st April,

1945. This officer showed great personal courage when it was necessary to organize the close protection of the tanks in harbour in close proximity of the enemy, as the harbour area was under considerable enemy fire during the initial stages of the operation. He was constantly to be seen moving about in the open under fire, organizing his troops into position. During the hours of darkness this officer personally led his company into Poggio Renatica and successfully cleared the town of enemy opposition.

Throughout this operation Major Dewhurst showed great courage, powers of leadership and initiative, and his action was a contributing factor to the success of the 17th/21st Lancers group on this occasion.

RFN. W. H. DOHERTY (2nd Battalion), *12th April*, 1945: M.M.

For courage and initiative. On the night of 9th/10th November, 1944, Rfn. Doherty was a member of a fighting patrol sent to Villa Mengone to get an identification. The patrol shot and killed a sentry outside the villa and withdrew after a sharp exchange of shots with the Germans inside. Rfn. Doherty remained with Rfn. Alldridge in a doorway of the villa, and after some forty minutes four Germans entered the courtyard. Both riflemen held their fire until the Germans were within a few yards; they then killed two and wounded the other two, who crawled away round the house. After another wait, Rfn. Doherty and Alldridge left the cover of the doorway and removed the identity documents from the two bodies in the courtyard. To do this Rfn. Doherty exposed himself to observation from a window some thirty feet away, where he knew there had been an automatic weapon which had fired on the patrol. About three hours later seven Germans came into the courtyard. When Rfn. Alldridge called upon them to surrender they withdrew behind a wall and opened fire. Rfn. Doherty, seeing that Rfn. Alldridge's T.S.M.C. had jammed when he tried to reply, threw a grenade, which caused groans and shouts. Both riflemen then withdrew and reached their company night position at 0430 hrs.

Rfn. Doherty showed initiative and disregard for his personal safety. His initiative in getting a useful identification and his offensive spirit in closing with the enemy have set a fine example to all ranks in the battalion.

BRIGADIER A. S. G. DOUGLAS, O.B.E., *23rd December*, 1943: C.B.E.

Brigadier Douglas has commanded the Persia Area since its inception in October, 1942.

In forming and organizing his command he has shown ability and enthusiasm in marked degrees. He has discharged with praiseworthy thoroughness his intricate responsibilities in connection with the security of his area; and, in particular, of the lines of communication used in forwarding supplies.

His duties have involved very close co-ordination with an Allied Power, and it is due in no small measure to his tact and thoroughness that close co-operation has been maintained.

22nd July, 1944: Order of Kutuzov (2nd Class).

SERGT. T. J. DRUMMOND, 13th August, 1942: M.M.

For conspicuous gallantry and devotion to duty on 13th June, 1942. This N.C.O., during a tank battle which took place near the blockhouse, was sent forward to rescue the injured crew of one of our leading tanks which had been knocked out by enemy anti-tank fire.

Without the slightest hesitation and under intense shelling and machine-gun fire, he drove his carrier to within a few yards of the knocked-out tank, jumped out and with the help of two other men of his carrier succeeded in extricating the wounded tank crew and brought them back to safety.

On this occasion, as throughout the operation from 27th May to 16th June, this N.C.O. displayed complete disregard for personal safety and set a fine example of coolness and bravery to those under his command.

T./CAPT. J. A. DUDGEON, 28th January, 1943: M.C.

On 25th October, 1942, Capt. Dudgeon, in order to co-ordinate the anti-tank guns which he commanded, showed complete disregard of danger in moving about, often in an unarmoured vehicle, over a comparatively wide area, under heavy shelling, considerable machine-gun fire and accurate sniping.

His success is measured by the fact that that afternoon fourteen enemy tanks were destroyed by his guns, the first time they had been in action.

On the night of 2nd/3rd November Capt. Dudgeon went forward with the leading companies in the attack on Pt. 40, near Tel el Aqqaqir, in order to reconnoitre the position, when won, for his guns. The attack failed and a number of men were killed or wounded.

In spite of heavy machine-gun fire, Capt. Dudgeon set about finding the wounded, and on this occasion, alone, was the direct means of saving three men's lives.

He had consistently tended the wounded when his other duties permitted, under considerable and often heavy fire throughout the battles from 25th to 28th October and 2nd and 3rd November.

His outstanding determination and disregard of danger, combined with coolness and clear thinking, were very fine examples in very unpleasant circumstances.

MAJOR J. A. DUDGEON, 1st June, 1943: Bar to M.C.

This officer commanded the anti-tank company when the Battalion captured the pass. At first light his company came under intense artillery, mortar and machine-gun fire.

Major Dudgeon, with complete disregard of his personal safety, and in spite of being wounded in the right foot early in the action, organized his company into a defensive position and in the absence of artillery support used his guns with great effect.

He was continually moving about in the open, encouraging his men and fighting his guns. In the final stages of this action when he was unable to walk and was obviously in great pain, this officer insisted on attending to the wounded (Major Dudgeon was a medical student for four years before the war) before they were evacuated.

Throughout the action Major Dudgeon's courage and leadership were an inspiration to all those with whom he came in contact.

LIEUT. (QRMR.) E. C. DUDMAN, 14*th October*, 1943 : M.B.E.

Lieut. E. C. Dudman has been Quartermaster since the arrival of the Battalion in the North African theatre of war, and has been in charge of the administration of the Battalion almost without leave, rest or relief of any kind.

Throughout the fighting of the winter of 1941-42, the summer of 1942, and since the Battle of El Alamein he has continued with unfailing cheerfulness, perseverance and determination to provide the Battalion with essential commodities and stores, often having to deliver them over tremendous distances. His handling of the petrol echelon on the pursuit from El Alamein to Tobruk, when many units ran short of petrol, was a classic example of the quartermaster's art, brought to a very rare standard of efficiency.

His devotion to duty, energy and, above everything else, his cheerfulness under all circumstances have been a source of great inspiration to the whole Battalion.

L./CPL. F. DYER (2nd Battalion), 24*th May*, 1945 : D.C.M.

For gallantry and devotion to duty during the attack on Tossignano. At 0600 hrs. on 14th December, 1944, L./Cpl. Dyer's platoon was ordered to seize a house on the southern side of Tossignano, to relieve pressure on " C " Company, 2nd Rifle Brigade, who were being counter-attacked in the western end of the village. The entry into the house was forced and the platoon established on the ground floor, which consisted of only one room. At first light the enemy counter-attacked and the Bren gunner covering the street was killed. L./Cpl. Dyer immediately manned the Bren gun and was himself hit in the leg almost at once. He refused attention and continued to fire the Bren with such good effect that the attack was temporarily stopped. Later the house was attacked with bazookas, the ceiling blown down and the room set on fire with petrol, so that the platoon was forced to withdraw down the hill. L./Cpl. Dyer, with his platoon commander and Rfn. Aldridge, covered this withdrawal, engaging the enemy at very short range.

Under cover of some rocks at the foot of the hill L./Cpl. Dyer tended three wounded men and then, on his own initiative, crossed 200 yards of open ground under observed machine-gun and mortar fire, to get help from the Company H.Q. Smoke was put down, but more men were hit near the Company H.Q. while crossing the open ground. Seeing this, L./Cpl. Dyer improvised a Red Cross flag from a white handkerchief and the blood of a wounded man and repeatedly went forward in face of heavy machine-gun and mortar fire, each time helping back a wounded man. Finally, as a result of L./Cpl. Dyer's determined and courageous efforts, the enemy recognized the Red Cross flag and it was possible for stretcher-bearers to collect the remaining wounded, who would otherwise have spent the day lying in the open exposed to enemy fire. Altogether, twelve wounded were brought in, and L./Cpl. Dyer continued for three hours to bring in and help tend the wounded.

L./Cpl. Dyer's gallantry was of the highest order and there is no doubt that by his determination and disregard for himself he saved the lives of several men of his platoon.

RFN. S. G. EAGLES, 20th September, 1945 : M.M.

For gallantry and distinguished service in the defence of Calais, May, 1940.

LIEUT. E. G. EAKINS (7th Battalion), 28th June, 1945 : M.C.

During the period September to December, 1944, this officer has been constantly in action as a platoon commander. He has continually shown quite outstanding qualities of leadership, determination and courage.

Two actions at Orsara on 30th/31st October and at Monteloro on 7th/8th November are typical of his gallant conduct. On the night of 30th/31st October, while in command of the Orsara platoon position, Lieut. Eakins defeated a determined enemy attempt to capture this isolated and dominating position, inflicting one dead and four wounded on the enemy while suffering no casualties himself. Again, on the night of 7th/8th November a German fighting patrol commanded by a company commander attacked Lieut. Eakins's platoon in position at Monteloro. The attack was defeated by Lieut. Eakins's platoon and the German patrol was routed, leaving three wounded, a bazooka and a Spandau in our hands.

Throughout this period Lieut. Eakins has inspired all with whom he came in contact with a very real desire to inflict the maximum casualties on the enemy at every possible opportunity.

W.O. CL. II J. EASEN, 20th September, 1945 : M.M.

For gallantry and distinguished service in the defence of Calais, May, 1940.

LIEUTENANT-GENERAL T. R. EASTWOOD, D.S.O., M.C., 1st January, 1941 :
    to be Companion of the Order of the Bath; 1st January, 1943 : to be Knight Commander of the Order of the Bath; 25th July, 1944 : Grand Cross, Ordre de Merite civil et militaire d'Adolphe de Nassau, Luxembourg.

CAPT. (T./MAJOR) HON. M. G. EDWARDES, 14th October, 1943 : M.B.E.

For continuous, outstanding, good service and devotion to duty as Brigade Major, 7th Motor Brigade, particularly during the operations at El Alamein, October, 1942, and subsequently.

Major Edwardes, during the battle periods, was in charge at Main Brigade H.Q., the Commander being away at Tactical H.Q. It fell to him to take decisions and to issue orders in conformity with the Commander's intentions, often without possibility of reference to the Commander.

By sound organization, clear understanding and unremitting attention he ensured the smooth working of the Brigade, relieved the Commander of all matters of detail and contributed in a very large measure to the success of the operations.

LIEUT.-COLONEL J. D. R. ELKINGTON, 13*th December*, 1945: O.B.E.

Lieut.-Colonel Elkington has been in charge of Tac. " A " Force at H.Q., A.A.I., and H.Q., Fifteenth Army, for approximately one year. During the last six months, which included the final campaign in Italy, of the spring of 1945 the major part of all " A " Force planning and operations has fallen on Colonel Elkington's shoulders.

The way in which he has carried out these duties has clearly been shown by both the results obtained in this successful campaign and the interrogation of the German Staff on its conclusion.

A./CPL. E. V. ELSMERE (7th Battalion), 7*th December*, 1944: M.M.

For showing the utmost gallantry and devotion to duty in the attack on Monte Malba on 20th June, 1944, and during the subsequent counter-attacks.

On 20th June L./Cpl. Elsmere acted as stretcher-bearer to the company detailed to capture Monte Malba.

Under intense mortar and machine-gun fire in an exposed position he personally carried in two men who had been wounded. Throughout the action he was continually tending the wounded in the most exposed positions.

By his complete disregard for his own safety and the greatest skill and determination, he undoubtedly saved the lives of many wounded and enabled them to be safely evacuated. His courage and devotion to duty were an inspiration to his company.

LIEUT. J. R. EMERSON-BAKER, 5*th November*, 1942: M.C.

On the night of 31st August/1st September, 1942, in the area west of Deirel Muhafid, Lieut. J. R. Emerson-Baker was in command of a scout platoon responsible for the left sector of the column front at its junction with the K.R.R.C. column.

During the night this officer's position was attacked by infantry escorted by eighteen tanks. He engaged the infantry at close range, causing many casualties and forcing the infantry to withdraw before they had succeeded in lifting any mines.

Later in the night, as a result of a report that enemy infantry had broken through to the north of his position, he was ordered to locate and stop the enemy.

He encountered 200 to 300 infantry closely packed together in process of passing through the minefield. He immediately attacked them, killing or wounding almost the entire party, his own carrier being hit by a 50-mm. shell during the engagement.

Throughout the whole action and during the subsequent withdrawal from the forward minefield, this officer continued to command his platoon with the utmost coolness and disregard for his personal safety. His cool judgment and the personal example he set in courage and devotion to duty were an inspiration to his platoon and his company.

P.S.M. A. ENDEAN, 1st *April*, 1941 : M.M.

For consistently good work during the period 10th June to 15th November, 1940. He led many night patrols with considerable skill.

When commanding his platoon in observation of a large enemy column he crawled forward to within 800 yards to get proper observation during the mirage period, and after burying a rifleman who had been killed on the previous day, returned with valuable information.

9th *May*, 1941 : Bar to M.M.

At Sidi Saleh, during the night of 6th/7th February, 1941, this warrant officer, who was C.S.M. of "A" Company, was laying mines on the main road Benghazi—Agedalia when an enemy column was heard approaching. He carried on and completed his task when the enemy column was only a few yards from him and plainly visible in the moonlight.

His courage and devotion to duty resulted in the destruction of the column and the capture of a hundred prisoners.

LIEUT. R. F. FAIRWEATHER, 23rd *September*, 1943 : M.C.

This officer was in command of the carrier platoon of "C" Company in the 17th/21st Lancers regimental group throughout the IX Corps advance from Djebel Rihane, starting on 22nd April, 1943.

On 24th April the group was held up by heavy anti-tank fire on the reverse slope of a hill. Lieut. Fairweather went forward on patrol with his carriers and when his carriers could go no farther he went on on foot and brought back accurate information as to the exact location and types of fourteen enemy tanks, which were in three different pockets, and two enemy guns, all on the reverse slope of the feature on which the regimental group was held up.

On this a plan was made and an attack launched which succeeded in knocking out ten out of twelve enemy tanks without loss to ourselves.

During the same operation Lieut. Fairweather carried out several other patrols, locating enemy armour.

In spite of his carriers being subjected to very heavy shelling and bombing, his leadership and disregard for personal safety were an example to his men at all times, and reports of his reconnaissance patrols were of vital value to the operations' successful accomplishment.

CPL. J. R. FARRER (1st Battalion), 24th *January*, 1946 : M.M.

Between October, 1944, and the end of hostilities in North-West Europe, Cpl. Farrer commanded a section in a motor platoon. Throughout this period he consistently distinguished himself in numerous actions by his courage, cheerfulness and ability. On two particular occasions Cpl. Farrer particularly distinguished himself. First at Geffen on the night of 10th/11th October, where his section of three riflemen, which was holding a street, was attacked by some fifty Germans supported by mortar and artillery fire. The enemy got to within ten yards of his po.ition before they were halted by the fire of his section and were forced to withdraw, leaving six dead behind. In beating off the assault by vastly superior forces Cpl. Farrer was in no small measure responsible for the fact that his company group, consisting of two platoons and a troop of tanks, were successful in repelling an attack by what turned out to be a battalion of enemy.

Later at Stadtlohn, on 29th March, 1945, when he was advancing at the head of his section, he was pinned down by heavy and accurate machine-gun fire. Ignoring his own safety, he rushed off to organize support and report to his platoon commander, and returned to his section to continue the advance.

Throughout his service with the Battalion his courage and cheerfulness have inspired all with whom he has worked.

LIEUT. A. R. FAULCONBRIDGE (1st Battalion), 2nd August, 1945 : M.C.

On 20th April, 1945, close to the village of Daerstorf, Lieut. Faulconbridge, who was commanding a scout platoon, proved himself not only an expert tactician but a bold and resourceful leader of men. The village had been turned into a strong-point, the enemy being about company strength with two 75-mm. A.T. guns, one 50-mm. A.T. gun and twelve Spandaus. It was essential that this strong-point be overrun, and accordingly this officer made sweeps in two directions with his carriers, but on each occasion was forced to withdraw by heavy fire. Quite undismayed, however, he made a third attempt from a new direction. Having edged up to within 300 yards of the enemy, he engaged them, and when an attack was put in from another flank by a mortar platoon and a troop of tanks he closed right in to finish off the enemy.

Throughout this action this officer displayed fierce determination to seek out and engage the enemy, and set an inspiring example of personal courage to his men.

SERGT. J. W. FELL (2nd Battalion), 13th December, 1945 : M.M.

This N.C.O. has commanded a section of carriers in the scout platoon throughout the past three months. On 22nd April, 1945, his section was leading a motor company group into Vigarano a Pieve during the advance on Bondeno. His orders were to secure two bridges in the southern part of the village, and while doing so his section was attacked by a group of Germans, amongst them six men armed with *Faustpatronen*. One of the carriers was destroyed, but Sergt. Fell beat off the enemy and his action undoubtedly saved the bridges, already prepared for demolition, from destruction.

Later during operations in the Belluno area his section was ordered to act as a covering party for a motor company to enable the latter to take up a defensive position. While doing so the section was strongly attacked by enemy infantry and subjected to heavy machine-gun fire, but Sergt. Fell fought the enemy off, inflicting severe casualties with his Brens and Brownings.

By his skilful handling of the section he enabled the motor company's position to be consolidated and the Germans' escape route to the north was thereby effectively cut.

Throughout the spring campaign Sergt. Fell's leadership and conduct have been of the highest order, and his complete disregard for personal safety has been an inspiration to his platoon and those around him.

SERGT. J. R. FERGUSON, 13*th June*, 1946: M.B.E.

MAJOR (T./BRIGADIER) F. W. FESTING, 16*th June*, 1942 (Madagascar): D.S.O.

In command of the assault brigade, he planned all details and carried his task through with great ability and dash. Showing almost complete indifference to shelling and sniping, he was continually in the more forward area, carrying out personal reconnaissances regardless of danger and cheering up the troops.

Accompanied by the C.P.O., he entered the town of Antsirang long before resistance had ended and accepted the personal surrender of the French Army commanders.

His leadership was always an inspiration and forceful as on occasions when he applied his walking-stick to the backsides of the few recalcitrants who appeared to have an unnecessary interest in rear areas.

MAJOR-GENERAL F. W. FESTING, D.S.O., 5*th July*, 1945: C.B.E.; 8*th November*, 1945: American Legion of Merit—Degree of Commander; 6*th June*, 1946: to be Companion of the Order of the Bath.

CPL. F. C. FIELD, 25*th April*, 1941: D.C.M.

This N.C.O. accompanied Lieut. C. H. Liddell on two reconnaissance patrols on the nights of 2nd/3rd and 7th/8th December, 1940. He and one other N.C.O. managed to crawl right up to the enemy defences, which had sentries posted about fifty yards apart. He got through these and climbed over the wall of the defences and got right inside the enemy camp. He then crept back over the wall and came away undiscovered.

He was thus able to bring back valuable information about the size and strength of the defences and the location of the mines. Again on the night of the 7th/8th he and one rifleman crept up to the camp on another side and found a line of tanks closely guarded by sentries.

He managed to penetrate these and got just inside. He crept back again and was able to report a gap in the defences closed only by tanks, which was of the greatest value. Both these patrols required great patience, courage and skill in locating and avoiding the enemy sentries.

CPL. G. FITZGERALD (8th Battalion), 19*th October*, 1944: M.M.

On the morning of 19th July, 1944, No. 6 Platoon, of "F" Company of the 8th Battalion of the Regiment, were holding the forward edge of the village of Grentheville, which had been captured the evening before.

Cpl. Fitzgerald was in command of a leading section. A machine-gun

42 suddenly opened fire on the section and wounded one of Cpl. Fitzgerald's men who was forward of the section position.

In full view of the enemy and showing complete disregard of his own safety, Cpl. Fitzgerald went forward and brought in the wounded man on his shoulder. Later on the same day Cpl. Fitzgerald's section was the first one into the village during the attack on Bras. Showing great dash and initiative, he cleared his sector of the village with speed, taking the enemy by surprise and capturing twenty-five prisoners.

He was a fine example and inspiration to all those with whom he came in contact.

2/LIEUT. K. J. FISH, 14*th January*, 1943 : M.C.

This officer showed exceptional gallantry on 27th October when his Battalion's positon was being attacked by more than twelve tanks. His platoon position was under heavy shell fire when he saw a Churchill tank hit by an 88-mm. shell and start burning some 600 yards away. The crew of this tank got out and moved away, except for one man, who was badly wounded and waved for help. 2/Lieut. Fish immediately walked out to the burning tank under shell and small-arms fire and bandaged the wounded man, who was in a dangerous condition.

He then carried him back to the shelter of a derelict tank, from where he waved for help, during which time he was sniped at by a machine gun and wounded.

A Bantam was brought up under 2/Lieut. Fish's instructions; the wounded man was taken to an ambulance, where it was found that he would live as the result of the prompt and gallant action by this officer.

Throughout four days of intermittent heavy shell fire and with practically no rest, 2/Lieut. Fish showed continuous leadership and imperturbability and was an excellent example to all ranks.

MAJOR P. T. FLOWER, 28*th June*, 1945 : M.B.E.

For service on the operational staff of the Eighth Army since November, 1943, first as G.3 and later as G.2.

His knowledge of forward troops and his constant efforts by visits and otherwise to get their picture have been of the greatest service in building up a true battle picture.

CAPT. R. A. FLOWER, 18*th June*, 1943 : M.C.

On the night of 26th/27th October, 1942, Capt. R. A. Flower was in command of a carrier platoon at the Snipe position.

At 0100 hrs. on the 27th his platoon was ordered forward through a gap in an enemy minefield to carry out a reconnaissance. The platoon went forward 2,000 yards, overran a strong infantry position, and took some prisoners.

Capt. Flower then attacked a tank leaguer of forty enemy tanks from 200 yards' range, setting fire to three vehicles and causing the leaguer to disperse. He was then heavily engaged at close range by the tanks, one carrier being knocked out. He withdrew his platoon slowly in front of the advancing tanks.

At 0900 hrs. Capt. Flower's platoon was ordered to patrol the south flank of Snipe threatened by an infantry attack. He attacked and dispersed the enemy infantry forming up to attack and inflicted many casualties.

Two enemy guns coming into action were also destroyed; the platoon continued to engage the enemy on the flank until all ammunition was expended and four carriers had been knocked out.

Throughout these actions Capt. Flower's personal coolness and courage were of the highest order and his fine offensive handling of his platoon played a large part in enabling his Battalion to hold its position.

CAPT. H. T. H. FOLEY, 1st January, 1944: M.B.E.

MAJOR S. FORSHALL, 30th August, 1945: M.B.E.

CPL. A. FRANCIS, 14th January, 1943: M.M.

Cpl. Francis was No. 3 of a 6-pounder anti-tank gun in the Snipe position, 866295, on 26th and 27th October, 1942.

He engaged enemy tanks, whenever they appeared, with accurate fire, although his gun was in an exposed position and continuously under shell and machine-gun fire. When there were no targets in sight he went across and attended to any wounded in the vicinity, and by his cheerfulness and unconcern was an inspiration to all in the area. Finally, when his gun was out of action, he fetched ammunition as it was needed to those guns still left firing, either carrying it on foot or driving it across the position under intensive fire.

His unflinching devotion to duty was a source of courage and confidence to all ranks in critical circumstances.

CPL. W. F. FRANCIS (2nd Battalion), 28th June, 1945: M.M.

For conspicuous gallantry and devotion to duty. This N.C.O. has been outstanding in his initiative and determination to destroy the enemy at all times. He has continually volunteered for all patrols carried out by his platoon, and by reason of his skill and resolute leadership as both patrol and section commander he has contributed much to the success of the operations carried out by his company.

In particular, on the night of 7th/8th December, 1944, he showed courage and disregard for his personal safety when, returning from a reconnaissance, his patrol was fired on from twenty yards' range. Cpl. Francis deliberately exposed himself, advanced on the enemy, and engaged them at close range, thereby drawing on himself their fire, which slightly wounded him in the foot, and covering the return of his patrol to our own lines with valuable information.

A few days later his platoon were occupying Casa Monte when they were attacked by a patrol. Cpl. Francis left the house, again drawing on himself the main enemy fire, thus assisting his platoon to observe and engage the enemy, and he himself killed two Germans.

By his initiative, coolness under fire and determination, this N.C.O. has set a fine example not only to his platoon but to his whole company

MAJOR J. FREEMAN, 25th November, 1943: M.B.E.

Major Freeman has been the D.A.Q.M.G. of the Brigade during the period under review. During this time the Brigade advanced from Medenine to Tunis and a heavy responsibility fell on Major Freeman.

At no time was the Brigade ever held up or delayed by shortage of supply and, in fact, everything ran with perfect efficiency and smoothness.

For this Major Freeman is deserving of the highest praise; indeed his energy, devotion to duty and attention to detail were of the first order. In particular, during the final stages of the advance to Tunis, when he accompanied the Tactical Brigade H.Q. in a tank in order to be in immediate touch with the situation.

Although at times under considerable shell fire, he handled the supply situation with cool and sure judgment, so that the Brigade went short of nothing, while the echelons suffered a minimum of casualties.

CPL. H. FULTON (8th Battalion), 24th January, 1946: D.C.M.

Cpl. Fulton fought with "H" Company, 8th Battalion, from Normandy, June, 1944, to the Baltic, May, 1945, firstly as a rifleman and later as a section commander. In his first battle on 28th June, 1944, at Hill 112, Rfn. Fulton showed by his complete coolness and bravery that he was admirably suited to command men in battle.

On 1st April, 1945, near Sterbeck, the platoon in which Cpl. Fulton commanded a section was clearing a wood. The right-hand section of the platoon was almost immediately held up by heavy 20-mm. fire from beyond the wood. Cpl. Fulton's section, which was on the left, without waiting for orders, continued the advance, and in spite of heavy mortar fire consolidated on the far edge of the wood and neutralized the 20-mm. guns.

The mortaring continued, but although his section suffered casualties and were not dug in, Cpl. Fulton held his position for a considerable time until ordered to move. There is no doubt that his initiative and coolness on this occasion were the deciding factor in his platoon's success.

On the night of 6th/7th April, 1945, Cpl. Fulton was ordered to take his section out in front of the Battalion bridgehead at Stolzenau to give warning of any approach of the enemy. So that his presence should not be revealed, Cpl. Fulton could not afford to dig his section in, and the area was heavily shelled and mortared all night.

In the early hours of the morning the enemy attacked and it was due to the excellent information given by Cpl. Fulton's section that the attack was completely broken up. Throughout this action Cpl. Fulton's gallantry and complete control of his section had a most heartening effect on the remainder of his platoon.

Throughout eleven months' fighting Cpl. Fulton has shown himself to be a brave and resolute leader and has been an outstanding section commander in every battle.

CPL. S. W. FULTON, 14th January, 1943: M.M.

This corporal was acting as a layer on a 6-pounder anti-tank gun in the Snipe position on 26th and 27th October, 1942.

Seven tanks approached to within 500 yards of the gun position. On orders from his No. 1 he opened fire and laid his sights so accurately that five tanks were set on fire and two immobilized. During the action he followed the orders of his No. 1 implicitly, waiting till he was absolutely certain that he could destroy the tank he was aiming at.

If it had not been for his coolness and his disregard of his safety, the position would have been overrun.

Eventually the gun received a direct hit and he was wounded and had to be evacuated.

His bravery was of the highest order.

MAJOR C. FUREY, 9th 9th September, 1942: M.B.E.

For service as Camp Commandant, H.Q., XIII Corps, in Cyrenaica. The manner in which his work has been performed, very often under enemy fire, has been quite exceptional.

LIEUT. L. R. K. FYFFE (7th Battalion), 1st June, 1943: M.C.

This officer commanded an anti-tank platoon when the Battalion to which he belonged captured the pass between Dj Zemlet el Beida and Dj Eadoudi, north of El Hamma, in the early hours of 31st March, 1943.

Throughout the action, from 0530 to 1030 hrs., in spite of being under intense artillery, mortar and small-arms fire at close range the whole time, this officer fought his guns and gave magnificent support with H.E. When he had expended all his ammunition he organized his anti-tank platoon as a rifle platoon and held his position until ordered to withdraw. During the withdrawal, which was carried out under extreme difficulties, in spite of being wounded himself, Lieut. Fyffe evacuated all his guns with their crews, the greater number of whom had by now been seriously wounded.

Throughout the action this officer showed tremendous courage and leadership and completely disregarded his personal safety in all his actions.

7th December, 1944: Bar to M.C.

For conspicuous gallantry and devotion to duty in the attack on Monte Malba on the night of 19th/20th June, 1944, and during the subsequent counter-attacks the following day.

On the night of 19th/20th June Major Fyffe was ordered with his company to capture the important feature of Monte Malba in order to allow the armoured brigade to pass through at first light the following morning. With the greatest skill and leadership, Major Fyffe captured the position in face of heavy enemy opposition and took twenty prisoners and a 210-mm. gun intact. During the following day the company was counter-attacked three times.

During one counter-attack, in a period of bad visibility, the enemy penetrated close to Company H.Q. Major Fyffe immediately collected all the men who were available and organized and led a counter-attack under heavy fire which restored the situation.

Throughout this action under continuous mortar, machine-gun and sniper fire, by his outstanding personal example and with complete disregard for his own safety, Major Fyffe enabled his company to hold their position in face of most strenuous efforts by the enemy to recapture this important feature. There is no doubt that as a result of Major Fyffe's action the position was held and the armoured brigade was enabled to pass through during the following day.

MAJOR R. A. FYFFE (10th Battalion), *8th April,* 1943 : M.C.

For conspicuous gallantry and devotion to duty at Thala from 21st to 23rd February, 1943.

By 1830 hrs. on 21st February, Major Fyffe's company had occupied a locality in the reserve position held by his Battalion. At about 1945 hrs. the enemy attacked the position with tanks, infantry and self-propelled artillery. He succeeded in establishing himself in the forward Battalion locality, but failed to penetrate Major Fyffe's position and was driven back.

Throughout the remainder of the night and the following day Major Fyffe succeeded in maintaining his now isolated and exposed position, which was constantly shelled and machine-gunned.

His company put up a most resolute defence during these operations. Major Fyffe's conduct and leadership were an inspiration to all ranks.

Major Fyffe has already proved his power of leadership in action on several occasions in the Bou Arada sector.

23rd August, 1945: D.S.O.

For outstanding leadership and devotion to duty while in support of the 2nd Lothian and Border Horse during the 26th Armoured Brigade's break-out from the Argenta Gap to Bondeno between 18th and 23rd April, and again on 1st May at Belluno.

At Belluno Lieut.-Colonel Fyffe was in charge of a battalion group which moved with such speed that it succeeded in cutting off a German force over 5,000 strong, fully armed and supported by tanks and S.P. guns. Twice this force tried to break out, but both attempts failed owing to Lieut.-Colonel Fyffe's conspicuous handling of the situation. Finally, owing to his personal tact he succeeded in negotiating the surrender of the whole force, including the commanding General.

There is no doubt that as a result of this officer's action the collapse of all German resistance in that area was greatly accelerated. This officer's complete disregard for personal safety has always been an inspiration to the troops under his command.

RFN. R. GALLOWAY, *9th September,* 1942: M.M.

For a period of two months, during which time his company was in almost continual contact with the enemy, this rifleman performed the duties of company signaller. During the whole period Rfn. Galloway was conspicuous for his courage, industry and cheerfulnes; on one occasion when he was operator in the command carrier of the scout platoon the driver was badly wounded.

Although the carrier was under heavy small-arms fire, Rfn. Galloway immediately got out, helped to lift the wounded man from the driver's seat, and was preparing to put him in the back of the carrier when the driver died.

On this and on every occasion when he has been in action, Rfn. Galloway's fearless courage and devotion to duty have had the highest possible influence on all those working with him.

CAPT. (T./MAJOR) THE VISCOUNT GARMOYLE, 20*th January*, 1942: D.S.O.

For conspicuous initiative and courage when he was with a troop of 25-pounders and part of a company of the Rifle Brigade one mile south of Sidi Rezegh aerodrome on 22nd November, 1941, when the main German tank attack came in from the west. When severe casualties, which included the G.P.O., were inflicted on the guns, Major Garmoyle took command, directed the fire of guns, assisted in the manning of one gun and played a very large part in checking this main German tank attack.

Moving from gun to gun, whilst under terrific fire from the anti-tank guns, machine guns and tanks, he encouraged the detachments, and undoubtedly by his example was the means of withstanding this attack.

When finally his H.Q. was more or less wiped out, one of his officers killed and a second wounded, and his guns ordered to be withdrawn, he went forward at last light and personally brought away what was left of his troop O.P. party.

3rd August, 1942: Bar to D.S.O.

On 27th May, 1942, Major Garmoyle was in command of his Battalion in the left sector of the Retma Box. The Battalion and guns on his left were completely overrun and he was ordered to withdraw his Battalion.

Under heavy machine-gun fire from 500 yards' range and shell fire he drove slowly round to each company in his staff car issuing his orders, and by his complete disregard of his personal safety withdrew his Battalion almost without loss. On 9th June, when this officer was dispatched with a mixed column thirty miles behind the enemy position, by his splendid leadership and judgment he succeeded in destroying forty-four lorries, four tanks, six guns, one self-propelled gun and three aircraft in addition to releasing fifty of our own prisoners and taking six prisoners in three days.

Frequently acting as O.P. officer himself, he guided his column right through the enemy lines to where it would inflict most damage.

It was mainly due to this officer's daring intuition and courage that these successful results were achieved.

MAJOR E. H. C. GARNIER, 25*th October*, 1943: M.C.

LIEUT. (T./CAPT.) B. G. GILBERT, 21*st December*, 1944: M.B.E.

MAJOR E. GILES, 1*st January*, 1945: M.B.E.

RFN. G. C. GILLAN, *9th May*, 1941 : D.C.M.

Rfn. Gillan was wireless operator of a command carrier advancing towards the defences of an important enemy position under heavy artillery, anti-tank and machine-gun fire. When the carrier was 600 yards from the wire he was wounded by an anti-tank shell in both legs, one of which had subsequently to be amputated, but he continued to send and receive messages for half an hour. When loss of blood made him too weak to carry on with his duties as wireless operator he continued to instruct the other occupant of the carrier how to manipulate the set.

His courage and devotion to duty while he was in great pain enabled the patrol commander to keep in touch with company headquarters throughout the operation.

SERGT. A. GILLINGS (1st Battalion), *31st August*, 1944 : M.M.

On 13th and 14th June, 1944, this N.C.O. commanded the most forward section on the southern front of his company. He established a position in and around a farm from which he patrolled continuously day and night. On the evening of 14th June a strong attack was launched and he came under considerable artillery, mortar and machine-gun fire, as a result of which the house received a direct hit and caught fire. The enemy advance continued, but Cpl. Gillings and his section remained in their position in an upstairs room and forced the enemy to withdraw except for one German machine gun, which continued to maintain a heavy fire on them. Owing to the fire, the house, by now burning well, became untenable and Cpl. Gillings was ordered to withdraw his section. He sent them back by a previously reconnoitred route to an alternative position, but he himself nevertheless remained in the upstairs room, which was well alight, and covered their withdrawal with Bren-gun fire against the German machine-gun position. When his section was established in its new position, and not until then, Cpl. Gillings made his way back to them, taking with him all the kit which the section had been unable to carry. He maintained the new position until the action ceased, and was at all times acting offensively.

He showed the greatest gallantry and devotion to duty throughout the engagement, and I most strongly recommend him for an immediate award.

R.Q.M.S. R. W. GLASGOW (8th Battalion), *11th October*, 1945 : M.B.E.

R.Q.M.S. Glasgow was Acting Quartermaster of the 8th Battalion from January to April, 1945. He was considerably handicapped in his task during this period by there being no one to help him as R.Q.M.S. and by a shortage of Quartermaster's staff.

During the very difficult period of improvisation for the Ardennes battle in January and the subsequent weeks in Holland with very bad communications, weather conditions and shortage of transport, R.Q.M.S. Glasgow showed himself to be a tireless worker and an exceptionally able administrator.

Since crossing the River Rhine on 28th March until 6th April on the arrival of the new Quartermaster, R.Q.M.S. Glasgow excelled himself in seeing that his Battalion never went short of anything, however difficult and however long the journey. Throughout this period R.Q.M.S. Glasgow has been a tremendous help and an inspiration to all ranks, and it is no exaggeration to say that the success of the Battalion has been largely due to his tremendous efforts to see that they never lacked anything.

LIEUT.-COLONEL P. GODFREY-FAUSSETT, 24th January, 1946: O.B.E.

Served with H.Q., I Corps, throughout the campaign in North-West Europe from 6th June, 1944, until 20th March, 1945, as A.P.M., and from 20th March until the end of the campaign on 8th May, 1945, as D.P.M.

He was responsible for the Provost planning for the assault and organizing the assembly areas behind the beaches through which all troops following up the assault were to pass.

He himself landed on D Day and immediately took charge of all Provost arrangements within the beach-head, working without sleep for over seventy-two hours.

W.O. CL. I E. C. GODLEY (1st Battalion), 20th September, 1945: D.C.M.

For gallant and distinguished service in the defence of Calais in May, 1940.

CAPT. J. C. C. GREEN-WILKINSON, 18th March, 1943: M.C.

Capt. Green-Wilkinson has shown outstanding devotion to duty and conspicuous gallantry in the performance of his duties as liaison officer.

During the battle which culminated in the capture of Tripoli he was frequently sent on journeys which necessitated being under enemy shell fire and going through mined areas which were unmarked.

He was eager to accept these dangerous missions and it was always possible to rely on his getting through with vital messages, whatever the difficulties might be.

L./SERGT. N. B. GRIFFITHS, 5th November, 1942: D.C.M.

For conspicuous gallantry and devotion to duty. On 31st August, 1942, at about 1830 hrs., his position was attacked by German tanks.

He held his fire until they were at close range and succeeded in knocking out five at least and damaging others.

Although it appeared likely that his position might be overrun, he continued to direct the fire of his gun in the coolest possible manner. His gallant conduct and good shooting were undoubtedly largely responsible for preventing the German tanks breaking into the position before it was possible for our own tanks to arrive.

Throughout the action, which lasted for about three-quarters of an hour, he was continuously under fire.

L./CPL. W. A. GROVES (8th Battalion), 12*th July*, 1945: M.M.

On the evening of the 5th/6th April, 1945, at Stolzenau, a platoon of 6-pdr. A.T. guns of the 8th Bn. Rifle Brigade were ferried across the River Weser into the battalion bridgehead. L./Cpl. Groves was second-in-command of a gun which was placed in a forward position covering the most likely enemy approach. On the morning of 6th April the N.C.O. in charge of the gun was wounded and L./Cpl. Groves took command. That morning the enemy counter-attacked this bridgehead with infantry supported by 88-mm. airbursts and mortar fire and also by self-propelled 20-mms. By engaging the self-propelled guns, although the range was long, L./Cpl. Groves's gun succeeded in keeping down the enemy fire and definitely hit one. L./Cpl. Groves also kept his Bren gun in action against the advancing infantry with great success.

That afternoon another member of L./Cpl. Groves's gun crew was wounded by mortar fire and the crew reduced to three.

On the night of the 6th/7th, the enemy again counter-attacked and L./Cpl. Groves successfully dealt with the enemy with his Bren gun.

Throughout these three days, and in spite of heavy artillery, mortar and machine-gun fire, and being heavily bombed from the air, L./Cpl. Groves was an inspiration to all. By his example and fine leadership he encouraged his crew to reply offensively at every opportunity, both with their 6-pdr. gun and small arms.

MAJOR J. B. GORDON-DUFF, 6*th January*, 1944: M.B.E.

CAPT. T. R. GORDON-DUFF, 20*th September*, 1945: M.C.

For gallantry and distinguished service in the defence of Calais in May, 1940.

LIEUT.-COLONEL A. C. GORE, 23*rd September*, 1943: D.S.O.

On 20th February, 1943, Lieut.-Colonel Gore was commanding a force consisting of a company of his own Battalion, a squadron of the Lothians Horse, "F" Battery, 12th R.H.A., and an anti-tank battery charged with the role of delaying the enemy north of the Kasserine Gap.

During the day this force was strongly attacked and was continually under shell fire. The situation on his flanks was confused and during the day it became apparent that the force was in danger of being encircled. Lieut.-Colonel Gore, however, maintained his position until dark and was a constant source of inspiration to his men by his own complete disregard of danger.

On the night of 21st/22nd February, when enemy tanks penetrated the position behind which his Battalion was in reserve and actually entered his Battalion position, Lieut.-Colonel Gore retained complete control of his unit and by his own steadying example to his men succeeded in holding his position intact and continuing to hold it throughout the following day.

23rd August, 1945: Bar to D.S.O.

Brigadier Gore has commanded the 61st Infantry Brigade since June, 1944. During the break-out through the Argenta Gap between 18th and 23rd April he did invaluable work, going around and encouraging the rifle battalions operating with the armour during the armoured battle. On 29th April, when located with two of his battalions just south of Monselice, he was ordered, at about 2200 hrs., to pass through the 2nd New Zealand Division and pursue enemy forces withdrawing to the north-east. He acted with such speed and imparted to his brigade such enthusiasm that by the early morning of 1st May one battalion had cut off enemy attempting to escape northwards from Belluno, ninety miles away, and another battalion had negotiated the crossing of the Tagliamento and was closing in on Udine, 130 miles away from the starting point.

For three days the operation continued at high speed, driving the enemy deep into the Alps and leading to the capture of thousands of prisoners and vast quantities of equipment, transport and stores. It was a pursuit battle carried out with great speed and skill.

The success of the operation was very largely due to the drive, enthusiasm and aggressiveness of Brigadier Gore.

The manner in which he kept up the momentum of the movement of the brigade for several days was an inspiration to everyone.

MAJOR SIR E. C. GOSCHEN, BT. (10th Battalion), *7th December*, 1944: D.S.O.

For conspicuous gallantry and devotion to duty between 18th and 22nd June, 1944, at Monte Pulito, outside Perugia, and at Monte Rentella, east of Maggione. On the night of 18th/19th June Major Goschen's company were ordered to cut the road leading west out of Perugia and to occupy Monte Pulito. After a long cross-country march in unusually difficult conditions of darkness and heavy rain, they reached their first objective at dawn and were met by intense fire. As a result, however, of the cool determination and skilful dispositions of the company commander, this opposition was overcome and heavy casualties, including one Mark IV tank, were inflicted on the enemy. Securing Monte Pulito in spite of further stiff resistance, the road was effectively cut and more casualties inflicted. Counter-attacks were beaten off throughout the day, during the whole of which the area was under intense shell, mortar and small-arms fire.

Showing complete disregard for his own safety, Major Goschen moved about encouraging his men and readjusting his dispositions to meet each new threat by the enemy. There is no doubt that as a direct result of the conspicuous tactical skill, personal courage and fine example of Major Goschen, the enemy plans for withdrawal were materially disrupted.

On the night of 21st/22nd June Major Goschen's company acted as a firm base while the Battalion attacked the Monte Rentella feature. On 22nd June the leading companies were overrun by enemy counter-attacks. Under intense machine-gun, mortar and shell fire Major Goschen moved about in the open incorporating in his defensive lay-out elements of the forward companies as they reached his position. As a direct result of his personal gallantry, cool appreciation and skilful dispositions, the enemy attack was halted without any exploitation of its initial success.

During the whole period from 18th to 22nd June Major Goschen has set a magnificent example of devotion to duty and complete disregard of personal safety, which example has been an inspiration to the whole Battalion.

CPL. A. G. GUISE, 13th August, 1942: D.C.M.

For most conspicuous gallantry on the afternoon of 14th June, 1942. The anti-tank platoon to which this N.C.O. belonged was, after successfully fighting the German tanks for some time, put completely out of action by enemy fire and was overrun by enemy tanks.

This N.C.O., seeing the plight of his comrades, drove a carrier forward under very heavy fire right among the German tanks and succeeded in bringing out from under the enemy's noses twenty-two men of his own unit and of the R.H.A. battery.

His action, which showed the most complete disregard of personal danger, undoubtedly saved these men, who must otherwise have been killed or captured by the advancing enemy infantry, and his bravery and disregard of personal danger were of the highest possible order.

RFN. F. GURR, 20th September, 1945: M.M.

For gallantry and distinguished service in the defence of Calais, May, 1940.

C.S.M. F. M. HAMILTON: U.S. Bronze Star.

CAPT. R. H. W. S. HASTINGS, 25th February, 1943: M.C.

"For consistent good work and devotion to duty as G.S.O.2 of this Division during operations from 23rd October to 16th November. Throughout this period he has been with me at my Tactical H.Q. and it is entirely due to his skill and energy and devotion to duty for long hours, frequently under fire, that I have been able to obtain the information required and issue the necessary orders to enable the Division to carry out its task."

31st August, 1944: D.S.O.

On 6th June, 1944, in the La Riviere area, Lieut.-Colonel Hastings was commanding the right assault Battalion of the 69th Infantry Brigade during the assault landings. The Battalion had a most difficult task to perform and its conspicuous success was very largely due to Lieut.-Colonel Hastings's detailed preparations before the landing and first-class leadership afterwards.

Shortly after touching down, Lieut.-Colonel Hastings ascertained that, although the attack on the Mont Fleury Battery had gone in successfully, the attack by the right reserve company on the strong locality at the quarry was held up by heavy machine-gun fire. He quickly organized effective smoke protection from destroyers and from his Battalion 3-inch mortars on the beach.

Wireless communication having failed, he succeeded in joining up with the company and redirected it to the attack. During this time he was under continuous machine-gun fire. The attack was successful, twenty or thirty prisoners were captured, and the beach was freed from aimed small-arms fire, thus ensuring the successful landing of the reserve battalion.

21st June, 1945: Bar to D.S.O.

Until 24th December, 1944, when he fell ill, Lieut.-Colonel Hastings was commanding the 2nd Bn. The King's Royal Rifle Corps. During most of this period his Battalion was actively engaged either in offensive operations or in holding the line of the River Maas.

Throughout the period he distinguished himself by his untiring energy, offensive spirit, persistent disregard of his own safety and great skill in handling his battalion.

In particular, on 22nd November, 1944, when the brigade was under command of the 49th Division, his battalion successfully cleared the enemy from the village of Tongerlo, although the whole area was waterlogged and infested with mines. The success of the operation was very largely due to his skill, drive and courageous personal example. During the whole period of his command he has brought his battalion up to a very high standard of morale and efficiency in every way.

21st April, 1946: O.B.E.

Lieut.-Colonel Hastings has been G.S.O.1 of the 11th Armoured Division since 27th January, 1945. During this time his work has been outstanding, and it has been largely due to his forethought and excellent staff work that this Division was able to exploit to the full the opportunities given at the crossing of the River Rhine.

Difficult moves of the Division have been organized by him at very short notice and slightly confused battles have been kept in hand due to his quick grasp of the tactical situation. A tireless worker, he has been a fine example to the rest of the staff and by his strong personality he has kept them happy and efficient.

SERGT. J. H. HAYDEN (1st Battalion), *29th March*, 1945: M.M.

Sergt. Hayden was platoon sergeant of a scout platoon during the months of August and September, 1944. During this period four successive officers of the platoon became casualties and consequently this N.C.O. commanded the platoon for the greater part of the time. The platoon was almost constantly in action and there were many difficult and important patrols to be carried out. Sergt. Hayden performed these with skill and courage and succeeded in obtaining much valuable information which was of the greatest assistance to the armoured regiment under whose command he was. On one occasion in Lillers his platoon commander was wounded. He at once took command and succeeded in repelling counter-attacks by a superior force of the enemy.

On another occasion, on the Albert Canal, Sergt. Hayden was instrumental in the destruction of a large number of Germans by shell and mortar fire directed from his observation post.

MAJOR P. T. HAYMAN, 21st June, 1945: M.B.E.

Major Hayman came to H.Q., Balkan Air Force, shortly after it was formed in June, 1944. His task was to form and afterwards take charge of an Inter-Services Secretariat which was set up to co-ordinate the political and military work of common concern to the various Services for whose activities this H.Q. was responsible.

This work has been of great volume and wide diversity and has entailed dealing with large numbers of people not only of different Services but of different nationalities.

MAJOR J. T. HARINGTON, 4th January, 1945 (service in Burma): D.S.O.; 4th January, 1945: M.B.E.

CPL. D. J. HEGARTY (2nd Battalion), 23rd August, 1945: M.M.

On 21st April, 1945, at S. Nicolo Ferrarese, Cpl. Hegarty's platoon was ordered to cross the river and form a bridgehead to the west of the town in face of the enemy, who were holding the houses on the far bank. The depth of the river was unknown, and Cpl. Hegarty's section was in the lead. Cpl. Hegarty led his section, but before they had gone half-way across the river the water rose above their heads and they had to retrace their steps.

It was then decided that the crossing must be made over the rubble of the demolished bridge, which, according to prisoners taken in the town, was sown with Schu-mines. It was under heavy and accurate shell fire and was in full view of two known enemy positions. Supplies of smoke were exhausted. Cpl. Hegarty volunteered once again to take the leading section over; this he did and assaulted the first houses on the far bank with great dash, capturing the enemy section defending them. The rest of the platoon then joined them.

Shortly afterwards two enemy supply wagons approached along the road towards the house held by his section, who ambushed them successfully, killing or capturing the occupants.

Throughout these operations Cpl. Hegarty displayed the highest possible standard of leadership and dash; and his determination to get to grips with the enemy played an outstanding part in the successful establishment of an important bridgehead.

CAPT. R. A. HENLEY, 13th December, 1945: M.B.E.

This officer was G.S.O.3 (Ops.) at H.Q., 6th British Armoured Division since October, 1944. Prior to this he had a similar appointment at 26th Armoured Brigade H.Q. from October, 1943, to June, 1944, and at the

61st Infantry Brigade H.Q. from June, 1944, to October, 1944. This Division was in action the whole of this period, including the Battle of Cassino, pursuit to Perugia and the winter campaign in the Apennines and final offensive in the spring of 1945.

During the last campaign Capt. Henley was in charge of A.C.V.1 and controlled the Divisional wireless net. His control of the net was, in spite of difficulties, unfaltering; relief was practically impossible and he was on duty for long spells without sleep.

The untiring efforts of this officer throughout the critical battle were beyond praise.

L./CPL. L. H. HENNELL (10th Battalion), 26*th October*, 1944 : M.M.

On 19th May, 1944, L./Cpl. Hennell was carrier commander of the leading carrier of his section, part of the scout platoon which had been ordered to make a detailed reconnaissance of the Hitler Line position in the southern sector of the town of Aquina; another section was making a similar reconnaissance in the northern sector. Information was soon received that this section had found the road blocked, was pinned to the ground by heavy fire, and was unable to proceed.

L./Cpl. Hennell's section, however, was ordered to advance down a track leading to the southern end of the town in order either to make contact with the enemy or to find his flank.

On rounding the bend, his carrier came face to face with a heavy-calibre anti-tank gun, which had just been put into position by the crew, at a distance of thirty yards. L./Cpl. Hennell immediately engaged the crew (approximately six men) with his 20-mm. Browning (mounted on the front of his carrier) and killed or wounded them all.

He followed this up by setting fire to the gun tower (a half-track) by successfully engaging it with incendiary bullets.

At this juncture enemy infantry, estimated at one platoon, were seen to be forming up on the left of the carrier section for a counter-attack. This was observed by the platoon commander, who put down 2-inch mortar fire on the area, under cover of which the section commander gave the order to disengage. L./Cpl. Hennell successfully withdrew his carrier from this extremely exposed position under heavy mortar and machine-gun fire.

L./Cpl. Hennell throughout the operation showed outstanding initiative and devotion to duty. The information acquired by the patrol was of great value to the planning of future operations, while L./Cpl. Hennell alone was responsible for putting out of action one enemy gun and tower in addition to killing or wounding the whole of its crew.

MAJOR J. P. C. HENNIKER-MAJOR, 22*nd February*, 1945 : M.C.

Major Henniker-Major has been working continuously in enemy-occupied Yugoslavia for over a year. He was dropped by parachute in September, 1943, and was attached to a partisan corps fighting in Bosnia throughout the winter. This corps was continuously in action against the Germans and fought under extreme hardships of snow, cold and hunger.

Major Henniker-Major during the different periods showed great courage and fortitude, setting a fine example to the partisans.

In the spring of 1944 he was sent as Senior B.L.O. to the partisans in Serbia and once again was dropped by parachute. At this time the partisan movement was only just starting in Serbia and the Germans for several months did their utmost to eliminate them. The partisan forces succeeded in remaining intact in spite of the grave hardships and difficulties which they underwent, and they gradually grew in numbers and did considerable damage to enemy communications.

This success was in no small measure due to the efforts of Major Henniker-Major, who organized the reception and distribution of supplies and passed back information of the greatest possible value, so that the maximum assistance could be given to the partisans.

Major Henniker-Major's courage and endurance under the most adverse and difficult conditions have been of an exceptionally high standard.

RFN. G. W. HENWOOD (2nd Battalion), 13*th December*, 1945: M.M.

During the final advance in Italy, Rfn. Henwood was the Bren gunner to his section. Throughout the entire period he showed a magnificent offensive spirit, and neglected no opportunity to engage the enemy, accounting for very many Germans killed and wounded. During one river-crossing operation at S. Nicolo Ferrarese Rfn. Henwood was covering the crossing of another platoon in face of machine-gun fire and under heavy shelling. The accuracy of Rfn. Henwood's fire played a large part in the success of the crossing, as he was scoring hits at ranges up to 800 yards. On another occasion, at Lendwara, where his section was doing a night patrol, Rfn. Henwood engaged a large enemy vehicle at short range, killing or wounding all the occupants. During this affray his section commander was wounded. Rfn. Henwood promptly took over his duties, and his complete coolness and control were of the greatest possible assistance to the patrol commander in withdrawing the section, though the enemy in considerable numbers were searching for the patrol.

In the ensuing village-clearing operation, made difficult by darkness and burning buildings, Rfn. Henwood continued to command his section with exemplary courage and skill. These incidents are typical of Rfn. Henwood throughout the campaign, during which his desire to engage the enemy at all times and his skill at arms have been of the very highest order and have had outstanding effect upon the confidence and morale of those around him.

LIEUT.-COLONEL K. B. HICKS, 21*st June*, 1945: O.B.E.

Lieut.-Colonel Hicks has acted as Commander, No. 2 District M.L., at Patras since his arrival in October, 1944. He arrived at a time of extreme difficulty, when conditions made it impossible for any reference to be made to his headquarters in respect of his work.

He found himself thwarted at every turn by the machinations of politics, and he was working in an atmosphere of unremitting tension and suspense, which increased with the developments in Athens.

In spite of the fact that there was an imminent likelihood of hostilities breaking out in Patras, Colonel Hicks continued his organization of relief and his military administration in the town with the utmost efficiency. He made himself well known and liked by all the leading Greek citizens and succeeded in getting their co-operation.

In addition to this arduous and thankless task, Colonel Hicks was called upon to act as Deputy Commander to the military forces concentrated at Patras when it seemed certain that E.L.A.S. would provoke hostilities.

RFN. C. W. HILLS, 1st *June*, 1943.

This rifleman was a member of the 6-pounder crew. Although his gun was in a forward and exposed position, under continuous and heavy artillery and mortar fire, he fought his gun alone for an hour after the crew had been wounded, loading and laying himself unaided. Rfn. Hills only stopped fighting when incapacitated by wounds.

SERGT. J. A. HINE, 5th *November*, 1942: M.M.

On the morning of 4th September, 1942, in the area north of Deir el Ragil, Sergt. Hine was in command of a 6-pounder which, with two other 6-pounders, was acting as part of the escort to an R.H.A. O.P. The escort became engaged before it was fully light with the rearguard of an enemy column, consisting of infantry covered by five Mark IV tanks. Sergt. Hine was obliged to bring his gun into action in a very exposed position, but in spite of this he continued to engage the tanks under very heavy shell fire from them, even after his gun had received three direct hits.

It was only when his gun was damaged and his vehicle burst into flames that he was forced to stop. He then proceeded to extinguish the fire with the assistance of the crew, though still under shell fire.

Sergt. Hine's courage and devotion to duty not only assisted in causing the enemy tanks to withdraw, thus allowing the O.P. officer to establish his position and so get the fire of his battery quickly on to the retreating column, but also enabled the scout section which accompanied the O.P. to round up thirty-seven German lorried infantry prisoners and to capture several vehicles and guns.

His quick action when the vehicle burst into flames saved both it and the gun.

14th *January*, 1943: Bar to M.M.

Sergt. Hine was No. 1 of a 6-pounder anti-tank gun in the Snipe position on 26th and 27th October, 1942.

Throughout the day he engaged enemy tanks, allowing them to come well within range without regard for their fire; and then accurately directed the fire of his layer.

At 1700 hrs. on 27th October his gun was put out of action and he led his men to another gun, whose crew had all been killed or wounded. Eight Mark IIIs were at this time approaching his position. He waited till they were 200 yards away and knocked out two of them, setting one on fire. During the day he and his crew accounted for three tanks, one gun burnt and several lorries.

His courage and leadership were of the highest order.

SERGT. G. J. HINES, 15*th October*, 1942: M.M.

On 29th June, 1942, one of our armoured cars was withdrawing down the Fuka—El Daba road in contact with an enemy column when it ran on to a mine and was abandoned. On discovering that its equipment was undamaged, Sergt. Hines at once volunteered to go out in an open truck and salvage it, in spite of the known proximity of the enemy tank column. Whilst he was dismantling the wireless signal set the disabled car came under heavy fire, but Sergt. Hines remained until he had destroyed everything in it except what he could carry back to his truck.

By his action this N.C.O. not only set a very fine example of coolness and resource but prevented valuable equipment from falling into enemy hands.

SERGT. W. A. HOLLANDS (5th Battalion), 19*th October*, 1944: M.M.

On 29th July, 1944, "G" Company of the Territorial Battalion to which Sergt. Hollands belonged were consolidating on Hill 112 after it had been captured.

The enemy began to mortar the position immediately. Sergt. Hollands, who commanded the mortar section, at once ordered his section into their slit trenches, and spotting one of the enemy mortars began to range on it by himself. His mortar was not yet dug in and he was therefore completely in the open.

Sergt. Hollands ranged successfully on the enemy mortar and destroyed it by fire, showing an utter disregard for danger, and in spite of heavy enemy mortar fire. Sergt. Hollands engaged another enemy mortar by himself and continued to do so until he was seriously wounded and forced to cease fire. There is no doubt that Sergt. Hollands's great gallantry was a major factor in reducing the intensity of the enemy fire.

LIEUT. A. B. HOLT-WILSON, 28*th January*, 1943: M.C.

Lieut. Holt-Wilson was commander of the reserve troop of 6-pounder anti-tank guns in the Snipe position on 26th/27th October, 1942. His troop hit and set alight two tanks during the night and was engaged in every subsequent attack, accounting for a further nine tanks destroyed.

Lieut. Holt-Wilson, as commander of the reserve troop, arranged the distribution of ammunition to the whole company. This necessitated his moving about under intense fire throughout the day, which he did with a disregard for his personal safety which was an example to all ranks.

At about 1700 hrs. the enemy made a final attack with about fifty tanks. Lieut. Holt-Wilson turned the last remaining gun of his troop completely round to face the attack, although this exposed to view and attracted concentrated machine-gun fire.

In face of this, with bullets hitting and piercing the shield of the gun, he waited until two enemy tanks had approached to within 200 yards and then directed the fire of the crew, so that both tanks were set on fire; his courage at this moment saved a critical situation.

As darkness fell he went round, still under fire, and rallied the company, of which he was the only unwounded officer remaining. Having personally satisfied himself that all the guns which could not be towed away had been rendered useless to the enemy, he withdrew the remainder of his company.

His courage and leadership were of the highest order.

LIEUT.-COLONEL H. S. P. HOPKINSON, 28*th June*, 1945 (Burma): O.B.E.

Throughout the period from 16th May, 1944, to 15th August, 1944, Lieut.-Colonel Hopkinson was A.A. and Q.M.G. of the 23rd Indian Division, which was operating in the very difficult hilly country between Palel and Sibong. Operations varied from the defence of the firm bases in the Shenam and Palel areas with a road L. of C. to wide outflanking movements over difficult hill tracks directed on the enemy L. of C. and rear.

The normal difficulties of supply and maintenance under such conditions were increased to a very considerable extent by the heavy monsoon rains which at times made supply routes almost impassable to animal transport. In addition, very considerable and detailed planning was necessary in order to build up supplies for the final assault on the Japanese positions covering the road between Shenam and Tamu, and to arrange for the maintenance of the two forces carrying out wide encircling movements on to the Japanese L. of C. and rear. During this period the work done by Lieut.-Colonel Hopkinson was beyond all praise.

In spite of very long and continuous hours of work with little time for rest, he was invariably cheerful and inspired others to exert the maximum effort to overcome difficulties in the shortest possible time.

It is not too much to say that the consistently high morale in the division throughout those difficult and trying times and the success of the final battles were due largely to Lieut.-Colonel Hopkinson's tireless and efficient work, and the confidence felt by formations and units that their supplies would turn up all right whatever the difficulties.

CPL. J. A. HORTON (7th Battalion), 20*th September*, 1945: M.M.

On the night of 27th/28th February, 1945, this N.C.O. was in charge of a section post in a forward position south of Tossignano which was attacked by an enemy patrol, which prisoners have since confirmed was twenty-five strong. A lucky shot from a bazooka concussed four members of his section. Cpl. Horton was undismayed and led his two remaining riflemen with such fury and courage that the enemy were unable to penetrate Cpl. Horton's post and were driven off after suffering casualties. This action was made all the more important, as Cpl. Horton at the time of the action was being visited by a member of an Italian formation which was shortly relieving the 7th Bn. Rifle Brigade in this sector.

Cpl. Horton realized it was essential that the enemy should not capture this Italian and obtain advance information of the relief. His personal courage and determination on this occasion thus not only inflicted a severe local defeat on the enemy but also prevented them from obtaining a very vital piece of information.

Throughout the period January to March, 1945, this N.C.O. has shown outstanding ability, courage and devotion to duty on many successful night patrols and in the defence of the isolated section position. His gallant conduct during this period has always been an inspiration to the riflemen under his command.

MAJOR T. P. C. G. B. HOUDRET, 20th September, 1945 : M.B.E.

For service as Staff Officer to No. 4 District, M.L., Greece, during the six or seven months of initial planning in order to prepare for the entry of No. 4 District into the Aegean islands.

During the extremely difficult period in December, 1944, in Mitylene, when this island, under E.A.M. and K.K.E. influences, was on the brink of revolution and constant strikes, the unfailing zeal and cheerfulness with which this officer carried out his many duties had a considerable amount to do with the successful carrying out of the M.L. charter in the face of acute political, administrative and considerably provocative difficulties.

LIEUT. D. HOWORTH (attached Gordon Highlanders), 21st *December*, 1944 : M.C.

On 11th July, 1944, Lieut. Howorth was in command of the leading platoon in a night attack on the village of Collombella. He led his men through to their objective under intense mortar and machine-gun fire and there reorganized.

Later the platoon was ordered to withdraw into a smaller perimeter, but by this time the enemy had cut him off from the rest of the company.

He organized his platoon and led them in a charge through the streets under heavy fire from close-range weapons and grenades, and himself killed eight of the enemy at close quarters. At the same time, he succeeded in bringing away several wounded men with him.

Through his leadership, personal example and disregard of danger, his platoon were able to rejoin the company intact and his daring leadership was an inspiration to everyone in the company.

RFN. S. HUMLY, 20th September, 1945 : M.M.

For gallantry and distinguished service in the defence of Calais, May, 1940.

COLONEL G. HUNT, 1st July, 1940 : O.B.E.; 20th September, 1945 : C.B.E.

When Colonel Hunt was appointed Deputy Military Secretary, Allied Armies in Italy, on 11th February, 1944, he himself had had no previous experience in M.S. work, and the staff, with few exceptions, were also inexperienced.

There were none of the necessary records available to him on which the M.S. Branch at a large H.Q. has to depend for its smooth, efficient working, and to complete such records without delay Colonel Hunt and his staff had to work very long hours under conditions of considerable strain, in addition to carrying out the heavy day-to-day work caused by active operations.

Colonel Hunt quickly overcame his difficulties and by his infectious energy and enthusiasm he succeeded in infusing into his staff a fine team spirit. His sound judgment, tact and impartiality soon gained him the confidence of all commanders and their staffs, and the high standard of his work over a long period which has contributed largely to the excellent state of morale existing in the Allied armies in Italy, is thoroughly deserving of recognition.

LIEUT. J. M. HUNTER, *25th November*, 1943 : M.C.

This officer was in charge of a carrier platoon for six months. By his skilful handling of this platoon, which he has trained to an exceptionally high standard, he has produced outstanding results. At Medenine, in March, he carried out a number of very successful patrols, bringing back information of the greatest value.

On one occasion he successfully attacked the enemy machine-gun posts and, although himself wounded, withdrew his patrol on completion of its task, bringing a number of prisoners with him.

Near Hamma, in April, he carried out several patrols through enemy minefields, on each occasion bringing back valuable information.

Finally, at a position near Kournine he was seriously wounded while out on patrol, but succeeded in bringing back the information that was required.

LIEUT. J. H. HUNTSMAN : U.S. Silver Star.

LIEUT. (A./CAPT.) R. C. HURLEY (attached Oxfordshire and Buckinghamshire Light Infantry), *20th July*, 1944 : M.C.

This officer commanded the carrier platoon as a rifle platoon at Battalion H.Q. when the Battalion was surrounded and overrun by the enemy between 15th and 21st February. On 18th February, when Battalion H.Q. was practically the only force left, Capt. Hurley accompanied Capt. Coates and two men to reconnoitre a house which had been occupied by the enemy, but had just received a direct hit by a shell. On nearing the house, heavy fire was opened on the party, which was forced to withdraw, Capt. Coates being severely wounded. Regardless of his personal safety, Capt. Hurley returned to his position and organized a stretcher party. As the state of the ground did not permit carriage by crawling, he ignored the intense enemy fire directed at him and calmly walked across the open with his party to fetch Capt. Coates.

For some time it seemed impossible that anyone could survive the intensity of the fire. Finally the enemy ceased fire in recognition of this gallant and unselfish conduct. Throughout the action this officer showed outstanding qualities of leadership and inspired all ranks to greater efforts.

SERGT. W. HUSSEY, *9th September*, 1942: M.M.

This N.C.O. has been platoon sergeant of a scout platoon throughout the campaign, during two months of which it was in almost continuous contact with the enemy. He has continually distinguished himself by his fearlessness, initiative and devotion to duty, and has carried out most valuable patrols by both day and night.

On several occasions he has remained calmly reporting enemy movements whilst under fire, and by his personal conduct has set a magnificent example.

LIEUT. P. C. INNES, *13th August*, 1942: M.C.

For conspicuous courage, initiative and leadership near Rotonda Mteifei on 9th June, 1942. This officer was commanding a carrier platoon of seven carriers. He was ordered to attack a convoy of seventy vehicles which were known to be escorted by tanks.

He led his carriers into action and in spite of enemy minefields on his course, and with utter disregard for the fire of a German Mark III tank at close range, succeeded in engaging the enemy supply vehicles with small-arms fire and grenades.

His platoon completely destroyed seventeen 10-ton supply lorries, damaged many more, inflicted considerable casualties to personnel, and returned with as many prisoners as the vehicles could carry.

This success was entirely due to this officer's determination and leadership.

LIEUT. J. B. D. IRWIN, *14th January*, 1943: M.C.

Lieut. Irwin was commander of a troop of 6-pounder guns on the Snipe position on 26th and 27th October, 1942. His troop was ordered to take up position on the northern flank. This flank was attacked by tanks once during the night and four times during the day; on each occasion Lieut. Irwin's troop repelled the attacks with losses to the enemy.

He went from gun to gun encouraging his men, and when one gun was knocked out he supervised the removal of wounded and the redistribution of ammunition under heavy fire.

In the final attack by some sixty German tanks at 1700 hrs. the troop had only twenty rounds left. He ordered his guns to hold their fire; and when the nearest enemy tanks were only a hundred yards away he gave orders to fire, setting four of them on fire and helping to turn the attack.

Under such cool leadership his troop accounted for nineteen enemy tanks burnt and other vehicles hit during the action. His courage was of the highest order.

RFN. T. IRVINE, *22nd July*, 1943: M.M.

On 27th March, 1943, Rfn. Irvine was a member of a motor section which was taking part in a company attack on a strong enemy position at Djebel Saikra.

Rfn. Irvine was the left-flank man of his section, which was pinned down by heavy rifle and machine-gun fire. Using his own initiative, he worked his way forward single-handed to a position where he could bring flanking fire to bear on an enemy strong-point.

His fire was so accurately applied that the fire of the enemy was silenced and his section was able to advance and overcome the enemy resistance. The ground over which he moved was heavily mined and swept by hostile fire; furthermore, there was a strong wire obstacle in his path.

His courage and daring were an important factor in the decisive defeat of the enemy, and his initiative turned a possible failure into a considerable success.

His action was a first-class example of individual initiative and bravery and an object lesson to all his comrades.

LIEUT. C. P. JAMES (1st Battalion), 2nd August, 1945: M.C.

On the evening of 20th April, 1945, Lieut. James was in command of a motor platoon mounted on a troop of tanks which was ordered to attack the village of Daerstorf under cover of smoke. Owing to bad visibility, the tanks reached a point far in advance of the place intended to set down infantry. As a result, the platoon found themselves in the midst of an enemy force which consisted of about a company with two 75-mm. and one 50-mm. A.T. guns and twelve Spandaus. Without a moment's hesitation, however, and under heavy fire, Lieut. James collected his small force, and in face of determined opposition attacked the enemy, causing considerable casualties in killed and wounded amongst them and putting the remainder to flight.

The platoon sergeant and runner became casualties almost immediately in the attack, but Lieut. James, encouraging his men, held on doggedly to his position against numerically superior enemy. After some time, reinforcements arrived, and Lieut. James then led his platoon in clearing the village, capturing a further thirty-nine prisoners.

The successful completion of this operation was undoubtedly the result of this officer's initiative, bravery and inspiring leadership at a critical moment, when events might well have taken an unfavourable turn.

P.S.M. E. H. JARVIS, 9th May, 1941: D.C.M.

For conspicuous gallantry at Sidi Saleh during the night of 6th/7th February. This warrant officer was commanding an isolated platoon on the beach when attacked in the moonlight by two enemy medium tanks. Accompanied by one rifleman, he ran up to the tanks on the move and fired through the slits with his rifle, wounding the crew. One of the officers fired at him with a pistol from the door of the tank and he thereupon hit him over the head with the butt of his rifle. The crew then surrendered.

LIEUT. B. W. JEPSON-TURNER, 26th October, 1942: M.C.

For conspicuous gallantry and devotion to duty. This officer was in charge of eight 6-pounder anti-tank guns. On 3rd July, 1942, at Ruweisat Ridge, just before first light, he took one of his sections about 500 yards forward of our own tanks, and as daylight came he saw ahead of him, approximately 700 yards away, some enemy anti-tank guns in the process of being dug in. Leaving his guns in a concealed position, he took forward a party of men armed with automatics and opened fire on the enemy, forcing them to withdraw and inflicting considerable casualties. A few minutes later a Mark IV tank appeared over a ridge some 600 yards away and opened fire on the party.

Immediately appreciating the situation, he ran back to where the guns were hidden, and, taking one of them forward, he quickly brought the gun into action and destroyed the tank with the first shot.

The success achieved by these two anti-tank platoons during recent operations was largely due to the skill and personal bravery shown by this officer.

W.S./CAPT. (T./MAJOR) B. W. JEPSON-TURNER, M.C.: Croix de Guerre with Gilt Star.

On 3rd September, 1944, Major Jepson-Turner was commanding "C" Company, 1st Rifle Brigade, which was part of the regimental group under my command. The group was ordered to push north through Lillers and seize crossings over the canal to the north of the town. After the armour had passed through Lillers, "C" Company, 1st Rifle Brigade, was ordered to clear the town of enemy in order that the "soft" vehicles might pass through and that the L. of C. might be kept open. This was done after some heavy street fighting, and throughout the day Major Jepson-Turner's company kept the enemy at bay in Lillers and the L. of C. clear, in spite of many determined counter-attacks by the enemy, including S.S. During the afternoon orders were received to withdraw, and "C" Company was accordingly pulled in from its forward positions, which were immediately occupied by the enemy. These orders were subsequently cancelled and the enemy had once more to be driven out of the outskirts of the town. Finally, the whole group withdrew successfully through Lillers while "C" Company acted as rearguard. Throughout the day Major Jepson-Turner was continuously at his forward section posts encouraging and directing his men. This officer's untiring energy and fine example were very largely responsible for the successful extrication of the force and for the destruction of many Germans.

LIEUT. R. L. JEPSON-TURNER, 13th August, 1942: D.S.O.

For conspicuous gallantry and devotion to duty during an attack by German tanks on a battery position in Libya on the evening of 14th June, 1942. This officer was in command of two 6-pounder anti-tank guns. He handled them with great skill and scored hits on no fewer than six enemy tanks, and when the whole crew of one gun became casualties he loaded and fired the gun single-handed until his right arm was shot off. He then continued to direct the fire of the remaining gun until that too was put out of action.

Throughout the action he showed courage and leadership of the highest order.

LIEUT.-COLONEL R. E. W. JOHNSON, T.D., 13th December, 1945: O.B.E.

This officer joined the W.T.S.F.F. in midsummer, 1943. In Italy he served with the advanced detachment attached to the Fifth Army and with the H.Q. of this unit.

In April, 1944, he was engaged in pursuing investigations in the Anzio bridgehead regarding sniping, etc. His efforts may be considered to have played no small part in sniping successes.

During the whole period he has been with W.T.S.F.F. he has done most painstaking and exceptionally good work.

C.S.M. B. W. JONES, 5th January, 1943: Croix de Guerre.

A./C.S.M. R. M. JONES, 14th January, 1943: M.M.

At El Wiskha on 25th October, 1942. This sergeant was directing machine-gun fire on enemy targets when one of his gunners was hit. He immediately took his place and continued firing. His No. 2 gunner was then hit and replaced by his platoon officer, who had already been wounded. He had fired about six belts when his officer was killed. He directed the withdrawal of his section to a less exposed position.

Throughout he continued steadily firing in the face of heavy enemy opposition. After this he took command of the platoon and showed considerable leadership for four more days.

His gallant conduct and coolness kept his platoon in action and inflicted heavy losses on the enemy.

RFN. F. G. JORDAN (1st Battalion), 1st March, 1945: M.M.

On the night of 10th/11th October, 1944, two motor platoons and a section of carriers of " A " Company, 1st Rifle Brigade, supported by a troop of tanks of the 5th Dragoon Guards, were holding the village of Geffen. This force was twice attacked by a battalion of enemy infantry supported by artillery and mortar fire. During the second attack and coincident with heavy shell fire, a half-track vehicle of one of the platoons received a direct hit from a shell, immediately bursting into flames. The burning vehicle was endangering other vehicles and houses in the vicinity and the flames were in danger of disclosing our positions to the enemy. Jordan accompanied his platoon sergeant to the courtyard where the vehicles were parked and, despite the danger of exploding ammunition on the burning vehicle, which was loaded with mines, 2-inch mortar bombs, grenades, S.A.A., etc., some of which was already exploding, drove three vehicles from the area. Having done this, he returned to his platoon sergeant and assisted him to put out the flames in two houses set on fire. This task completed, Jordan assisted the sergeant to rescue civilians trapped in a cellar by blazing petrol. He then returned to his platoon position.

This work was carried out with complete disregard for his own safety and with the ever-present danger of the mines, etc., exploding, in addition to the enemy shell and mortar fire, which intensified when the vehicle began to burn.

MILITARY AWARDS, 1939-46   119

MAJOR F. H. V. KEIGHLEY, 24th January, 1946: O.B.E.

This officer was Provost Staff Officer, H.Q., Second Army. In addition to his ordinary military duties, owing to the disorganized and absent civil police force in liberated enemy countries he had grave responsibilities added to his work. By his capacity for careful thought and hard work the larceny of petrol and rations was almost entirely stopped and Government property of enormous value was recovered for use in operations.

LIEUT.-COLONEL J. E. S. KING-SALTER, 24th April, 1943: D.S.O.; 1st January, 1946: O.B.E.

CPL. G. H. KINGSMILL (8th Battalion), 1st March, 1945: M.M.

On 30th August, 1944, at Amecourt, Cpl. Kingsmill was signal corporal in the command half-track of " G " Company, 8th Rifle Brigade. Heavy fire was opened on the vehicle by a 20-mm. gun from about 200 yards away. Several of the crew were wounded, including the company commander. Those who were able to get out of the vehicle immediately came under machine-gun fire, and the driver of the vehicle was killed. Cpl. Kingsmill, the only one who was not wounded, remained on his wireless set, continued to send in valuable information which ultimately led to the destruction of the enemy position, and looked after the wounded men.

Cpl. Kingsmill showed great courage and disregard for danger, and his action not only led to the destruction of the enemy but also saved the lives of his comrades.

SERGT. (A./CLR.-SERGT.) A. J. KIRK (10th Battalion), 7th December, 1944: M.M.

For outstanding leadership and devotion to duty at Monte Pulito, two miles west of Perugia.

On 19th June, 1944, Sergt. Kirk was in command of a platoon which was in a vital position astride the Perugia—Maggione road. Perugia was still occupied by the enemy, to whom the continued use of the road was of the highest importance.

In spite of counter-attacks and intense mortar and shell fire throughout the day, Sergt. Kirk inspired his platoon to hold on and by calm judgment and cool control of fire destroyed three enemy trucks and two motorcycle combinations, killing most of the occupants and taking three prisoners.

Finding that opposition centred in a village which overlooked the company position, Sergt. Kirk on his own initiative planned and carried out an attack which cleared the village and greatly relieved pressure on the company.

As a result of Sergt. Kirk's calmness, judgment and outstanding example under fire the platoon and company positions were maintained and the important road was denied to the enemy throughout the day.

LIEUT.-COLONEL R. M. C. KITTOE, 13th December, 1945: O.B.E.

For services when in charge of the Historical Section at H.Q., A.A.I., and A.F.H.Q.

CPL. G. C. KLANKE (10th Battalion), 7th December, 1944: M.M.

During the attack on Monte Rentella on 22nd June, 1944, for conspicuous gallantry and devotion to duty.

Cpl. Klanke was commanding a section in a platoon which was ordered to capture a house occupied by the Germans as a strong-point.

Cpl. Klanke's section was the assault section. Heavy mortar and shell fire was falling in the area, and intense machine-gun fire coming from the house itself. Using most difficult ground with the greatest skill and leading his section to the objective with the utmost determination and entire disregard of his own safety, Cpl. Klanke successfully entered the house and ejected the enemy. As a result of this action, carried out under intense fire but with barrack-square precision and dash, a most dangerous salient into the companies' position was eliminated, enabling two companies to link up and form a vital firm base.

RFN. L. R. LADMORE (8th Battalion), 12th August, 1945: M.M.

On 17th April, 1945, Rfn. Ladmore's platoon was advancing in its vehicles with a troop of tanks towards the village of Barum. As the platoon went over the crest and came into full view of the village, the enemy opened fire with 88-mm. guns, 20-mms. and machine guns, all firing from a range of about 400 yards. The leading section half-track, of whose crew Rfn. Ladmore was a member, was struck in the suspension by a solid shot and crashed into a ditch. The crew abandoned the vehicle and lay in a ditch. Heavy fire from machine guns was opened on these men, both from the village and a hitherto undisclosed position on the right flank. One rifleman, a member of the same section, was hit in the lower jaw by a bullet. Rfn. Ladmore, without waiting for orders, went forward to where the rifleman lay and applied a field dressing. He then carried and dragged the rifleman up the slope in direct view and under fire from the village for a distance of 300 yards. By some miracle he was not hit, though fire was deliberately opened on him. Owing to the fact that blood from the wound hindered the casualty's breathing, the majority of the journey was done by crawling. Having handed over the casualty to the stretcher-bearers, Rfn. Ladmore returned to his section in the ditch.

Rfn. Ladmore's conduct throughout was an inspiration to all. He was completely impervious to all danger and at no time took any thought for his own safety. His prompt action undoubtedly saved his comrade's life.

CPL. E. J. LANE, 20th September, 1945: M.M.

For gallantry and distinguished service in the defence of Calais, May, 1940.

LIEUT.-COLONEL G. E. W. LANE (Commanding 7th Bn. Surrey Home Guard), 15th December, 1944: O.B.E.

SERGT. L. G. V. LANGENSCHEID (1st Battalion), 1st *March*, 1945: M.M.

On the night of 10th/11th October, 1944, two motor platoons and a section of carriers of " A " Company, 1st Rifle Brigade, supported by a troop of tanks of the 5th Dragoon Guards, were holding the village of Geffen. This force was twice attacked by a battalion of enemy infantry supported by artillery and mortar fire.

During the first attack Sergt. Langenscheid (platoon sergeant of one of the motor platoons) set the highest example of tenacity and bravery. He was manning and firing a .30 Browning mounted on the front of his vehicle and remained at his post despite heavy enemy fire of all descriptions, including grenades thrown at short range.

As the second attack developed, one of the platoon vehicles received a direct hit from a shell and immediately burst into flames. He personally drove away another burning vehicle from very close proximity to the one in flames, which was full of ammunition, exploding anti-tank mines and Piat bombs, and supervised reparking the other vehicles, all the time under heavy fire. He then put out the fire in two houses, which had also been set ablaze, the flames from which were lighting up some of our positions and giving away their location to the enemy. Having got the fires under control, he went to the rescue of civilians trapped in a cellar by blazing petrol. He then returned to his platoon area and again got the .30 Browning into action against the attacking enemy.

Not only did his prompt action save the vehicles and civilians but, more important still, the fire from the weapons he was manning had a decided effect on the course of the battle. Both attacks were beaten off.

W.O. CL. II C.S.M. W. J. LAWSON (2nd Battalion), 13*th December*, 1945: M.M.

For outstanding devotion to duty. C.S.M. Lawson has fought throughout the Italian campaign as a platoon sergeant and later as C.S.M. His conduct in action has at all times been of the highest order. His aggressive spirit, courage and initiative have been beyond all praise.

At Bondeno " B " Company, 2nd Rifle Brigade, was ordered to force an entry into the town and cut off a large number of retreating Germans. C.S.M. Lawson immediately volunteered for this patrol as patrol commander, working under very great difficulties owing to pouring rain and being continuously subjected to aimed small-arms fire. He successfully led his patrol to their objective, thereby causing very heavy casualties to the enemy and resulting in the taking of a very large number of prisoners.

Throughout the campaign C.S.M. Lawson has proved himself to be an outstandingly reliable, efficient and courageous N.C.O. There is no doubt that the excellent example he set has proved to be the turning point in many different operations.

W.O. CL. III A. LEDLEY, 20*th September*, 1945: M.M.

For gallantry and distinguished service in the defence of Calais, May, 1940.

SERGT. W. W. LEE (1st Battalion), 21*st December*, 1944: M.M.

On 2nd August, 1944, at Breuil, 7752 L./Sergt. Lee was ordered to lead a patrol of three to locate enemy positions in the wooded area 781525 which were holding up the advance. On reaching the area of the woods L./Sergt. Lee found the road mined and the area strongly held by enemy machine guns and mortars. Undeterred, he advanced stealthily to the edge of the wood. Then he surprised a party of enemy and shot them up, killing several and capturing fourteen prisoners. The patrol was then engaged from a house near by. L./Sergt. Lee left the prisoners in charge of his two men and, single-handed, destroyed the enemy post, capturing three more Germans.

By this time very heavy fire was being directed on the patrol from the wood. With complete calm and disregard for his own safety, L./Sergt. Lee formed up his party of prisoners and doubled them smartly down the road under the very noses of their comrades. Two prisoners were seriously wounded and had to be abandoned. The two riflemen of the patrol were slightly wounded, but were able to reach our lines.

Without any doubt, this excellent patrol and the discomfiture of the enemy played a large part in the successful attack on this area later in the day.

2/LIEUT. J. W. O'N. LENTAIGNE, 13*th August*, 1942: M.C.

For conspicuous gallantry and devotion to duty during operations from 27th May to 10th June, 1942. On the night of 30th/31st May he carried out a patrol behind the enemy leaguers and succeeded in locating accurately the enemy guns in rear, and provided information of very great value.

On the night of 9th/10th June, with his platoon as protection, he took a recovery vehicle one and a half miles forward of our lines and brought back a damaged Grant tank at times under very heavy fire and within some one hundred yards of the enemy tanks.

Throughout the operations this officer has shown great daring and resource and his leadership of the platoon has been of the highest order.

LIEUT. J. C. M. LEYLAND, 19*th August*, 1943: M.C.

On the night of 29th/30th April Lieut. Leyland was in command of a motor platoon when the Battalion carried out an attack on Djebel Kournine.

Lieut. Leyland led his platoon with great determination up the steep slopes of the hill under heavy fire against practically an inaccessible enemy position.

When his platoon had received several casualties, Lieut. Leyland made his way right up to the enemy position and threw grenades until he was seriously wounded.

This officer's great gallantry and determination brought his platoon to within an ace of storming what was a practically impregnable position, and his action at the last enabled the platoon to get their casualties away and withdraw without further loss.

LIEUT. C. H. LIDDELL, 25*th April*, 1941 : M.C.

This officer was in command of a night patrol round Nibeiwa Camp on the nights of 2nd/3rd and 7th/8th December, 1940. On the first occasion, accompanied by two N.C.Os., he crawled through the defences between enemy sentry groups only fifty yards apart and located the minefields and also a gap in the defences.

On the second occasion, accompanied by the same N.C.Os., he found enemy tanks patrolled by sentries, stationed apparently in the minefield. Although the tanks were only twenty yards apart, he succeeded in getting in between them unseen by the patrolling sentries and locating the gap in the minefield leading to the camps. The information gained by this officer's gallant action was of great value and was probably instrumental in saving many casualties when the tank attack took place on 9th December.

2/LIEUT. A. J. LING, 20*th January*, 1942 : M.C.

For conspicuous bravery and leadership at Sidi Rezegh on 20th November, 1942.

2/Lieut. Ling was second-in-command of a carrier platoon of "S" Company of his Battalion. One of his carriers was hit by shell fire in an exposed position in full view of the main German tank force.

2/Lieut. Ling drove out in his truck under heavy fire, rescued the crew and later towed the vehicle to safety.

Later, on 21st November, when his position was attacked by over sixty German tanks and infantry at 800 yards' range, he moved out under heavy fire and carried two wounded men to safety.

Later in the day this officer was wounded.

His conduct throughout this action was an inspiration to all under his command.

LIEUT. R. W. B. LLOYD (attached to 1st Bn. The Middlesex Regiment), 13*th March*, 1945 : M.C.

On 30th October, 1944, the 2nd Gloucestershire Hussars were reorganizing in the wood at 6613 when a counter-attack, supported by mortars and an S.P. gun, was launched against " D " Company. Lieut. Lloyd, commanding the M.M.G. platoon in support of the battalion, was at that moment siting positions for his guns. These were still mounted in their carriers, notwithstanding which he at once drove them, conspicuous as they were, through the fringe of the wood and engaged the enemy in the open. He was quickly discovered and was subjected to all types of fire, including mortaring and direct fire from the S.P. gun, as a result of which over half of his platoon were casualties within a few minutes and two guns were disabled. Calling upon the remaining gun numbers, Lieut. Lloyd threw himself into the task of reallocation and repair. Directing the surviving N.C.O. to one gun, he applied himself to the second with such coolness and dexterity that he quickly had it in action again. He was thus in time to engage the enemy reserve, and this, in the face of renewed aimed fire, he did with such deadly determination as completely to pin it down. The assaulting enemy troops, profiting by the temporary neutralization of Lieut. Lloyd's platoon, had meantime succeeded in penetrating between our forward sections. He, however, by separating them from their reserve, arrested further progress and caused them embarrassment and indecision.

It was his complete disregard for personal safety and vigorous example of leadership which alone enabled Lieut. Lloyd to rally his surviving gun numbers. It was by his resuscitating action and by the achievement of his own hand that he succeeded in reviving the fire of a unit which to all appearances had been silenced. The resulting surprise and confusion, apart from disorganizing the enemy, had a most uplifting influence on the hard-pressed infantry, and this, by enabling them to hold their ground, was largely responsible for the repulse of the enemy attack.

SERGT. J. LONGSTAFF: U.S. Bronze Star.

MAJOR J. F. LONSDALE (10th Battalion), 20*th April*, 1945: D.S.O.

For continual gallantry and distinguished service during the period 11th May to 30th August, 1944.

Major Lonsdale has commanded a motor company throughout the campaign with outstanding success and distinction. On the Gustav Line, on the Liri, at Fontana Lire Inferiore, at Piglio, Monte Rotondo, Perugia, Corgiano and Castellione, Major Lonsdale's company has been in the thick of the fighting and by these successes has materially affected the course of the battle at each stage.

Major Lonsdale himself has repeatedly led his company into the assault, has invariably exposed himself to the heaviest fire in order to control and encourage his men, and has shown throughout the very highest qualities of leadership.

His calm judgment and skilful dispositions have time after time turned the scale in our favour, while his exceptional devotion to duty and absolute disregard of personal safety have been for many months an inspiration to his own men and to the whole battalion.

LIEUT.-COLONEL THE HON. N. A. S. LYTTON-MILBANK, 13*th December*, 1945: O.B.E.

Lieut.-Colonel Lytton-Milbank has shown outstanding singleness of purpose in his efforts to make the operation of Land Forces, Adriatic, succeed. With great determination and conscientious personal sacrifice, he produced most satisfactory results from an inadequate administrative machine at a time when four operations were in progress in three different Balkan countries.

He then built up the administration of this force so that by the spring of 1945 it reached a high pitch of efficiency. His consistent devotion to duty and his long hours of application to detail contributed in a large measure to the success of operations in Greece, Albania and Yugoslavia in the past autumn and winter.

W./Capt. (T./Major) P. A. C. Luke (1st Battalion), 12th April, 1945: M.C.

On 20th January, 1945, Major Luke's company was ordered to do an attack on the village of Saint Joost, supported by a squadron of tanks and a troop of Crocodiles. Soon after the attack started it became apparent that the enemy, who were paratroops, were in much greater strength than was at first thought, and from the start they put up a fierce fight. For over six hours the company battled its way slowly forward against this very stubborn enemy, armed with large numbers of machine guns and bazookas and supported by assault guns and mortars. Large numbers of the enemy were killed in hand-to-hand fighting and over 40 prisoners were taken, and there is no doubt that the action of the company made it possible for a battalion attack the next day to capture this important strong-point.

The success of the operation, which in view of the strength of the enemy was out of all proportion to the size of the attacking company, was in large measure due to the personal courage and determination of Major Luke, as well as to the members of his company. He personally directed the operation from start to finish, although he was subjected to very heavy and accurate mortar fire and shelling. His coolness and determination undoubtedly communicated themselves to his whole company, which fought with great courage from start to finish.

Lieut. J. W. MacAlpine (7th Battalion), 23rd August, 1945: M.C.

At 1800 hrs. on 21st April, 1945, this officer was ordered to advance with his platoon in close support of the leading armoured squadron on to Poggio Renatica; on approaching the objective, the platoon was heavily engaged by snipers from either side of the road after the tanks had passed through.

Lieut. MacAlpine in the leading carrier immediately engaged them and enabled the platoon to continue the advance without casualties. This action was so successful that the enemy surrendered immediately to the next troops to pass through. The platoon then covered the tank leaguer of the leading squadron during the night from the outskirts of Poggio Renatica. Lieut. MacAlpine led a reconnaissance patrol to the far side of the town, bringing back valuable information concerning a complete flak battery of 88-mm., which were subsequently destroyed.

Shortly after returning at about 0100 hrs. a 20-mm. and a Spandau opened fire on the tank leaguer at 200 yards' range. Lieut. MacAlpine immediately seized an L.M.G., advanced beyond his forward section's position into the open, and engaged the enemy, effectively silencing both weapons and causing ten casualties.

At 0400 hrs. the platoon was ordered to advance into the town and seize a strategic building to allow the tanks to advance through at first light. The platoon quickly seized their objective and began to mop up the left half of the town. One section was pinned down by Spandau fire and sniping and the Platoon Sergeant was hit. Showing complete disregard for his own safety, Lieut. MacAlpine went out alone and organized the recovery of the wounded man.

Throughout this action, which lasted continuously for more than twelve hours, Lieut. MacAlpine set a magnificent example to his platoon of courage, leadership and tireless energy. His conduct throughout was an inspiration to all ranks.

2/Lieut. R. S. McColl, *15th October*, 1942 : M.C.

On 14th July, 1942, on Ruweisat Ridge, some machine gunners of his company, having suddenly come under heavy machine-gun and shell fire, were ordered to withdraw.

When Lieut. McColl, who was just returning from a patrol with his carriers, saw that the machine gunners were in difficulties, he at once ordered the carriers with him to continue on their course while he himself went to the assistance of the stranded machine gunners.

He took the guns and their crews on his carrier in turn, depositing each in their new position and returning for the next, entirely undaunted by heavy enemy fire.

By his prompt and courageous action he prevented heavy casualties and loss, and displayed qualities of quick decision and coolness under fire, for which he has been noted on many occasions during the campaign.

Sergt. D. A. Main, *1st June*, 1943 : D.C.M.

Sergt. Main was a member of the company ordered to capture a pass. The company came under heavy machine-gun fire soon after the commencement of the advance and was temporarily held up by a machine-gun post fifty yards to the right flank. Sergt. Main, on his own initiative, led his section to the attack and silenced the gun, being wounded in the thigh. He then continued successively to silence four more machine-gun posts, killing most of the crew in each case, which were causing casualties on the right flank. Throughout, Sergt. Main acted entirely on his own initiative without waiting for orders from a superior officer.

He continued fighting with his company, in spite of his wound, until ordered to withdraw.

2/Lieut. D. A. Main, D.C.M. (7th Battalion), *7th December,* 1944 : M.C.

For conspicuous gallantry during a counter-attack on Monte Castiglion Maggio.

On the morning of 7th July, 1944, 2/Lieut. Main's company was consolidating on a reverse slope position at the top of Maggio when an enemy counter-attack developed.

Leading elements of the enemy had advanced to within fifteen yards of the company position when an officer charged forward with a section to drive them back, but was mortally wounded by a sniper.

2/Lieut. Main immediately went forward to him, shot the German sniper and then advanced upon the enemy by himself, firing his T.S.M.C. from the hip. He killed three Germans and forced the remainder to retire over the hill. Throughout this time enemy small-arms fire was heavy, but 2/Lieut. Main arranged for the evacuation of the wounded and did not return to dead ground until this task was completed.

It was due to 2/Lieut. Main's gallantry that the counter-attack was repulsed and control of the height regained.

CPL. J. A. MALKIN (Italy), 19*th April*, 1945: B.E.M.

This N.C.O. is a G.P.O.A. who, apart from performing his duties very efficiently over two years, was also in charge of a pioneer party and therefore responsible for mine clearance when occupying new sites. As N.C.O. in charge of the pioneer party he has tackled the often hazardous task of mine-lifting with great courage and perseverance.

Always he has been an example to those working with him, and through his excellent work he has enabled gun positions to be occupied with speed and safety.

SERGT. A. H. MANNING, 25*th November*, 1943: M.M.

Sergt. Manning was platoon sergeant of a scout platoon (carriers) for the period 18th February to 31st March, 1943.

On 9th March he was proceeding on patrol in the Mareth area when the carrier in which he was travelling blew up on mines. Sergt. Manning, though thrown some fifteen yards, picked himself up and continued the patrol in another carrier.

On the night of 23rd/24th March Sergt. Manning was on standing patrol with three carriers and one machine-gun section at a point named Cross Tracks (Tunisia). At about 0300 hrs. on the 24th the position was attacked by an enemy patrol. The enemy succeeded in getting to close quarters, using grenades and tommy-guns. Sergt. Manning, aided by the remainder of his patrol, successfully beat off the attack after half an hour. Though wounded in the eye, he brought the whole party safely back to the leaguer area.

This non-commissioned officer has repeatedly shown complete disregard for personal danger and has at all times provided an excellent example to the men under his command.

SERGT. A. F. MANSELL, 18*th February*, 1943: M.M.

During operations from 23rd to 28th January, from 5th to 12th April, and from 27th May to 8th June, this N.C.O. showed resourcefulness and great power of leadership. On 23rd January he was separated from his platoon and chased some fifty miles by an armoured car and rejoined his company three days later, having covered a matter of 250 miles.

On 9th April he was part of a patrol which attacked an enemy defensive position. During the operation his platoon commander became separated and he collected the remainder of the patrol inside the enemy lines and led them back to his own lines, a distance of about ten miles, on 30th May.

After his platoon commander was killed he led his platoon, with coolness and courage and complete disregard of personal safety, in spite of periods of intense shell fire and dive-bombing attacks until relieved by another officer in 5th June.

His example and the confidence which he inspired are an example to all.

MAJOR F. W. MARTEN, 14*th October*, 1943 : M.C.

At El Alamein from 22nd to 24th October, Capt. Marten was acting as Chief Staff Officer to the 1st Armoured Division, Minefield Task Force.

During this phase of operations he never ceased to co-ordinate progress reports and information coming in from the parties in the enemy minefields. The smooth running of the advance headquarters was largely due to his foresight and planning prior to the battle and by his devotion to duty and fine example during the battle. On 26th and 27th October at Snipe, as adjutant, he remained at the Battalion rear link set for fourteen hours. All through this period his position was under heavy shell and small-arms fire, but he never ceased to send clear and concise reports of the operation.

At 1630 hrs. on the 27th, when his commanding officer was wounded, the Battalion being isolated and out of ammunition, of his own initiative he issued detailed orders for the evacuation of the position should the enemy attack during the night.

These orders enabled the Battalion to withdraw from the position without loss and in good order when the enemy advanced, and all equipment that could be moved was saved.

This officer's outstanding courage and example ensured that the Battalion was never out of communication with the Brigade, and his calm reports of the situation to companies inspired them with confidence when all seemed lost and the Battalion position penetrated by enemy tanks.

SERGT. H. J. MATHEWS, 20*th September*, 1945 : M.M.

For gallantry and distinguished service in the defence of Calais, May, 1940.

T./CAPT. E. P. MAY (8th Battalion), 13*th March*, 1945 : M.C.

On 18th August, 1944, Capt. May was in command of the vanguard, consisting of a section of carriers and a mortar platoon of " H " Company, 8th Rifle Brigade, supported by a troop of tanks of the 23rd Hussars. West of Launay enemy opposition was met and heavy fire from artillery was opened on the vanguard. There was also considerable small-arms fire. Capt. May organized an attack on the village by the infantry, supported by the tanks. During the attack, Capt. May saw that the supporting fire from the tanks was ineffective and he immediately jumped on to the troop commander's tank to secure better supporting fire.

All this time the tanks were under machine-gun fire and Capt. May was completely exposed. Shortly after this, two riflemen were killed in a farmyard. Disregarding his own safety and in spite of enemy small-arms and mortar fire, Capt. May went forward by himself to see whether the men were wounded or killed.

The infantry under Capt. May's command continued to attack and harass the enemy with great effect until ordered to withdraw by his company commander.

Heavy casualties were suffered by the vanguard in this action and Capt. May's gallantry and complete disregard of danger were an inspiration to the men under his command.

LIEUT. G. T. MAY, 22nd July, 1943 : M.C.

On the morning of 27th March, 1943, Lieut. May was commanding a rifle platoon which was to form part of a company attack on a strongly held enemy position at Djebel Saikra.

When the barrage lifted, Lieut. May, who was leading his platoon, was short of the object and the platoon on his left had been held up.

With complete disregard for his own personal safety, he led his men through the belts of armour-piercing mines, over a double apron of barbed-wire fence and reached a position whence he could outflank a strongly held enemy stronghold.

He directed the fire of his platoon with such accuracy that all the defenders were forced to surrender.

By his courage, skill and leadership he turned what might have been a serious reverse into a complete success. Thereafter he was tireless in consolidating the position against a threat of counter-attack.

His action set a fine example of bravery and leadership to all ranks in the Battalion.

CAPT. (T./MAJOR) T. H. MELDRUM, 18th February, 1943 : D.S.O.

On approximately 6th June, in the middle of the Knightsbridge battle, the Battalion was issued with 6-pounder anti-tank guns which were joined into a company under the command of Major Meldrum.

This company was in action throughout the fighting in the Knightsbridge area, on Ruweisat Ridge on 2nd July, at Alam el Dahmaniya on 17th July, and in the fighting on 31st August. Major Meldrum has commanded the company throughout. Starting with untrained personnel when actually in contact with the enemy, he brought his company up to a high state of efficiency, so that under his leadership it is known to have destroyed at least thirty German tanks in the above operations, and damaged many others.

He fought his company throughout all these operations with great skill and bravery.

He has been tireless in training his men under all circumstances, and without previous experience achieved great results.

Largely through his own courage and leadership, through his own devotion to duty and skill in battle, his company has never been engaged without inflicting loss on the enemy; at times he has had guns destroyed, but he has never allowed a single gun to fall into the hands of the enemy.

This officer throughout has rendered services of exceptional merit.

LIEUT. C. H. MELVILLE (1st Battalion), 24*th August*, 1944: M.C.

During the period 1st June to 15th November, 1943, this officer has consistently shown an extremely high standard of leadership, courage and initiative.

On 6th October, 1943, the day after joining his company, he led an extremely successful day patrol up to the bank of the River Volturno in spite of mortar and machine-gun fire, and obtained valuable information. This patrol gained the commendation of the Divisional Commander.

On 22nd October he led a reconnaissance patrol through the enemy covering position to Francolise and obtained useful information. On 23rd October he led a patrol up the main road to Francolise and brought back information of enemy dispositions covering the road. On 24th October he led a day patrol into the village of Francolise and obtained very valuable information on the river crossings there. On 25th October, after dark, he took his platoon across the river at Francolise to cover an R.E. party clearing the bridge. He met strong opposition from Germans there with machine guns.

Although his party was heavily outnumbered, he withdrew and returned the fire, whereupon he was very heavily and accurately shelled by nebelwerfers. He has subsequently led other reconnaissance patrols with great skill and determination.

CAPT. G. E. MERRICK (7th Battalion), 23*rd August*, 1945: M.C.

On 1st May, 1945, Capt. Merrick's platoon of 6-pdr. A.T. guns was part of a force ordered to destroy three enemy tanks which were preventing the 7th Battalion column crossing the River Tagliamento south of St. Vito. Owing to the deep ditches, it was possible to get only one gun into action on the road, in full view of the enemy. Although the extreme danger of such a course of action was obvious to all, Capt. Merrick unhesitatingly got one gun into action under heavy enemy fire and engaged the enemy with such speed that they were forced to withdraw and the way across the River Tagliamento to Udine was open to us.

In the afternoon of the same day Capt. Merrick was in charge of a 6-pdr. A.T. gun accompanying a small force of carriers which had been sent out to effect the surrender of five enemy tanks which were reported to be willing to surrender. The enemy tanks treacherously opened fire on our carriers while the surrender was in progress and three tanks charged down the road towards the remainder of the force. Capt. Merrick immediately got his gun into action in the open on the road under heavy fire. He personally directed the fire to such effect that the leading tank was knocked out at 100 yards' range and the remainder were forced to withdraw.

On both these occasions Capt. Merrick showed great personal courage and initiative, and his speed of action on both occasions resulted in two very difficult situations being turned into an enemy defeat.

MILITARY AWARDS, 1939-46   131

SERGT. K. C. MEYER (1st Battalion), 21*st December*, 1944: M.M.

On 3rd September, 1944, the battalion was in position holding crossroads on the main road north of St. Pol at Cauchy. A section of carriers was sent out to some high ground to watch the east flank of the position. From this position L./Sergt. Meyer contacted some Maquis, who reported a troop of German field guns three kilometres down the road to the east. Having reported this, he received permission to investigate and, continuing in that direction, he contacted other Maquis, who gave him the troop location fairly accurately. L./Sergt. Meyer then took his section forward until he was able to observe one gun and its crew in an " action " position. L./Sergt. Meyer himself then patrolled forward on foot until he had located each gun. He then returned to his section and made a quick plan, which was to collect as many Maquis as possible to create a diversion while he attacked the troop position with his carriers. This he did, taking the German gunners completely by surprise; by suddenly pouring on them a deadly fire from three .5 Brownings at the critical moment when their attention was drawn to rifle fire from the Maquis to their flank. With his Brownings L./Sergt. Meyer knocked out three 105-mm. field guns, " brewed up " two ammunition lorries and one Opel staff car and killed one officer and five other ranks, taking eight others prisoner—an action requiring cool judgment, good leadership and considerable daring and personal bravery.

The following day this N.C.O.'s section "liberated" Bethune at approximately 1100 hrs. and for the rest of the day proceeded to engage the enemy north of the canal. With his heavy machine gun and a Bren placed in a house he knocked out a heavy lorry and a staff car and killed or wounded several men who attempted to bale out. This fire was returned by a numerically very superior enemy, and the section signaller and another rifleman were wounded. L./Sergt. Meyer, though slightly wounded by a mortar fragment, remained in action, called for medical help on the 19 set himself, and then proceeded to neutralize the enemy fire with H.E. from his own 2-inch mortar. He remained in position until reinforced at approximately 2000 hrs. the same day.

RFN. J. MICALLIF, 15*th March*, 1945: M.M.

SERGT. H. H. MILES, 14*th January*, 1943: M.M.

This sergeant was acting as layer on a gun on 27th October, 1942. Five tanks came to within 500 yards of his position and on orders from his platoon commander, who was doing No. 1, he opened fire, and his shooting was so accurate that all five tanks were set on fire and completely destroyed. He also accounted for two assault guns.

It was directly attributable to this N.C.O.'s coolness and high courage amidst heavy and accurate shell fire that the attack was beaten off with severe losses to the enemy.

His behaviour during the whole day was of an exemplary order and an inspiration to the rest of the crew.

CAPT. G. R. MILLAR (Special Duty), 27*th April*, 1944 : M.C.

3rd *April*, 1945 : D.S.O. (service in Burma).

LIEUT. R. J. MILLAR (1st Battalion), 24*th January*, 1946 : M.C.

Lieut. Millar has served with the Battalion since June, 1944, first as Intelligence Officer and later, from September, 1944, as Motor Platoon Commander. During this period he has carried out many arduous duties with outstanding success. His unflagging courage, energy and cheerfulness have never failed to act as an inspiration to his men.

Particularly was his great power of leadership and bravery demonstrated near Welle on 17th April, 1945. His platoon was in support of a squadron of tanks and was given the task of clearing a road block defended by a numerically stronger enemy. He led his men without hesitation in to the attack and in the face of heavy and accurate small-arms fire succeeded in putting the enemy to flight after inflicting heavy casualties on them.

Throughout this action, as in many similar ones, he has shown a complete disregard for his own safety and his example inspired his men to further efforts.

CPL. (A./SERGT.) R. W. MILLER (1st Battalion), 27*th January*, 1944 : M.M.

This N.C.O. assumed command of his platoon when the platoon commander was wounded in the first few minutes of the attack by "I" Company on 3rd October, 1943. Throughout the advance he displayed fearless devotion to duty and such qualities of leadership which resulted in the destruction of five machine-gun posts.

As the first to reach the objective on the left flank, he reorganized his remaining eight men and established his L.M.G. post. Under continuous and heavy fire from snipers the post maintained its position until the arrival of a carrier section some fifteen minutes later. It was entirely due to this N.C.O. that the left flank consolidated its objective and remained during the vital period before the carriers arrived to forestall a counter-attack.

W./CAPT. (T./MAJOR) C. F. MILNER (1st Battalion), 12*th July*, 1945 : M.C.

On the evening of 29th March, 1945, the regimental group to which " A " Company, commanded by Major C. F. Milner, was attached were preparing to halt for the night at Sudlohn (4073) when orders were received to try to secure Stadtlohn (4377), 4,000 yards farther on. Demolitions and craters made it impossible for tanks or half-tracks to go forward; Major Milner, however, succeeded in getting four carriers through and in advancing with these and the three motor platoons in the quickly failing light. The enemy on the outskirts of Stadtlohn held their fire until the leading platoon was within 150 yards, and then opened up with small arms and bazookas, destroying one of the carriers. Major Milner then organized an attack and secured not only the first houses but several more in addition. Throughout this period enemy small-arms fire was intense and owing to the darkness everything had to be organized by one man—Major Milner.

After storming as many houses as could be held by the enemy against strong opposition, Major Milner reorganized his company and withstood a number of determined efforts by the enemy, now at battalion strength, to dislodge the company.

He showed considerable initiative in getting such a firm footing in the town in spite of many difficulties, and this had a very considerable effect on the following day's operations. Throughout both its capture and retention he set a magnificent example of personal courage.

SERGT. A. R. MINKOFF (7th Battalion), 20*th September*, 1945: M.M.

On the night of 1st/2nd March, 1945, Sergt. Minkoff was in charge of three riflemen detailed to cover an R.E. working party in the neighbourhood of Pt. 307, 800 yards south of Tossignano. At 2000 hrs. Sergt. Minkoff observed two enemy going into a house while the remaining five men of the German patrol took up a fire position to cover them into the house. Sergt. Minkoff ordered his three riflemen to cover the German covering party and immediately went himself to deal with the two Germans in the house. He stalked them to the cellar and forced them out with grenades. He shot one dead as he emerged and took the other prisoner. The remainder of the German patrol immediately retreated on seeing their comrades dealt with so expeditiously and the R.E. were able to continue their work undisturbed.

Throughout the period from January to March, 1945, this N.C.O. has shown many examples of his courage, resource and initiative which have resulted in casualties being inflicted on the enemy and have been an inspiration to all those with whom he came in contact.

LIEUT. J. I. MITCHELL (2nd Battalion), 23*rd August*, 1945: M.C.

On 20th April, 1945, " B " Company, 2nd Bn. The Rifle Brigade, was ordered to cross the Po Morte at S. Nicolo Ferrarese in company with " B " Squadron, 2nd Lothian and Border Horse, and to establish a bridgehead on the west bank of the river. The crossing was defended by the enemy with infantry supported by tanks and S.P. guns, while S. Nicolo itself, through which it was necessary to pass in order to cross the river, was heavily and accurately shelled throughout the day.

As commander of the leading platoon of " B " Company, Lieut. Mitchell had the task of advancing 400 yards up to the village of S. Nicolo, crossing the river and then advancing 800 yards level with the leading troop of tanks, in order to provide anti-bazooka protection. Lieut. Mitchell led his platoon through the town in face of intense enemy shelling and mortaring, and, despite casualties, succeeded in establishing his platoon on its objective on the far side of the river. Here he observed a party of enemy infantry about to attack the leading troop of tanks with a bazooka. Lieut. Mitchell, with great presence of mind, ordered a Bren gunner to engage this party of the enemy with tracer in order to attract the attention of the tanks. This proved entirely successful and enabled the tanks successfully to engage and kill, wound or put to flight the enemy party.

For the remainder of the day Lieut. Mitchell maintained his platoon in their exposed position despite heavy enemy artillery and mortar fire, in addition to small-arms fire from enemy tanks and infantry. During this period this officer displayed splendid powers of leadership and a complete disregard for his own safety as he moved from section to section encouraging and controlling his platoon.

Lieut. Mitchell's example, determination to engage the enemy, and bravery were an inspiration to his whole platoon and were largely responsible for the successful holding of an important sector of the bridgehead over the river.

LIEUT. P. A. N. MITCHELL (1st Battalion), 12*th July*, 1945: M.C.

On the afternoon of 2nd April, 1945, this officer, the only surviving platoon commander in his company, and who had already carried out three attacks in two days, was ordered to attack some infantry with bazookas in the woods about 593979 between Nienborg and Ochtrupp. These enemy were holding up the armoured column to which the company was attached. With splendid dash and spirit Lieut. Mitchell cleared the first wood with two platoons. Just outside he found an air-raid shelter which he investigated with four men. A German officer was captured and almost immediately heavy and accurate fire from at least four Spandaus was opened on Lieut. Mitchell. With great initiative he threw down smoke bombs and led his men to a house fifty yards away. He then located the enemy in an adjoining house and, encouraging his men, he organized them in such a manner that the enemy thought his position was far stronger than it really was. He ordered his men to go from window to window firing their automatic weapons, thus giving an impression of great strength, and he drove the Germans out of the house, causing many casualties. He then proceeded to the next farmhouse and drove out the enemy, who attempted to filter away down a hedge. Great execution was inflicted on the enemy, and by last light the situation was secure. Prisoners were taken who stated that there were 250 men of the Parachute Regiment Hemmer in the area, at least a quarter of whom had been either wounded or killed. One prisoner stated that out of his section of twelve six only were left after the attack.

The whole success of this operation was entirely due to Lieut. Mitchell's great courage, his splendid personal example under heavy fire, and his dashing leadership.

LIEUT.-COLONEL I. C. MONTFORD, D.S.O., 21*st December*, 1944: O.B.E.

The successful establishment of any new training system is dependent, in the first instance, on the efficiency of its administrative lay-out and organization.

The C.M.T.C. has been exceptionally fortunate in the appointment of

Lieut.-Colonel Montford as its administrative Commandant. From the moment this officer was selected for these duties in anticipation of the forming of the Centre, and since its earliest days of existence he has displayed unremitting zeal, initiative and enthusiasm.

His foresight, imagination and control of the many and varied administrative factors and problems have been outstanding, and he has displayed exceptional ability.

The success achieved in the early stages of the C.M.T.C. and development can largely be attributed to Lieut.-Colonel Montford's administrative standards and achievements.

RFN. G. MORGAN, *5th November, 1942*: M.M.

On 22nd July, 1942, we were supporting the advance along the Ruweisat Ridge. The carrier platoon in making a reconnaissance attracted the attention of some eight German heavy tanks, by whom they were engaged. A number of men were wounded, but transport to get them back was very limited, and in the circumstances time was vital. Among the wounded was Rfn. Jones, who had both legs broken and was difficult to move. In spite of the fact that Rfn. Jones was a heavy-weight and helpless, Rfn. Morgan, a small man, volunteered to bring him in.

This he did on his back, walking through a minefield under considerable shell fire and some small-arms fire over a distance of 800 yards.

This was Rfn. Morgan's first day in action in unknown conditions in a strange country. His steadiness and bravery were an excellent example to his comrades.

This action took place north of El Mireir on 22nd July, 1942.

COLONEL THE HON. T. MORGAN-GRENVILLE, D.S.O., M.C., *24th January, 1946*: O.B.E.

Colonel Morgan-Grenville was G.S.O.1 at H.Q., L. of C., from its inception and throughout the campaign. For the greater part of the period he was the head of the General Staff Branch. As such, the calls made upon him were many and varied, often urgent and covering a wide field of responsibility, which have been borne with consistent success.

At all times this officer has displayed an intense and unsurpassed devotion to duty which has been an example to all with whom he has had contact.

His unflagging zeal, outstanding determination to give always of his best, and unsparing effort have been a material contribution to the successful discharge of the considerable General Staff commitments on the L. of C.

MAJOR (T./LIEUT.-COLONEL) G. W. R. MORLEY, *21st December, 1944*: O.B.E.

Lieut.-Colonel Morley has been A.Q.M.G. of a Corps since January, 1944, the maintenance of which has been carried out under the most diverse conditions, varying from mud and snow on the Adriatic coast to mule and porterage in the Cassino sector.

During March, 1944, he was responsible for the "Q" planning for the relief of a number of formations.

In April the task fell on him of making the very considerable "Q" preparations for the spring offensive and subsequent advance beyond Cassino. In these last tasks he showed outstanding ability and abundant initiative. He never spared himself. He maintained his cheerfulness under difficult conditions and continually displayed a most helpful attitude to all with whom he came in contact. There is no doubt that Lieut.-Colonel Morley's work in March and April was a large factor in making the Corps to which he belonged administratively well found in the battle which opened in May.

2/Lieut. M. H. Mosley, *9th May*, 1941: M.C.

For conspicuous gallantry and initiative at Sidi Saleh on the night of 6th/7th February, 1941, when this officer was in command of a mobile patrol consisting of two platoons and one section of Bofors guns.

For three hours he engaged and harassed an enemy column with guns and tanks, and, despite heavy fire, succeeded in bringing it to a standstill and forcing the surrender of the entire column.

The daring and initiative shown by this officer in repeatedly engaging a strong column throughout its length of three miles at various points undoubtedly convinced the enemy that much larger forces were opposed to them.

Lieut N. Mosley (attached to 2nd Bn. The London Irish Rifles), *24th April*, 1945: M.C.

During the attack on Casa Spinello, near Monte Spaduro, on the evening of 23rd October, 1944, Lieut. Mosley commanded the assault platoon which was first into the farm buildings. After bitter fighting amongst the buildings, they were cleared of the enemy except for two, who maintained resistance from beneath the floor of a building. Lieut. Mosley personally disposed of these two with his tommy-gun and a grenade. When his company commander became a casualty, Lieut. Mosley took over temporary command of the company and rapidly prepared for counter-attack under very heavy shelling and mortaring. Another officer arrived and took over command of the company, but Lieut. Mosley throughout the three counter-attacks which followed in the early part of the night behaved with the greatest gallantry, exposing himself frequently to enemy fire with complete disregard for his own safety, in order to direct fire and to keep alert his men, who were very tired.

This officer's leadership, gallantry and tirelessness were in large part responsible for the capture, and still more in the holding, of this important position.

Lieut. The Viscount Morpeth (10th Battalion), *28th June*, 1945: M.C.

On 23rd October, 1944, Lieut. Morpeth's platoon was ordered to attack and capture Villa Monteloro, known to be held by the enemy. After a long approach march over difficult country, Lieut. Morpeth carried out a skilful personal reconnaissance and made a plan which was so successful that the enemy were taken entirely by surprise and the position, which was a strong one, was captured. Enemy losses were six prisoners, one Spandau, two Schmeisers and two rifles. That evening Lieut. Morpeth laid an ambush in the vicinity of the position and intercepted a strong patrol of Germans, and as a result of a fire fight the enemy were put to flight, leaving three of their number prisoners, together with a Spandau and two Schmeisers. A daylight search showed a morphia syrette, blood, etc., indicating that at least one of the remaining enemy had been badly wounded.

On the night of 28th/29th December, Lieut. Morpeth was on a night patrol when he intercepted and captured an enemy runner. Discovering from him the whereabouts of the German position the man had come from, Lieut. Morpeth planned and led a fighting patrol to attack the farm concerned. Following a daring personal reconnaissance right up to the walls of the farm, Lieut. Morpeth made a plan which resulted in the capture of the complete enemy post with their arms: five men, a Spandau, three Schmeisers and one rifle; our own losses were nil.

During this period Lieut. Morpeth's high standard of leadership and planning resulted in the large area for which he was responsible being entirely dominated by his platoon; and the sure casualties which he inflicted on the enemy were as follows: fourteen prisoners; at least one wounded; three Spandaus; seven Schmeisers; three rifles.

Throughout the past six months Lieut. Morpeth has shown the greatest determination to get to grips with the enemy, and his powers of leadership and fighting spirit based on careful planning have been an example and an inspiration to all ranks of the battalion.

SERGT. H. C. MULFORD, 15*th October*, 1942: M.M.

For conspicuous bravery and devotion to duty. This N.C.O. has been in charge of a section of two anti-tank guns during the recent fighting.

On 4th July, 1942, he went forward by himself on foot and under heavy shelling and machine-gun fire reconnoitred suitable positions for his guns some 500 yards forward of our tanks. He then brought his guns into position and succeeded in knocking out two Mark IV tanks at short range. Then, realizing that the position of his guns was no longer tenable, he ordered them to withdraw behind the next ridge while he himself remained behind with an L.M.G. to cover their withdrawal.

After this had been successfully carried out without loss, he returned on foot to his section. This action was repeated later in the day when another enemy tank was destroyed without any casualties being sustained by the section. Again, on 14th July, in the area of the depression, this N.C.O. advanced his gun to a position 900 yards from seven German Marks III and IV tanks.

He engaged them at once, destroyed one and caused the others to withdraw. In the face of considerable shelling he then withdrew his equipment and crew to a place of safety without loss.

This N.C.O. set the highest example to the men under his command and showed a complete disregard for his own safety.

SERGT. H. R. MURRAY (1st Battalion), 12*th April*, 1945: M.M.

This N.C.O. commanded the only infantry platoon present in the early stages of the operation at Aandenberg on 22nd/23rd January, 1945. The platoon was heavily outnumbered and Sergt. Murray showed great enterprise in pushing forward against strong opposition and in withstanding heavy enemy counter-attacks. Two of his sections were cut off and Sergt. Murray led his Platoon H.Q. in an attack on the house next door to his H.Q. Although he was badly wounded in this, he insisted on being given his weapon and in continuing the fight himself when the enemy re-entered the house where his H.Q. was. He refused to be evacuated until the situation was completely restored.

His inspiring leadership and most courageous example were directly responsible for the success of his platoon, which, though reduced to eight men, held off the enemy until reinforcements arrived, and thus kept the enemy from overrunning a position of the utmost tactical importance.

LIEUT. N. W. I. NAPER, 28*th February*, 1946: M.C.

SERGT. D. NEWMAN, 14*th January*, 1943: M.M.

Sergt. Newman was No. 1 of a 6-pounder anti-tank gun in the Snipe position on 26th/27th October, 1942. On the afternoon of the 27th he allowed seven tanks to get near his position; then with the utmost courage, paying no heed to heavy and accurate shell fire, he directed the fire of his guns so well that his layer was able to set five tanks on fire and immobilize the other two.

His gun was then knocked out by a direct hit. Sergt. Newman, paying no attention to machine-gun fire or to his personal safety, first made the gun useless to the enemy and then helped carry away the wounded men among his crew.

Throughout the whole day's action he behaved with great bravery and resource.

By his gallant and unconcerned bearing he was an inspiration to his crew and afforded a fine example to his whole troop.

LIEUT.-COLONEL J. D. G. NIVEN, 8*th November*, 1945: American Legion of Merit—Degree of Legionnaire.

RFN. J. P. NOONAN (1st Battalion), 2*nd August*, 1945: M.M.

On 17th April, 1945, south of Welle, Rfn. Noonan was in the leading section of the motor platoon supporting " A " Squadron, 1st Royal Tank Regiment. The object of this section was to clear the enemy from a well-dug-in position behind a road block, the enemy being armed with automatics and bazookas. Rfn. Noonan displayed great courage, closing with the enemy despite their concentrated fire, and in the killing of two of them with a grenade just as they were about to shoot one of his comrades. Soon afterwards he succeeded in shooting a bazooka-man as he was firing on a tank, and by lobbing smoke grenades prevented the tank from being hit.

Throughout the action Rfn. Noonan showed a complete disregard for his own safety, and the calm and deliberate manner in which he destroyed the enemy was a shining example to the remainder of his section.

RFN. J. O'BRIEN, *9th May*, 1941 : M.M.

For conspicuous gallantry at Sidi Saleh during the night of 6th/7th February, he accompanied P.S.M. Jarvis when attacked by two enemy tanks. He ran up to the tanks on the move and fired through the slits with his rifle, wounding the crews, who thereupon surrendered.

CPL. E. OSBORNE (1st Battalion), *1st March*, 1945: M.M.

On 21st August, 1944, at 494793 Cpl. Osborne was in command of a rifle section. At approximately 2230 hrs. his platoon advanced with a squadron of tanks in support to capture the cross-roads at this reference. It became apparent at once that there was at least a company of enemy infantry in the area.

Cpl. Osborne advanced with his section in the most daring and deliberate manner and, having driven out the enemy posts, consolidated his section position astride the road facing north. He was counter-attacked immediately, but despite heavy fire and fierce hand-to-hand fighting he succeeded in holding his position and inflicting heavy casualties on the enemy. After a fight lasting over an hour his section had disarmed and captured twenty enemy infantry.

Cpl. Osborne's coolness and courage were an inspiration to the remainder of his section, and his success in holding on to his positions contributed largely to the satisfactory outcome of the engagement in that area.

L./SERGT. H. E. PAIN (2nd Battalion), *7th December*, 1944 : M.M.

For conspicuous leadership in action. On 21st June, 1944, this N.C.O.'s company occupied a position in the Monti Rentella area.

During the day the position was strongly counter-attacked by the enemy three times. During the second counter-attack the company was forced to give some ground temporarily. This was regained and was largely due to L./Sergt. Pain's leadership. His platoon commander had been wounded. L./Sergt. Pain quickly regrouped the platoon and led them back on to the position under heavy fire from enemy mortars and machine guns.

His determination and coolness throughout the day were an inspiration to the rest of the company, and without doubt his actions and personal example were most influential in enabling the company to resist for many hours superior forces with strong supporting fire. The conduct of this N.C.O. has been noteworthy on two previous occasions.

MAJOR A. G. V. PALEY, *1st April*, 1941 : O.B.E.

LIEUT.-COLONEL A. G. V. PALEY, O.B.E. (1st Battalion), 29th March, 1945: D.S.O.

Lieut.-Colonel Paley has commanded the Motor Battalion in this Division throughout the campaign. A great deal has been asked of this battalion and they have never failed to respond.

During the advance from Caen to the Seine Lieut.-Colonel Paley commanded a force consisting of part of his battalion and a tank regiment. After a most difficult night march they seized an important bridge at Fervaques, and held it against strong attacks. This place turned out to be on the line of retreat of the 21st Panzer Division.

During the advance from the Seine to the Scheldt a force composed of the 1st Rifle Brigade and 1st Royal Tank Regiment operated far into territory occupied by the enemy, in the area Lillers—Bethune—Estaires, and were cut off from the remainder of the division for more than two days. The 1st Rifle Brigade was involved in a lot of fighting, including the capture of Lillers.

Throughout the past three months there has seldom been a time when at least one company of the battalion has not been in contact with the enemy. Lieut.-Colonel Paley has been tireless in visiting his men in the most forward positions, and he has proved himself to be a fearless and inspiring commanding officer. The high morale and the fighting spirit of the 1st Rifle Brigade are largely due to Lieut.-Colonel Paley's energy and personal example.

LIEUT. (A./MAJOR) A. G. D. PALMER, 1st April, 1941: M.C.

On the night of 3rd/4th August this officer commanded a patrol, creeping forward to within twenty-five yards of an enemy post north of Capuzzo. He threw five grenades into the post, inflicting severe casualties.

On 12th September, again in command of a patrol shadowing the enemy near Birchirba, he was cut off from the rest of the Battalion. He continued, however, to shadow the column and send back valuable information. At night he successfully withdrew his patrol round the enemy flank. He has consistently shown great skill and boldness.

LIEUT.-COLONEL F. A. PARKER, 28th June, 1945: O.B.E.

Lieut.-Colonel F. A. Parker has been A.A. and Q.M.G. at my H.Q. for seventeen months. Both in Tunisia and later in Italy his work has been outstanding and he has at all times given the most loyal and unstinted service.

In particular, his work on the opening of the advanced base port of Ancona has been of inestimable value. It was with his co-operation that this port was opened within four days of the town being captured, thereby enabling vital supplies to go forward to meet the needs of the armies operating in Eastern Italy.

His forethought, the keen way in which he deals with the many problems continually arising in an advanced base post and the way in which he has brought together all services into an organized loyal team, together with his own absolute loyalty and devotion to duty are worthy of the highest praise, and an example to all with whom he comes into contact.—H.Q., No. 1 DISTRICT, C.M.F.

RFN. G. R. PAYNE, *5th November*, 1942: M.M.

For conspicuous gallantry and devotion to duty on 31st August, 1942. At 1830 hrs. his platoon was attacked by twenty German Mark III tanks. He was No. 3 on a 6-pounder gun and held his fire until they were at close range and then succeeded in knocking out four.

Early in the action the No. 1 of his gun was killed, but in spite of this he continued to lay and fire his gun in action until he was wounded in both arms and the chest from a direct hit on the gun.

His coolness and good shooting were undoubtedly responsible for preventing the position being overrun before reinforcements could arrive.

W.O. CL. III C.S.M. A. E. PEARCE (1st Battalion), *3rd April*, 1945: Croix de Guerre with Silver Star.

This W.O. was C.S.M. of "C" Company, 1st Rifle Brigade, which was in close contact with the enemy in the fighting in France. His cheerfulness and disregard for danger have been a constant aid to the general morale. He was wounded when the company came under heavy enemy shell fire, but continued to carry out his duties, although he was in considerable pain and heavy shell fire was still being directed on the company. When he was evacuated he contrived to return to the company before he was really fit.

His splendid example of devotion to duty has been an inspiration to all ranks.

LIEUT. (T./CAPT.) T. C. H. PEARSON, *9th May*, 1941: D.S.O.

On 6th February this officer was in command of the advance-guard company and one section of anti-tank guns and ordered to hold both sides of the road Benghazi—Agedablia. In spite of heavy machine-gun and Breda fire, he succeeded in driving the enemy from their positions on the west of the road. Subsequently he held the position against repeated enemy tank and infantry attacks delivered with very superior forces throughout the two days and nights. On at least two occasions his position was surrounded.

This officer's initiative in originally seizing the position against considerably superior forces, and his courage, were chiefly responsible for preventing the enemy forces from breaking through.

19th August, 1943: Bar to D.S.O.

For conspicuous gallantry and leadership on 9th/10th May, 1943. When the armour was held up by anti-tank fire from positions which could not be observed, to the north and north-east of Djebel Ressas, Lieut.-Colonel Pearson brought his Battalion forward with great speed, and by brilliant personal leadership established them during the night in positions from which the enemy guns could be observed and neutralized in the morning. His reconnaissance was carried out under heavy shell fire and at considerable personal risk from enemy small arms, as he himself was a long way forward of the leading tanks. The success of this manœuvre of his Battalion secured the observation necessary for the artillery and led to the eventual advance of the armour on to Grombalia, and the capture of a very large number of prisoners. The manœuvre was rendered possible only by Lieut.-Colonel Pearson's complete disregard of danger and his magnificent personal leadership.

CAPT. P. PEEL, M.C., 20*th September*, 1945: M.C.

For gallantry and distinguished service in the defence of Calais, May, 1940.

RFN. A. J. PERRY, 1*st April*, 1941: M.M.

During the Italian advance a truck and a motor-cycle were disabled by enemy air attack and had to be abandoned. After his company had withdrawn, Rfn. Perry returned alone to within 400 yards of the enemy and set fire to the disabled M.T.

Later, when "B" Echelon was heavily bombed, he showed great coolness throughout in attending to wounded and salvaging arms and stores from burning vehicles.

During the whole period Rfn. Perry had set an outstanding example.

CPL. R. L. PETTITT, 22*nd July*, 1943: M.M.

During the dawn attack on Djebel Saikra on 27th March, 1943, while advancing under heavy machine-gun fire through the enemy minefields, Cpl. Pettitt discovered three enemy mines.

Notwithstanding the fact that he had never seen mines of that type before, he placed them where they would not endanger further lives. On continuing his advance up the hill, Cpl. Pettitt saw an enemy machine-gun post firing on our troops. He attacked and the majority of his platoon became casualties. Carrying on single-handed, he finally captured the post by himself, taking prisoner the four occupants.

His complete contempt for danger and his leadership and initiative were largely responsible for the success of the operation.

His action throughout was a fine example.

CPL. S. W. PEVALIN, 13*th August*, 1942: D.C.M.

On 18th June, 1942, this N.C.O. was in command of a patrol of carriers of "B" Company of his Battalion near El Adem when his platoon commander ordered him to engage a German Mark III tank and a troop carrier advancing towards him.

He led his carrier round behind the tank, dismounted and with one other rifleman jumped on to the tank. He was able to fire through a slot at the crew as they were about to fire on the platoon commander's carrier, wounding three of the crew and capturing the whole party.

The leadership, resource and courage of this N.C.O. saved his platoon commander and enabled this valuable capture to be made.

L./CPL. L. E. PIGGOTT (8th Battalion), 24th January, 1946: M.M.

L./Cpl. Piggott has fought with "F" Company, 8th Battalion, from Normandy, June, 1944, to the Baltic, May, 1945. As Rfn. Piggott, on 28th June, 1944, he took part in the attack on Hill 112 and was a constant source of inspiration to the rest of the men in the platoon. Very few of them had been in action before, and Rfn. Piggott in his first battle showed himself to be a good leader in addition to being a very brave man.

At De Rips in September, 1944, Rfn. Piggott went out on a reconnaissance patrol. In the middle of the patrol the officer in charge fell ill and Rfn. Piggott immediately took charge. Leaving the patrol lying up, he brought the officer back through difficult country and then led another officer out to continue a successful patrol.

In March, 1945, on the River Waal at Tiel, L./Cpl. Piggott was a member of a night reconnaissance patrol that crossed the river in an assault boat. The boat became caught in the current and landed on the far bank in an enemy position. The officer in charge was killed and several members of the patrol were wounded. L./Cpl. Piggott immediately took charge and in spite of heavy enemy fire made several attempts to get the officer's body back into the boat. This eventually became impossible and L./Cpl. Piggott brought the remainder of the patrol, including the wounded, back to our own bank.

Throughout the campaign L./Cpl. Piggott has shown great courage and initiative. His actions have been an inspiration to the other men in his platoon, and he was ready at all times to take over responsibility.

R.S.M. E. T. PINNOCK, 18th February, 1943: M.M.

W.O.I Pinnock has served continuously with the Battalion as R.S.M. during twenty-eight months in Libya since the outbreak of war in that country in May, 1940, twenty-four of which he has spent in active operations in the Western Desert, only going back when the Battalion was withdrawn to re-equip. On several occasions he has shown courage in the face of the enemy, notably at Sidi Saleh in February, 1942, when he continued to engage with anti-tank-rifle fire Italian tanks which overran Battalion H.Q. until they were halted and knocked out only a hundred yards from where he lay.

During the campaign from November, 1941, to January, 1942, and from May to September, 1942, he frequently brought the Battalion and column replenishment vehicles up to the leaguer position, skilfully negotiating enemy forces in his path and bringing essential supplies many miles past the enemy's easternmost points of penetration.

His record has been one of consistent devotion to duty. His superb personal example, combined with the standard of discipline and tradition of service, which he has always maintained, have been of the utmost assistance to successive commanding officers and have formed one of the main contributions to the success of operations carried out by the Battalion during two and a half years of desert warfare.

SERGT. G. PRATT (8th Battalion), 1st *March*, 1945: D.C.M.

On 10th September, 1944, in the attack on Helchteren, Sergt. Pratt was commanding a section in the leading platoon. Shortly after crossing the start line his platoon sergeant was killed. The platoon then came under heavy mortar and machine-gun fire and the platoon commander was wounded. Sergt. Pratt immediately took command of the platoon and with great courage led them to their objective. The objective was captured, many Germans being killed and several taken prisoner. Sergt. Pratt consolidated on the objective and reorganized the platoon, which had suffered many casualties.

Throughout the action Sergt. Pratt showed a complete lack of fear and set a fine example to his platoon. There is no doubt that his initiative in taking over the platoon at a critical time contributed greatly to the final capture of the whole position.

CPL. R. G. PRITCHARD (10th Battalion), 28*th June*, 1945: M.M.

For conspicuous gallantry and devotion to duty. Throughout the period from September to December, 1944, Cpl. Pritchard has led a section with most gallant determination and complete success. He himself has taken part in more patrols than any other man in his platoon and has on every occasion brought to this exacting task the very highest standard of personal skill and unflagging enthusiasm and keenness, and an utter disregard for his own personal safety.

On 23rd November Cpl. Pritchard and his section were holding a platoon position in the area of Monteloro, the remainder of the platoon being away on a night patrol. At 0100 hrs. the position was attacked by an enemy raiding party of approximately twice the strength of Cpl. Pritchard's section. Despite the fact that he was outnumbered and the enemy attack being pressed home with the utmost ferocity and with great weight of L.M.G., machine-carbine and grenade fire at very close quarters, Cpl. Pritchard continued personally to command his section, which had suffered two casualties in the initial onslaught, with the greatest coolness and gallantry. As a result of his clear judgment and complete devotion to duty, Cpl. Pritchard's section, though depleted, held the enemy for ten minutes and then, having inflicted casualties, threw them back as they were forming up to rush the position.

During this period, which culminated in an action in which the very highest standard of coolness and personal courage was displayed, Cpl. Pritchard has shown himself to be an exceptional example to the men of his section, his platoon and his company.

COLONEL D. J. PURDON, 17*th October*, 1946: American Legion of Merit
—Degree of Legionnaire.

SERGT. T. A. PUXLEY (1st Battalion), 21*st June*, 1945: M.M.

On 9th April, 1945, the regimental group was advancing east from Twistringen to Colnrade. This N.C.O. was ordered to take a section of carriers on a reconnaissance to the west of the C.L. through the woods to the outskirts of Wildeshausen, due north of Colnrade.

Enemy S.S. troops had been putting up a stubborn resistance in the area, and just after Sergt. Puxley had started out he was told over the wireless that several strong enemy bazooka patrols were reported in the area through which he was travelling. Accordingly, Sergt. Puxley took two men and advanced ahead of the carrier on foot. Whilst doing this he heard an enemy patrol of eight men working round to the right of the carriers in order to take them in the rear. He immediately returned and warned the section and then advanced towards the enemy patrol, who, after a slight show of force, surrendered.

After this brush with the enemy Sergt. Puxley ordered the section to make all possible speed in the direction of their objective. After some time they reached a particularly thick part of the wood, added to which it was getting dark. Sergt. Puxley therefore went off by himself, armed only with a pistol, to ensure that there were no enemy in the vicinity. He shortly heard movement to his right and identified nine enemy led by an officer, and armed with bazookas and automatic weapons, making towards the carriers from the flank. He accordingly returned and warned the section. Immediately afterwards the enemy charged, but owing to Sergt. Puxley's warning they were met by very heavy fire from the Brownings and Brens on the carriers. After a sharp engagement, during which five of the enemy (including the officer) were wounded, they surrendered.

It being by now almost completely dark, and the patrol having reached the point to which it was ordered to go, Sergt. Puxley ordered it to return to the company. This it did, bringing with it seventeen prisoners, having suffered no casualties itself.

The success of this patrol speaks for itself and was due in a very large measure to the contribution of personal bravery, skill and initiative shown by Sergt. Puxley.

LIEUT.-COLONEL M. B. RATHBONE, 1st January, 1945: O.B.E.

LIEUT. W. B. G. RAYNOR (7th Battalion), 13th December, 1945: M.C.

This officer has commanded a motor platoon throughout the Italian campaign until March, 1945. He has frequently been in action with the enemy and has at all times displayed gallantry and coolness under fire.

He has had to do more patrolling than any other officer in the battalion, and has invariably carried out his task with outstanding courage, determination and efficiency, setting a magnificent example to those whom he has commanded.

In March he took command of the Scout Platoon, which he commanded throughout the final Italian offensive.

His work during this period has been above all praise and he played a conspicuous part in the joint operations of the 7th Rifle Brigade and the 17th/21st Lancers in their break-out of the Argenta Gap.

On 20th April he was ordered to follow up the leading tanks at Poggio Renatico. He was heavily shelled passing through Segni and suffered casualties, but he succeeded in keeping his carriers together and pressed on to join the tanks.

Between Segni and Poggio Renatico his carriers were fired at by a bazooka at point-blank range. Lieut. Raynor himself shot the bazooka man dead with his T.S.M.C. His carrier was then engaged by Spandau fire at short range, killing one man on his carrier. Lieut. Raynor immediately engaged the Spandau with all available weapons and silenced it, thus clearing the way for those who followed him.

In this sharp action Lieut. Raynor displayed great coolness and a complete disregard for his own safety. He set a fine example to all around him.

LIEUT. T. E. REDFERN, 13*th August*, 1942: M.C.

For conspicuous gallantry and devotion to duty during operations from 27th May to 9th June, 1942. This officer was in command of a scout platoon engaged on close reconnaissance during the armoured action on 29th May. Under the heaviest fire he carried out his task with complete disregard of personal danger, though his carrier was repeatedly hit, furnishing valuable information throughout. Subsequently he undertook many difficult and dangerous patrols within close range of the enemy tanks, and during the whole period he led his scout platoon with courage and resource and showed fine leadership, skill and determination.

RFN. S. A. READ, 1*st June*, 1943: M.M.

This rifleman was a member of an anti-tank company which, for four hours, held an exposed position under continual close-range artillery, mortar and machine-gun fire when the Battalion attacked the pass.

When the order to evacuate the position was given Rfn. Read walked back 500 yards from the most forward gun, whose crew had all been wounded and the portee knocked out; he found a serviceable 3-tonner and drove it back and rescued the gun under very heavy fire. After placing the gun in a position of safety, Rfn. Read once more took the 3-tonner in the shell-swept area and rescued all the wounded crew, bringing them safely back.

By his bravery and coolness under fire Rfn. Read saved his gun and its crew.

MAJOR-GENERAL J. T. W. REEVE, D.S.O., 1*st July*, 1941 (Birthday Honours): C.B.E.; 1*st January*, 1946: to be Companion of the Order of the Bath.

LIEUT.-COLONEL J. M. L. RENTON, D.S.O., 9*th May*, 1941:

This officer held a line three and a half miles long, defended only by three and a half companies of infantry and one battery, for thirty-six hours against great odds.

Four separate night attacks and several attacks by day, all supported by artillery fire and led by medium tanks, were beaten off and eventually fifteen thousand of the enemy, including generals and their staffs, were made prisoner. In addition, twenty-seven medium tanks and large numbers of guns, Breda guns and armoured cars were destroyed.

Lieut.-Colonel Renton displayed great ability in the selection of the position to be held, and in the use of cover and cross-fire, and in his expert tactical handling of the situation as it developed; and his imperturbability and personal courage in difficult circumstances were a splendid example to the men under his command.

MAJOR (T./BRIGADIER) J. M. L. RENTON, D.S.O., O.B.E., 13*th August,* 1942: Bar to D.S.O.

During the operations in Libya from 27th May to 19th June, 1942, Brigadier Renton has directed the operations of the 7th Motor Brigade with the utmost skill.

During the whole period his troops were engaged on harassing tactics against the enemy's flanks and rear.

Every day his column struck with vigour and tenacity in spite of the exhausting nature of this form of activity. The enemy was caused heavy casualties both in personnel and transport, and he has had to make detachments from his main effort to meet this constant threat. These successes have been largely due to Brigadier Renton's skilful handling, vigour and personality.

LIEUT. (QRMR.) A. W. RICHARDSON, 28*th June,* 1945: M.B.E.

During the period 1st October, 1944, to 31st December, 1944, the 7th Bn. The Rifle Brigade has been continuously operating in the most difficult country in the Central Apennines.

By perseverance, personal supervision, improvisation, tremendous drive and the will-power to surmount all difficulties, Lieut. Richardson has ensured that the troops in the forward area, sometimes situated in the most inaccessible places, have never lacked their full requirements of supplies of all kinds.

The operational efficiency of the Battalion throughout this period has been very greatly helped by the outstanding administrative work of this officer, and mud, snow, swollen rivers, impassable tracks, mountains and intense cold have failed to produce difficulties which this officer has not been able to overcome during this period.

MAJOR J. C. ROBINSON, 17*th October,* 1946: American Legion of Merit —Degree of Legionnaire.

CAPT. K. A. ROGERS, 28*th June,* 1945: M.B.E.

Served in the S.D. Branch of X Corps H.Q. In Italy he helped to run all road traffic over a high pass in the Apennines, and it was largely due to his efforts that the Mandriali Pass was made to take over 1,200 vehicles a day over a period of days and thus enabled the concentration of Polcorps to be completed quickly and in secret.

2/LIEUT. A. P. R. ROLT, 20*th September,* 1945: M.C.

For gallantry and distinguished service in the defence of Calais, May, 1940.

1*st November,* 1945: Bar to M.C.

SERGT. W. F. J. ROOTS (7th Battalion), 8*th February*, 1945: M.M.

This N.C.O. was commander of one of the sections of a fighting patrol ordered to go to Mt. Fredo on 3rd October, 1944, at first light. Sergt. Roots was ordered to take his section over the summit to investigate a probable enemy position. Directly he came on the forward slope of this mountain he was subjected to heavy and accurate Spandau and mortar fire. The platoon was ordered to withdraw after suffering casualties, but Sergt. Roots was unable to evacuate a badly wounded rifleman, who was lying in an exposed position on the forward slope. Sergt. Roots refused to accompany the fighting patrol back and went forward in full view of the enemy, under heavy fire, and dragged the wounded rifleman to a less exposed position with the help of two other riflemen who remained with him. At last light Sergt. Roots returned 2,000 yards to our forward position and guided a stretcher party back in the dark to the wounded rifleman, whose life was thus saved.

Throughout this action Sergt. Roots showed complete disregard for his personal safety and gave a very fine example of courage and devotion to duty.

RFN. W. ROWETT, 13*th August*, 1942: M.M.

On 18th June, 1942, south-west of El Adem, this rifleman was in a carrier of "B" Company of his Battalion which had crept up behind a German Mark III tank and troop carrier. With his patrol commander he dismounted from his carrier, jumped on to the tank and fired on the crew through a slot, wounding three and taking the whole party prisoners.

The exceptional courage, presence of mind and daring of the rifleman saved the rest of his patrol and enabled a valuable capture to be made.

CAPT. S. H. RUSSELL, 9*th May*, 1941: O.B.E.

CAPT. (T./MAJOR) W. R. V. RUSSELL, 28*th October*, 1942 (Burma): M.C.

During operations subsequent to 11th March, 1942, Major Russell was in command of F.F.I., a column which through no fault of his had lost touch by wireless with the remainder of the force and had of necessity to be left behind during the withdrawal. In spite of many vicissitudes and brushes with Japanese cavalry (the column was some time behind the Japanese lines), Major Russell managed to bring out his column complete, men and animals, down the Pegu Yomas, living on the country, wherever food could be found, for two weeks and marching some twenty-five miles a day. The morale of this small force under Major Russell's leadership never waned, and on rejoining the Division, although tattered, thin and exhausted, their spirit was magnificent.

This, I am convinced, was due to the personality and character of their leader.

LIEUT. J. P. SEDGWICK (8th Battalion), 19*th October*, 1944: M.C.

On the evening of 18th July, 1944, "F" Company of a Territorial Battalion of the Regiment was ordered to clear the village of Grenthevide. Lieut. Sedgwick commanded No. 6 Platoon, which was the leading platoon into the village. He showed great dash and determined leadership in overrunning two orchards full of the enemy and capturing twenty prisoners and twelve nebelwerfers. Throughout the evening and the ensuing night Lieut. Sedgwick's platoon were under heavy artillery and mortar fire and he showed great coolness and courage, being a really good example to his men.

On 19th July "F" Company was the leading company in the attack on the village of Bras. Lieut. Sedgwick's platoon, now considerably reduced in numbers, was again in the lead. Although the enemy was in strength in the village, Lieut. Sedgwick led his platoon with such skill and speed that a considerable number of the enemy were killed and the remainder taken prisoner.

RFN. A. C. SHELCOCK, *9th May*, 1941: M.M.

For conspicuous gallantry at Sidi Saleh on 6th February, when this rifleman was the only unwounded man left in his position. He remained firing with his Bren gun, protecting the anti-tank guns from advancing enemy infantry until they themselves were withdrawn.

This rifleman's action undoubtedly prevented the capture, or destruction, of the section of anti-tank guns.

MAJOR P. C. SHEPHERD-CROSS (7th Battalion), *7th December*, 1944: M.C.

Major Shepherd-Cross was vanguard commander to the Battalion group in the advance north from Acuto on 3rd June, 1944. An enemy position consisting of two 88-mm. and two 150-mm. guns and a company of enemy infantry was encountered. After making a very close personal reconnaissance of the enemy position, Major Shepherd-Cross led his company with such skill and determination that the enemy position was taken from the rear with very few casualties.

Throughout the action Major Shepherd-Cross was constantly leading his company in the most advanced and exposed position, and his inspired leadership was largely responsible for the success of this action.

CPL. J. H. SHUTZ (8th Battalion), *1st March*, 1945: M.M.

At Louvain on the night of 2nd/3rd September, 1944, the platoon in which Cpl. Shutz commanded a section was holding a bridge. During the night the enemy began to mortar the bridge, the platoon commander and platoon sergeant were both killed, and several men were wounded. Cpl. Shutz immediately took command of the platoon and reorganized it. The mortar fire continued and the enemy put in an infantry attack. Cpl. Shutz showed a complete grasp of the situation and commanded the platoon so well that the enemy attack was broken up and beaten off. He continued to control the situation in spite of continuous enemy fire until relieved the following morning.

During the whole night Cpl. Shutz's conduct was an inspiration to the platoon and there is no doubt that his initiative and gallantry under difficult circumstances prevented the enemy from destroying a bridge, which was of great value to us in our subsequent advance.

CAPT. C. K. SIMOND, 16*th September*, 1943 : M.B.E.

For setting a fine example of devotion to duty when a Staff officer and suffering from the effect of wounds.

RFN. T. C. SIMPSON, 13*th August*, 1942 : M.M.

For conspicuous gallantry and devotion to duty on 14th June, 1942. This rifleman was loader of a 6-pounder anti-tank gun, and during an attack made on his gun position by enemy tanks, in spite of being under heavy fire and the fact that his gun had been hit five times before it was finally knocked out, continued to load with remarkable coolness.

Eventually he was hit in the arm, and after having dressed his own wound he returned to the gun and helped his platoon officer, at that time the only other person on the gun, to keep the gun in action until it was finally destroyed.

Throughout the action he displayed great disregard of personal danger and a fine example of determination and courage.

LIEUT. (T./CAPT.) T. C. SINCLAIR, 8*th July*, 1941 : M.C.

For continuous good work during the whole period 15th November, 1940, to 17th February, 1941, and in particular during the action at Sidi Saleh on 6th and 7th February, 1941, when this officer was in command of a company responsible for preventing any enemy forces penetrating south from an area west of the main road.

He held the position for forty-eight hours despite repeated tank and infantry attacks by greatly superior forces. It was largely due to this officer's courage and example that the position was held, though several times penetrated.

12*th February*, 1942 : Bar to M.C.

At Sidi Rezegh on 21st and 22nd November, 1941, Major Sinclair was commanding during our attack on the Sidi Rezegh ridge.

During the subsequent holding of the ridge and the final German assault with infantry and tanks on the aerodrome, this officer displayed the most outstanding qualities. In particular, when the main German attack was launched on 22nd November this officer remained with his company until it was completely overrun by enemy tanks. During this phase he was taken prisoner and most of his company wounded or taken prisoner. During the night of 22nd/23rd he managed to escape, bringing back two wounded men of the company.

His magnificent leadership, courage and resource were of the very highest standard.

W./SERGT. J. A. SKIPPER (1st Battalion), 12*th April*, 1945 : M.M.

This N.C.O. commanded the scout platoon on 22nd/23rd January, 1945, in Aandenberg. In the early part of the engagement there were present only one infantry platoon and the scout platoon, and, to make the position firm, it was necessary to push forward against a numerically very much stronger enemy and to beat off determined counter-attacks. During this difficult operation Sergt. Skipper was mainly responsible for the excellent work done by his platoon. He kept magnificent control of the operation under the most confused and difficult circumstances, and was constantly moving from one section to another under very heavy fire from three sides, from mortars, bazookas and Spandaus, encouraging and heartening his men. He also did the most valuable work in evacuating the wounded under heavy fire.

Altogether, the success of the action was in no small measure due to his courage and his constant leadership of the platoon.

LIEUT. (QRMR.) W. SMITH (2nd Battalion), 20*th September*, 1945: M.B.E.

Lieut. (Qrmr.) Smith was Quartermaster of the 10th Battalion from December, 1942, when the Battalion landed in North Africa until its disbandment in March, 1945, and he is now Quartermaster of the 2nd Battalion.

He carried an exceptionally heavy burden during the disbandment of the 10th Battalion, and his efficiency during this period was typical of the standard which he always set himself during his service in that battalion. His work has always been of an exceptional standard and was especially notable during the winter period from November, 1944, to March, 1945, when the Battalion was operating in the mountains and efficient maintenance over snow and mud-bound mule and jeep tracks from a most inadequate base presented problems requiring outstanding initiative and efficiency.

Lieut. Smith's influence upon the operational efficiency and morale of the Battalion cannot be over-estimated, both by his devotion to duty and his personal example of cheerfulness in the face of the most difficult problems. In his determination to ensure the administrative well-being of all ranks, he showed industry and initiative much beyond the normal call of duty.

Lieut. Smith's work was also exceptional during three other periods in the past: (*a*) the North African campaign, when very mobile operations demanded the highest standards of maintenance to ensure the speed of the advance; (*b*) the move of the 10th Battalion from North Africa to Italy; and (*c*) the Liri Valley campaign in May, 1944, when he never failed to deliver supplies in person under the most difficult conditions and often actually under fire.

2/LIEUT. I. S. K. SOBOLEFF, 13*th August*, 1942: M.C.

For conspicuous bravery and devotion to duty on 14th June, 1942. During an attack by German tanks on a position held by another regiment, some way to his front, this officer observed a number of men withdrawing on foot and suffering severe casualties. He took his trucks some 2,000 yards forward, through our own tanks, close into the German tanks, no fewer than three times and succeeded in bringing back 210 of all ranks. By his action he saved to fight again these men, who otherwise must have become casualties and prisoners. His complete fearlessness and disregard of personal danger were an inspiration to the whole of his company, who witnessed it.

LIEUT.-COLONEL A. R. C. SOUTHBY, 13*th December*, 1945: O.B.E.

Lieut.-Colonel Southby rendered distinguished service during the Italian campaign during 1944. Throughout the whole advance from Cassino to Florence he commanded the 10th Bn. The Rifle Brigade with distinction. This battalion, in the 6th Armoured Division, was most actively and successfully employed under his leadership. Since August, 1944, as G.S.O.1, 50th B.L.U., with the Italian Friuli Gruppo, Lieut.-Colonel Southby has displayed the utmost devotion to duty in a difficult task. Largely thanks to his untiring efforts, the Friuli Gruppo took part with distinction in the great Eighth Army offensive between 9th and 22nd April, 1945.

The Gruppo was continuously engaged in the difficult mountainous Apennines country south of Route 9, when the enemy was driven from a succession of strong positions between Faenza and Bologna. These successful operations were a fitting culmination to eight months' intensive hard work on the part of Lieut.-Colonel Southby.

50th B.L.U., under Lieut.-Colonel Southby's direction, played a great part in the training, organization and development of the Friuli Gruppo. This officer's work has been quite outstanding and is deserving of special recognition.

LIEUT. G. E. SPARROW (10th Battalion), 8*th February*, 1945: M.C.

For conspicuous gallantry, leadership and devotion to duty near Faella on 30th July, 1944.

Lieut. Sparrow's platoon was the leading platoon of a company ordered to occupy a vital feature. On reaching the first of the three crests which constituted the feature, Lieut. Sparrow's platoon came under heavy shell and machine-gun fire, and at the same time found themselves involved in an extensive anti-personnel minefield.

Lieut. Sparrow went forward alone, under fire and in view of the enemy, and showed the utmost skill in the use of ground and the very highest degree of personal courage and determination.

He personally cleared a lane 150 yards long through the minefield, in the process neutralizing a large number of mines and booby-traps. A patrol passed safely through the gap, but 250 yards farther on ran into another minefield, all the patrol becoming casualties. Lieut. Sparrow again went out, picked up a badly wounded N.C.O. and, still under fire and after neutralizing yet a further number of booby-traps on the way, carried the wounded man back to the safety of our own lines.

CPL. V. E. STEGGLES, 8*th July*, 1943: M.M.

"B" Company was under command of the Lothians and Border Horse during the operations from 6th to 12th May.

At 0530 hrs. on 9th May Cpl. Steggles was commanding a section of his platoon which was ordered to advance into Hammam Lif. When his platoon officer and two other ranks were seriously wounded he assisted Sergt. Coad in evacuating them to a place of safety.

This was done in consecutive journeys in the face of heavy mortar and small-arms fire.

He returned into the battle and rallied the remainder of his section and continued to engage the enemy until ordered to withdraw.

When his platoon was attacking the town later in the morning at 0830 hrs. Cpl. Steggles's section again suffered casualties. He returned to his section three times to evacuate wounded men in spite of intense machine-gun fire, knowing that at least four snipers were waiting for him to show himself.

He encouraged his section and carried out an orderly withdrawal when ordered to do so.

By his fearless example and complete disregard of his own personal safety Cpl. Steggles displayed qualities of courage and determination which were an inspiration to the men under him.

MAJOR (T./LIEUT.-COLONEL) F. STEPHENS, 31st December, 1942: D.S.O.

During the night of 23rd/24th October, 1942, the Brigade was engaged in penetrating the first enemy minefields (January) north of Himeimat at 882256. Considerable casualties had been inflicted on the leading troops and owing to enemy strong-points on the flank of the penetration area the whole operation was in danger of being temporarily held up.

Colonel Stephens, taking immediate advantage of the one gap which had been successfully made, got his Battalion through and in spite of heavy fire, which caused many casualties, led them with such determination that the enemy strong-points were captured. Lieut.-Colonel F. Stephens's leadership and determination were a fine example not only to his own unit but to the rest of the Brigade, and it was undoubtedly due to his efforts that the operation was finally successful.

W.O. CL. III H. L. STEVENS (1st Battalion), 20th September, 1945: D.C.M.

For gallant and distinguished service in the defence of Calais in May, 1940.

LIEUT. R. S. STEWART-WILSON (7th Battalion), 7th December, 1944: M.C.

At dawn on 19th May, 1944, Lieut. Stewart-Wilson was platoon commander of a scout platoon which had been ordered to carry out a detailed reconnaissance of the defences of Aquino, one of the key points of the Adolf Hitler Line. One section was held up on the outskirts of the village by a road block, covered by heavy small-arms and machine-gun fire.

The second, accompanied and controlled by Lieut. Stewart-Wilson, met an A.T. gun at thirty yards' range. The tractor was destroyed and the crew killed, but the party came under concentrated mortar fire and were pinned to the ground.

Lieut. Stewart-Wilson's carrier was now knocked out and set on fire. He himself, however, dismounted and, his wireless being now useless, in full view of the enemy and under concentrated mortar and machine-gun fire, he moved across the open giving orders and personally directing the fire of his two sections. With entire disregard for his own safety, Lieut. Stewart-Wilson continued to command his platoon from an exposed position in the open, causing casualties to the enemy and making him revise his dispositions. Having discovered the details of the enemy position and that the enemy was in strength, Lieut. Stewart-Wilson ordered his platoon to withdraw under his platoon sergeant. He himself, however, remained out alone within 100 yards of the enemy for a further six hours under heavy fire, making his way from point to point in order to confirm previous dispositions and collect fresh information which he personally brought back to our own lines.

Lieut. Stewart-Wilson had been deliberately moving about exposed under heavy fire and within a stone's-throw of the enemy for eight hours.

The information which he thus obtained was of the utmost importance in planning an eventual attack on Aquino.

SERGT. W. R. STOCKDALE, 3rd October, 1942 (Dieppe operations): D.C.M.

Sergt. Stockdale took command of the troop after all his officers had been killed or become casualties.

While leading a bayonet charge he had part of his foot blown away by an enemy stick bomb; although in very great pain, Sergt. Stockdale continued to engage the enemy.

He set a splendid example and was an inspiration to his men.

CAPT. (T./MAJOR) D. R. STOKES, 21st August, 1944: M.B.E.

CPL. H. W. STONELL (8th Battalion), 12th July, 1945: M.M.

On the night of the 6th/7th April, at Stolzenau, No. 6 Platoon, 8th Bn. The Rifle Brigade, was holding the right flank of the battalion bridgehead over the River Weser. During the whole night Spandau fire and airbursts from 88-mms. were falling on the position. At about 0400 hrs. the platoon was handing over to a troop of Commandos. As Cpl. Stonell was withdrawing his section, having completed the hand-over, German S.S. troops counter-attacked the position. The enemy infiltrated round the flanks and at the same time brought down heavy machine-gun and mortar fire. Cpl. Stonell's section suffered casualties both from enemy fire and from the fire of a neighbouring troop of Commandos, who mistook them for Germans.

In spite of the intense fire and the darkness, Cpl. Stonell led the remnants of his section to a fire position, and, completely disregarding his own safety, went over to the Commando troop to stop them firing, and then went back four times to his wounded men in the open to bring

MILITARY AWARDS, 1939-46   155

them in. Even at this stage he did not forget to recover his Bren gun, which was with the wounded men.
Throughout the action until Cpl. Stonell's section was finally brought back over the river, his coolness and courage were an inspiration and an example to all ranks, and there is no doubt that his conduct throughout a very difficult time was largely instrumental in preventing the enemy counter-attacks from having any success at all.

BRIGADIER M. G. N. STOPFORD, M.C., 11th July, 1940: D.S.O.

GENERAL M. G. N. STOPFORD, D.S.O., M.C., 1st June, 1943: to be Companion of the Order of the Bath.

29th September, 1944: to be Knight Commander of the Order of the British Empire.

T./CAPT. J. J. STRAKER (8th Battalion), 13th March, 1945: M.C.
At Helchteren on 10th September, 1944, Capt. Straker was in command of a force consisting of one mortar platoon and one section of carriers of his battalion, and one troop of tanks. This force was ordered to clear the houses which extended for about 100 yards along the road. The enemy was holding each house in strength and refused to surrender on any occasion until actually overrun. Under considerable and accurate mortar and machine-gun fire, Capt. Straker organized his attack to such effect that the enemy position was destroyed.
Early on in the action Capt. Straker was wounded in the hand. He refused medical attention until the battle was over, and showed such courage and leadership that he was an inspiration to all under his command. The success of the attack and the small number of casualties suffered were largely due to Capt. Straker's skill and initiative.

LIEUT.-COLONEL V. W. STREET, 30th December, 1941, M.C.; 31st August, 1944 (on Special Service): D.S.O.

2/LIEUT. J. F. H. SURTEES, 20th September, 1945: M.C.
For gallantry and distinguished service in the defence of Calais, 20th May, 1940.

COLONEL O. SUTTON-NELTHORPE, H.M. Birthday Honours List, 1942: C.B.E.

SERGT. J. E. SWANN, 14th January, 1943: D.C.M.
Sergt. Swann was troop sergeant of a troop of 6-pounder anti-tank guns during the action on the Snipe position on 26th/27th October, 1942.
As troop sergeant he should have gone back when the portee was withdrawn during the first night, but he was at the time firing a gun and the portee withdrew without him.
In this night action he personally accounted for two lorries and one

80-mm. gun which was firing into the position at near range. During the day he acted as No. 1 on a gun, at the same time giving all possible help to his troop commander in controlling the fire of the troop.

Whenever tanks appeared he engaged them as soon as the range was suitable, even though his flank was exposed to machine-gun fire from other tanks, which were in dead ground and could not be engaged by any gun in the position.

In the afternoon a shell landed behind the gun, killing the loader and wounding the No. 4; he carried on firing with the No. 3 until the latter was also wounded.

He then crawled across to another gun in the troop which was out of action and fetched its crew and ammunition to man his own gun. In the evening attack at 1700 hrs. eight Mark IIIs advanced head-on towards his position; he saw that the gun on his right, belonging to another troop, was not being fired, as the crew were all wounded. He crawled across to it under shell and machine-gun fire, loaded and laid it and hit the turret of the nearest tank, halting and putting it out of action.

He then took on the second tank, at 200 yards, and set it on fire.

This gallant action, under intense fire, when there were only twenty rounds of ammunition left in the whole position and sixty German tanks were attacking south-eastwards down the valley, turned the enemy and saved the day.

LIEUT.-COLONEL W. J. K. TAYLOR, 13th June, 1946 : O.B.E.

SERGT. A. THOMPSON (2nd Battalion), 23rd August, 1945 : M.M.

Sergt. Thompson is platoon sergeant of No. 8 Platoon, " B " Company, 2nd Rifle Brigade. On the night of 26th/27th April, 1945, his platoon was ordered to advance as a fighting patrol ahead of the company and secure the cross-roads at Cavazzana. The platoon reached their objective without difficulty. They were shortly afterwards strongly counter-attacked by a force of fifty enemy, suffered nine casualties and were forced to withdraw to a house dominating the cross-roads. Despite heavy small-arms and bazooka fire, Sergt. Thompson went forward and recovered two wounded men from positions in the open. On his return he discovered that the platoon had lost one L.M.G. previously manned by a rifleman who had become a casualty. Without hesitation Sergt. Thompson went forward in face of sustained enemy fire and successfully recovered the L.M.G., which he then manned himself.

At daylight orders were received to hold on until a counter-attack by the rest of the company could be launched to clear the village. Sergt. Thompson assisted his platoon commander in reorganizing the defences and made a plan to give covering fire for the rest of the company when they attacked. At the same time, he lost no opportunity of engaging the enemy with his L.M.G., killing seven of them, whose bodies were subsequently found, and wounding others.

Very largely as a result of this N.C.O.'s efforts, the platoon were able to hold out successfully and maintain the initiative until the remainder of the company reached them.

Throughout the whole action Sergt. Thompson displayed a complete disregard for his own safety and a devotion to duty beyond praise. His skill at arms and personal courage were a magnificent example and inspiration to his whole platoon and made possible the subsequent operation by which the remainder of his company captured Cavazzana.

MAJOR J. H. THOMSON, 24*th January*, 1946: M.B.E.

Capt. Thomson was G.S.O.3 of the 29th Armoured Brigade from the Normandy landing until 20th July, 1944. He was then promoted to Brigade Major, which appointment he held until he was wounded on 25th September, 1944.

During the whole of this period his work was always of a very high order. He was quite unmoved in battle, was always cheerful and a fine inspiration to all in the Brigade H.Q.

On 25th September, 1944, whilst on a dismounted reconnaissance, he was badly wounded, being shot through the chest and liver. Despite his wound, he engaged the enemy with his pistol until they had been driven off. His personal courage was a fine example to all ranks.

He returned to the 29th Armoured Brigade H.Q. at the beginning of April, 1945, and continued to perform the most invaluable work.

LIEUT. A. THRIFT (7th Battalion), 19*th April*, 1945: M.C.

Lieut. Thrift has commanded a carrier platoon in action for the past four months with the utmost gallantry. Throughout the advance in Italy his platoon has been almost continually in action, he himself going out every time a section has been employed.

On 25th July, 1944, when accompanying some tanks on a reconnaissance to Coro, two of his carriers received direct hits, as a result of which several men, including Lieut. Thrift, were wounded. Despite his wounds, he organized the evacuation of the wounded and reorganized his platoon to carry on with the tanks. He then returned and reported the situation to his company commander, and not until he was satisfied that everything was in order would he go to the R.A.P., some three hours after he had been wounded.

Again, on 27th September, 1944, he led his platoon in an attack on the village of Bocconi. Having occupied the village, it was promptly heavily shelled, two carriers received direct hits, wounding or killing the crews. Under this heavy shell fire Lieut. Thrift collected the wounded and saw them safely evacuated. Then, having received orders to withdraw from the village, he successfully extricated the remainder of his platoon.

By his continuous gallant leadership his platoon has been able to carry out successfully many difficult operations with a minimum of loss.

2/LIEUT. J. E. B. TOMS, 13*th August*, 1942: M.C.

For gallantry and exemplary conduct in action in the El Adem area on 13th June, 1942. 2/Lieut. Toms was in command of a section of 6-pounder anti-tank guns.

A small armoured force of Honey tank carriers and a 6-pounder surprised and attacked a large concentration of enemy transport south of El Adem box.

Toms was the first to come under fire from anti-tank guns and small arms just before the attack.

He manœuvred his two guns most skilfully to take advantage of dead ground near by and he himself stood up to keep the enemy under observation. When the attack was launched he led his two guns into the thick of it, directing their fire from his open 15-cwt. truck under heavy small-arms, artillery and anti-tank fire, and his was the only unarmoured vehicle in the fight.

Throughout the action he showed absolute fearlessness and fine powers of leadership and judgment.

14*th January*, 1943: Bar to M.C.

2/Lieut. Toms was commander of a troop of 6-pounder anti-tank guns in Snipe position on 26th and 27th October, 1942. His troop took up position on the western flank and was immediately counter-attacked by tanks before the guns could be dug in. His guns waited till the enemy were a hundred yards away and then set three tanks on fire.

During the following morning three more tank attacks developed, but were repulsed with heavy loss to the enemy. At the end of these actions only one of his guns remained in action, the other three having been knocked out. At about 1300 hrs. an attack by fifteen tanks developed. He went to his remaining gun, which was manned by the No. 1 and the Commanding Officer, and observed for it. Nine of the advancing tanks had been set alight when the gun ran out of ammunition. 2/Lieut. Toms ran a hundred yards back to his jeep, which carried some ammunition, and under intense machine-gun fire from the tanks, which were only 600 yards away, drove it almost to the gun position before it was hit and set on fire.

He got the ammunition out and assisted No. 1 to set on fire three more tanks in as many shots, which turned the enemy attack. Shortly after this, Toms was wounded in the arm, but he continued to command his troop for the rest of the day, walking out with them on foot when orders were received to withdraw.

During the day his troop accounted for twenty-three enemy tanks burnt as well as other vehicles and guns hit. His leadership and courage in critical circumstances were outstanding, and although his troop suffered severe losses under his command it continued to engage the enemy until all attacks had been finally beaten off.

CAPT. H. R. TOWNSHEND, 24*th January*, 1945: M.B.E.

MAJOR S. R. TRAPPES-LOMAX, 28th January, 1943: M.C.

On 2nd/3rd November, 1942, Major Trappes-Lomax was with the leading company in the night advance on Pt. 40. This strong-point had been reported as occupied by an isolated party of our own troops. On approaching it, however, heavy and close-range machine-gun fire was opened, and it was obvious that it was strongly held by the enemy.

Major Trappes-Lomax sized up the situation extremely quickly and led a spirited charge right through the enemy position, killing a number of the occupants in so doing.

This action raised such a storm of fire as to pin the remainder of the Battalion, at which it was directed. Finding himself isolated, Major Trappes-Lomax then led another charge, this time with some twenty men only, back through the enemy position and eventually rejoined the Battalion.

His determined action had no immediate effect, but the enemy retired five hours later, leaving a gap through which the tanks were able to advance.

L./SERGT. S. J. TRIGGS (8th Battalion), 19th October, 1944: M.M.

On 18th July, 1944, L./Sergt. Triggs was in command of a section of carriers. His section was attached to a platoon which had been ordered to carry out an attack on and clear the village of Grentheville. While taking up position covering the village L./Sergt. Triggs had his carrier hit and destroyed. He immediately evacuated his wounded gunner, jumped into another carrier and continued with the action.

During the clearing of the village L./Sergt. Triggs captured a 75-mm. gun and towed it behind his carrier.

On 19th July L./Sergt. Triggs took part in the attack on Bras. With great dash he led his carriers into the village and captured an anti-tank gun complete with crew. This anti-tank gun had been causing casualties to our armour. L./Sergt. Triggs then took up position with his section covering the exits from the village.

During both days' fighting L./Sergt. Triggs showed great coolness under heavy fire and shell fire and was an inspiration to his section and to all around him.

RFN. D. J. TRINDER, 19th August, 1943: M.M.

Rfn. Trinder was a company runner on the night of 29th/30th April when his company carried out an attack on Djebel Kournine.

Throughout the operation this rifleman showed great courage and devotion to duty in carrying messages between company headquarters and his platoon under very heavy mortar and small-arms fire. Messages with which he was entrusted invariably reached their destination, in spite of the darkness of the night and heavy enemy fire.

His complete disregard for his personal safety and his determination to get his messages through at all costs played a considerable part in extracting his company when forced to withdraw.

MAJOR SIR G. E. TRITTON, BT., *8th November*, 1945: American Legion of Merit—Bronze Medal.

LIEUT.-COLONEL VICTOR BULLER TURNER, *21st November*, 1942: Victoria Cross.

On 21st November, 1942, it was announced that H.M. The King had approved the award of the Victoria Cross to Lieut.-Colonel Turner.

Lieut.-Colonel Victor Buller Turner is the son of the late Major Charles Turner, Royal Berkshire Regiment, and Mrs. Turner, of Thatcham House, Thatcham, near Newbury, Berks. He was born on 17th January, 1900, and educated at Wellington.

His elder brother, 2/Lieut. Alexander Buller Turner, 1st Bn. The Royal Berkshire Regiment, was awarded the Victoria Cross, posthumously, for great gallantry at Vermelles in 1915.

Vic was gazetted as second-lieutenant in the Regiment from the Royal Military College on 20th December, 1918, and has long been an outstanding figure in all matters of regimental interest.

No matter how hard-worked he was, and Vic was always busy, he always found, or made, time to help with any matter dealing with the Regiment.

All members of the Regiment, past and present, will wish to congratulate him on his award, and the honour he has brought to the Regiment.

The official citation reads as follows:

"The King has been graciously pleased to approve the award of the Victoria Cross to:

"Major (Temporary Lieut.-Colonel) Victor Buller Turner, The Rifle Brigade (Prince Consort's Own) (Thatcham, Berks).

"For most conspicuous gallantry and devotion to duty on the 27th October, 1942, in the Western Desert."

Lieut.-Colonel Turner led a battalion of the Rifle Brigade at night for 4,000 yards through difficult country to their objective, where forty German prisoners were captured. He then organized the captured position for all-round defence; in this position he and his Battalion were continuously attacked from 5.30 a.m. to 7 p.m., unsupported and so isolated that replenishment of ammunition was impossible owing to the concentration of the enemy fire.

During this time the Battalion was attacked by not less than ninety German tanks, which advanced in successive waves. All of these were repulsed with a loss to the enemy of thirty-five tanks.

Throughout the action Lieut.-Colonel Turner never ceased to go to each part of the front as it was threatened. Wherever the fire was heaviest there he was to be found. In one case, finding a solitary 6-pounder gun in action (the others being casualties) and manned only by another officer and a sergeant, he acted as loader and with these two destroyed five enemy tanks. While doing this he was wounded in the head, but he refused all aid.

His personal gallantry and complete disregard of danger as he moved about encouraging his Battalion to resist to the last resulted in the infliction of a severe defeat on the enemy tanks. He set an example of leadership and bravery which inspired his whole Battalion.

This award of the Victoria Cross brings the number earned by the Regiment since the decoration was instituted in 1858 to twenty-seven, which is a record for any one Infantry regiment.

LIEUT.-COLONEL U. O. V. VERNEY, 13th June, 1946: O.B.E.

CPL. V. W. WARNER, 20th January, 1942: M.M.

At Sidi Rezegh on 21st November, 1941, this N.C.O. was an operator on the wireless of Column H.Q. when it was attacked and pinned by the fire of sixty German tanks and infantry. While the control set which Cpl. Warner was manning was hit and set on fire, he recovered the set, got it into another vehicle, and although under continuous fire in a very exposed position brought it to safety.

His promptness and resource in face of great danger enabled the column to remain in communication with H.Q., S.P. and G.P.

His complete disregard for his personal safety and his quick action were a fine lesson to all ranks.

RFN. F. A. WALKER, 14th October, 1943: M.M.

Rfn. Walker was the driver of a 6-pounder anti-tank portee at Snipe on 27th October, 1942. The Battalion was counter-attacked by enemy tanks before it could consolidate the position it had captured.

Rfn. Walker drove his portee on to a ridge which was being swept by fire and helped to get his gun into action. It was then in a position to fire, destroyed a Mark IV and halted the attack. This success at a critical moment was mainly due to Rfn. Walker's skill and courage.

Rfn. Walker has served over two years in the Western Desert, first as a carrier driver and later as a portee driver. He has always inspired those around him by his unfailing cheerfulness, his coolness under fire and his confidence in action.

MAJOR C. P. WARREN, 11th June, 1940: M.B.E.; 30th April, 1941: Order of the Nile, 4th Class; 15th August, 1946: American Legion of Merit—Degree of Officer.

RFN. A. A. WEBB, 22nd July, 1943: M.M.

Rfn. Webb was the layer of a 6-pounder gun which accompanied the leading company when the Battalion was ordered to capture the White House, Argoubel Regas, on the night of 26th/27th April, 1943.

After proceeding for 1,000 yards, the Battalion came to a narrow defile guarded by six Mark VI German tanks, which were protected by at least one company of German infantry.

Under the direction of his platoon commander, Rfn. Webb exchanged shot for shot with the enemy tanks, hitting them repeatedly at short range.

When his gun received a direct hit Rfn. Webb accompanied his platoon commander on two attempts in Bantams to salvage his own gun and one other, both of which had received direct hits. On both occasions the Bantams were set on fire by direct hits when on the point of towing the damaged guns out of action.

Rfn. Webb then dragged his platoon commander, who had been rendered unconscious by wounds, back to safety and then returned under fire to try to rescue some more wounded men.

Throughout the action, under greatly superior enemy fire at point-blank range, Rfn. Webb showed great personal courage and devotion to duty.

SERGT. J. J. WEBSTER, 13*th August*, 1942 : M.M.

For conspicuous gallantry and devotion to duty throughout the operations from 27th May to 15th June, 1942. In particular, on 7th June this N.C.O. carried out a carrier patrol, covering some four miles along the enemy's front, the whole time under shell fire and for a great deal of it under machine-gun fire.

He then reconnoitred the enemy position on foot and was able to confirm where the enemy had, and had not, dug in. As platoon sergeant of a scout platoon he did invaluable work, and throughout showed the greatest gallantry and determination and set a fine example to his whole platoon.

LIEUTENANT-GENERAL SIR R. M. WEEKS.

21*st January*, 1939 : C.B.E.

1*st June*, 1943 : K.C.B.

LIEUT. T. A. A. WHITAKER (8th Battalion), 13*th March*, 1945 : M.C.

On 17th October, 1944, Lieut. Whitaker was commanding a group consisting of one mortar platoon and one section of carriers of the 8th Rifle Brigade, and one troop of tanks of the 23rd Hussars. The road south of Meerseld was cratered by the enemy and trees had been felled across the road. These demolitions had been registered by the enemy and under heavy mortar fire Lieut. Whitaker at once began to clear the road blocks and fill in the craters. Enemy mortar fire was continuous and great difficulty was experienced in dealing with the demolitions. In spite of this, Lieut. Whitaker carried on with his task with great courage and determination and was a fine example to all under his command. Casualties were incurred and Lieut. Whitaker was wounded in the leg. He carried on with his task and refused to be evacuated until his force was ordered to stop work on the road, as another route had been found.

Lieut. Whitaker's conduct during this operation was of the highest order and he was the finest possible example to the men under his command.

MAJOR I. H. D. WHIGHAM, *19th April*, 1945: M.B.E.

Was G.S.O.2 (Intelligence), H.Q., XIII Corps, throughout the operations which began with the assault on the Gustav Line on 11th May.

On several occasions he has indicated accurately the enemy's immediate intentions before they have started to carry them out, thus enabling full advantage to be taken of a favourable situation.

R.Q.M.S. G. F. WHITE (2nd Battalion), *19th August*, 1941: M.B.E.

For meritorious service as C.S.M. over a long period in the field. His fine example of devotion to duty and his imperturbable manner in the presence of danger have been most inspiring to all ranks of his company.

SERGT. G. C. WIGHTMAN, *19th August*, 1941: D.C.M.

On 8th May, 1941, when approaching enemy defences at Halfaya Pass, sudden and very heavy fire was opened on this N.C.O.'s carrier platoon from about 500 yards by two field guns, five anti-tank guns and numerous heavy and light machine guns. The leading carrier was immediately hit, the officer in charge of the platoon was seriously wounded (he subsequently died), and the driver killed. Sergt. Wightman went forward in his carrier under this very heavy fire to tow the damaged carrier and the occupants to safety.

He made two attempts, each time leaving his vehicle under close-range fire to adjust the tow ropes, but another direct hit made the carrier impossible to tow. He therefore removed the wounded officer and put him in his carrier. He then removed the weapons from the damaged carrier and rendered the wireless set unserviceable before abandoning the vehicle and drove his carrier to safety. This was all carried out under heavy close-range fire of all calibres of weapons.

His action under heavy fire in full view of the enemy showed the greatest coolness, gallantry and unselfish devotion to duty and to his platoon commander.

BRIGADIER E. S. B. WILLIAMS, *1st June*, 1943: C.B.E.

MAJOR A. J. WILSON (2nd Battalion), *23rd August*, 1945: M.C.

For outstanding leadership and devotion to duty as company commander of " B " Company, 2nd Bn. The Rifle Brigade, on the night of 26th/27th April, 1945. Major Wilson's company was ordered to advance from Saguedo to Cavanazza across country, and to capture the latter village, which was known to be held by the enemy. The five-mile approach march was made in pitch darkness across difficult country in pouring rain, and just before first light contact was established with the enemy by means of a fighting patrol, which discovered them to be in much greater strength than was anticipated, and became dangerously pinned in the village. Major Wilson therefore immediately made a plan, employing artillery, 3-inch mortars, a Wasp and a troop of tanks for attacking Cavanazza at first light. So effective was the plan and so well did Major Wilson direct the operation that the company quickly captured the village, relieved the beleaguered fighting patrol and killed at least twenty of the enemy, captured another thirty, and put the remainder to flight.

During the day the enemy counter-attacked the village several times in a most determined manner, but by outstanding personal leadership, regardless of his own safety, Major Wilson beat them off, inflicting heavy casualties on the enemy and taking another thirty prisoners.

During the period from 18th April to 5th May, 1945, Major Wilson's company has been continually in action, and this officer has invariably shown outstanding qualities of leadership, initiative, planning and an intense desire to engage the enemy whenever possible. His example has resulted in his company obtaining outstanding results, and has been an inspiration to all ranks of the battalion.

SERGT. D. WILSON, *1st June*, 1943 : D.C.M.

This N.C.O. commanded a portee 6-pounder in the action between Dj Zemlet el Bieda and Dj Hadoudi, north of El Hamma, on 31st March, 1943. He gave magnificent support with high explosive from a forward and exposed position and personally directed the fire without a thought of his personal safety, in spite of being continuously, for three hours, under very heavy artillery, mortar and rifle fire.

After all his high explosive had been expended he organized the unwounded riflemen of his gun and a neighbouring gun into a defensive position and continued to fight his position with Bren and rifles.

When ordered to withdraw, Sergt. Wilson kept the advancing enemy infantry at bay until the remaining equipment had been withdrawn.

Throughout the action, under continuous and heavy German fire, Sergt. Wilson showed great courage and determination, which inspired all those under him to fight to the last.

FIELD-MARSHAL THE LORD WILSON, D.S.O., *4th March*, 1941 : to be Knight Grand Cross of the Order of the British Empire.

8th June, 1944 : to be Knight Grand Cross of the Order of the Bath.

10th April, 1942 : Greek Military Cross, 1st Class.

7th December, 1944 : Polish Order of Virtute Militari Velais, Vth Class.

24th January, 1946 : American Distinguished Service Medal.

4th April, 1946 : American Legion of Merit—Degree of Officer.

LIEUT. J. K. WOOD (2nd Battalion), 19*th April*, 1945: M.C.

For conspicuous gallantry during the period 1st May to 31st August, 1944. During this period this officer continually led his carrier platoon with great initiative and untiring energy. His qualities of leadership have been proved frequently.

On 6th July, 1944, during operations on Monte Lignano, his platoon was held up by intense and accurate shell fire and casualties were incurred. He disregarded his personal safety and dressed the wounds of those injured in the open under continuous shell fire. Throughout the day his coolness and cheerfulness in unpleasant circumstances were an encouragement and example to all near him. Again, on 24th July, during operations in the Terranuova area, this officer showed great initiative over a period of forty-eight hours in establishing O.Ps. and carrying out daring patrols into the enemy lines, bringing back valuable information which affected operations over the whole brigade front.

At all times, the initiative and untiring efforts of this officer have set a fine example to the members of his platoon, whose achievements have consequently been of the highest order.

LIEUT.-COLONEL E. F. C. WRIGHT, 13*th June*, 1946: O.B.E.

CAPT. SIR W. F. WRIXON-BECHER, BT., 1*st June*, 1943: M.C.

This officer personally led his company in the bayonet charge which captured the pass in the early hours of 31st March, 1943. From 0530 hrs. to 1030 hrs., although in a very exposed position and under very heavy artillery, mortar and rifle fire at close range, Capt. Wrixon-Becher maintained his position until ordered to withdraw.

The success achieved by his company in the face of very heavy opposition was entirely due to his leadership and courage.

Throughout this period with complete disregard of his personal safety he was constantly moving about in all exposed positions encouraging and cheering on his men.

CPL. W. J. WYETH, 24*th September*, 1942: M.M.

On the night of 25th/26th July, 1942, this N.C.O. commanded a section on a night patrol to the north of Gebel Kalakh.

He led his section on to the objective over 2,700 yards of open ground, during the last half of which heavy machine-gun fire was encountered. He took his section in with outstanding dash and gallantry and played a leading part in the capture of two infantry posts and the crew of an anti-tank gun, totalling two officers and fifteen other ranks.

His section also inflicted other casualties, using tommy-guns and cold steel.

Cpl. Wyeth's courage and powers of leadership in attacking this strongly defended position and in covering prisoners and escort away from the objective under intense machine-gun and mortar fire from numerous enemy posts were exemplary and contributed in large measure to the success of the patrol.

LIEUT. E. R. C. YETMAN (8th Battalion), 21*st December*, 1944: M.C.

On 31st July, 1944, the company to which Lieut. Yetman belonged was attacking St. Martin de Besaces from the north. Lieut. Yetman, commander of No. 12 Platoon, was ordered to take his platoon round the right flank and establish himself on the level crossing. Lieut. Yetman's platoon advanced and immediately came under heavy mortar fire and sustained five casualties. In spite of this, Lieut. Yetman led his platoon forward with such great skill and courage that they reached the level crossing and held it. For the next four and a half hours Lieut. Yetman's platoon held out alone on the level crossing, under heavy mortar and machine-gun fire, and out of touch with the rest of the company, as no runners could get through.

On being relieved, this platoon was only eleven men strong. Lieut. Yetman was wounded twice during this action, but refused either to be evacuated or to be looked after, and there is no doubt that his great personal courage and complete disregard for his own safety enabled his platoon to hold out in most difficult circumstances and thereby hastened the capture of the village.

MENTIONED IN DESPATCHES
1940—1946

26th July, 1940
BRIGADIER M. G. N. STOPFORD, D.S.O., M.C.

20th December, 1940
GENERAL SIR T. R. EASTWOOD, D.S.O., M.C.

20th January, 1941
MAJOR THE VISCOUNT GARMOYLE.

1st April, 1941
GENERAL SIR H. M. WILSON, D.S.O.
2/LIEUT. D. W. BASSET.
LIEUT.-COLONEL F. O. CAVE.
LIEUT.-COLONEL H. S. R. HOPKINSON.
CAPT. HON. A. H. P. HORE-RUTHVEN.
MAJOR A. G. D. PALMER.
LIEUT.-COLONEL J. M. L. RENTON.
RFN. D. F. BARTLETT.

8th July, 1841
CAPT. R. A. A. FRANKLYN.
CAPT. R. H. W. S. HASTINGS.
LIEUT. A. H. S. MELLOR.
R.S.M. E. T. PINNOCK.
CLR.-SERGT. H. ANDREWS.
L./CPL. T. CAHILL.
P.S.M. R. C. EVANS.
RFN. H. S. HAWDON.
P.S.M. F. G. HERIES.
RFN. H. H. HASIER.
SERGT. A. H. MCPHERSON.
C.S.M. A. T. WILLIS.

30th December, 1941
BRIGADIER M. G. N. STOPFORD, D.S.O., M.C.
CAPT. C. R. BILLARD-LEAKE.
MAJOR F. E. A. FULFORD.
LIEUT.-COLONEL H. S. P. HOPKINSON.
MAJOR R. D. D. POOLE.
C.S.M. G. F. WHITE.

20th January, 1942
MAJOR (T./BRIGADIER) THE VISCOUNT GARMOYLE.

30th June, 1942
MAJOR C. ANDREWS.
MAJOR C. FUREY.
CAPT. O. H. J. FOSTER.

15th December, 1942

CLR.-SERGT. R. C. ANTOINE.
L./CPL. D. ATKINS.
MAJOR N. A. BARKER
MAJOR B. C. BAYLAY.
RFN. J. J. EVANS.
CAPT. R. H. W. S. HASTINGS.
LIEUT. P. C. INNES.
RFN. K. F. JONES.
LIEUT.-CCLONEL D. J. PURDON.
RFN. O. H. S. RUTTLEY.
CAPT. I. H. D. WHIGHAM.
MAJOR D. O. WILSON.

24th June, 1943

H. M. WILSON.
CAPT. (T./MAJOR) J. M. FRANCIS.
CAPT. (T./MAJOR) G. W. R. MORLEY
CAPT. P. S. MORRIS-KEATING.

25th June, 1943

CLR.-SERGT. R. C. ANTOINE.
LIEUT. (A./CAPT.) R. A. FLOWER.
LIEUT. J. M. HAWKES.
L./CPL. E. G. PUDDEFOOT.
CAPT. (T./MAJOR) W. E. SUTER.
RFN. F. A. WALKER.

22nd July, 1943

LIEUT.-COLONEL N. BLOCKLEY.

23rd December, 1943

BRIGADIER A. S. G. DOUGLAS, C.B.E.

16th September, 1943

CAPT. (T./MAJOR) G. W. R.

13th January, 1944

SERGT. H. C. AYRIS.
LIEUT. J. L. BARROW.
RFN. R. W. BOLT.
LIEUT.-COLONEL F. O. CAVE, O.B.E., M.C.
LIEUT. J. L. CLAY.
RFN. W. G. COATES, M.M.
RFN. R. A. E. COOPER.
SERGT. A. M. COULSON.
R.Q.M.S. F. DAY.
LIEUT. J. G. H. S. W. DAW.
SERGT. A. F. DOE.
RFN. A. B. GAUNTLETT.
C.Q.M.S. J. L. GORDON.
C.Q.M.S. A. J. F. HAWKER.
LIEUT. J. M. HAWKES (second mention).
RFN. H. G. JACOB.
RFN. J. LEE.
LIEUT. W. R. MCBRIEN.
CAPT. J. E. B. NAUMANN.
CPL. J. F. RAY.
LIEUT. A. W. RICHARDSON.
C.S.M. S. J. SIMMONDS.
C.S.M. G. A. WORBOYS.

3rd February, 1944

SERGT. D. W. WELSH (service at Calais).

24th February, 1944
LIEUT. F. C. HALL (killed in action).

2nd March, 1944
CPL. (A./SERGT.) T. A. H. FROST.   RFN. W. D. COBBETT (posthumously).

6th April, 1944
CPL. (F./A./SERGT.) R. E. ALLBERRY.
P./L./CPL. G. A. ANGEL.
SERGT. M. C. BROOKE.
LIEUT. G. A. BUDIBENT, M.M.
L./CPL. E. S. EDWARDES.
SERGT. F. FORD.
MAJOR J. B. GORDON-DUFF, M.B.E
LIEUT. (T./CAPT.) K. S. HANCOCK.
RFN. P. KELLY.
SERGT. J. LYDEN.
SERGT. C. F. MILLER.
MAJOR (T./LIEUT -COLONEL) D. J. PURDON (second mention).
RFN. W. J. SCANES.
MAJOR (T./LIEUT.-COLONEL) D. J. SINCLAIR, M.C.
RFN. H. D. SHUCKHARD.
RFN. J. W. WOHLGEMUTH.

27th April, 1944
CPL. M. DOUGLAS.

10th May, 1944
CAPT. G. HAMLYN.

15th June, 1944
For gallant and distinguished services whilst prisoners of war:
LIEUT. A. D. V. HOUGH.   SERGT. C. E. C. MEE.
SERGT. W. J. HUGHES.

29th June, 1944
L./CPL. S. DENT.

24th August, 1944
RFN. (A./CPL.) E. C. ELDON.
MAJOR (T./LIEUT.-COLONEL) K. B. HICKS.
CAPT. (T./MAJOR) P. R. C. MORGAN.
CAPT. (T./MAJOR) I. H. D. WHIGHAM.
RFN. (A./CPL.) E. C. ELDON.

9th November, 1944
For gallant and distinguished services whilst prisoners of war:
CAPT. H. C. WHEELER.   CPL. N. WILLSMER.

11th December, 1944

LIEUT. M. S. ATKIN-BERRY, M.C.   LIEUT. R. S. STEWART-WILSON, M.C.

24th December, 1944

CAPT. P. S. MORRIS-KEATING.

11th January, 1945

CAPT. (T./MAJOR) A. J. S. DUCK-   LIEUT. (T./CAPT.) J. R. S.
WORTH.   MITCHELL.
RFN. T. D. KING.   CAPT. (T./MAJOR) G. E. M.
CPL. C. LIPMAN.   NORMAN.

25th January, 1945

RFN. B. K. BROMLEY.

22nd February, 1945

BRIGADIER R. C. J. CHICHESTER-   LIEUT.-COLONEL H. R. NICHOLL.
CONSTABLE, D.S.O.   SERGT. F. H. TRAYLER.

1st March, 1945

For gallant and distinguished services whilst prisoners of war:

RFN. J. GOODWIN.
RFN. J. STRANGE.   RFN. L. F. WELLS.

13th March, 1945

LIEUT.-COLONEL E. P. A. DES GRAZ (posthumously).

22nd March, 1945

SERGT. T. H. BRAY.   RFN. A. C. LINCOLN.
SERGT. R. J. FARMER.   SERGT. J. E. LOWE.
CAPT. N. T. A. FIENNES.   SERGT. J. MACAULEY.
RFN. E. A. HOPKINS.   COLONEL HON. T. MORGAN-
MAJOR J. O. HOPPER.   GRENVILLE, D.S.O., M.C.
L./SERGT. A. I. JAMES.   MAJOR J. H. THOMPSON.
MAJOR F. H. V. KEIGHLEY.

27th April, 1945

MAJOR M. G. KERR.

10th May, 1945

MAJOR F. A. V. KEIGHLEY.   MAJOR E. H. SARGENT.
CAPT. G. HAMLYN.   SERGT. N. D. MILLWOOD.
LIEUT. R. B. M. ADAMS.

MILITARY AWARDS, 1939-46 171

15th June, 1945
For gallant and distinguished services whilst prisoners of war:

CAPT. C. G. JOHNSTON.
SERGT. C. E. C. MEE.
SERGT. T. F. SMITH.

SERGT. G. A. TULLY.
RFN. H. A. G. WEYMAN.

28th June, 1945

L./SERGT. M. W. CARTER, M.M.
MAJOR P. T. FLOWER.

CPL. P. H. ST. J. FAIRHOLM.

19th July, 1945

CAPT. F. BAILEY (Burma).
L./CPL. A. G. BATES.
MAJOR A. J. G. BOOTH.
SERGT. P. N. W. BREWSTER.
RFN. D. F. BRIGHTMAN.
CPL. M. W. CARTER, M.M.
COLONEL F. O. CAVE, O.B.E., M.C. (Burma)
LIEUT.-COLONEL D. L. DARLING, D.S.O., M.C.
MAJOR T. L. DEWHURST.
RFN. W. C. R. GROOM.
SERGT. T. W. GROOM.
SERGT. R. HARRIS.
R.S.M. W. J. IRVINE.
SERGT. A. LEMAR.
CPL. A. T. MERSH.
SERGT. L. A. METCALFE.
RFN. R. MORHAIM.

CPL. J. OLIVER.
MAJOR H. H. PETLEY.
LIEUT. W. B. G. RAYNOR.
RFN. V. O. SAWYER.
MAJOR N. C. SELWAY.
CAPT. C. D. G. SEVERN.
LIEUT.-COLONEL T. C. SINCLAIR, M.C.
RFN. R. D. SKINGLE.
LIEUT.-GENERAL SIR M. G. N. STOPFORD, K.B.E., D.S.O., M.C. (Burma)
L./CPL. C. D. SUGG.
COLONEL C. E. TEMPERLEY, O.B.E., M.C.
LIEUT. W. R. TREVELYAN.
MAJOR A. W. WIGGLESWORTH.
CPL. N. D. WIGLEY.
MAJOR H. A. WILSON.

27th July, 1945

RFN. S. J. MILTON.

2nd August, 1945

MAJOR F. O. A. G. BENNETT.
MAJOR R. D. HOLLIS.

MAJOR (T./LIEUT.-COLONEL) P. G BURFORD.

9th August, 1945

SERGT. G. BATT.
MAJOR P. J. D. FURSE.
LIEUT.-COLONEL P. GODFREY FAUSSETT.
MAJOR J. D. HASLAM.

CAPT. J. H. J. MAIDLAW.
RFN. F. A. POCOCK.
MAJOR C. M. ROSE.
MAJOR I. S. K. SÖBOLEFF.
RFN. R. A. SOFFE.

24th August, 1945

MAJOR P. R. C. MORGAN.

30th August, 1945
CAPT. J. DE W. WALLER.

20th September, 1945 (CALAIS)

LIEUT.-COLONEL C. B. A. HOSKYNS (died of wounds).
MAJOR A. G. L. HAMILTON-RUSSELL (died of wounds).
MAJOR J. A. TAYLOR.
CAPT. (QRMR.) W. STRAIGHT.
LIEUT. J. P. DUNCANSON (died of wounds).
LIEUT. D. R. SLADEN (killed in action).
2/LIEUT. E. A. BIRD (died of wounds).
2/LIEUT. C. J. J. CLAY.
2/LIEUT. HON. J. D. C. FELLOWES.
2/LIEUT. G. J. KANE.
2/LIEUT. HON. T. C. F. PRITTIE.
2/LIEUT. A. SAUNDERSON.
2/LIEUT. A. J. B. VAN DE WEYER (killed in action).
2/LIEUT. C. R. C. WELD FORESTER.

W.O. CL. II L. CHANNON.
W.O. CL. II E. W. CURTIS.
W.O. CL. III F. W. BURMAN.
W.O. CL. III R. A. V. JOHNSTON (killed in action).
W.O. CL. III I. WILLIAMS.
SERGT. G. E. HEDLWY.
SERGT. K. MAHONEY.
SERGT. D. M. PHILLIPS.
SERGT. W. J. TAYLOR.
SERGT. J. L. D. WELCH.
A/.CPL. T. JOHNSTON.
L./CPL. M. J. MURPHEY.
L./CPL. W. STEELS.
RFN. J. E. BARRETT.
RFN. W. P. BYRNE.
RFN. R. G. J. COBLEY.
RFN. J. M. DUCK.
RFN. V. J. SEABROOK.

1st November, 1945
For gallant and distinguished services whilst prisoners of war:

RFN. A. DIAMOND.
LIEUT. C. R. C. WELD-FORESTER.

8th November, 1945

MAJOR A. S. AMBLER.
MAJOR G. E. ANSELL.
L./SERGT. W. E. C. BENN.
CAPT. D. C. GLENNY.
LIEUT. M. E. JOHNSTON.

SERGT. H. R. LAWGRISH.
LIEUT. R. J. MILLAR.
SERGT. P. C. RODWELL.
MAJOR A. P. ROWAN.
MAJOR C. K. SIMOND.

29th November, 1945

COLONEL R. R. CRIPPS, T.D.
LIEUT.-COLONEL J. D. R. ELKINGTON, M.B.E.
MAJOR R. B. ADAMS.
MAJOR L. E. AHLBERG.
MAJOR H. C. BARING, M.C.
MAJOR A. J. G. BOOTH.
MAJOR W. S. BROWNLOW.
MAJOR J. E. EELES.
MAJOR I. E. WILLIAMS.

MAJOR A. J. WILSON.
MAJOR I. R. S. COSBY.
MAJOR J. L. MASON.
CAPT. C. F. ADAMS.
CAPT. R. A. HENLEY.
CAPT. E. A. JONES.
CAPT. J. I. MITCHELL, M.C.
CAPT. M. E. DAY.
LIEUT. J. A. C. COWAN.
LIEUT. H. EASTWOOD.

MILITARY AWARDS, 1939-46   173

Lieut. D. E. Head.
Lieut. J. H. Huntsman.
Lieut. J. S. Longrigg.
W.O. Cl. II W. D. Basten.
W.O. Cl. II J. A. Goy.
W.O. Cl. II F. M. Hamilton.
W.O. Cl. II E. Kelsey.
W.O. Cl. II W. A. C. Rawlings.
W.O. Cl. II F. H. Roberts.
A./W.O. Cl. II K. Bishop.
A./W.O. Cl. II S. Bonney.
Clr.-Sergt. A. E. Britton.
Clr.-Sergt. S. Duggan.
Clr.-Sergt. J. G. Harris.
Clr.-Sergt. F. W. Restorick.
C.Q.M.S. G. Lane.
Sergt. J. Dowsett.
Sergt. M. Handebode.
Sergt. H. J. O'Grady.
Sergt. A. R. Pittman.
Sergt. C. W. Plummer.
Sergt. E. Pool.
Sergt. C. H. Thornborough.
Sergt. P. G. Wright.
Sergt. S. Wright.
A./Sergt. W. Taylor.
L./Sergt. F. S. Pamington.
L./Cpl. S. G. Dawson.
Rfn. W. S. Ball.
Rfn. R. L. Longstaff.
Rfn. J. F. Northover.

21st February, 1946

For gallant and distinguished services whilst prisoners of war:

R.S.M. L. E. B. Munday.
W.O.II J. A. Riley.
Sergt. D. M. Phillips.
Rfn. C. W. Barton.

28th February, 1946

Sergt. R. W. Bosley.
Sergt. P. A. Kennedy.
L./Cpl. J. E. A. Godwin.
L./Cpl. M. W. Wells.

6th June, 1946

For gallant and distinguished services whilst prisoners of war:

Sergt. G. Wilton.
Rfn. M. A. Moss.

4th April, 1946

Lieut.-Colonel C. K. Simond, M.B.E.
Major A. H. Farrell-Barrs.
Major J. T. Borthwick, M.B.E.
Major B. H. Gibson.
Major P. C. E. Russell.
Major H. B. Shepherd.
Major I. S. K. Soboleff, M.C.
Major J. C. Witt.
Major G. R. Tibbett.
Capt. G. S. B. Cohen.
Capt. Hon. K. G. Kinnaird.
Capt. I. P. Purvis.
Lieut. D. A. O. Davies.
Lieut. P. S. Hodge.
W.O.I. W. G. Page.
W.O.II E. J. Durey.
W.O.II H. J. Hewstone.
Sergt. G. Batt.
Sergt. W. G. Bonner.
Sergt. J. R. Ferguson.
Sergt. F. J. Richens.
L./Cpl. W. C. Prior.
Rfn. R. E. Elmes.

23rd May, 1946

LIEUT.-COLONEL I. C. MONTFORD, D.S.O., O.B.E.
LIEUT.-COLONEL C. E. WALTERS.
MAJOR F. P. BARRY.
MAJOR R. E. WORSLEY.
MAJOR W. CALLARD.
MAJOR A. I. FAIRWEATHER.
MAJOR SIR E. C. GOSCHEN, Bt., D.S.O.
CAPT. C. E. McGRIGOR.
CAPT. R. J. PARKER.
CAPT. D. M. PONTIFEX.
LIEUT. H. F. W. L. VATCHER.
LIEUT. P. BOWRING.
LIEUT. R. W. EARLEY.
W.O.II W. J. LAWSON.
W.O.II J. E. HUSSELBY.
W.O.II R. G. ROBERTS.
CLR.-SERGT. B. ASHWORTH.
CLR.-SERGT. J. BUTTERFIELD.

CLR.-SERGT. P. CABLE.
CLR.-SERGT. F. FOWLER.
SERGT. H. L. COLE.
SERGT. T. FEARON.
SERGT. W. F. MOORE.
SERGT. W. O'HARA.
SERGT. N. W. SMITH.
SERGT. A. L. KING.
SERGT. R. J. PRICKETT.
SERGT. W. H. TAPPING.
L./SERGT. J. WHEELER.
L./SERGT. S. G. PEARSON.
CPL. K. R. COMPTON.
CPL. S. HAYES.
CPL. F. G. LOVE.
CPL. H. R. WHITCHELO.
RFN. C. W. HILL.
RFN. A. G. MARCHANT.
RFN. R. SOWTER.

6th June, 1946

LIEUT. C. J. J. CLAY.

19th September, 1946 (BURMA)

CLR.-SERGT. W. S. HAWKINS.
LIEUT. H. A. MOLE.

W.O. CL. II A. A. WILKIE.